www.wadsworth.com

www.wadsworth.com is the World Wide Web site for Wadsworth and is your direct source to dozens of online resources.

At www.wadsworth.com you can find out about supplements, demonstration software, and student resources. You can also send email to many of our authors and preview new publications and exciting new technologies.

www.wadsworth.com
Changing the way the world learns®

Voices of the American Past

Documents in U.S. History

Volume I

Voices of the American Past

Documents in U.S. History

Volume I

Third Edition

Raymond M. Hyser
J. Chris Arndt
James Madison University

THOMSON

WADSWORTH

Australia • Canada • Mexico • Singapore • Spain • United Kingdom • United States

THOMSON
WADSWORTH

Publisher: Clark Baxter
Acquisitions Editor: Ashley Dodge
Senior Development Editor:
Margaret McAndrew Beasley
Assistant Editor: Julie Yardley
Editorial Assistant: Anne Gittinger
Technology Project Manager: Melinda Newfarmer
Marketing Manager: Lori Grebe Cook
Marketing Assistant: Mary Ho
Advertising Project Manager: Stacey Purviance
Senior Project Manager, Editorial Production:
Kimberly Adams

Print/Media Buyer: Rebecca Cross
Permissions Editor: Stephanie Lee
Production Service and Compositor:
Lachina Publishing Services
Photo Researcher: Linda Sykes
Copy Editor: Lachina Publishing Services
Cover Designer: Lisa Henry
Cover Image: Smithsonian American Art Museum,
Washington, DC/Art Resource, NY
Printer: Malloy Incorporated

For more information about
our products, contact us at:
**Thomson Learning Academic
Resource Center
1-800-423-0563**

For permission to use material from this text
or product, submit a request online at
http://www.thomsonrights.com.
Any additional questions about permissions
can be submitted by email to
thomsonrights@thomson.com.

Thomson Wadsworth
10 Davis Drive
Belmont, CA 94002-3098
USA

Asia
Thomson Learning
5 Shenton Way #01-01
UIC Building
Singapore 068808

Australia/New Zealand
Thomson Learning
102 Dodds Street
Southbank, Victoria 3006
Australia

Canada
Nelson
1120 Birchmount Road
Toronto, Ontario M1K 5G4
Canada

Europe/Middle East/Africa
Thomson Learning
High Holborn House
50/51 Bedford Row
London WC1R 4LR
United Kingdom

**Library of Congress
Control Number:** 2004105197

ISBN: 0-534-64300-0

To our children,

Kelsey, Marshall, and Christopher Hyser

and Olivia Arndt

Thanks for all of your love

and inspiration

About the Authors

Raymond M. Hyser is a professor of history at James Madison University in Harrisonburg, Virginia, where he teaches courses in U.S. history, U.S. business history, Gilded Age America, and historical methods. He focuses his research interests on the study of race and ethnicity in the Gilded Age.

J. Chris Arndt is a professor of history at James Madison University in Harrisonburg, Virginia, where he teaches courses in U.S. history, the American Revolution, the early Republic, and historical methods. He focuses his research interests on the study of state's rights and economic change in antebellum America.

Contents

CHAPTER 8 The New Nation and Its Place in the World 120

CHAPTER 9 The Democratic Republic 137

CHAPTER 10 Diversifying Society and Economy 158

CHAPTER 11 Social Reform 177

CHAPTER 12 Manifest Destiny and American Expansion 193

CHAPTER 13 Slavery and the Old South 211

Preface to the Third Edition

We are delighted with the opportunity to produce a revised third edition of *Voices of the American Past*. This allows us to better represent the ever-evolving approaches that historians employ to interpret the past, but it also enables us to provide more documents covering a greater variety of issues. Those who use this edition will find significant changes. Our selection of new documents was guided by a desire to provide greater diversity of voices while also offering readable selections that spoke to larger issues.

The revised reader offers well known primary sources such as *Federalist 10,* and President Eisenhower's farewell address, as well as Cotton Mather's admonitions on the evils of "self-pollution," a women's description of the southern homefront during the Civil War, John Muir's essay on American forests, and a critique of East Asians as the "model minority." The most significant change, however, is the addition of visual images. As historians have increasingly adopted more interdisciplinary approaches and expanded the types of sources they use both as scholars and in the classroom, we thought it essential to add a different type of primary source to the more traditional use of documents. The result is a collection of more than thirty images that provide a unique approach to interpreting and understanding the key issues of U.S. history.

We are again indebted to our colleagues in the James Madison University Department of History for their contributions and inspiration. Their high standards of teaching excellence coupled with their strong sense of collegiality provide the perfect atmosphere for quality instruction. Our students have contributed greatly by showing us where a document was contradictory or less readable, and perhaps more important, they helped to make us aware of the issues that are central to the current generation of young people. Many of our colleagues in the profession, particularly those who participate in the annual Advanced Placement U.S. History grading, have made more important contributions than they could ever realize. We appreciate the criticisms and suggestions of the following reviewers:

Sharon L. Arnoult, Midwestern State University

Robert A. Becker, Weber State University

Mario Bennekin, Georgia Perimeter College

Kirk Burnett, Mt. San Antonio College

Dominick Cavallo, Adelphi University

Stacy A. Cordery, Monmouth College

Brian Daugherity, University of Richmond

Gregory Michael Dorr, University of Alabama

Lisa Lindquist Dorr, University of Alabama

Harvey Green, Northeastern University

Robert R. Hollander, St. Louis Community College at Forest Park

Todd Kerstetter, Texas Christian University

Suzanne Marshall, Jacksonville State University

Timothy J. McMannon, North Seattle Community College

Stephen Middleton, North Carolina State University

William Howard Moore, University of Wyoming

Rick Moniz, Chabot College

John T. Payne, North Harris Montgomery Community College District/ Tomball College

Emily S. Rosenberg, Macalester College

Norman L. Rosenberg, Macalester College

Thomas Schoonover, University of Southwestern Louisiana

Sandra Strohhofer Pryor, University of Delaware

Paul Searls, University of Vermont

Vernon L. Volpe, University of Nebraska at Kearney

Their insight did much to improve this edition, enabling us to refocus our attention in some areas and leading us to some excellent documents in others. Special thanks go to our friends at Wadsworth Publishers. Margaret Beasley is a terrific editor with a wonderful sense of humor, a necessary ingredient for successfully bringing this project to fruition. Finally, we thank our wives, Pamela and Andi, for their love and support.

A Guide to Reading and Interpreting Documents and Images

This volume contains edited documents about American history. Historians refer to documents as written *primary sources*. These are the raw materials, the basic building blocks to reconstructing past events. In the same way that a detective searches a crime scene for clues, a historian draws on primary sources and uses the weight of the evidence to determine what happened, and to help support an interpretation of the event. While primary sources might be described as any evidence that is contemporary to the event described, historians rely heavily on first-hand, eyewitness accounts or recollections of events of the time, as well as speeches or official reports produced at that time. All primary sources, however, are not created equal. The closer the evidence is in time and space to the event described, the less bias that it contains, and the more reliable it tends to be. The interpretations that historians produce from these primary sources are called *secondary sources*. Secondary sources are books and articles written about past events, such as a textbook, the introductions to the documents in this volume, or a history of the American Civil War.

Reading and analyzing documents require particular skills. You should examine documents with a critical eye; that is, ask questions about the document. We recommend that you develop the ability to perform a twofold reading of a document. First, try to understand the document as the people in the time and place in which it was produced would have comprehended it. What did the document mean to them? Always remember that people live within a historical context—they inhabit a different time and place. They do not know what the future holds. Careful analysis of a document will enable you to examine the thoughts and actions of the people of a particular time. Second, read the document and consider the similarities and differences between that time period and your own. Students of history are often called upon to make judgments about the past. Documents should be analyzed to see how they fit into the broader sweep of history.

We have included the following pointers that will be useful in introducing you to this spirit of historical inquiry and enable you to better understand documents. It is our hope that equipped with these guidelines, you will be better able to read primary sources in a critical manner. And in so doing, you will gain more insight into past events, add some real-life views to historical facts, and better understand the complexities of the American past.

Interpreting Written Documents

1. **Context:** Each document has an introduction. You should read it, as well as review notes from your instructor's lecture. This will provide you with some background about events, people, and ideas of the time period in which the document was created.

   • What major political, social, and economic events may have affected the author of the document?

   • How does this document fit into the historical context?

   • How does this document better our understanding of the event?

   • Does the document help to explain the cause-and-effect relationship of this event?

2. **Thesis:** Most documents have a central point that is being conveyed. This is known as the thesis. It is critical for any reader to understand the core argument—the thesis—of a document. Identifying the thesis is the important first step in making sense of a document's overall impact.

   • Can you summarize the document in three or four sentences?

   • What is the thesis?

   • What does the author emphasize?

   • What are the key words that define the argument?

   Keep in mind that the meaning of words changes over time, so try to understand the use of language in the historical time period of the document. For example, students in the 21st century might refer to "icon" as a clickable symbol on their computer's desktop, while prior to the widespread use of computers, "icon" would refer to a sacred, religious image.

3. **Perspective:** The author's point of view, including his or her prejudices and beliefs, can dramatically affect the content of a document. It is essential to consider the author of a document when reading. Biographical information can be helpful in deciding the author's point of view. For example, a slave owner would have a different view of slavery than a slave. Factory workers would certainly have a different perception of life in America than the owner of the factory where they worked.

   • Who is the author of the document?

   • What is his or her background?

   • When was the document created?

   • Was it prepared during the event, immediately afterwards, within a short time period, or years later?

Such timing is important, as memories often fade or become distorted over time. An individual's life experience often shapes perspective or views about events in his or her time. Seek to determine the authors' gender, class, ethnicity (where appropriate), their regional background, and their political, economic, or social position.

- Do you detect any prejudices?
- What evidence indicates the bias of the author?
- Can you determine the author's motive in producing the document?
- What did he or she hope to accomplish?

4. **Audience:** Knowing the intended audience of an account can be useful in better understanding why the document was created.

   - Was the document prepared for a specific audience—women, members of Congress, African Americans, wealthy businessmen, immigrants, a friend, for example?
   - Was the document prepared for public distribution?
   - Was it a speech, a newspaper or a magazine article or editorial, an official government report, a published memoir or autobiography, to name a few possibilities?
   - Was it produced for personal and private reflection, such as a diary, journal entry, or an exchange of letters between friends?

Public consumption documents tend to be carefully worded, often guarded in presentation, while private ones tend to be less cautious and more honest. Classifying or identifying the document can be helpful in understanding its contents.

5. **Significance:** Finally, one should determine why a document is important.

   - Why is the document important or significant?
   - How has it shaped our understanding of the event?
   - How has it shaped our understanding of historical change or continuity over time?
   - What does it tell us about the historical time period?

Interpreting Visual Images

Many of the techniques used to interpret visual images are similar to those used to make sense of written documents. It is as important to ask questions about context, thesis, perspective, audience, and significance when analyzing an image as it is when reviewing a written text. The major difference with visual images is that there is more room for interpretation since the author/artist/photographer does not specifically describe what he or she is thinking. In analyzing visual images, one should consider the following:

- Carefully study the image. What is your overall impression? What thoughts or emotions does it conjure?
- What activities are depicted in the image? How and why are these activities significant?
- Does the artist make use of symbols? If so, what are they? What is the significance of these symbols?
- Who or what is portrayed positively? Negatively? What can you infer from this?

1

Diverse Beginnings

American history began not in 1607, but tens of thousands of years earlier with the first arrivals, the Native Americans. Native Americans spent millennia living beyond the contact of the outside world until the late 15th-century arrival of European explorers. The contact of cultures initiated a process that radically transformed societies throughout the world. The rush to conquer and colonize the area of the present-day United States began with the Spanish, but soon came to include other Europeans. Native Americans were not passive bystanders in the process and responded to the contact in a variety of ways. The following documents collectively reveal European motives in North America and provide a glimpse of the impact this presence had on the native population.

1

The Spanish Letter of Columbus to Luis Sant' Angel (1493)

Christopher Columbus was born Cristoforo Colombo in Genoa, Italy, in either 1451 or 1452. He went to sea early in life, and by the early 1490s had sailed as far north as Iceland and as far south as the modern-day country of Ghana, West Africa. By the mid-1480s, he began to seek support for a voyage of exploration westward into the Atlantic, primarily to open a trade route with East Asia. By 1492, the Spanish kingdom of Castile, under the leadership of Queen Isabella, was ready to support his endeavor. He left Palos, Spain, on August 3, and on October 12, 1492, his three ships, the Niña, Pinta, and Santa María, touched land in the West Indies. After three months of sailing and exploring the Caribbean, he returned to Spain. Three later voyages would establish the primary transatlantic sailing routes and allowed Columbus to conduct a thorough reconnaissance of the Caribbean. Although he went to his grave believing he was skirting the coast of Asia, his legacy was the discovery of a continent formerly unknown to Europeans. This letter describes what Columbus saw on his first visit.

Questions to Consider

1. What is the perspective of the author of this document?
2. According to this account, what does Christopher Columbus seem interested in achieving?
3. What can you deduce about Spanish attitudes toward Native Americans from this document?

. . . There are wonderful pine-groves, and very large plains of verdure, and there is honey, and many kinds of birds, and many various fruits. In the earth there are many mines of metals; and there is a population of incalculable number. Spanola is a marvel; the mountains and hills, and plains, and fields, and land, so beautiful and rich for planting and sowing, for breeding cattle of all sorts, for building of towns and villages. There could be no believing, without seeing, such harbours as are here, as well as the many and great rivers, and excellent waters, most of which contain gold. In the trees and fruits and plants, there are great differences from those of Juana. In this, there are many spiceries, and great mines of gold and other metals. The people of this island, and of all the others that I have found and seen, or not seen, all go naked, men and women, just as their mothers bring them forth; although some women cover a single place with the leaf of a plant, or a cotton something which they make for that purpose. They have no iron or steel, nor any weapons than the stems of reeds in their seeding state, on the end of which they fix little sharpened stakes. . . . I gave gratuitously a thousand useful things that I carried, in order that they may conceive affection, and furthermore may be made Christians; for they are inclined to the love and service of their Highnesses and of all the Castilian nation, and they strive to combine in giving us things which they have in abundance, and of which we are in need. And they knew no sect, nor idolatry; save that they all believe that power and goodness are in the sky; and in such opinion, they received me at every place where I landed, after they had lost their terror. And this comes not because they are ignorant; on the contrary, they are men of very subtle wit, who navigate all those seas, and who give a marvellously good account of everything—but because they never saw men wearing clothes nor the like of our ships. And as soon as I arrived in the Indies, in the first island that I found, I took some of them by force to the intent that they should learn [our speech] and give me information of what there was in those parts. And so it was, that very soon they understood [us] and we them, what by speech or what by signs; and those [Indians] have been of much service. To this day I carry them [with me] who are still of the opinion that I come from heaven, [as appears] from much conversation which they have had with me. And they were the first to proclaim it wherever I arrived; and the others went running from

---

The Spanish Letter of Columbus to Luis Sant Angel, (February 15, 1493), *Personal Narrative of the First Voyage of Columbus to America* (Boston, 1827), 303.

house to house and to the neighbouring villages, and loud cries of "Come! come to see the people from heaven!" Then, as soon as their minds were reassured about us, every one came, men as well as women, so that there remained none behind big or little; and they all brought something to eat and drink, which they gave with wondrous lovingness. They have in all the islands very many canoes, after the manner of rowing-galleys, some larger, some smaller; and a good many are larger than a galley of eighteen benches. They are not so wide, because they are made of a single log of timber, but a galley could not keep up with them in rowing, for their motion is a thing beyond belief. And with these, they navigate through all those islands which are numberless, and ply their traffic. I have seen some of those canoes with seventy, and eighty, men in them, each one with his oar. In all those islands, I saw not much diversity in the looks of the people, nor in their manners and language; but they all understand each other, which is a thing of singular towardness for what I hope their Highnesses will determine, as to making them conversant with our holy faith, unto which they are well disposed. . . .

2

Images of 16th-Century Native American Life

Artists have left important clues about the Native American societies that existed before they had extensive contact with Europeans. The first selection depicts members of the Timucua tribe planting crops in what is now Florida. The second selection is an engraving by Theodore DeBry, based on a painting by John White. It shows a Native American village in what is now North Carolina. Taken together, these images dispel later claims by whites that Indians were an "uncivilized" people who had not yet mastered agriculture and who lacked the sophisticated social structures necessary for urban life.

Questions to Consider

1. What can you deduce about Timucua gender roles from the first image?
2. How well organized does the town of Secoton appear? What types of institutions would likely be necessary to support what you see in the picture?
3. What conclusions can you draw from these images about 16th-century Native American life?
4. Compare and contrast Mary Rowlandson's description of Native Americans with what you see here ("'Captivity Account' of Mary Rowlandson," Document 7). What seems different? How do you account for this?

"Timucua planting crops"

The town of Secoton, 16th-century North Carolina

3

Jesuit Comparison of French and Native Life (1657–1658)

France established its most important North American outposts in Nova Scotia and along the St. Lawrence River valley. Faith and fortune were the primary reasons for French involvement along the St. Lawrence. Control of the region enabled French traders to tap the lucrative fur trade of the interior, while the conversions of many local tribes to Roman Catholicism enhanced French influence in the region. The bulk of the French missionaries were Jesuits. Created in response to the Protestant Reformation, the Society of Jesus sought to convert individuals to Roman Catholicism and fight heresy; by the 17th century, the Jesuits had become a formidable missionary force. Often sent alone to live among those whom they sought to convert, the Jesuits endured years of hardship to achieve their mission. The accounts left by the missionaries in the Jesuit Relations *provide excellent insights into the structure and folkways of Native American life. In the following account, a Jesuit compares French and native habits.*

Questions to Consider

1. How do European and Native American dress, eating habits, and social customs differ?
2. Why do you think this account was written?
3. What can you deduce about European and Native American contact from this selection?
4. In what ways does this description of Native culture differ from that contained in the "'Captivity Account' of Mary Rowlandson" (Document 7) and "The Pueblo Revolt" (Document 8)? How do you account for these differences?

. . . In Europe, the seam of stockings is behind the leg. . . . Among the Savages it is otherwise; the seam of stockings worn by men is between the legs, and here they fasten little ornaments—made of porcupine quills, stained scarlet, and in the form of fringe or of spangles—which meet when they walk, and make . . . a pretty effect, not easily described. The women wear this ornamentation on the outer side of the leg.

In France, patterns and raised shoes are considered the most beautiful. . . . The Savages' shoes are as flat as tennis-shoes, but much wider, especially in winter, when they stuff and line them amply to keep away the cold.

The Jesuit Relations and Allied Documents, ed. Reuben G. Thwaites, vol. 44, *Iroquois, Lower Canada, 1656–58* (Cleveland, 1899), 293–309.

Shirts are in Europe worn next to the skin, under the other garments. The Savages wear them usually over their dress, to shield it from snow and rain. . . .

The end of a shirt protruding from under the coat is an indecorous thing; but not so in Canadas. You will see Savages dressed in French attire, with worsted stockings and a cloak, but without any breeches; while before and . . . behind are seen two large shirt-flaps hanging down below the cloak. . . . That fashion seems all the more tasteful in their eyes because they regard our breeches as an encumbrance. . . .

Politeness and propriety have taught us to carry handkerchiefs. In this matter the Savages charge us with filthiness—because, they say, we place what is unclean in a fine white piece of linen, and put it away in our pockets as something very precious, while they throw it upon the ground. . . .

Most Europeans sit on raised seats, using round or square tables. The Savages eat from the ground. . . .

In France, food and drink are taken together. The Algonquins follow quite the contrary custom in their feasts, first eating what is served them, and then drinking, without touching food again. . . .

We wash meat to cleanse it of blood and impurities; the Savages do not wash it, for fear of losing its blood and a part of its fat. . . . We usually begin the dinner with soup, which is the last dish among the Savages, the broth of the pot serving them for drink. Bread is eaten here with the meat and other courses; if you give some to a Savage, he will make a separate course of it and very often eat it last. Yet they are gradually adapting themselves to our way.

In most parts of Europe, when any one makes a call he is invited to drink; among the Savages he is invited to eat. . . .

When the Savages are not hunting or on a journey, their usual posture is to recline or sit on the ground. They cannot remain standing, maintaining that their legs become swollen immediately. Seats higher than the ground they dislike; the French, on the contrary, use chairs, benches, or stools, leaving the ground and litter to the animals.

A good dancer in France does not move . . . his arms much, and holds his body erect, moving his feet so nimbly that, you would say, he spurns the ground and wishes to stay in the air. The savages, on the contrary, bend over in their dances, thrusting out their arms and moving them violently as if they were kneading bread, while they strike the ground with their feet so vigorously that one would say they are determined to make it tremble, or to bury themselves in it up to the neck. . . .

In France, children are carried on the arm, or clasped to the breast; in Canadas, the mothers bear them behind their backs. In France, they are kept as well covered as possible. . . . The cradle, in France, is left at home; there the women carry it with their children; it is composed merely of a cedar board, on which the poor little one is bound like a bundle.

. . . In France, a Workman does not expect his pay until he completes his task; the Savages ask it in advance. . . .

Europeans have no hesitation about telling their names and conditions, but you embarrass a Savage by asking him his name; if you do ask him, he will say that he does not know, and will make a sign to some one else to tell it. . . .

In France, when a father gives his daughter in marriage, he allows her a dowry. There, it is given to the girl's father.

In Europe, the children inherit from their parents; among the Hurons the nephews, sons of the father's sister, are their uncle's heirs; and the Savage's small belongings will be given to the friends of the deceased, rather than to his children. . . .

In France, the man usually takes to his house the woman whom he marries; there, the man goes to the woman's house to dwell.

In France, if any one fall into a fit of anger, or harbor some evil purpose, or meditate some harm, he is reviled, threatened, and punished; there, they give him presents, to soothe his ill-humor, cure his mental ailment, and put good thoughts into his head again. This custom, in the sincerity of their actions, is not a bad one; for if he who is angry, or is devising some ill . . . to resent an offense, touch this present, his anger and his evil purpose are immediately effaced from his mind.

In a large part of Europe, ceremonies and compliments are indulged in to such an excess as to drive out sincerity. There quite on the contrary sincerity is entirely naked. . . .

In Europe, we unclothe the dead as much as we can, leaving them only what is necessary to veil them and hide them from our eyes. The Savages, however, give them all that they can, anointing and attiring them as if for their wedding, and burying them with all their favorite belongings.

The French are stretched lengthwise in their graves, while the Savages, . . . in burying their dead make them take in the grave the position which they held in their mothers' wombs. In some parts of France, the dead are placed with their heads turned toward the East; the Savages make them face the West.

4

Captain John Smith Describes the Founding of Jamestown (1607)

The English were latecomers in colonizing the Americas. During the last quarter of the 16th century, English mariners began an intensive reconnaissance of the east coast of North America with an eye toward establishing a permanent outpost. Initial attempts at colonization met with failure until the successful settlement at Jamestown in 1607. Organized as a business venture by the Virginia Company of London, Jamestown was established on a small, swampy peninsula along the James River in Virginia. The site's selection resulted from military considerations; it afforded a defensible position against attack from the neighboring Powhatan Confederacy. Most of the new arrivals were unprepared for the rigors of colonizing a strange land, although a handful would prove their mettle. John Smith was among the first group of settlers. He was an adventurer and soldier of fortune whose experiences had taken him from the Low Countries to wars against the Turks, and, in 1607, to Virginia. In the following excerpt, he describes the conditions facing his fellow settlers during the first months of colonization.

Questions to Consider

1. According to John Smith's account, why were conditions in Jamestown so poor?
2. How were conditions improved?
3. How did the colony survive?
4. What seems to be the nature of the relationship between the English and the Native Americans?

Being thus left alone to our fortunes, it fortuned that, within ten days, scarce ten amongst us could either go, or well stand; such extreme weakness and sickness oppressed us. And thereat none need mervaile, if they consider the cause and reason; which was this.

Whilest the ships stayed, our allowance was somewhat bettered by a daily proportion of bisket which the sailers would pilfer to sell, give, or exchange with us, for mon[e]y, saxefras, furs, or loue. But when they departed, there remained neither tavern, beer-house, nor place of releif but the common kettle. Had we been as free from all sins as gluttony and drunkeness, we might have been canonized for Saints. But our President would never have bin admitted, for ingrossing to his private [i.e., his own use], Oatmeal, sacke [sweet wine], oil, aquavitae [aromatic brandy], beef, eggs, or what not, but the kettle; that indeed he allowed equally to be distributed: and that was half a pint of wheat, and as much barley, boiled with water, for a man a day; and this having fryed some 26. weeks in the ships hold, contained as many worms as grains, so that we might truly call it rather so much bran than corne. Our drink was water; our lodgings, castles in the air [i.e., in the trees].

With this lodging and diet, our extreme toil in bearing and planting pallisadoes, so strained and bruised . . . us, and our continual labor in the extremity of the heat had so weakened us, as were cause sufficient to have made us as miserable in our native country, or any other place in the world.

John Smith, "The Proceedings of the English Colony of Virginia," *Travels and Works of Captain John Smith,* ed. Edward Arber (Edinburgh, 1910), 1: 94–96.

From May to September, those that escaped lived upon Sturgeon and sea-Crabs. 50. in this time we buried.

The rest seeing the Presidents projects to escape these miseries in our Pinnas by flight (who all this time, had neither felt want nor sickness), [this] so moved our dead spirits, as we deposed him [10 *Sept.* 1607]; and established *Ratcliffe* in his place: *Gosnoll* being dead [22 *Aug.* 1607], [and] *Kendall* deposed [? *Sept.* 1607]. *Smith* newly recovered; *Martin* and *Rat[c]liffe* was, by his care, preserved and relieved.

But now was all our provision spent, the Sturgeon gone, all helps abandoned, each hour expecting the fury of the Savages; when God, the patron of all good endeavours, in that desperate extremity, so changed the hearts of the Savages, that they brought such plenty of their fruits and provision, as no man wanted.

And now where some affirmed it was ill done of the Councel to send forth men so badly provided, this incontradictable reason will show them plainly they are too ill advised to nourish such ill concepts. First, the fault of our going was our own. What could be thought fitting or necessary we had: but what we should find, what we should want, where we should be, we were all ignorant [of]. And supposing to make our passage in two months, with victual to live, and advantage of the spring to work: we were at sea 5. months, where we both spent out victual and lost the opportunity of the time and season to plant. . . .

Such actions have ever since the worlds beginning been subject to such accidents, and every thing of worth is found full of difficulties: but nothing [is] so difficult as to establish a common wealth so far remote from men and means; and where mens minds are so untoward as neither do well themselves, nor suffer others. But to proceed.

The new President, and *Martin,* being little beloved, of weak judgement in dangers and less industry in peace, committed the managing of all things abroad [*i.e., out of doors*] to captain *Smith:* who, by his own example, good words, and fair promises, set some to mow, others to bind thatch; some to build houses, others to thatch them; himself always bearing the greatest task for his own share: so that, in short time, he provided most of them lodgings, neglecting any for himself.

This done, seeing the Savages superfluity begin to decrease, [he] (with some of his workmen) shipped himself in the shallop, to search the country for trade. The want of the language, knowledge to manage his boat without sailers, the want of a sufficient power [*forces*] (knowing the multitude of the Savages), [of] apparel for his men, and [of] other necessaries; [these] were infinite impediments, yet no discouragement.

Being but 6 or 7 in company, he went down the river to *Kecoughtan;* where at first they scorned him, as a starved man: yet he so dealt with him, that the next day they loaded his boat with corn. And in his return, he discovered and kindly traded with the *Weraskoyks.*

In the mean time, those at the fort so glutted the Savages with their commodities, as they became not regarded.

5

"General Considerations for the Plantation in New England" (1629)

The Puritans established the first extensive English settlement in North America at Massachusetts Bay in 1630. Dissatisfied with the Church of England and determined to create a church free of corruption, the Puritans became interested in the region with the establishment of a fishing concern on Cape Ann, Massachusetts, in 1623. By the end of the decade, many Puritans, whose attempts to create a purified church had alienated the Crown, sought to establish a model community in which they could practice their religion without interference. In 1629, they obtained a charter for the Massachusetts Bay Company. In the following selection, the leaders of the company give their reasons for establishing a colony in New England. The Massachusetts Bay Colony attracted 20,000 Englishmen in the ensuing Great Migration of 1630–1643.

Questions to Consider

1. What is the thesis of this document?
2. Why was the Massachusetts Bay Colony established?
3. What role do economic factors play in this colony? What might that say about the Puritans?
4. Why would this colony be so attractive to English settlers?

First, it will be a service to the Church of great consequence, to carry Gospel into those parts of the world, and to raise a bulwark against the kingdom of Antichrist, which the Jesuits labor to rear up in all places of the world.

Secondly, all other churches of Europe are brought to desolation, and it may be justly feared that the like judgment is coming upon us; and who knows but that God hath provided this place to be a refuge for many whom he means to save out of the general destruction?

Thirdly, the land grows weary of her inhabitants, so that man, which is the most precious of all creatures, is here more vile and base than the earth they tread upon; so as children, neighbors and friends, especially of the poor, are counted the greatest burdens, which, if things were right, would be the chiefest earthly blessings.

Fourthly, we are grown to that excess and intemperance in all excess of riot, as no mean estate almost will suffice [a man] to keep sail with his

"General Considerations for the Plantation in New England; with an Answer to Several Objections," *Chronicles of the First Planters of the Colony of Massachusetts Bay, from 1623–1636,* ed. Alexander Young (Boston, 1846), 271–273.

equals; and he that fails in it, must live in scorn and contempt. Hence it comes to pass, that all arts and trades are carried in that deceitful manner and unrighteous course, as it is almost impossible for a good, upright man to maintain his charge, and live comfortably in any of them.

Fifthly, the schools of learning and religion are so corrupted as, (besides the unsupportable charge of their education), most children, even the best, wittiest, and of fairest hopes, are perverted, corrupted, and utterly overthrown by the multitude of evil examples and licentious governors of those seminaries.

Sixthly, the whole earth is the Lord's garden, and he has given it to the sons of Adam to be tilled and improved by them. Why then should we stand starving here for places of habitation, (many men spending as much labor and cost to recover or keep sometimes an acre or two of lands as would procure him many hundreds of acres, as good or better, in another place) and in the mean time suffer whole countries, as profitable for the use of man, to lie waste without improvement?

Seventhly, what can be a better work, and more noble, and worthy a Christian, than to help to raise and support a particular church while it is in its infancy, and to join forces with such a company of faithful people as by a timely assistance may grow stronger and prosper, and for want of it may be put to great hazard, if not wholly ruined?

Eighthly, if any such as are known to be godly, and live in wealth and prosperity here, shall forsake all this to join themselves with this church, and run in hazard with them of a hard and mean condition, it will be an example of great use both for the removing of scandal and sinister and worldly respects, to give more life to the faith of God's people in their prayers for the Plantation, and also to encourage others to join the more willingly in it.

6

William Bradford on Sickness among the Natives (1633)

The arrival of Europeans had a devastating impact on Native Americans. European demand for land, the introduction of new flora and fauna, and the disruption of traditional intertribal relations all created severe dislocation for America's original inhabitants, but European diseases had the greatest repercussions. Long isolated from the disease pool shared by Europeans, Asians, and Africans, Native Americans had no resistance to the microbial invaders that accompanied the newcomers after 1492. The following account, written by William Bradford, describes the catastrophic effect disease had on the New England tribes. A native of England, Bradford had become a Pilgrim as a youth and lived in the Netherlands before arriving in North America aboard the Mayflower. As leader of Plymouth during most of the period from 1622 until 1656, he greatly influenced the development of the Pilgrim colony.

Questions to Consider

1. What was the impact of smallpox on the Native Americans?

2. How does William Bradford explain why Indians die and Europeans survive the disease? What does this say about the 17th-century Pilgrim worldview?

3. How did the Native Americans react?

4. In what ways would disease assist European conquest of the New World?

I am now to relate some strange and remarkable passages. There was a company of people [who] lived in the country, up above in the river of Conigte-cut [Connecticut], a great way from their trading house there, and were enemies to those Indians which lived about them, and of whom they stood in some fear (being a stout people). About a thousand of them had enclosed them selves in a fort, which they had strongly palisaded about. 3. or 4. Dutch men went up in the beginning of winter to live with them, to get their trade, and prevent them for bringing it to the English, or to fall into amity with them; but at spring to bring all down to their place. But their enterprise failed, for it pleased God to visit these Indians with a great sickness, and such a mortalitie that of a 1000. above 900. and a half of them died, and many of them did rot above ground for want of burial, and the Dutch men almost starved before they could get away, for ice and snow. But about Feb: they got with much difficulty to their trading house; whom they kindly relieved, being almost spent with hunger and cold. Being thus refreshed by them diverse days, they got to their own place, and the Dutch were very thankful for this kindness.

This spring, also, those Indians that lived about their trading house there fell sick of the small pox, and died most miserably; for a sorer disease cannot befall them; they fear it more than the plague; for usually they that have this disease have them in abundance, and for want of bedding and lining and other helps, they fall into a lamentable condition, as they lie on their hard mats, the pox breaking and mattering, and running one into another, their skin cleaving (by reason thereof) to the mats they lie on; when they turn them, a whole side will flee off at once, (as it were,), and they will be all of a gore blood, most fearful to behold; and then being very sore, what with cold and other distempers, they die like rotten sheep. The condition of this people was so lamentable, and they fell down so generally of this disease, as they were (in the end) not able to help one another; no, not to make a fire, nor to fetch a little water to drink, nor any to bury the dead; but would strive as long as they could, and when they could procure no other means to make fire, they would burn the wooden trays and dishes they ate their meat in, and their very bows and arrows; and some would crawl out on all four to get a little

William Bradford, *History of Plimouth Plantation* (Boston, 1898), 388–389.

water, and some times die by the way, and not be able to get in again. But those of the English house, (though at first they were afraid of the infection,), yet seeing their woeful and sad condition, and hearing their pitiful cries and lamentations, they had compassion of them, and daily fetched them wood and water, and made them fires, got them victuals whilst they lived, and buried them when they died. For very few of them escaped, notwithstanding they did what they could for them, to the hazard of them selves. The chief Sachem him self now died, and almost all his friends and kindred. But by the marvelous goodness and providence of God not one of the English was so much as sick, or in the least measure tainted with this disease, though they daily did these offices for them for many weeks together. And this mercy which they showed them was kindly taken, and thankfully acknowledged of all the Indians that knew or heard of the same; and their mrs. here did much commend and reward them for the same.

7

"Captivity Account" of Mary Rowlandson (1675)

The spread of white settlement in southern New England had placed many of the native tribes in a precarious position. Pressed by white land hunger and decimated by European diseases, a coalition of the Wampanoag, Narragansett, Nipmuck, Mohegan, and Podunk allied under the leadership of the Wampanoag sachem (leader) Metacom, or King Philip, to attack the white settlements. During the 1675–1676 campaign, the natives enjoyed great success, including the burning of Lancaster in 1676. As they fled the town, they left with several captives, including Mary White Rowlandson. The daughter of one of Lancaster's wealthiest proprietors and wife of the village's first minister, Mary spent her captivity making shirts and stockings. After she had spent eleven weeks with the natives, a ransom freed her. The following excerpt describes some of her experiences and reveals how her captors managed to feed themselves while on the run.

Questions to Consider

1. To what audience is this document addressed?
2. What is Mary Rowlandson's opinion of the Native Americans?
3. Why does Rowlandson place the Native Americans and their actions within a religious context?
4. How does this description of native culture differ from that contained in the "Jesuit Comparison of French and Native Life" (Document 3) and "The Pueblo Revolt" (Document 8)? How do you account for these differences?

It was thought, if their corn were cut down, they would starve and die with hunger; and all that could be found was destroyed and they driven from that little they had in store, into the woods, in the midst of winter; and yet how to admiration did the Lord preserve them for his holy ends, and the destruction of many still among the English! Strangely did the Lord provide for them, that I did not see (all the time I was among them) one man, woman, or child die with hunger. Though many times they would eat that, that a hog or a dog would hardly touch; yet by the God strengthened them to be a scourge to his people.

Their chief and commonest food was ground-nuts, they eat also nuts and acorns, artichokes, lily roots, ground beans, and several other weeds and roots that I know not.

They would pick up old bones, and cut them in pieces at the joints, and if they were full of worms and maggots, they would scald them over the fire, to make the vermin come out, and then boil them, and drink up the liquor, and then beat the great ends of them in a mortar, and so eat them. They would eat horses' guts, and ears, and all sorts of wild birds which they could catch. Also bear, venison, beavers, tortoise, frogs, squirrels, dogs, skunks, rattlesnakes. Yea, the very bark of trees; besides all sorts of creatures and provision which they plundered from the English. I can but stand in admiration to see the wonderful power of God, in providing for such a vast number of our enemies in the wilderness, where there was nothing to be seen, but from hand to mouth.

8

The Pueblo Revolt (1680)

By 1598, Spanish expansion north from the Valley of Mexico had established settlements in the Rio Grande Valley of modern-day New Mexico. For nearly a century, the Pueblo Indian villages in the region tolerated Spanish demands for labor and Spanish insistence on conversion to Roman Catholicism. By the 1670s, a group of Pueblo Indian leaders began to emphasize a reassertion of traditional customs as a means of resisting outside domination. In 1675, Spanish authorities rounded up forty-seven, executing three and publicly whipping the rest. Resistance continued in secret, and by the summer of 1680, insurgent leader Popé was prepared to drive out the Spanish and resurrect traditional Pueblo Indian practices. The Pueblos revolted on August 11, 1680; within just a few days, the Spanish fled south to El Paso and would not reassert their control over the region until the mid-1690s. In the meantime, the Pueblo Indians set about destroying all elements of Spanish culture. The following excerpt discusses a Spanish official's account of the revolt.

Mary Rowlandson, *A Narrative . . . of Mrs. Mary Rowlandson* (Boston, 1856), 104–105.

Questions to Consider

1. What can you deduce from this document about Spanish attitudes toward Native Americans?

2. Why are the Spanish under attack? Why do some of the Native Americans cooperate with the Spanish?

3. Why are priests being killed? What might this say about the role of religion in Spanish and native cultures?

On the eve of the day of the glorious San Lorenzo, having received notice of the said rebellion from the governors of Pecos and Tanos, who said that two Indians had left the Teguas, and particularly the pueblos of Tesuque, to which they belonged, to notify them to come and join the revolt, and that they [the governors] came to tell me of it and of how they were unwilling to participate in such wickedness and treason, saying that they now regarded the Spaniards as their brothers, I thanked them for their kindness in giving the notice and told them to go to their pueblos and remain quiet. I busied myself immediately in giving the said orders, which I mentioned to your reverence, and on the following morning as I was about to go to mass there arrived Pedro Hidalgo, who had gone to the pueblo of Tesuque, accompanying Father Fray Juan Pio, who went there to say mass. He told me that the Indians of the said pueblo had killed the said Father Fray Pio and that he himself had escaped miraculously. He told me also that the said Indians had retreated to the sierra with all the cattle and horses belonging to the convent, and with their own.

The receipt of this news left us all in the state that may be imagined. I immediately and instantly sent the maestre de campo [military commander], Francisco Gomez, with a squadron of soldiers sufficient to investigate this case and also to attempt to extinguish the flame of the ruin already begun. He returned here on the same day, telling me that the report of the death of the said Fray Juan Pio was true. He said also that there had been killed that same morning Father Fray Tomas de Torres, guardian of Nambe, and his brother, with the latter's wife and a child, and another resident of Taos, and also Father Fray Luis de Morales, guardian of San Ildefonso, and the family of Francisco de Ximenez, his wife and family, and Dona Petronila de Salas with ten sons and daughters; and that they had been robbed and profaned the convents and had robbed all the haciendas of those murdered and also all the horses and cattle of that jurisdiction and La Canada.

Upon receiving this news I immediately notified the alcalde [chief] mayor of that district to assemble all the people in his house in a body, and told him to advise at once the alcalde mayor of Los Taos to do the same. On this same day I received notice that two members of a convoy had been killed in the

"Letter of the Governor and Captain-General, Don Antonio de Otermin," September 8, 1680 C. W. Hackett, ed., *Historical Documents Relating to New Mexico, Nueva Vizcaya, and Approaches Thereto, to 1773* (Washington, DC, 1937), 3: 327–335. Reprinted by permission.

pueblo of Santa Clara, six others having escaped by flight. Also at the same time the sargento [deputy] mayor, Bernabe Marquez, sent to ask me for assistance, saying that he was surrounded and hard pressed by the Indians of the Queres and Tanos nations. Having sent the aid for which he asked me, and an order for those families of Los Cerrillos to come to the villa, I instantly arranged for all the people in it and its environs to retire to the casas reales [royal houses]. Believing that the uprising of the Tanos and Pecos might endanger the person of the reverend father custodian, I wrote to him to set out at once for the villa, not feeling reassured even with the escort which the lieutenant took, at my orders, but when they arrived with the letter they found that the Indians had already killed the said father custodian; Father Fray Domingo de Fernando de Velasco, guardian of Los Pecos, near the pueblo of Galisteo, he having escaped that far from the fury of the Pecos. The latter killed in that pueblo Fray Juan de la Pedrosa, two Spanish women, and three children. There died also at the hands of the said enemies in Galisteo Joseph Nieto, two sons of Maestre de Campo Leiva, Francisco de Anaya, the younger, who was with the escort, and the wives of Maestre de Campo Leiva and Joseph Nieto, with all their daughters and families. I also learned definitely on this day that there had died, in the pueblo of Santo Domingo, Fathers Fray Juan de Talaban, Fray Francisco Antonio Lorenzana, and Fray Joseph de Montesdoca, and the alcalde mayor, Andres de Peralta, together with the rest of the men who went as escort.

Seeing myself with notices of so many and such untimely deaths, and that not having received any word from the lieutenant general was probably due to the fact that he was in the same exigency and confusion, or that the Indians had killed most of those on the lower river, and considering also that in the pueblo of Los Taos the father guardians of that place and of the pueblo of Pecuries might be in danger, as well as the alcalde mayor and the residents of that valley, and that at all events it was the only place from which I could obtain any horses and cattle—for all these reasons I endeavored to send a relief of soldiers. Marching out for that purpose, they learned that in La Canada, as in Los Taos and Pecuries, the Indians had risen in rebellion, joining the Apaches of the Achos nation. In Pecuries they had killed Francisco Blanco de la Vega; a *mulata* [woman of mixed race ancestry] belonging to the maestre de campo, Francisco Xavier; and a son of the said *mulata*. Shortly thereafter I learned that they also killed in the pueblo of Taos the father guardian, Fray Francisco de Mora; and the Father Fray Mathias Rendon, the guardian of Pecuries; and Fray Antonio de Pro; and the alcalde mayor, as well as another fourteen or fifteen soldiers, along with all the families of the inhabitants of that valley, all of whom were together in the convent. . . .

2

Emerging Colonial Societies

Colonists came to North America in the 17th and early 18th centuries for a variety of reasons. Some sought the right to worship as they wished, others came for economic opportunity, and still others arrived as forced labor or slaves. By 1740, much of the Atlantic coastline of what is now the United States came under English control, but the local population was not necessarily like that of Britain. The American colonies exhibited far more ethnic diversity than was found in England, while providing many white inhabitants with greater personal freedom and more social mobility. As such, an increasingly American society had begun to emerge. The following documents provide insights into the diverse nature of colonial society and culture.

9

Images of 17th-Century European and Native American Combat

Vast cultural differences and disputes over land are generally given as major reasons for Native American and white conflict throughout American history. Although these factors certainly help explain such conflict, the ensuing images show that a greater complexity was at work. The first image depicts combat during the Pequot War. The Pequots, who traded with the Dutch, lived along Long Island Sound near the Connecticut River, which enabled them to control the production of wampum, a sea shell that was used as currency by Native Americans and European settlers alike. The Pequots' traditional enemy, the Narragansett of present-day Rhode Island, made common cause with the English, who sought to displace the Dutch in the region. The second selection is a woodcut from Samuel de Champlain's account of his adventures in North America. The French presence in the St. Lawrence River Valley made them trading partners of the Hurons, ancient rivals of the Iroquois Confederacy of upstate New York. The image shows the role of the French in one of these battles.

Questions to Consider

1. Why are Indians fighting Indians in these pictures?
2. How involved are the Europeans in these battles?
3. Based on what you see in these images, how decisive are Europeans in these conflicts?

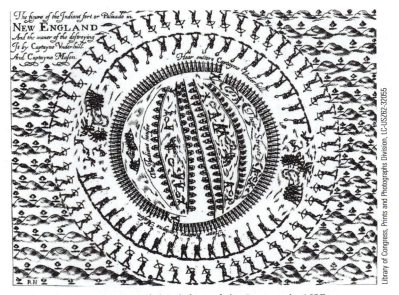

Contemporary engraving of the defeat of the Pequots in 1637

Contemporary engraving of the 1609 battle between Champlain and the Iroquois

10

A Treaty Between the Five Nations and the New England Colonies (1689)

In 1689, Britain engaged in the first of a series of wars against the French. Known as King William's War, the conflict had European roots but quickly spilled across the Atlantic. Native Americans often held the balance of power in this and later conflicts. The Five Nations of the Iroquois (Mohawk, Oneida, Onondaga, Cayuga, and Seneca) dominated the fur trade along the northern frontier and controlled the region of upstate New York between New England and New France. Their support was vital in a conflict between Britain and France. In the following excerpted account, the New England colonies negotiate a treaty with the Five Nations. The author of this tract was one of the leading figures in colonial America. Scottish-born Cadwalader Colden was one of America's leading scientists and a major figure in New York politics. His works on the Iroquois are among the best surviving accounts of the Five Nations.

Questions to Consider

1. Why are the Five Nations willing to fight the French? Why are they unwilling to fight Indian tribes from New England?
2. What can you deduce from this document about the religious views of the Iroquois?
3. What items seem valuable to the Five Nations? Why?
4. Compare and contrast this document with "The Pontiac Manuscript" (Document 22). What similarities do you notice? Differences?

About the beginning of September 1689, Colonel John Pynchon, Major John Savage, and Captain Jonathan Bull, Agents for the Colonies of Massachuset's Bay, New Plymouth, and Connecticut, arrived at Albany, to renew the Friendship with the Five Nations, and to engage them against the Eastern Indians, who made War on the English of those Colonies, and were supported by the French. . . .

"*Brethren,*

"You are welcome to this House, which is appointed for our Treaties and publick Business with the Christians; we thank you for renewing the Covenant-chain. It is now no longer of Iron and subject to Rust, as formerly, but of pure Silver, and includes in it all the King's Subjects, from the Senekas Country eastward to Virginia. Here he gave a Bever.

Cadwallader Colden, "A Treaty between the Agents of Massachuset's Bay, New-Plymuth, and Connecticut, and the Sachems of the Five Nations, at Albany, in the Year 1689," *The History of the Five Indian Nations of Canada* (New York, 1922), 1: 119–126.

"We are glad to hear of the good Success our great King has had over the French by Sea, in taking and sinking so many of their Men of War. You tell us in your Proposals that we are one People, let us then go hand in hand together, to ruin and destroy the French in our common Enemy. Gives a Bever.

"The Covenant-chain between us is ancient (as you tell us) and of long standing, and it has been kept inviolably by us. When you had Wars some time ago with the Indians, you desired us to help you; we did it readily, and to the Purpose; for we pursued them closely, by which we prevented the Effusion of much of your Blood. This was a certain Sign that we loved truly and sincerely, and from our Hearts. Gives a Belt.

"You advise us to pursue our Enemies, the French, vigorously; this we assure you we are resolved to do to the utmost of our Power: But since the French are your Enemies likewise, we desire our Brethren of the three Colonies to send us an hundred Men for the Security of this Place, which is ill provided, in Case of an Attack from the French; the Christians have Victuals enough for their Entertainment. Gives one Belt.

"We patiently bore many Injuries from the French, from one Year to another, before we took up the Axe against them. Our Patience made the Governor of Canada think, that we were afraid of him, and durst not resent the Injuries we had so long suffered; but now he is undeceived. We assure you, that we are resolved never to drop the Axe, the French never shall see our Faces in Peace, we shall never be reconciled as long as one Frenchman is alive. We shall never make Peace, though our Nation should be ruined by it, and every one of us cut in Pieces. Our Brethren of the three Colonies may depend on this. Gives Bever.

"As to what you told us of the Owenagungas and Uragees, we answer: That we were never so proud and haughty, as to begin a War without just Provocation. You tell us that they are treacherous Rogues, we believe it, and that they will undoubtedly assist the French. If they shall do this, or shall join with any of our Enemies, either French or Indians, then we kill and destroy them. Gives a Bever."

. . . the Speaker continued his Speech, and said: "We have spoke what we had to say of the War, we now come to the Affairs of Peace: We promise to preserve the Chain inviolably, and wish that the Sun may always shine in Peace over all our Heads that are comprehended in this Chain. We give two Belts, one for the Sun, the other for its Beams.

"We make fast the Roots of the Tree of Peace and Tranquility, which is planted in this Place. Its Roots extend as far as the utmost of your Colonies; if the French should come to shake this Tree, we would feel it by the Motion of its Roots, which extend into our Country: But we trust it will not be in the Governor of Canada's Power to shake this Tree, which has been so firmly and so long planted with us. Gives two Bevers."

Lastly, He desired the Magistrates of Albany to rember what he had said, and gave them a bever.

But the Agents perceiving, that they had not answered any Thing about the Owenagunga messengers, and had answered indistinctly about the War with the Eastern Indians, desired them to explain themselves fully on these two points, about which the Agents were chiefly concerned.

The Five Nations answered:

"We cannot declare War against the Eastern Indians, for they have done us no Harm; Nevertheless our Brethren of New-England may be assured, that we will live and die in friendship with them. When we took up the Axe against the French and their Confederates, we did it to revenge the Injuries they had done us; we did not make War with them at the Persuasions of our Brethren here; for we did not so much as acquaint them with our Intention, till fourteen Days after our Army had begun their March."

. . . Now we assure our Brethren, that we are resolved to look on your Enemies as ours, and that we will first fall on the Owaragees; and then on the Owenagungas, and lastly on the French; and that you may be convinced of our Intention, we design to send five of our young Men along with our Brethren to New-England, to guard them, who have Orders to view the Country of the Owaragees, to discover in what Manner it can be attacked with the most Advantage. This we always do before we make an Attempt on our Enemies. In a Word, Brethren, your War is our War, for we will live and dye with you. . . .

"WE have a hundred and forty Men out skulking about Canada; it is impossible for the French to attempt any Thing, without being discovered and harassed by these Parties: If the French shall attempt any Thing this Way, all the Five Nations will come to your Assistance, for our Brethren and we are but one, and we will live and dye together. . . . The Great God hath sent us Signs in the Sky to confirm this. We have heard uncommon Noise in the Heavens, and have seen heads fall down upon Earth, which we look upon as a certain Presage of the Destruction of the French: Take Control! On this they all immediately joined in singing and crying out, Courage! Courage!"

11

Petition of an Accused Witch (1692)

The Salem witchcraft trials remain one of the most compelling events in American history. The cause for the hysteria remains an area of lively debate, as theories of causation have looked at the event from political, social, economic, geographic, gender, and pharmacological perspectives. The historical record does show that the craze began early in 1692, when a group of adolescent girls experienced "fits" and claimed that they had been bewitched. Widespread belief in witches (more than 300 individuals had been accused of witchcraft in 17th-century New England) combined with community stresses to fuel the frenzy. Over the next ten months, authorities in Salem Village, Massachusetts, condemned twenty individuals to death and jailed more than one hundred on charges of witchcraft. In the following account, Mary Esty [or Easty] responds to the charges of witchcraft leveled against her. Her impassioned plea was to no avail, as she would be put to death for practicing witchcraft.

Questions to Consider

1. What is the historical context of this document?
2. In what ways does Mary Esty defend herself from the charges of witchcraft?
3. Why would Esty (or someone else) be accused of witchcraft?
4. What can you deduce from this document about the status of women in late 17th-century Massachusetts?

To the Honorable Judge and Bench now sitting in Judicature in Salem and the Reverend Ministers, humbly sheweth, That whereas your humble poor Petitioned being Condemned to die, doth humbly beg of you, to take it into your Judicious and Pious Consideration, that your poor and humble Petitioned knowing my Innocency (blessed be the Lord for it) and seeing plainly the Wiles and Subtilty of my Accusers, by my self, cannot but judge charitably of others, that are going in the same way with my self, if the Lord step not mightily in. I was confined a whole Month on the same account that I am now condemned for, and then cleared by the Afflicted persons, as some of your Honours know, and in two days time I was cried out upon by them, and have been confined, and now am condemned to die. The Lord above knows my innocency then, and likewise doth now, as at the great day will be known to Men and Angels. I Petition to your Honours not for my own Life, for I know I must die, and my appointed time is set; but the Lord he knows it is, if it be possible, that no more Innocent blood be shed, which undoubtedly cannot be avoided in the way and course you go in. I question not, but your Honours do to the utmost of your powers, in the discovery and detecting of witchcraft and Witches, and would not be guilty of Innocent Blood for the World; but by my own Innocency I know you are in the wrong way. The Lord in his infinite Mercy direct you in this great work, if it be his blessed will, that Innocent Blood be not shed; I would humbly beg of you, that your Honours would be pleased to Examine some of those confessing Witches, I being confident there are several of them have belyed themselves and others, as will appear, if not in this World, I am sure in the World to come, whither I am going; and I question not, but your selves will see an alteration in these things: They say, my self and others have made a league with the Devil, we cannot confess. I know and the Lord he knows (as will shortly appear) they belye me, and so I question not but they do others; the Lord alone, who is the searcher of all hearts, knows that as I shall answer it at the Tribunal Seat, that I know not the least thing of Witchcraft, therefore I cannot, I durst not belye my own Soul. I beg your Honours not to deny this my humble Petition, from a poor dying Innocent person, and I question not but the Lord will give a blessing to your Endeavours.
—Mary Esty

Narratives of the Witchcraft Cases, 1648–1706, ed. George L. Burr (New York, 1914), 368–369.

12

"Pennsylvania, the Poor Man's Paradise" (1698)

William Penn established the colony of Pennsylvania on land he received from the Crown in lieu of a debt owed to his father. The colony was initially founded as a religious haven and land of opportunity for English Quakers; its 1692 proclamation supporting liberty of conscience and Penn's extensive promotion of the area attracted immigrants from throughout Western Europe. One of these early settlers was Gabriel Thomas, a Quaker who lived in Pennsylvania and western New Jersey from 1682 until 1697. His An Historical and Geographical Account of the Province and Country of Pensilvania and West New Jersey, *published in 1698, was among the more widely read works by an American author. In the following excerpt, Thomas discusses conditions facing those who chose to colonize Pennsylvania.*

Questions to Consider

1. Who was the intended audience for this document?
2. According to Thomas, what made Pennsylvania attractive to settlers?
3. Was Pennsylvania a "poor man's paradise"?
4. In what ways was late 17th-century Pennsylvania different from early 17th-century Virginia ("Captain John Smith Describes the Founding of Jamestown," Document 4)? Why was it different?

And now for their Lots and Lands in City and Country, in their great Advancement since they were first laid out, which was within the compass of about Twelve Years, that which might have been bought for Fifteen or Eighteen Shillings, is now sold for Fourscore Pounds in ready Silver; and some other Lots, that might have been then Purchased for Three Pounds, within the space of Two Years, were sold for a Hundred Pounds a piece. . . .

Now the true Reason why this Fruitful Country and Flourishing City advance so considerably in the Purchase of Lands both in the one and the other, is their great and extended Traffic and Commerce both by Sea and Land, viz. to New-York, New-England, Virginia, Maryland, Carolina, Jamaica, Barbadoes, Nevis, Monsserat, Antigua, St. Christophers, Bermuda, New-Foundland, Madeiras, Saletudeous, and Old-England; besides several other places. Their Merchandize chiefly consists in Horses, Pipe-Staves, Pork and Beef Salted and Barreled . . . Bread, and Flower, all sorts of Grain, Peas, Beans, Skins, Furs, Tobacco, or Pot-Ashes, Wax &c. which are Barter'd for Rum, Sugar, Molasses, Silver, Negroes, Wine, Linen, Household-Goods, &c. . . .

Gabriel Thomas, *An Historical and Geographical Account of the Province and Country of Pensilvania . . .* (London, 1698), 23–45.

. . . the Countrey at the first, laying out, was void of Inhabitants (except the Heathens, or very few Christians not worth naming) and not many People caring to abandon a quiet and easy (at least tolerable) Life in their Native Country (usually the most agreeable to all Mankind) to seek out a new hazardous, and careful one in a Foreign Wilderness or Desert Country, wholly destitute of Christian Inhabitants, and even to arrive at which, they must pass over a vast Ocean, expos'd to some Dangers, and not a few Inconveniences: But now all those Cares, Fears and Hazards are vanished, for the Country is pretty well Peopled, and very much Improv'd, and will be more every Day, now the Dove is return'd with the Olive-branch of Peace in her Mouth.

I must needs say, even the Present Encouragements are very great and inviting, for Poor People (both Men and Women) of all kinds, can here get three times the Wages for their Labor they can in England or Wales. . . .

Corn and Flesh, and what else serves Man for Drink, Food and Rayment, is much cheaper here than in England, or elsewhere; but the chief reason why Wages of Servants of all sorts is much higher here than there, arises from the great Fertility and Produce of the Place; besides, if these large Stipends were refused them, they would quickly set up for themselves, for they can have Provision very cheap, and Land for a very small matter, or next to nothing in comparison of the Purchase of Lands in England; and the Farmers there, can better afford to give that great Wages than the Farmers in England can, for several Reasons very obvious.

As first, their Land costs them (as I said but just now) little or nothing in comparison, of which the Farmers commonly will get twice the increase of Corn for every Bushel they sow, that the Farmers in England can from the richest Land they have.

In the Second place, they have constantly good price for their Corn, by reason of the great and quick vent into Barbadoes and other Islands; through which means Silver is become more plentiful than here in England, considering the Number of People, and that causes a quick Trade for both Corn and Cattle; and that is the reason that Corn differs now from the Price formerly, else it would be at half the Price it was at then; for a Brother of mine (to my own particular knowledge) sold within the compass of one Week, about One Hundred and Twenty fat Beasts, most of them good handsome large Oxen.

Thirdly, They pay no Tithes, and their Taxes are inconsiderable; the Place is free for all Persuasions, in a Sober and Civil way; for the Church of England and the Quakers bear equal Share in the Government. They live Friendly and Well together; there is no Persecution for Religion, nor ever like to be; 'tis this that knocks all Commerce on the Head, together with high Imposts, strict Laws, and cramping Orders. Before I end this Paragraph, I shall add another Reason why Womens Wages are so exorbitant; they are not yet very numerous, which makes them stand upon high Terms for their several Services, in Sempstering, Washing, Spinning, Knitting, Sewing, and in all the other parts of their Employments; for they have for Spinning either Worsted or Linen, Two Shillings a Pound, and commonly for Knitting a very Coarse pair of Yarn Stockings, they have half a Crown a pair; moreover they are usually Marry'd before they are Twenty Years of Age, and when once in that Noose, are for the most part a little uneasy, and make their Husbands so too, till they procure them a Maid Servant to bear the burden of the Work, as also in some measure to wait on them too. . . .

. . . what I have here written, is not a Fiction, Flam, Whim, or any sinister Design, either to impose upon the Ignorant, or Credulous, or to curry Favor with the Rich and Mighty, but in mere Pity and pure Compassion to the Numbers of Poor Laboring Men, Women, and Children in England, half starv'd, visible in their meager looks, that are continually wandering up and down looking for Employment without finding any, who here need not lie idle a moment. . . . Here are no Beggars to be seen (it is a shame and Disgrace to the State that there are so many in England) nor indeed have any here the least Occasion or Temptation to take up that Scandalous Lazy Life. . . .

13

Of the Servants and Slaves in Virginia (1705)

During the 17th century, the English colonies hoped to meet their labor with indentured servants. Individuals entered into a contractual relationship promising to serve a master for a fixed number of years, after which the servants became free. Many individuals entered into such arrangements in order to gain passage to North America, but some convicts could escape imprisonment or execution by agreeing to become indentured labor in America. Despite the numerous indentured servants who crossed the Atlantic, they were too few and their labor too temporary to serve the needs of the South's emerging plantation economy. Virginia and other southern colonies responded by turning to African slaves for their workforce. The first Africans arrived at Jamestown in 1619, but it was not until later in the century that distinctions emerged between the institutions of slavery and indentured servitude. In the following excerpt, Robert Beverly differentiates between the two conditions. Virginia-born and English-educated, Beverly served as clerks of the General Court, Assembly, and Council, and represented Jamestown in the House of Burgesses.

Questions to Consider

1. What is the thesis of this document?
2. Who is the intended audience of this document?
3. What are the similarities and differences between slaves and indentured servants?
4. In what ways were women slaves and servants treated differently?
5. What does this document tell you about emerging racial consciousness in Virginia?

Their servants they distinguish by the names of slaves for life, and servants for a time.

Slaves are the negroes and their posterity, following the condition of the mother. . . . They are called slaves, in respect of the time of their servitude, because it is for life.

Servants, are those which serve only for a few years, according to the time of their indenture, or the custom of the country. The custom of the country takes place upon such as have no indentures. The law in this case is, that if such servants be under nineteen years of age . . . they must serve until they reach four and twenty; but if they be adjudged upwards of nineteen, they are then only to be servants for the term of five years.

. . . The male servants, and slaves of both sexes, are employed together in tilling and manuring the ground, in sowing and planting tobacco, corn, &c. Some distinction indeed is made between them in their clothes, and food; but the work of both is no other than what the overseers, the freemen, and the planters themselves do.

Sufficient distinction is also made between the female servants, and slaves; for a white woman is rarely or never put to work in the ground, if she be good for anything else; and to discourage all planters from using any women so, their law makes female servants working in the ground tithables, while it suffers all other white women to be absolutely exempted; whereas, on the other hand, it is a common thing to work a woman slave out of doors, nor does the law make any distinction in her taxes, whether her work be abroad or at home.

. . . Because I have heard how strangely cruel and severe the service of this country is represented in some parts of England, I can't forebear affirming, that the work of their servants and slaves is no other than what every common freeman does; neither is any servant required to do more in a day than his overseer; and I can assure you, with great truth, that generally their slaves are not worked near so hard, nor so many hours in a day, as the husbandmen, and day laborers in England. An overseer is a man, that having served his time, has acquired the skill and character of an experienced planter, and is therefore entrusted with the direction of the servants and slaves.

But to complete this account of servants, I shall give you a short relation of the care their laws take, that they be used as tenderly as possible:
BY THE LAWS OF THEIR COUNTRY,

1. All servants whatsoever have their complaints heard without fee or reward; but if the master be found faulty, the charge of the complaint is cast upon him, otherwise the business is done *ex officio.*

Robert Beverly, *The History of Virginia, in Four Parts,* 2nd revised ed. (Richmond, VA, 1855), 219–222.

2. Any justice of the peace may receive the complaint of a servant, and order everything relating thereto, till the next country court, where it will be finally determined.

3. All masters are under the correction and censure of the county courts, to provide for their servants food and wholesome diet, clothing and lodging.

4. They are always to appear upon the first notice given of the complaint of their servants, otherwise to forfeit the service of them until they do appear.

5. All servants' complaints are to be received at any time in court, without process, and shall not be delayed for want of form; but the merits of the complaint must be immediately enquired into by the justices; and if the master may cause any delay therein, the court may remove such servants, if they see cause, until the master will come to trial.

6. If a master shall at any time disobey an order of court, made upon any complaint of a servant, the court is empowered to remove such servant forthwith to another master who will be kinder, giving to the former master the produce only (after fees deducted), of what such servants shall be sold for by public outcry.

7. If a master should be so cruel, as to use his servant ill, . . . and thereby rendered unfit for labor, he must be removed by the church wardens out of the way of such cruelty, and boarded in some good planter's house, till the time of his freedom, the charge of which must be laid before the next county court, which has power to levy the same, from time to time, upon the goods and chattels of the master, after which, the charge of such boarding is to come upon the parish in general.

8. All hired servants are entitled to these privileges.

9. No master of a servant can make a new bargain for service, or other matter with his servant, without the privity and consent of the county court, to prevent the masters overreaching, or scaring such servant into an unreasonable compliance.

10. The property of all money and goods sent over thither to servants, or carried in with them, is reserved to themselves, and remains entirely at their disposal.

11. Each servant at his freedom receives of his master ten bushels of corn (which is sufficient for almost a year), two new suits of clothes, both linen and woolen, and a gun, twenty shillings value, and then becomes as free in all respects, and as much entitled to the liberties and privileges of the country, as any of the inhabitants or natives are, if such servants were not aliens.

12. Each servant has then also a right to take up fifty acres of land, where he can find any unpatented. . . .

14

Cotton Mather on the Evils of "Self-Pollution" (1723)

Cotton Mather was one of the most important figures in late 17th-century and early 18th-century Massachusetts. At the height of his considerable powers, he wielded great political influence, lent support to the shameful witchcraft trials in Salem, and endorsed the use of an early smallpox vaccination. But he is best remembered in his role as Puritan minister. From the pulpit of Boston's Old North Church, he exhorted his congregation to remain faithful to traditional Puritan beliefs of living in the world without succumbing to worldliness. The following tract, The Pure Nazarite: Advice to a Young Man, *reveals much about Mather's sexual outlook and his views toward the purpose of marriage and family.*

Questions to Consider

1. In what ways does Cotton Mather believe "self-pollution" to be harmful? Why?
2. What can you deduce from this document about Mather's views concerning marriage and the family?
3. What can you deduce from this document about early 18th-century sexual mores?
4. Are Mather's attitudes about sex, marriage, and the family still prevalent today? To what extent?

IT is time for me to tell you, that the *Crime* against which I warn you, is that *Self-Pollution,* which from the Name of the Person that stands for ever stigmitiz'd for it in our Holy Bible bears the Name of ORANISM. Among the *Libidinous Practices* of them who *do Evil with both hands earnestly,* they have the cursed way of procuring a *Discharge,* which the God of *Nature* has ordered only to be made in a Way which a *Lawful Marriage* leads unto. But, *My Son, be Admonished,* and let no such *Vile Thing* be practiced with you. It is the Unhappiness of the Subject now fallen upon the Sins, without some hazard of stirring up the Commission of them. Such a *Corruption* are the Children of Men sunk into, that when the Sins of *Unchastity* are to be Rebuked, every Word that raises the *Ideas* of them, gives hazard of their being the *Sooner* Perpetrated. *Lord, what wretched Creatures are we! How shall we be delivered from such a Body!* But I hope, the *Crime* against which you are now Cautioned, has been sufficiently *Explained,* and yet there is not Trespass upon the Rules of *Purity* in too broad an *Explanation.*

[Cotton Mather], *The Pure Nazarite: Advice to a Young Man* (Boston, 1723).

THIS *Crime* is not least among those *Unfruitful Works of Darkness,* upon which the *pure Word* of our God had that Remark, *It is a shame even to speak of those things, which are done of them in Secret.* But I am to *write* of those things which it is a *shame* to *speak* of; and I shall hope to do it so that you will be *Ashamed,* and also *Afraid* of doing them.

ONE would think, there should be little need for producing any *Sentences* from the *sacred Scriptures,* to do the part of *Thunderbolts* on this *Impiety,* and assure you that it is a grievous Offence unto an Holy GOD, who will not *hold them Guiltless,* that *abuse* his Creatures Impious Purposes. They who commit this Enormity, do *Immediately* upon the *Act,* find a Dismal Check and Sting of their *Conscience* upon them. An *Horror of Darkness does Immediately* seize upon their Minds; They feel *something within* them, with an Hideous Twitch telling of them, *You have done wickedly; . . .*

NEVERTHELESS you shall hear, how the *GOD of Glory Thunders* more Particularly and more Articulately in the *Voice* of His Holy Word, against this *Impiety.* The *Seventh* of the *Ten Commandments,* uttered by the *Voice of the Lord full of Majesty,* when He *came* with *His Holy Myriads* down upon the Burning Mountain, and *from His Right Hand there went forth a Fiery Law,* by which we shall one day be *Judged* of the Lord; forbids all Pranks of *Unchastity;* and certainly this *Unnatural Prostitution,* is to be numbered among the Pranks of *Unchastity. . . .*

AT the same time, take into your most serious Consideration, the *Dreadful Consequences* of indulging this *Impiety;* For there is a *Strange Punishment reserved* for *the workers* of this *Iniquity. . . .*

Such Transgressors, GOD *will Judge them!* In a *Future State* there will most certainly be a *Day of Judgment,* in which *the Unjust shall be punished,* but among the *Unjust,* the *Unchast* will make a great Figure, . . . *Chiefly they that walk after the Flesh, in the Lust of Uncleaness.* The *Bodies* that have now been defiled with much *Unchastity,* will be *Raised* on purpose, that Men may *receive the things in the Bodies,* which will answer to what had been *done in them.* And then, the *Bodies* which have been kept like an *Oven,* by the *Burning of Unchastity* ever cherished there, will be most grievously Tormented in *the day of the Lord that shall burn like an Oven,* and God shall *make them as a fiery Oven in the time of His Anger.* For a *Nasty Delight,* which is but the *crackling of Thorns under a Pot,* the forlorn Fools incur the Torments of a *Devouring Fire, and Everlasting Burnings.* Oh, that you may be *persuaded* unto a due Care to avoid the least Approach towards the *Impiety,* concerning which you now *know in the Terror of the Lord. . . .*

Every time a young Man commits this *impiety,* he makes a new *Resignation* of himself unto the *Unclean Spirit,* and gives the *Unclean Spirit* a new Invitation to take *Possession* of him. . . .

Young Men that have been more frequent Actors of this Wickedness, if the *Long-Suffering of God* permit them to come into the *Married Life,* they will find, that their former Lewdness, has upon *unmentionable Accounts,* brought various and lasting Mischief upon them. Why may not so much as this be *mentioned!* They strangely *Disable* themselves for Things expected by them, and from; and they render themselves *unacceptable,* where they would much desire to be otherwise. However, what may be more freely *mentioned*, is, That wonderful *Trouble* in the *Married Life* may befall them, to chaise the Faults committed before they came into it. Besides the *uneasiness* which they that are now Inseparably, and perhaps Unadvisedly *Yoked*, may give to one another, their not having of any *offspring*.

15

Early New Orleans (c. 1728)

Founded near the mouth of the Mississippi River in the early 18th century, New Orleans was among France's few outposts along the Gulf Coast. By the late 1720s, the future Crescent City had already shown signs of dramatic growth. In 1724, its population was less than 400 inhabitants. Three years later, the city had 794 white inhabitants and 144 slaves, mostly Africans who had begun to replace Native Americans as the preferred source for labor.. The village had no wall, and nearly all of its inhabitants lived within four blocks of the river. Woods and bayous surrounded the town, and mosquitoes that carried tropical fevers abounded. By this time, efforts had been begun to build levees to protect New Orleans, and the food supply, which was precarious in previous years, became more reliable because of the arrival of cattle. The following selection describes the town as it appeared in the late 1720s.

Questions to Consider

1. To what audience is this document addressed?
2. What role does religion play in the community?
3. Why does the author seem optimistic about the town's future?

...When the foundation of the new capital, which took the name of New Orleans, was laid, the houses, as I have said, were mere palisade cabins, like those of Old and New Biloxi; the only difference being, that in the latter places the posts were pine, while at the capital they were cypress. But since they began to make brick there, no houses but brick are built, so that now the government-house, church, barracks, &c., and almost all the houses are brick, or half-brick and half-wood.

About this time arrived a third vessel, loaded with young women, but these were of a superior class to their predecessors, from the fact of their being called "casket-girls," because, on leaving France, each had received from the liberality of the company a little trunk of clothes, and linens, caps, chemises, stockings, &c. They had, too, the advantage of being brought over by

Historical Memoirs of Louisiana, ed. B. F. French (New York, 1853), 5: 25–26.

nuns. They had not time to pine away in the houses assigned for their abode on their arrival, but soon found husbands.

The parish church of New-Orleans is built facing the Place d'Armes, and is served by the Capuchins, one of whom is vicar-general of the Bishop of Quebec. At some distance from the city is a very fine house, the residence of the Jesuit Fathers. It formerly belonged to M. Bienville, commandant-general in the country, who sold it to them.

Out of the city on the right was also built a brick convent, for the Ursuline nuns, who came to the country, a few at a time, but at last formed an establishment. They employed their time in instructing youth and teaching children to read. Beside the convent is a military hospital, served by these good nuns. This hospital, for many years, was used also by the citizens and country people, but at last another was built especially for them.

In this city there is a council, which meets generally every Tuesday and Saturday. It is composed of six councilors, an attorney-general, and an intendant, who is also commissaire of ordinance; there is also a register and a secretary to the council. Law-suits are settled there without attorneys or counselors, and consequently without expense, on the pleadings of the party. In conclusion, this place, which at first was hardly a good-sized village, may now justly be called a city. On the levee, to the left, a little above the intendant's, is the market, and opposite the place, beside the storehouses, is the anchorage for vessels, and beside it the guard-house. To avoid accident by fire the powder-magazine is at a distance from the city. In a word, it may be said that this capital wants only fortifications, which have not yet been begun. On the whole, you will find there very fine brick houses, and a great many buildings four and five stories high.

16

Eliza Lucas, a Modern Woman (1741–1742)

First settled in 1669, the area around Charleston at the confluence of the Ashley and Cooper Rivers quickly became the hub of life in South Carolina. The young colony grew rapidly, attracting a cosmopolitan population of New Englanders, New Yorkers, Virginians, and West Indians. By the early 18th century, the establishment of plantation agriculture and slavery had begun to dominate the local economy. Many of the early planters came from the British West Indies to cultivate rice in the tidal flats along the coast. One of the more uncommon early planters was Eliza Lucas. The daughter of Antigua's Lieutenant Governor George Lucas, the English-educated Eliza came to South Carolina in 1783 when she was only sixteen. Over the next several years, she managed several family plantations. Among Lucas's most significant contributions to the local economy was her development of indigo cultivation, which soon became an important cash crop. In the following selection, Lucas discusses the business of running the plantations under her care, as well as other tasks she performs in the community.

Questions to Consider

1. What tasks did Eliza Lucas perform on her plantation and for the local community?
2. Were these responsibilities typical for women of the time?
3. How did Lucas acquire such authority?
4. How does the status of women in 18th-century South Carolina compare with that of mid-19th-century America as described in "Sarah Grimké Argues for Gender Equality" (Document 84)?

June 4 [1741]. . . . After a pleasant passage of about an hour we arrived safe at home as I hope you and Mrs. Pinckney did at Belmont. But this place appeared much less agreeable than when I left it, having lost the agreeable company & conversation of our friends—I am engaged now with the rudiments of the Law to w[hi]ch I am but a Stranger and what adds to my mortification is that Doctr Wood wants the Politeness of your Uncle who with a graceful ease & good nature peculiar to himself is always ready to instruct the ignorant—but this rustic seems by no means to court my acquaintance for he often treats me with such cramp phrases I am unable to understand him nor is he civil enough to explain them when I desire it. However I hope in a short time we shall be better friends nor shall I grudge a little pains and application that will make me useful to my poor neighbors. We have some in this Neighbourhood who have a little Land and a few slaves and Cattle to give their children, that never think of making a Will till they come upon a sick bed and find it too expensive to send to town for a Lawyer. If you will not laugh too immoderately at me I'll trust you with a secret. I have made two Wills ready. I know I have done no harm for I conn'd my lesson very perfect. and know how to convey by Will Estates real and personal and never forget in it's proper place him and his heirs for Ever. nor that tis to be sign'd by 3 Witnesses in presence of one another. but the most comfortable remembrance of all is that Doctr Wood says the Law makes great allowance for last Wills and Testaments presuming the Testator could not have Council learned in the Law. but after all what can I do if a poor creature lies a dying and the family takes it into their head that I can serve them, I cann[o]t refuse but when they are well and able to employ a Lawyer I always shall. A Widow here abouts with a pretty little fortune teazed me intolerably to draw her a marriage settlement but it was out of my depth and I absolutely refused it— so she got an able hand to do it—indeed she could afford it—but I could not get off from being one of the Trustees to her settlement and an old Gent . . . the other I shall begin to think myself an old woman before I am a young one having such weighty affairs upon my hands. . . .

Septr 20. 1741. Wrote to my father on plantation business and Concerning a planter's importing negroes for his own use. Colo Pinckney thinks

Eliza Lucas, *Journal and Letters*, ed. H. P. Holbrook (Wormsloe, GA, 1850), 13–16.

not—but thinks twas proposed in the assembly and rejected—promised to look over the act and let me know. also informed my father of the alteration tis Supposed there will be in the value of our money occasioned by a late Act of Parliament that Extends to all America w[hi]ch is to dissolve all private banks by the 30th of last Month or be liable to lose their Estates and put themselves out of the King's protection. informed him of the Tyranical Govrt at Georgia.

Octr 29. 1741 Wrote to my father acknowledging the receipt of a ps of rich yellow Lustring consisting of 19 yards for myself do of blue for my Mama. also for a ps of Holland and Cambrick received from London at the same time. Tell him we have had a moderate and healthy summer and preparing for the King's birth day next day. Tell him [we] shall send the rice by Bullard.

Novr. 11. 1741. Wrote to Mr. Murray to send down a boat load of white oak staves, bacon and salted beef for the West Indies. sent up at the same time a barl. salt 1/2 wt salt peter. some brown sugar for the bacon. Vinegar and a couple of bottles Wine for Mrs. Murray and desire he will send down all the butter and hogs lard.

Jany 1741/2 Wrote my father about the Exchange with Colo Heron. the purchasing [of] his house at Georgia. . . . Returned my father thanks for a present I received from him by Capt Sutherland of twenty pistols. and for the sweetmeats by Capt Gregory. Shall send the preserved fruit as they come in season. . . . shall try different soils for the Lucern grass this year. The ginger turns out but poorly. We want a supply of Indigo Seed. Sent by his Vessel a waiter of my own Japaning my first Essay. Sent also the Rice and beef. Sent Govr. Thomas of Philadelphia's Daughter a tea chest of my own doing also Congratulate my father on my brother's recovery from the small pox and having a Commission. . . .

[Feb. 6] I received yesterday the favor of your advice as a physician and want no arguments to convince me I should be much better for both my good friends Company. A much pleasanter Prescription that Doctr Meads w[hi]ch I have just received. To follow my inclination at this time I must endeavor to forget that I have a Sister to instruct and a parcel of little Negroes whom I have undertaken to teach to read . . . I am a very Dunce, for I have not acquird ye writing short hand yet with any degree of Swiftness but I am not always so for I give a very good proof of the brightness of my Genius when I can distinguish well enough to Subscribe my Self with great Esteem.

3

Toward an American Identity

By the 18th century, the American colonies had evolved from small, struggling outposts into prosperous, growing societies. During the first half of the century, American culture became increasingly distinct from that of Great Britain, as large numbers of Germans, Scots-Irish, and West Africans joined the English in America. British authorities were eager to exercise some control over the American possessions, but with their authority constrained—in part by a worldwide struggle for empire—Americans were relatively free to manage their own affairs. The prosperity and independence of the colonies caused some to ponder whether the colonies might ultimately sever their ties with Britain. The following excerpts detail the emergence of an increasingly American culture.

17

Navigation Act of 1660

During the second half of the 17th century, most Western European states pursued an economic policy known as mercantilism. Mercantilists measured a nation's economic health by the amount of bullion it held. To increase the supply of bullion, these economic theorists argued that a favorable balance of trade was essential and could be secured by having colonies produce raw materials and buy finished goods. During the political turmoil that gripped England during the first half of the 17th century, much of its foreign trade had fallen into Dutch hands. In an effort to guarantee a favorable trade balance and to stimulate the British carrying trade, the Puritan government of Oliver Cromwell passed the Navigation Act of 1660, excerpted as follows.

Questions to Consider

1. What is the thesis of this document?
2. What is England trying to accomplish with the Navigation Act?

3. In what ways does the Navigation Act affect the relationship between England and her colonies?

4. Does the Navigation Act have a positive or negative impact on England's economy? Why?

AN ACT FOR THE ENCOURAGING AND INCREASING OF SHIPPING AND NAVIGATION

For the increase of shipping and encouragement of the navigation of this nation, wherein, under the good providence and protection of God, the wealth, safety and strength of this kingdom is so much concerned; be it enacted by the King's most excellent majesty, and by the lords and commons in this present parliament assembled, and by the authority thereof, That from and after the first day of December one thousand six hundred and sixty, and from thenceforward, no goods or commodities whatsoever shall be imported into or exported out of any lands, islands, plantations or territories to his Majesty belonging or in his possession, or which may hereafter belong unto or be in the possession of his Majesty, his heirs and successors, in Asia, Africa or America, in any other ship or ships, vessel or vessels whatsoever, but in such ships or vessels as do truly and without fraud belong only to the people of England or Ireland, dominion of Wales or town of Berwick upon Tweed,* or are of the built of and belonging to any the said lands, islands, plantations or territories, as the proprietors and right owners thereof, and whereof the master and three fourths of the mariners at least are English; under the penalty of the forfeiture and loss of all the goods and commodities which shall be imported into or exported out of any the aforesaid places in any other ship or vessel, as also of the ship or vessel. . . .

II. And be it enacted, That no alien or person not born within the allegiance of our sovereign lord the King, his heirs and successors, or naturalized, or made a free denizen, shall from and after the first day of February, 1661, exercise the trade or occupation of a merchant or factor in any the said places; upon pain of the forfeiture and loss of all his goods and chattels, . . .

III. . . . no goods or commodities whatsoever, of the growth, production or manufacture of Africa, Asia or America, or of any part thereof, or which are described or laid down in the usual maps or cards of those places, be imported into England, Ireland or Wales, islands of Guernsey and Jersey, or town of Berwick upon Tweed, in any other ship or ships . . . but in such as do truly and without fraud belong only to the people of England or Ireland, dominion of Wales, or town of Berwick upon Tweed or of the lands, islands,

---

Danby Pickering, *Statutes at Large* (Cambridge, England, 1762–1807), 2: 452.

*Berwick enjoyed direct trading rights with the Netherlands under a 15th-century agreement and was likely singled out to show that the same rules applied here as elsewhere in England.

plantations or territories in Asia, Africa or America, to his Majesty belonging, as the proprietors and right owners thereof, and whereof the master, and three fourths at least of the mariners are English; (2) under the penalty of the forfeiture of all such goods and commodities, and of the ship or vessel in which they were imported. . . .

IV. . . . no goods or commodities that are of foreign growth, production or manufacture, and which are to be brought into England, Ireland, Wales, the islands of Guernsey and Jersey, or town of Berwick upon Tweed, in English-built shipping, or other shipping belonging to some of the aforesaid places, and navigated by English mariners, as aforesaid, shall be shipped or brought from any other place or places, country or countries, but only from those of the said growth, production or manufacture, or from those ports where the said goods and commodities can only, or are, or usually have been, first shipped for transportation, and from none other places or countries; under the penalty of the forfeiture of all such of the aforesaid goods as shall be imported from any other place or country contrary to the true intent and meaning hereof, as also of the ship in which they were imported. . . .

V. . . . any sort of ling, stock-fish, pilchard, or any other kind of dried or salted fish, usually fished for and caught by the people of England, Ireland, Wales, or town of Berwick upon Tweed; or any sort of cod-fish or herring, or any oil or blubber made or that shall be made of any kind of fish whatsoever, or any whale-fins or whale-bones, which shall be imported into England, Ireland, Wales, or town of Berwick upon Tweed, not having been caught in vessels truly and properly belonging thereunto as proprietors and right owners thereof, and the said fish cured saved and dried, and the oil and blubber aforesaid (which shall be accounted and pay as oil) not made by the people thereof, and shall be imported into England, Ireland or Wales, or town of Berwick upon Tweed shall pay double aliens custom.

VI. . . . from henceforth it shall not be lawful to any person or persons whatsoever, to load or cause to be loaden and carried in any bottom or bottoms, ship or ships, vessel or vessels whatsoever, whereof any stranger or strangers-born (unless such as shall be denizens or naturalized) be owners, part-owners or master, and whereof three fourths of the mariners at least shall not be English, any fish, victual, wares, goods, commodities or things, of what kind or nature soever the fame shall be, from one port or creek of England, Ireland, Wales, islands of Guernsey or Jersey, or town of Berwick upon Tweed, to another port or creek of the same, or of any of them; under penalty for every one that shall offend contrary to the true meaning of this branch of this present act, to forfeit all such goods shall be loaden and carried in any such ship or vessel, together with the ship or vessel, . . .

XVIII. . . . from and after the first day of April, 1661, no sugars, tobaccos, cotton-wool, indicoes, ginger, fustick, or other dying wood, of the growth, production or manufacture of any English plantations in America, Asia or Africa, shall be shipped, carried conveyed or transported from any of the said English plantations to any land . . . other than to such other English plantations as do belong to his Majesty. . . .

18

Two Views of Early Merchant Capitalism

During the 17th century, European nations began to construct a worldwide trading system with far-flung effects. Initially, the Dutch dominated the trade, becoming the envy of Europe, but soon other Western European states such as Britain began to compete for overseas markets. The spread of commercial capitalism brought great wealth to many societies, as the first image indicates. However, among the most lucrative trade items were human beings. Europe's almost insatiable demand for commodities, such as tobacco, cotton, and especially sugar, necessitated large quantities of labor that contributed to the spread of slavery in the Americas. A comparison of these images shows both sides of the new commercial economy, which clearly creates great gulfs between "winners" and "losers."

Questions to Consider

1. What can you deduce about the ethics of commercial capitalism from these images?

2. To what extent might race determine status in the European-dominated parts of the world?

3. What can you deduce from the first image about gender roles in Europe?

From Edward Ward, *Vulgus Britannicus*, London (1711)

"The Coffeehous Mob"

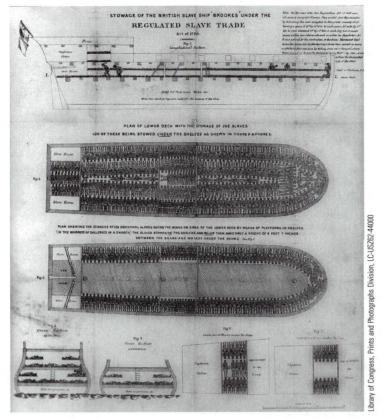

"Interior of a slave ship"

19

***

"Sinners in the Hands of an Angry God" (1741)

The Great Awakening was the single most important religious event in 18th-century America. Part of a larger movement that occurred in Western Europe, the evangelical emotionalism of the Great Awakening enabled its adherents to experience a more intense religious fervor than that offered by most existing churches. Although widespread throughout the colonies between 1730 and 1750, the movement was strongest in New England's Connecticut River Valley, where Jonathan Edwards had begun to deliver sermons that ignited local religious fervor. Following his graduation from Yale, Edwards returned to his hometown of Northampton, Massachusetts, to serve in the Congregationalist (Puritan) church headed by his grandfather, Solomon Stoddard, whom he ultimately succeeded. Using enlightenment rationalism to support traditional church beliefs, Edwards epitomized the New England Awakening. The movement divided established churches into the rationalist "Old Light" and the evangelical "New Light" factions, a split that anticipated some later divisions during the American Revolution. The following selection is an excerpt from Edwards' most famous work, "Sinners in the Hands of an Angry God."

Questions to Consider

1. What is Jonathan Edwards' view of humanity? Why might he be so concerned about people's behavior?
2. Why does Edwards frequently refer to God's control over people's lives, especially the sinners?
3. What impact did such sermons have on the people of New England?
4. How are Edwards' views similar to those found in "General Considerations for the Plantation in New England" (Document 5)? How are they different?

. . . This that you have heard is the case of every one of you that are out of Christ. That world of misery, that lake of burning brimstone, is extended abroad under you. There is the dreadful pit of the glowing flames of the wrath of God; there is hell's wide gaping mouth open; and you have nothing to stand upon, nor any thing to take hold of; there is nothing between you and hell but the air; 'tis only the power and mere pleasure of God that holds you up. . . .

Your wickedness makes you as it were heavy as lead, and to tend downwards with great weight and pressure towards hell; and, if God should let you go, you would immediately sink, and swiftly descend and plunge into the bottomless gulf; and your healthy constitution, and your own care and prudence, and best contrivance, and all your righteousness, would have no more influence to uphold you and keep you out of hell, than a spider's web would have to stop a falling rock. Were it not that so is the sovereign pleasure of God, the earth would not bear you one moment; for you are a burden to it; the creation groans with you; the creature is made subject to the bondage of your corruption, not willingly; the sun don't willingly shine upon you, to give you light to serve sin and Satan; the earth don't willingly yield her to increase to satisfy your lusts, nor is it willingly a stage for your wickedness to be acted upon; the air don't willingly serve you for breath to maintain the flame of life in your vitals, while you spend your life in the service of God's enemies. God's creatures are good, and were made for men to serve God with, and don't willingly subserve to any other purpose, and groan when they are abused to purposes so directly contrary to their nature and end. And the

Jonathan Edwards, "Sinners in the Hands of an Angry God," *The Works of President Edwards,* ed. Samuel Austin (Worcester, MA, 1808), 2: 72–79.

world would spew you out, were it not for the sovereign hand of him who hath subjected it in hope. There are the black clouds of God's wrath now hanging directly over your heads, full of the dreadful storm, and big with thunder. . . . The sovereign pleasure of God for the present stays his rough wind; otherwise it would come with fury, and your destruction would come like a whirlwind, and you would be like the chaff of the summer threshing-floor. . . .

Thus are all you that never passed under change of heart, by the mighty power of the spirit of God upon your souls; all that were never born again and made new creatures, and raised from being dead in sin, to a state of new, and before altogether unexperienced light and life. However you may have reformed your life in many things, and may have had religious affections, and may keep up a form of religion in your families and closets, and in the house of God, and may be strict in it, you are thus in the hands of an angry God; 'tis nothing but his mere pleasure that keeps you from being this moment swallowed up in everlasting destruction.

However unconvinced you may now be of the truth of what you hear, by and by you will be fully convinced of it. Those that are gone from being in the like circumstances with you, see that it was so with them; for destruction came suddenly upon most of them, when they expected nothing of it, and while they were saying, peace and safety. Now they see, that those things that they depended on for peace and safety, were nothing but thin air and empty shadows.

The God that holds you over the pit of hell, much as one holds a spider or some loathsome insect over the fire, abhors you, and is dreadfully provoked; his wrath towards you burns like fire; he looks upon you as worthy of nothing else but to cast into the fire; he is of purer eyes than to bear to have you in his sight; you are ten thousand times so abominable in his eyes as the most hateful venomous serpent is in ours. You have offended him infinitely more than ever a stubborn rebel did his prince; and yet 'tis nothing but his hand that holds you from falling into the fire every moment. . . .

O' Sinner! Consider the fearful danger you are in . . . you have no interest in any mediator, and nothing to lay hold of to save yourself, nothing to keep off the flames of wrath, nothing of your own, nothing that you ever have done, nothing that you can do, to induce God to spare you one moment. . . .

How dreadful is the state of those that are daily and hourly in danger of this great wrath, and infinite misery! But this is the dismal case of every soul in this congregation that has not been born again, however moral and strict, sober and religious they may otherwise be. Oh that you would consider it, whether you be young or old! There is reason to think, that there are many in this congregation, now hearing this discourse, that will actually be the subjects of this very misery to all eternity. We know not who they are, or in what seats they sit, or what thoughts they now have. It may be they are now at ease, and hear all these things without much disturbance, and are now flattering themselves that they shall escape. . . . And it would be a wonder if some that are now present should not be in hell in a very short time, before this year is out; and it would be no wonder if some person that sits here in some seat of this meeting-house, in health, and quiet and secure, should be there before to-morrow morning. . . .

20

Pennsylvania Assembly Comments on German Immigration (1755)

In 1700, roughly 250,000 people inhabited the American colonies; by 1775, the population had increased to 2.5 million. Although natural increase accounted for much of the ten-fold rise in population, immigration also contributed to the American colonies' explosive growth. Where 17th-century immigrants had been overwhelmingly English, the new immigrants were more diverse, including large numbers of Scots-Irish, West Africans, and Germans. Chronic warfare, religious persecution, and crop failures forced many Germans to flee to America. In the late 17th century, the first group of German settlers came to Pennsylvania, which sought to lure settlers with cheap, fertile soil and religious tolerance. In the 18th century, Pennsylvania continued to attract large numbers of Germans, many of whom came to be known as Pennsylvania Dutch, a corruption of Deutsch. *The following selection contains an excerpt of a resolution issued by the Pennsylvania Assembly in 1755.*

Questions to Consider

1. What changes were taking place in the German immigration?
2. Why was the Pennsylvania Assembly issuing this resolution?
3. Compare this response to immigration with the earlier description found in "Pennsylvania, the Poor Man's Paradise" (Document 12) and the later description found in "What Is an American?" (Document 23).
4. What characteristics does the Pennsylvania Assembly seem to value in immigrants? Why?

. . . The German Importations were at first and for a considerable Time of such as were Families of Substance and industrious sober People, who constantly brought with them their Chests of Apparel and other Necessaries for so long a voyage. But these we apprehend have for some time past been shipped on board other Vessels in order to leave more Room for crowding

"Message to the Governor from the Assembly," May 15, 1755, *Minutes of the Provincial Council of Pennsylvania,* 6: 384–386.

their unhappy Passengers in greater Numbers, and to secure the Freights of such as might perish during the voyage, which experience has convinced us must be the Case of very many where such Numbers (as have been lately imported in each Vessel) are crowded together without Change of Raiment or any other Means of keeping themselves sweet and clean. But this Provision the Governor has been pleased to throw out of our Bill; and yet we think it so essentially necessary that the Want of it must necessarily poison the Air those unhappy Passengers breathe on Shipboard, and spread it wherever they land to infect the Country which receives them, especially as the Governor has likewise altered the Provision We had made by the Advice of the Physicians for accommodating them with more Room and Air upon their Arrival here.

We have reason to believe the Importations of Germans have been for some Time composed of a great Mixture of the Refuse of their People, and that the very Jails have contributed to the Supplies We are burthened with. But as there are many of more Substance and better Character, We thought it reasonable to hinder the Importer from obliging such as had no connections with one another to become jointly bound for their respective Freights or Passages; but the Governor has thought fit to alter this also in such a manner as to elude the good Purposes intended by the Act, by which means those who are of more Substance are involved in the Contracts and Debts of Others, and the Merchants secured at the Expence of the Country where they are necessitated and do become very frequently common Beggars from Door to Door, to the great Injury of the Inhabitants and the Increase and Propagation of the Distempers they have brought among us. Many who have indented themselves for the Payment of their Passages have frequently been afflicted with such secret and loathsome Diseases at the Time as have rendered them altogether unfit for the Services they had contracted to perform. . . .

21

Edmund Burke on British Motives in the Seven Years' War (1762)

Great Britain and France's struggle for empire culminated in the Seven Years' (French and Indian) War. Britain's victory in the worldwide conflict established it as the leading European power. The following selection comes from the Annual Register of World Events, a periodical established in 1759. Edmund Burke served as its principal author and editor. After studying law at Great Britain's prestigious Middle Temple, Burke, a Dublin native, abandoned the legal profession for a career as a writer. Burke later established himself as the leading conservative political theorist of his time. In the ensuing excerpt, Burke reviews the proposed treaty to end the Seven Years' War and discusses the importance of North America in England's future considerations.

Questions to Consider

1. What is the historical context of this document?
2. According to Edmund Burke, what are the advantages of keeping the British colonies after this war? Who would be the chief beneficiary?
3. For what reasons does Burke support removing France from North America?
4. How are relations strained between mother country and colony in the years after this war?

. . . That the original object of the war was the security of our colonies upon the continent; that the danger to which these colonies were exposed, and in consequence of that danger, the immense waste of blood and treasure which ensued to Great Britain, together with the calamities, which were from the same source, derived upon the four quarters of the world, left no sort of doubt that it was not only our best, but our only policy, to guard against all possibility of the return of such evils. Experience has shown us that while France possesses any single place in America, from whence she may molest our settlements, they can never enjoy any repose, and of course that we are never secure from being plunged again into those calamities, from which we have at length, and with so much difficulty, happily emerged. To remove France from our neighborhood in America, or to contract her power within the narrowest limits possible, is therefore the most capital advantage we can obtain; and is worth purchasing by almost any concessions.

They insisted that the absolute security derived from this plan, included itself an indemnification. First; by saving us, more effectually than any other method could, from the necessity of another war, and consequently by giving us an opportunity of increasing our trade, and lowering our debt. Secondly; by permitting our colonies on the continent to extend themselves without danger or molestation. They showed the great increase of population in those colonies within a few years. They showed, that their trade with the mother country had uniformly increased with this population. That being now freed from the molestation of enemies, and the emulations of rivals, unlimited in their possessions, and safe in their persons, our American planters would, by the very course of their natural propagation in a very short time, furnish out a demand of our manufactures, as large as all the working hands of Great Britain could possibly supply. That there was therefore no reason to dread that want of trade, which their adversaries insinuated, since North America alone would supply the deficiencies of our trade in every other part of the world.

. . . That the value of our conquests thereby ought not to be estimated by the present produce, but by their probable increase. Neither ought the value

---

Edmund Burke, *A Complete History of the Late War: From the Annual Register of World Events* (Dublin, 1774): 621–622.

of any country to be solely tried on its commercial advantages; that extent of territory and a number of subjects, are of as much consideration to a state attentive to the sources of real grandeur, as the mere advantages of traffic. . . .

22

"The Pontiac Manuscript" (1763)

At the end of the Seven Years' (French and Indian) War, Native Americans in the Great Lakes region faced a difficult choice. As long-time trading partners with the French, they were allies during the war. British efforts to reduce the tribes to dependence and the tribes' feared loss of land had led to some sporadic frontier attacks as early as 1761. Native Americans began planning for a coordinated uprising in 1763. The Ottawa leader Pontiac was nearly 50 years old when he hammered out an alliance between his tribe, the Potawatomies, and some Wyandots. He struck at Detroit in May 1763, laying a siege that would not be lifted until October. Attacks against other frontier posts were more successful, and other tribes joined in. By midsummer, nine of Britain's eleven western posts had been taken, and the other two (Detroit and Pitt) were under siege. After the failure of the rebellion, Pontiac concluded a peace in July 1766. The following excerpt describes Pontiac's reasons for war and his plans for its prosecution.

Questions to Consider

1. What role do the French appear to play in the formation of this Native American alliance?
2. What is the nature of the relationship between Native Americans and the English? What are the major sources of complaint in this relationship?
3. Why might other tribes be willing to cooperate with Pontiac?
4. What does Pontiac hope to accomplish?

The day fixed having arrived, all the Ottawas, with Pondiak [Pontiac] at their head, and the band of the Hurons, with Také [Yaka] at their head, all proceeded to the village of the Foxes [Potawatomies], where the council was intended to be held, taking care to send the women out of the village so as not to be interrupted in their deliberations. After all these precautions had been made, each Indian took his place in a circle, in accordance with his rank, and Pondiak at the head, as the great chief of all. He took the floor, and, as chief of the league, said:

"The Pontiac Manuscript" (1763) in *Historical Collections,* coll. by Michigan Pioneer and Historical Society (Lansing, MI, 1900–13), 8: 273–274.

"It is important for us, my brothers, that we exterminate from our land this nation which only seeks to kill us. You see, as well as I do, that we cannot longer get our supplies as we had them from our brothers, the French. The English sell us the merchandise twice dearer than the French sold them to us, and their wares [are worth] nothing. Hardly have we bought a blanket, or something else to cover us, than we must think of having another of the kind. When we want to start for our winter quarters they will give us no credit, as our brothers, the French, did. When I go to the English chief to tell him that some of our comrades are dead, instead of weeping for the dead, as our brothers, the French, used to do, he makes fun of me and of you. When I ask him for something for our sick, he refuses, and tells me that he has no need of us. You can well see by that that he seeks our ruin. Well, my brothers, we must all swear to destroy them! Nor will we wait any longer, nothing impedes us. There are very few of them, and we can easily overcome them. All the nations who are our brothers are ready to strike a blow at them; why should we not? Are we not men like them? Have I not shown you the war-belts which I have received from our great father, the Frenchman? He tells us to strike; why should we not listen to his words? Whom fear we? It is time. Are we afraid that our brothers, the French, who are here amongst us, would hinder us? They know not our designs, and could not if they wanted to. You know as well as I do, that when the English came to our country to drive out our father, Bellestre, they took away all the guns of the Frenchmen, and that they have no weapons to defend themselves. Thus it is. Let us strike all together! If there are any French who take up for them, we shall strike them as we do the English. Remember what the Master of Life has said to our brother, the Wolf. That concerns us all as well as them. I have sent war-belts and word to our brothers, the Sauteux, of the Saginaw, and to our brothers, the Ottawas, of Michelimakinak, and to those of the river's mouth to join them with us, and they will not tarry to come. While waiting for them, let us commence the attack. There is no more time to lose, and when the English shall be defeated, we shall see what to do, and we shall cut off the passage so that they cannot come back to our country."

This address, which Pondiak delivered with a voice full of energy, made upon the whole assembly the full effect which he had desired, and all swore, as in one voice, the complete extermination of the English nation.

It was decided at the end of the council that Pondiak, at the head of sixty picked men, should go into the fort to ask the English commander for a great council, that those should have weapons concealed under their blankets and that the rest of the village should follow them, armed with tomahawks, dirks and knives hid under their clothes and enter the fort as if taking a walk, so as not to create any suspicion, while the first should hold council with the commander. The women of the Ottawas should also enter, carrying guns, cut short, and other arms of attack hid under their blankets and take position in the back of the street of the fort, waiting for the signal, which should be a [war] cry uttered by the great chief, when all together should throw themselves upon the English and take good care not to hurt the Frenchmen who lived in the fort. The Hurons and Foxes [Potawatomies] should divide into bands, one to go down the river to stop those who might come, and the other band to be around the fort at a distance to kill those who were at work outside the fort, and that each one should shout the war song in his own village. All these measures being taken, each nation returned to their village with the resolution to execute the orders of their great chief; but although they had taken all these precautions not to be discovered, God permitted that they were discovered, as I am going to tell. . . .

23

"What Is an American?" (1770)

By the middle of the 18th century, America's bounty of opportunity had attracted large numbers of immigrants. Many of these new arrivals came in search of religious freedom, but most sought economic opportunity, specifically land. The possibility for upward mobility profoundly affected the outlook of those who ventured across the Atlantic. In the ensuing selection, J. Hector St. John Crèvecoeur [Michel-Guillaume-Jean de Crèvecoeur] describes how the American environment transformed Europeans into Americans. A native of France, he fought with Montcalm's army in the Seven Years' War before moving to the British colonies in 1759. Crèvecoeur received his naturalization papers in 1765 and four years later settled on a New York frontier farm, where he probably wrote much of his famous Letters of an American Farmer. *He remained loyal to the Crown during the Revolution and left America from 1780 until 1783.*

Questions to Consider

1. According to Crèveceour, what are the differences between Europe and America?

2. In what ways are Europeans transformed into Americans?

3. What are the characteristics of an American? How does this help shape a distinct American identity?

4. How do you think Olaudah Equiano ("Olaudah Equiano Describes the 'Middle Passage,'" Document 94) would respond to this document?

. . . The rich stay in Europe, it is only the middling and the poor that emigrate. Would you wish to travel in independent idleness, from north to south, you will find easy access, and the most cheerful reception at every house; society without ostentation, good cheer without pride, and every decent diver-

Hector St. John de Crèvecoeur, *Letters from an American Farmer* (London, 1782), 58–65.

sion which the country affords, with little expense. It is no wonder that the European who has lived here a few years, is desirous to remain; Europe with all its pomp, is not to be compared to this continent, for men of middle stations, or laborers.

An European, when he first arrives, seems limited in his intentions, as well as in his views; but he very suddenly alters his scale; two hundred miles formerly appeared a very great distance, it is now but a trifle; he no sooner breathes our air than he forms schemes, and embarks in designs he never would have thought of in his own country. There the plenitude of society confines many useful ideas, and often extinguishes the most laudable schemes which here ripen into maturity. Thus Europeans become Americans.

But how is this accomplished in that crowd of low, indigent people, who flock here every year from all parts of Europe? I will tell you; they no sooner arrive than they immediately feel the good effects of that plenty of provisions we possess: they fare on our best food, and they are kindly entertained; their talents, character, and peculiar industry are immediately inquired into; they find countrymen everywhere disseminated, let them come from whatever part of Europe. Let me select one as an epitome of the rest; he is hired, he goes to work, and works moderately; instead of being employed by a haughty person, he finds himself with his equal, placed at the substantial table of the farmer, or else at an inferior one as good; his wages are high, his bed is not like that bed of sorrow on which he used to lie: if he behaves with propriety, and is faithful, he is caressed, and becomes as it were a member of the family. He begins to feel the effects of a sort of resurrection; hitherto he had not lived, but simply vegetated; he now feels himself a man, because he is treated as such; the laws of his own country had overlooked him in insignificancy; the laws of this cover him with their mantle. Judge what an alteration there must arise in the mind and thoughts of this man; he begins to forget his former servitude and dependence, his heart involuntarily swells and glows; this first swell inspires him with those new thoughts which constitute an American. . . . He looks around, and sees many a prosperous person, who but a few years before was as poor as himself. This encourages him much, he begins to form some little scheme, the first, alas, he ever formed in his life. If he is wise he thus spends two or three years, in which time he acquires knowledge, the use of tools, the modes of working the lands, felling trees, etc. This prepares the foundation of a good name, the most useful acquisition he can make. He is encouraged, he has gained friends; he is advised and directed, he feels bold, he purchases some land; he gives all the money he has brought over, as well as what he has earned, and trusts to the God of harvests for the discharge of the rest. His good name procures him credit. He is now possessed of the deed, conveying to him and his posterity the fee simple and absolute property of two hundred acres of land, situated on such a river. What an epocha in this man's life! He is become a freeholder, from perhaps a German boor—he is now an American, a Pennsylvanian, an English subject. He is naturalized, his name is enrolled with those of the other citizens of the province. . . . From nothing to start into being; from a servant to the rank of a master; from being the slave of some despotic prince, to become a free man, invested with lands, to which every municipal blessing is annexed! . . . It is in consequence of that change that he becomes an American. . . . Ye poor Europeans, ye, who sweat, and work for the great—ye, who are obliged to give so many sheaves to the church, so many to your lords, so many to your government, and have hardly any left for yourselves—ye, who are held in less estimation than favorite hunters or useless lap-dogs—ye, who only breathe the air of nature, because it cannot be withheld from you; it is here that ye can conceive the possibility of those feelings I have been describing; it is here the laws of naturalization invite every one to partake of our great labors and felicity, to till unrented, untaxed lands! Many, corrupted beyond the power of amendment, have brought with them all their vices, and disregarding the advantages held to them, have gone on in their former career of iniquity, until they have been overtaken and punished by our laws. It is not every emigrant who succeeds; no, it is only the sober, the honest, and industrious: . . . Others again, have been led astray by this enchanting scene; their new pride, instead of leading them to the fields, has kept them in idleness; the idea of possessing lands is all that satisfies them—though surrounded with fertility, they have mouldered away their time in inactivity, misinformed husbandry, and ineffectual endeavors. How much wiser, in general, the honest Germans than almost all other Europeans; they hire themselves to some of their wealthy landsmen, and in that apprenticeship learn everything that is necessary. They attentively consider the prosperous industry of others, which imprints in their minds a strong desire of possessing the same advantages. This forcible idea never quits them, they launch forth, and by dint of sobriety, rigid parsimony, and the most persevering industry, they commonly succeed.

4

Coming of the Revolution

A lthough the roots of the American Revolution can be traced back to the first half of the 18th century, it was not until the 1760s that differences between Britain and the colonies became obvious. After the Seven Years' War, British policy makers were determined to consolidate their empire and raise funds to pay their enormous war debts. They turned to the American colonies as a source of revenue. Americans saw British attempts to exercise authority—such as levying taxes on such varied items as public documents, tea, newspapers, and playing cards—as a tyrannical encroachment on their liberty. British officials, on the other hand, interpreted opposition to their policies as a potential source of anarchy. The following documents illustrate the various positions taken by those on both sides of the Atlantic and provide insights into the growing intensity of the confrontation.

24

John Locke on Political Society and Government (1689)

John Locke was one of the leading philosophers of the Enlightenment. Educated at Oxford, Locke eschewed a career as a physician to become one of the most influential thinkers of his day. As an advisor to Anthony Ashley Cooper (later Lord Shaftesbury), Locke helped create the "Fundamental Constitutions" for early South Carolina. The Constitutions were aristocratic, but they did guarantee religious toleration and the right to representative assemblies. As Shaftesbury emerged as a leading opponent of the Crown in the early 1680s, Locke was pulled into the constitutional crisis and even fled to Holland in 1683. By this time, he had begun to write Two Treatises of Government, *which called for a limited government. Following the Glorious Revolution in 1688–89, Locke published his work. His ideas would influence Anglo-American concepts of liberty over the next century. The following selection is excerpted from* Two Treatises of Government.

Questions to Consider

1. What is the historical context for this document?
2. According to John Locke, what is the chief purpose of government?
3. What limits does the author wish to place on government?
4. What does Locke consider to be the greatest threats to liberty?

OF THE ENDS OF POLITICAL SOCIETY AND GOVERNMENT

123. If Man in the state of Nature be so free, as has been said; if he be absolute Lord of his own Person and Possessions, equal to the greatest and subject to no Body, why will he part with his Freedom? Why will he give up this Empire, and subject himself to the Dominion and Controul of any other Power? To which 'tis obvious to answer, that though in the state of Nature he hath such a Right, yet the Enjoyment of it is very uncertain, and constantly exposed to the Invasion of others. For all being Kings as much as he, every man his Equal and the greater Part no strict Observers of Equity and Justice, the enjoyment of the Property he has in this State, is very unsafe, very unsecure. This makes him willing to quit this Condition, which however free, is full of Fears and continual Dangers: And 'tis not without Reason, that he seeks out, and is willing to joyn in Society with others, who are already united, or have a Mind to unite, for the mutual *Preservation* of their Lives, Liberties and Estates, which I call by the general Name, *Property.*

124. The great and *chief End* therefore, of Mens uniting into Commonwealths, and putting themselves under Government, *is the Preservation of their Property.* To Which in the state of Nature there are many things wanting.

First, There wants an *establish'd,* settled, known *Law,* received and allowed by common consent to be the Standard of right and wrong, and the common Measure to decide all Controversies between them. For though the Law of Nature be plain and intelligible to all rational Creatures; yet Men being biassed by their Interest, as well as ignorant for want of Study of it, are not apt to allow of it as a Law binding to them in the application of it to their particular Cases.

125. *Secondly,* In the State of Nature there wants *a known and indifferent Judge,* with Authority to determine all Differences according to the established Law. For every one in that State being both Judge and Executioner of the Law of Nature, Men being partial to themselves, Passion and Revenge is very apt to carry them too far, and with too much Heat, in their own Cases; as well as Negligence, and unconcernedness, to make them too remiss in other mens.

John Locke, "Two Treatises of Government," *Works of John Locke* (London, 1714), 2: 193–194.

126. *Thirdly,* In the State of Nature there often wants *Power* to back and support the Sentence when right, and to *give* it due *Execution.* They who by any Injustice offended, will seldom fail, where they are able, by Force to make good their Injustice; such Resistance many times makes the Punishment dangerous, and frequently destructive, to those who attempt it.

127. Thus Mankind, notwithstanding all the Privileges of the State of Nature, being but in an ill Condition, while they remain in it, are quickly driven into Society. Hence it comes to pass, that we seldom find any number of Men live any time together in this State. The Inconveniences that they are therein exposed to, by the irregular, and uncertain exercise of the Power every Man has of punishing the transgressions of others, make them take Sanctuary under the establish'd Laws of Government, and therein seek the *preservation of their Property.* 'Tis this makes them so willingly give up every one his single Power of punishing, to be exercised by such alone, as shall be appointed to it, amongst them; and by such Rules as the Community, or those authorized by them to that purpose, shall agree on. And in this we have the original *right and rise of both the Legislative and Executive power,* as well as of the Governments, and Societies themselves. . . .

128. But though Men when they enter into Society, give up the Equality, Liberty, and Executive Power they had in the State of Nature, into the hands of the Society, to be so far disposed of by the Legislative, as the good of the Society shall require; yet it being only with an intention in every one the better to preserve himself his Liberty and Property; (For no rational Creature can be supposed to change his condition with an intention to be worse) the Power of the Society, or *Legislative* constituted by them, can *never be suppos'd to extend farther than the common good;* but is obliged to secure every ones Property, by providing against those three defects above-mentioned, that made the State of Nature so unsafe and uneasie. And so whoever has the Legislative or supream Power of any Commonwealth, is bound to govern by establish'd *standing Laws,* promulgated and known to the People, and not by Extemporary Decrees; by *indifferent* and upright *Judges,* who are to decide Controversies by those Laws, And to imploy the force of the Community at home, *only in the Execution of such Laws,* or abroad to prevent or redress Foreign Injuries, and secure the Community from Inroads and Invasion. And all this to be directed to no other *End,* but the *Peace, Safety,* and *publick good* of the People. . . .

25

Cato's Letters (1721)

Cato's Letters, *published by John Trenchard and Thomas Gordon, represent the radical Whig critique of British government during the 1720s. Trenchard began to write in favor of political reform in the late 17th century, initially warning of the dangers of a standing army. By the early 18th century, he had become one of the most vocal critics of the High Church or Court party that dominated British politics. His collaboration with Gordon began in 1719, and they published letters under the pseudonym Cato until Trenchard's death in 1723. Alarmed by the growing corruption of the British political system, the two men pointed out in Cato's Letters the sources of tyranny that undermined British liberty. Although largely ignored in Britain, Trenchard and Gordon's views were widely disseminated among the American colonists on the eve of the revolution. The following selection presents the authors' views on liberty and the role of government in protecting this right.*

Questions to Consider

1. How do the authors define liberty?
2. What do the authors see as the role of government?
3. What do the authors fear about government?
4. In what ways are the ideas expressed in this document similar to those found in Thomas Paine's "Introduction to *Common Sense*" (Document 31)? How are they different?

By Liberty, I understand the Power which every-Man has over his own Actions, and his Right to enjoy the Fruits of his Labour, Art, and Industry, as far as by it he hurts not the Society, or any Members of it, by taking from any Member, or by hindering him from enjoying what he himself enjoys. The Fruits of a Man's honest Industry are the just Rewards of it, ascertained to him by natural and eternal Equity, as is his Title to use them in the Manner which he thinks fit And thus, with the above Limitations, every Man is sole Lord and Arbiter of his own private Actions and Property—A Character of which no Man living can divest him but by Usurpation, or his own Consent.

   The entering into political Society, is so far from a Departure from this natural Right, that to preserve it, was the sole Reason why Men did so, and mutual Protection and Assistance is the only reasonable Purpose of all reasonable Societies. To make such Protection practicable magistracy was formed, with power to defend the innocent from violence, and to punish those that offered it; nor can there be any other presence for magistracy in the world. In order to this good end, the magistrate is entrusted with conducting and applying the united force of the community; and with exacting such a share of every man's property, as is necessary to preserve the whole, and to defend every man and his property from foreign and domestick injuries. These are the boundaries of the power of the magistrate, who deserts his function whenever he breaks them. By the laws of society, he is more limited and restrained than any man amongst them; since, while they are absolutely free in all their actions, which purely concern themselves; all his actions, as a publick person, being for the sake of society, must refer to it, and answer the ends of it.

T. Gordon, "An Enquiry into the Nature and Extent of Liberty, 20 January 1721," *Cato's Letters,* 3rd ed., ed. John Trenchard (1733), 2: 244–247.

It is a mistaken Notion in Government, that the Interest of the Majority is only to be consulted, since in Society every Man has a Right to every Man's Assistance in the Enjoyment and Defence of his private Property; otherwise the greater Number may sell the lesser, and divide their Estates amongst themselves; and so, instead of a Society, where all peaceable Men are protected, become a Conspiracy of the Many against the Minority. With as much Equity may one Man wantonly dispose of all, and Violence may be sanctified by mere Power. . . .

Let people alone, and they will take care of themselves, and do it best; and if they do not, a sufficient Punishment will follow their Neglect, without the Magistrate's Interposition and Penalties. It is plain that such busy Care and officious Intrusion into the personal Affairs, or private Actions, Thoughts, and Imaginations of Men, has in a more Craft than Kindness; and is only a Device to mislead People, and pick their Pockets, under the false Pretence of the publick and their private Good. To quarrel with any Man for his Opinions, Humours, or the Fashion of his Cloaths, is an Offence taken without being given. What is it to a Magistrate how I wash my Hands, or cut my Corns, what Fashion or Colours I wear, or what Notions I entertain, or what Gestures I use, or what Words I pronounce, when they please me, and do him and my Neighbor no hurt? As well may he determine the Colour of my Hair, and controul my Shape and Features.

True and impartial Liberty is therefore the Right of every Man to pursue the natural, reasonable, and religious Dictates of his own Mind; to think what he will, and act as he thinks, provided he acts not to the Prejudice of another; to spend his own Money himself, and lay out the Produce of his Labour his own Way; and to Labour his own Way; and to labour for his own Pleasure and Profit, and not for others who are idle, and would live and riot by pillaging and oppressing him and those that are like him.

So that Civil government is only a partial Restraint put by the Laws of Agreement and Society upon natural and absolute Liberty, which might otherwise grow licentious; And Tyranny is an unlimited restraint put upon natural Liberty, by the Will of one or a few. Magistracy, amongst a free People, is the Exercise of Power for the sake of the People and Tyrants abuse the People, for the sake of Power. Free Government is the protecting the People in their Liberties by stated Rules: Tyranny is a brutish Struggle for unlimited Liberty to one or a few, who would rob all others of their Liberty; and act by no Rule but lawless Lust.

26

Stamp Act Riots (1765)

British officials had been considering imperial reorganization since 1750, but the experience of the Seven Years' War served as the catalyst for reform. In addition to governing newly conquered French territories, the government also had to find a way to reduce the staggering debt it had amassed during the war. English leaders, who were reluctant to tax an already burdened population at home, turned to the American colonies. Following the war, Parliament passed several pieces of legislation to raise money in North America and to enforce existing taxes. The passage of the Stamp Tax was one of these revenue-producing laws. Similar to an existing British tax, the new law required that a duty be placed on legal documents and nearly all forms of printed materials. Many of Boston's citizens found the new tax threatening. Mired in an economic slump that the tax might exacerbate and fearful of encroachments against their rights, the well-organized and highly politicized Boston mob offered their response, which is described in this document.

Questions to Consider

1. What is the mob trying to accomplish? Are they successful?
2. Does the mob seem organized?
3. How do you think Joseph Galloway, author of "A Loyalist Perspective of the Coming of Revolution" (Document 29), responded to news of the mob in Boston?
4. Explain the symbolism in the mob's use of effigies discussed in the first paragraph.

EXTRACTED FROM A LETTER FROM BOSTON, IN NEW ENGLAND, AUGUST 26.

"Very early on Wednesday morning, the 14th instant, were discovered hanging, on a limb of the great trees, so called, at the South part of this town, two effigies, one of which, by the labels, appeared to be designed to represent a stamp officer; the other a jack boot with a head and horns peeping out of the top. The report of the images soon spread through the town, brought a vast number of spectators, and had such an effect on them, that they were immediately inspired with a spirit of enthusiasm, which diffused itself through the whole concourse; so much were they affected with a sense of liberty, that scarce any could attend to the task of day-labor. About dusk, the images were taken down, placed on a bier (not covered with a sheet, except a sheet of paper which bore the inscription) supported in procession by six men, followed by a great concourse of people, and in the greatest order, echoing forth, Liberty and Prosperity! No Stamp, &c.—Having passed through the town-house, they proceeded with their pageantry down King-street, and thro' Kilby-

John Almon, comp., *A Collection of Interesting, Authentic Papers Relative to the Dispute Between Great Britain and America* (London, 1777), 10–11.

street, where an edifice had been lately erected, which was supposed to be designed for a stamp-office. Here they halted, and went to work to demolish that building, which they soon effected, without receiving any hurt, excepting one of the spectators, who happened to be rather too nigh the brick wall when it fell. This being finished, many of them loaded themselves with the wooden trophies, and proceeded (bearing the two effigies) to the top of Fort-hill, where a fire was soon kindled, in which one them was burnt. The populace after this went to work on the barn, fence, garden, &c. and here it would have ended had not some indiscretions, to say the least, been committed by his friends within, which so enraged the people they were to be restrained, though hitherto no violence had been offered to any one. But it is very remarkable, though they entered the lower part of the house in multitudes, yet the damage done to it was not so great as might have been expected.

The next day the honourable gentleman, who had been appointed to the duty of distributor of the stamps when they should arrive, supposing himself to be the object of their derision, informed the principal gentlemen of the town, that as it appeared so disagreeable to the people, he should request the liberty of being excused from that office, and in the evening the populace re-assembled, erected a pyramid, intending a second bonfire; but upon hearing of the resignation, they desisted, and repaired to the gentleman's gate, gave three cheers, and took their departure without damage; but having heard it propagated that an honourable gentleman, at the north part of town, had been accessory in laying on the stamp duties, &c. they repaired to his house, where, upon being informed by some gentlemen of integrity and reputation, that he had not only spoke, but wrote to the contrary, they retired, and having patrolled the streets, returned to their respective habitations, as quietly as they had done the night before."

27

The Boston Massacre (1770)

In few places was colonial hostility toward Parliament stronger than in Boston. Massachusetts' opposition to royal authority had become so brazen by 1768 that British officials dispatched troops to the city to preserve order. Within a year, more than 3,000 soldiers patrolled Boston's streets. Their presence not only conjured threats to American liberties, but because many British enlisted men worked as laborers in their spare time, they also competed for colonial jobs. Tension turned to violence when, in March 1770, a near brawl broke out between British soldiers and local citizens. Feeling threatened, the soldiers fired on the crowd, killing five. The following account of the Boston Massacre and its aftermath is an excerpt from the diary of John Tudor, a local merchant. In the ensuing trial, John Adams defended the British soldiers, who were acquitted.

Questions to Consider

1. Why did the Boston Massacre take place?
2. What was the reaction of some Bostonians to the massacre? Why did they take this position?
3. How did this massacre and the acquittal of Captain Thomas Preston affect relations between Boston residents and the government?
4. Compare and contrast the depiction of the mob described here and in "Ann Hulton, Loyalist View of Colonial Unrest" (Document 28).

On Monday Evening the 5th current, a few Minutes after 9 O'Clock a most horrid murder was committed in King Street before the Customhouse Door by 8 or 9 Soldiers under the Command of Capt Thos Preston drawn from the Main Guard on the South side of the Townhouse.

This unhappy affair began by Some Boys & young fellows throwing Snow Balls at the sentry placed at the Customhouse Door. On which 8 or 9 Soldiers Came to his assistance. Soon after a Number of people collected, when the Capt commanded the Soldiers to fire, which they did and 3 Men were Kil'd on the Spot & several Mortally Wounded, one of which died next morning. The Capt soon drew off his Soldiers up to the Main Guard, or the Consequences might have been terrible, for on the Guns firing the people were alarm'd & set the Bells a Ringing as if for Fire, which drew Multitudes to the place of action. Levt Governor Hutchinson, who was commander in Chief, was sent for & Came to the Council Chamber, where some of the Magistrates attended. The Governor desired the Multitude about 10 O'Clock to separate & go home peaceable & he would do all in his power that Justice should be done &c. The 29 Regiment being then under Arms on the south side of the Townhouse, but the people insisted that the Soldiers should be ordered to their Barracks 1st before they would separate, Which being done the people separated about 1 O'Clock.—Capt Preston was taken up by a warrant given to the high Sheriff by Justice Dania & Tudor and came under Examination about 2 O'clock & we sent him to jail soon after 3, having Evidence sufficient, to commit him, on his ordering the soldiers to fire: So about 4 O'clock the Town became quiet. The next forenoon the 8 Soldiers that fired on the inhabitants was also sent to jail. Tuesday A.M. the inhabitants met at Faneuil Hall & after some pertinent speeches, chose a Committee of 15 Gentlemen to wait on the Levt. Governor in Council to request the immediate removal of the Troops. The message was in these Words: That it is the unanimous opinion of this Meeting, that the inhabitants & soldiery can no longer live together in safety; that nothing can Rationally be expected to restore the peace of the Town & prevent Blood & Carnage, but the removal of the Troops: and that we most fervently pray his Honor that his power & influence may be exerted for their instant removal. His Honor's Reply was: Gentlemen I am extremely sorry for the unhappy difference & especially of

William Tudor, ed., *Deacon Tudor's Diary* (Boston, 1896), 30–34.

the last Evening & Signifying that it was not in his power to remove the Troops &c &c.

The Above Reply was not satisfactory to the Inhabitants, as but one Regiment should be removed to the Castle Barracks. In the afternoon the Town Adjourned to Dr. Sewill's Meetinghouse, for Faneuil Hall was not large enough to hold the people, their being at least 3,000, some suppos'd near 4,000, when they chose a Committee to wait on the Levt. Governor to let him & the Council Know that nothing less will satisfy the people, than a total & immediate removal of the Troops out of the Town.—His Honor laid before the Council the Vote of the Town. The Council thereon expressed themselves to be unanimously of opinion that it was absolutely Necessary for his Majesty service, the good order of the Town &c that the Troops Should be immediately removed out of the Town.—His Honor communicated this advice of the Council to Col Dalrymple & desir'd he would order the Troops down to Castle William. After the Col. had seen the Vote of the Council He gave his Word & honor to the Town's Committee that both the Regiments should be remov'd without delay. The Committee return'd to the Town Meeting & Mr Hancock, chairman of the Committee Read their Report as above, which was Received with a shout & clap of hands, which made the Meetinghouse Ring: So the Meeting was dissolved and a great number of Gentlemen appear'd to Watch the Center of the Town & the prison, which continued for 11 Nights and all was quiet again, as the Soldiers was all moved . . . to the Castle.

(Thursday) Agreeable to a general request of the Inhabitants, were follow'd to the Grave (for they were all Buried in one) in succession the 4 Bodies of Messrs. Saml Gray, Saml Maverick, James Caldwell & Crispus Attucks, the unhappy Victims who fell in the Bloody Massacre. On this sorrowful Occasion most of the shops & stores in Town were shut, all the Bells were order'd to toll a solemn peal in Boston, Charleston, Cambridge & Roxbury. The several Hearses forming a junction in King Street, the Theatre of that inhuman Tragedy, proceeded from thence thro' the main street, lengthened by an immense Concourse of people, So numerous as to be obliged to follow in Ranks of 4 & 6 abreast and brought up by a long Train of Carriages. The sorrow Visible in the Countenances, together with the peculiar solemnity, Surpass description, it was suppos'd that the Spectators & those that follow'd the corps amounted to 15000, some supposed 20,000. Note Capt Preston was tried for his Life on the affair of the above Octobr 24 1770. The Trial lasted 5 Days, by the Jury brought him in not Guilty.

28

Ann Hulton, Loyalist View of Colonial Unrest (1774)

Colonial opposition to British authority grew more heated following the passage of the Tea Act in 1773. Designed as a means to bail out the financially troubled East India

Company and provide Americans with inexpensive tea, the act instead elicited heated opposition. Believing that the act was yet another attempt by British officials to force their will on America, colonists responded by refusing to allow the importation of the tea. Colonial intimidation made it impossible to land the tea anywhere other than Charleston, South Carolina. In Philadelphia, opponents of the tax organized tar-and-feathering committees; at the Boston Tea Party, British tea was dumped into the harbor. In New York, Governor William Tryon was determined to land the tea, but its late arrival prevented a showdown with the local Sons of Liberty. By 1774, physical intimidation of those loyal to British authority became increasingly common in many colonial towns. In the ensuing document, Ann Hulton describes treatment meted out to a New York loyalist.

Questions to Consider

1. What is the historical context of this document?
2. What were the reasons for tarring and feathering this man?
3. Why was Ann Hulton fearful of mob actions?
4. How does Hulton's view of the mob differ from that described in the "Stamp Act Riots" (Document 26)?

The most shocking cruelty was exercised a few nights ago, upon a poor old man, a tidesman, one Malcolm. . . . A quarrel was picked with him. He was afterward taken, and tarred and feathered. There's no law that knows a punishment for the greatest crimes beyond what this is, of cruel torture. And this instance exceeds any other before it. He was stripped stark naked, one of the severest cold nights this winter, his body covered all over with tar, then with feathers, his arm dislocated in tearing off his clothes. He was dragged in a cart, with thousands attending, some beating him with clubs and knocking him out of the cart, then in again. They gave him several severe whippings, at different parts of the town. This spectacle of horror and sportive cruelty was exhibited for about five hours.

The unhappy wretch they say behaved with the greatest intrepidity and fortitude. All the while before he was taken, he defended himself a long time against numbers; and afterwards, when under torture they demanded of him to curse his masters, the king, governors, etc. which they could not make him do, but still he cried, Curse all Traitors. They brought him to the gallows and put a rope about his neck saying that they would hang him; he said he wished they would, but that they could not for God was above the Devil. The doctors say his flesh comes off his back in stakes.

It is the second time he has been tarred and feathered and this is looked upon more to intimidate the judges and others than a spite to the unhappy

---

Ann Hulton, *Letters of a Loyalist Lady* (Cambridge, MA, 1927), 70–71.

victim, though they owe him a grudge for some things, particularly, he was with Governor Tryon in the Battle with the Regulators. . . . The Governor has declared that he was of great service to him in that affair, by his undaunted spirit encountering the greatest dangers.

Governor Tryon had sent him a gift of ten guineas just before this inhuman treatment. He has a wife and family and an aged father and mother who, they say, saw the spectacle which no indifferent person can mention without horror.

These few instances among many serve to show the abject state of government and the licentiousness and barbarism of the times. There's no magistrate that dare or will act to suppress the outrages. No person is secure. There are many objects pointed at, at this time, and when once marked out for vengeance, their ruin is certain.

29

A Loyalist Perspective on the Coming of the Revolution (1780)

Many Americans refused to support the Whig cause during the American Revolution and remained loyal to the Crown. Disparate in background and without real organization, Loyalists had numerous reasons for their stance. Many ultimately fled America, leaving everything they owned behind. Joseph Galloway was one of the foremost Loyalists. A prominent figure in the Quaker party (along with his close friend Benjamin Franklin) that represented the Philadelphia establishment, he served as the Speaker of the Pennsylvania Assembly from 1766 until 1775. A firm believer that colonial liberties could only be preserved within an imperial union, Galloway offered his Plan for Union that the First Continental Congress rejected in the fall of 1774. Determined to remain loyal to Britain, he refused election to the Second Continental Congress and left the Pennsylvania Assembly. In 1778, he and his family abandoned their homes and moved to London. In the following selection, Galloway presents his views on the cause of the American Revolution.

Questions to Consider

1. What is the author's purpose in writing this document?
2. Does the author see widespread support for the Revolution?
3. What does Joseph Galloway see as the leading cause of the American Revolution?
4. To what extent are Galloway's views influenced by "John Locke on Political Society and Government" (Document 24) and "Cato's Letters" (Document 25)?

When the Tea-act passed, the same men, determined to lose no opportunity of promoting their favourite scheme of independence, stirred up the rabble in several of the sea-ports, headed by the smuggling merchants, whose interest alone was affected by the act, to seize the Tea, and in one of the Colonies to destroy it. But in this the people at large took no part.

In consequence of the illegal and unjustifiable destruction of the Tea in Boston, the Act for stopping up that port was passed; this afforded another opportunity for the exercise of violent spirits. Every art was used to draw the people of that town into violent measures. The country was called upon to join them, but in vain; far from any views of independence, the people honestly declared, that a violent act of injustice had been committed, and that reparation ought to be made.

These daring spirits having, however, by various arts and incessant exertions, procured in most of the Colonies, a party of men immediately interested in the repeal of the Tea-act, of the most restless dispositions,—of bankrupt fortunes, and dishonest principles, proposed a general Congress, under pretence of uniting in *decent and proper measures,* for obtaining a repeal of these statutes. But they carefully concealed their principle design of separating the two countries, and establishing independent Governments, because they knew the minds and affections of the people, and even of some of those who were zealous opposers of the acts, were too firmly attached to the British government to endure the thought; and they had not as yet obtained a power sufficient to enforce the measure.

This proposal of a Congress was by no means generally approved by the people. They thought, that their respective Assemblies were most proper to petition, and to obtain a redress of their grievances; they knew, that the Assemblies were their legal Representatives, that the appointment of a Congress would be by themselves a violation of those rights which they complained of in others; and they were apprehensive, that persons illegally appointed, might not pursue reasonable and legal measures; or if they did, that they would not be so successful in the event, as if proposed and pursued under a constitutional authority. For these reasons they relied on their Assemblies. But, while the great bulk of the people acted on such rational and loyal principles, the violent few proceeded to chuse their Committees and Conventions, and these to chuse their Delegates in Congress. Under this circumstance, it was an easy task for the independent faction, to prevail on a few restless and weak men to appoint many of their own number. However zealous the electors might be in opposing the Statutes of which they wished for a repeal, yet there were many among them whose opposition was meant to extend no further; and therefore we find, that the instructions given to the Delegates in Congress were too far from authorising them to promote the independence of the Colonies, or to take up arms, that all of them, either expressly, or by the fullest implication, prohibited it. I have inclosed, for your

Joseph Galloway, *Letters to a Nobleman on the Conduct of the War in the Middle Colonies,* 3rd ed. (London, 1780), 12–15.

Lordship's perusal, extracts of those instructions, from which it will clearly appear, that the Congress were not authorised to pursue any measures, except those that were *legal,* that perfectly corresponded with their *allegiance to their Sovereign,* and that tended to *unite, and not to separate* the two countries. Your Lordship will perceive, on comparing these instructions with the proceedings of Congress, particularly in their approbation of the Suffolk resolves, inciting the people to arms, their resolve to make reprisals, and their seditious letters to the people of England, Ireland, and Canada, that the Delegates violated their trust, acted in every measure which tended to violence and sedition, without authority, and contrary to the directions of those who appointed them; and that the people in general were so far from intending the least deviation from their loyalty, that all they fought for was a redress of what they thought grievances, by "prudent and legal measures, and a more perfect union of the two countries upon constitutional principles."

30

Lord Chatham's Motion to Withdraw the Troops from Boston (1775)

Parliament passed the Coercive Acts in response to Boston's resistance to the Tea Act. Designed to discipline and make an example of the city, the measures closed the port until the tea was paid for, put a military governor with increased power in charge of the colony, and allowed the British to quarter troops in private homes. Despite passage of the bill, many within Parliament believed that the legislation would only further alienate the colonies. One of the leading spokesmen opposing British policy in America was William Pitt (Lord Chatham). The engineer of victory in the Seven Years' War, Pitt had been elevated to the peerage after the conflict and took his seat in the House of Lords. As early as the Stamp Act, Pitt opposed British policy in America. In the following excerpt, the British statesman offers his solution to the impasse in a January 1775 speech.

Questions to Consider

1. According to Lord Chatham, who is to blame for the state of affairs between the colonies and Great Britain?
2. Why does Chatham want to remove the troops from the colonies?
3. For what reasons does Chatham argue that "the kingdom is undone"?

When I state the importance of the colonies to this country, and the magnitude of the danger hanging over this country, from the present plan of misadministration practiced against them, I desire not to be understood to argue for a reciprocity of indulgence between England and America. I contend not for indulgence, but for justice to America; and I shall ever contend that the Americans justly owe obedience to us in a limited degree,—they owe obedience to our ordinances of trade and navigation. But let the line be skillfully drawn between the objects of those ordinances and their private, internal property; let the sacredness of their property remain inviolate; let it be taxable only by their own consent, given in their provincial assemblies, else it will cease to be property. As to the metaphysical refinements, attempting to show that the Americans are equally free from obedience and commercial restraints as from taxation for revenue, as being unrepresented here, I pronounce them futile, frivolous, and groundless.

. . . When I urge this measure of recalling the troops from Boston, I urge it on this pressing principle, that it is necessarily preparatory to the restoration of your peace, and the establishment of your prosperity. It will then appear that you are disposed to treat amicably and equitably, and to consider, revise, and repeal, if it should be found necessary, as I affirm it will, those violent acts and declaration which have disseminated confusion throughout your empire.

. . . Resistance to your acts was necessary as it was just; and your vain declarations of the omnipotence of Parliament, and your imperious doctrines of the necessity of submission, will be found equally impotent to convince or to enslave your fellow-subjects in America, who feel that tyranny, whether ambitioned by an individual part of the legislature or the bodies who compose it, is equally intolerable to British subjects.

. . . The means of enforcing this thraldom are found to be as ridiculous and weak in practice as they are unjust in principle. Indeed, I cannot but feel the most anxious sensibility for the situation of General Gage and the troops under his command; thinking him, as I do, a man of humanity and understanding; and entertaining, as I ever will, the highest respect, the warmest love, for the British troops. Their situation is truly unworthy, penned up pining in inglorious inactivity. They are an army of impotence. You may call them an army of safety and of guard; but they are in truth an army of impotence and contempt; and, to make the folly equal to the disgrace, they are an army of irritation and vexation.

. . . Allay the ferment prevailing in America by removing the obnoxious, hostile cause,—obnoxious and unservicable, for their merits can be only in inaction: . . .—their victory can never be by exertions. . . . But our Ministers say, the Americans must not be heard. They have been condemned unheard; the discriminating hand of vengeance has lumped together innocent and guilty; with all the formalities of hostility, has blocked up the town, and reduced to beggary and famine thirty thousand inhabitants.

. . . But his Majesty is advised that the union in America cannot last! Ministers have more eyes than I, and should have more ears; but, with all the information I have been able to procure, I can pronounce it—an union solid, permanent, and effectual. . . .

"Lord Chatham's Speeches on the American Revolution," *Old South Leaflets,* no. 199 (Boston, n.d.), 15–21.

. . . This resistance to your arbitrary system of taxation might have been foreseen. It was obvious, from the nature of things and of mankind; and, above all, from the Whiggish spirit flourishing in that country. The spirit which now resists your taxation in America is the same which formerly opposed loans, benevolences, and ship-money in England,—the same spirit which called all England on its legs, and by the Bill of Rights vindicated the English constitution; the same spirit which established the great, fundamental, essential maxim of your liberties, that no subject of England shall be taxed but by his own consent.

. . . This glorious spirit of Whiggism animates three millions in America; who prefer poverty with liberty to gilded chains and sordid affluence; and who will die in defense of their rights as men, as freemen. What shall oppose this spirit, aided by the congenial flame glowing in the breasts of every Whig in England, to the amount, I hope, of double the American numbers? . . .

. . . We shall be forced ultimately to retract; let us retract while we can, not when we must. I say we must necessarily undo these violent oppressive acts: they must be repealed. You will repeal them; I pledge myself for it, that you will in the end repeal them; I stake my reputation on it. I will consent to be taken for an idiot if they are not finally repealed. Avoid, then, this humiliating, this disgraceful necessity. With the dignity becoming your exalted situation make the first advances to concord, to peace, and to happiness; for that is your true dignity, to act with prudence and justice. That you should first concede is obvious, from sound and rational policy. . . .

. . . To conclude, my Lords: if the Minister thus preserve in misadvising and misleading the King, I will not say that they can alienate the affections of his subjects from his crown; but I will affirm that they will make the crown not worth his wearing. I will not say that the king is betrayed; but I will pronounce that the kingdom is undone.

5

The War for Independence

The American Revolution pitted Americans, united by a determination to preserve their liberties, against the British, who resolved to uphold the authority of Parliament. Militarily, the American strategy was to avoid losing while somehow luring France into the war, an act that would drain off British forces and likely assure American independence. To achieve this end, American forces first had to secure a major victory. Eighteenth-century battles could be particularly brutal, especially when American Whigs faced their Loyalist neighbors. In such engagements, victors sometimes left the field without prisoners. The principles over which the Americans fought the war—to preserve their liberty—became embedded into the political culture and would shape the political dialogue in the United States for decades to come. The following documents illustrate various aspects of the wartime experience, including the expanded view of liberty held in some quarters of the nation.

31

Introduction to *Common Sense* (1776)

The publication of the 47-page pamphlet Common Sense *in early 1776 marked an important turning point in the American colonists' decision to leave the British Empire. Despite the outbreak of hostilities in 1775, many Americans were hesitant to support independence.* Common Sense *questioned the colonies' relationship with England and influenced many previously wavering Americans to support the Revolution. The author of* Common Sense, *Thomas Paine, grew up in a humble English household and received only a rudimentary education. After failing at a variety of jobs, including that of a lobbyist for British excise collectors, Paine left for Philadelphia in 1774 with letters of introduction from Benjamin Franklin. After arriving in America, Paine landed a job writing for the* Pennsylvania Magazine. *(One of his first articles called for the abolition of slavery.) The following selection contains excerpts from the introduction to* Common Sense.

Questions to Consider

1. To what audience is this document addressed?

2. On what basis does Thomas Paine argue for American independence?

3. In what ways would this presentation help convince wavering colonists to support the Revolution?

4. To what extent was Paine influenced by John Locke ("On Political Society and Government," Document 24) and "Cato's Letters" (Document 25)?

. . . The cause of America is in a great measure the cause of all mankind. Many circumstances have, and will arise, which are not local, but universal, and through which the principles of all lovers of mankind are affected, and in the event of which their affections are interested. The laying a country desolate with fire and sword, declaring war against the natural rights of all mankind, and extirpating the defenders thereof from the face of the earth, is the concern of every man to whom nature hath given the power of feeling. . . .

. . . government; namely, [is] a mode rendered necessary by the inability of moral virtue to govern the world; here too is the design and end of government, viz. freedom and security. And however our eyes may be dazzled with show, or our ears deceived by sound; however prejudice may warp our wills, or interest darken our understanding, the simple voice of nature and reason will say, 'tis right. . . .

The sun never shone on a cause of greater worth. 'Tis not the affair of a city, a county, a province, or a kingdom; but of a continent—of at least one eighth part of the habitable globe. 'Tis not the concern of a day, a year, or an age; posterity are virtually involved in the contest, and will be more or less affected even to the end of time, by the proceedings now. Now is the seed-time of continental union, faith and honor. The least fracture now will be like a name engraved with the point of a pin on the tender rind of a young oak; the wound would enlarge with the tree, and posterity read it in full grown characters.

By referring the matter from argument to arms, a new era for politics is struck—a new method of thinking has arisen. All plans, proposals, &c. prior to the nineteenth of April, i.e. to the commencement of hostilities, are like the almanacs of the last year; which tho' proper then, are superceded and useless now. Whatever was advanced by the advocates on either side of the question then, terminated in one and the same point, viz. a union with Great Britain; the only difference between the parties was the method of effecting it; the one proposing force, the other friendship; but it hath so far happened that the first has failed, and the second has withdrawn her influence. . . .

I have heard it asserted by some, that as America has flourished under her former connection with Great Britain, the same connection is necessary towards her future happiness, and will always have the same effect. Nothing

Thomas Paine, *The Writings of Thomas Paine,* ed. Moncure D. Conway (New York, 1902), 1: 68, 71, 84–87.

can be more fallacious than this kind of argument. . . . America would have flourished as much, and probably much more, had no European power taken any notice of her. The commerce by which she hath enriched herself are the necessaries of life, and will always have a market while eating is the custom of Europe. . . .

We have boasted the protection of Great Britain, without considering, that her motive was interest not attachment; and that she did not protect us from our enemies on our account; but from her enemies on her own account, from those who had no quarrel with us on any other account, and those who will always be our enemies on the same account. Let Britain waive her pretensions to the continent, or the continent throw off the dependance, and we should be at peace with France and Spain, were they at war with Britain. The miseries of Hanover's last war ought to warn us against connections. . . .

But Britain is the parent country, say some. Then the more shame upon her conduct. Even brutes do not devour their young, nor savages make war upon their families; wherefore, the assertion, if true, turns to her reproach; but it happens not to be true, or only partly so, and the phrase parent or mother country hath been jesuitically adopted by the king and the parasites, with a low papistical design of gaining an unfair bias on the credulous weakness of our minds. Europe, and not England, is the parent country of America. This new world hath been the asylum for the persecuted lovers of civil and religious liberty from every part of Europe. Hither have they fled, not from the tender embraces of the mother, but from the cruelty of the monster; and it is so far true of England, that the same tyranny which drove the first emigrants from home, pursues their descendants still.

In this extensive quarter of the globe, we forget the narrow limits of three hundred and sixty miles (the extent of England) and carry our friendship on a larger scale; we claim brotherhood with every European Christian, and triumph in the generosity of the sentiment.

32

A Speech against Independence (1776)

Before declaring independence in the summer of 1776, the Continental Congress was the scene of heated debate about whether the colonies should sever their relationship with Britain. John Dickinson was one of those who spoke on the issue. Born in Maryland, Dickinson began his professional training in a Philadelphia law office and continued his education at London's prestigious Middle Temple. Dickinson first gained notoriety in 1767–68 with the publication of Letters from a Farmer in Pennsylvania. *Written in response to the Townshend Duties, the* Letters *distinguished between external and internal taxes and expressed colonists' opposition to taxes levied on them by Parliament. In the ensuing excerpt, Dickinson offers his views just days before the signing of the Declaration of Independence. Dickinson ultimately supported American independence and later served in the 1787 Constitutional Convention.*

Questions to Consider

1. For what reasons does John Dickinson believe the colonies should resolve their differences with Great Britain?

2. What had Great Britain offered the American colonies that Dickinson did not want to lose?

3. What does Dickinson fear will happen if the colonies declare independence?

4. Compare and contrast the views contained in this document with those found in Thomas Paine's "Introduction to *Common Sense*" (Document 31). How do you account for similarities? Differences?

. . . I know the name of liberty is dear to each one of us; but have we not enjoyed liberty even under the English monarchy? Shall we this day renounce that to go and seek it in I know not what form of republic, which will soon change into a licentious anarchy and popular tyranny? In the human body the head only sustains and governs all the members, directing them, with admirable harmony, to the same object, which is self-preservation and happiness; so the head of the body politic, that is the king, in concert with the Parliament, can alone maintain the union of the members of this Empire, lately so flourishing, and prevent civil war by obviating all the evils produced by variety of opinions and diversity of interests. And so firm is my persuasion of this that I fully believe the most cruel war which Great Britain could make upon us would be that of not making any; and that the surest means of bringing us back to her obedience would be that of employing none. For the dread of the English arms, once removed, provinces would rise up against provinces and cities against cities; and we shall be seen to turn against ourselves the arms we have taken up to combat the common enemy.

Insurmountable necessity would then compel us to resort to the tutelary authority which we should have rashly abjured, and, if it consented to receive us again under its aegis, it would be no longer as free citizens but as slaves. Still inexperienced and in our infancy, what proof have we given of our ability to walk without a guide?

. . . [O]ur union with England . . . is no less necessary to procure us, with foreign powers, that condescension and respect which is so essential to the prosperity of our commerce, to the enjoyment of any consideration, and to the accomplishment of any enterprise. . . . From the moment when our separation shall take place, everything will assume a contrary direction. The nations will accustom themselves to look upon us with disdain; even the pirates of Africa and Europe will fall upon our vessels, will massacre our seamen, or lead them into a cruel and perpetual slavery. . . .

Independence, I am aware, has attractions for all mankind; but I maintain that, in the present quarrel, the friends of independence are the promoters of

---

"Speech of John Dickinson of Pennsylvania, Favoring a Condition of Union with England, Delivered July 1, 1776," *Principles and Acts of the Revolution in America*, ed. Hezekiah Niles (Baltimore, 1822), 493–495.

slavery, and that those who desire to separate us would but render us more dependent, . . . to change the condition of English subjects for that of slaves to the whole world is a step that could only be counseled by insanity. . . .

But here I am interrupted and told that no one questions the advantages which America derived at first from her conjunction with England; but that the new pretensions of the ministers have changed all, have subverted all. If I should deny that, . . . I should deny not only what is the manifest truth but even what I have so often advanced and supported. But is there any doubt that it already feels a secret repentance? These arms, these soldiers it prepares against us are not designed to establish tyranny upon our shores but to vanquish our obstinacy, and to compel us to subscribe to conditions of accommodation.

. . . to pretend to reduce us to an absolute impossibility of resistance, in cases of oppression, would be, on their part, a chimerical project. . . . [But only] an uninterrupted succession of victories and of triumphs could alone constrain England to acknowledge American independence; which, whether we can expect, whoever knows the instability of fortune can easily judge.

If we have combated successfully at Lexington and at Boston, Quebec and all Canada have witnessed our reverses. Everyone sees the necessity of opposing the extraordinary pretensions of the ministers; but does everybody see also that of fighting for independence?

. . . By substituting a total dismemberment to the revocation of the laws we complain of, we should fully justify the ministers; we should merit the infamous name of rebels, and all the British nation would arm, with an unanimous impulse, against those who, from oppressed and complaining subjects, should have become all at once irreconcilable enemies. The English cherish the liberty we defend; they respect the dignity of our cause; but they will blame, they will detest our recourse to independence, and will unite with one consent to combat us.

The propagators of the new doctrine are pleased to assure us that, out of jealousy toward England, foreign sovereigns will lavish their succors upon us, as if these sovereigns could sincerely applaud rebellion; as if they had not colonies, even here in America, in which it is important for them to maintain obedience and tranquility. . . . under the most benevolent pretexts they will despoil us of our territories, they will invade our fisheries and obstruct our navigation, they will attempt our liberty and our privileges. We shall learn too late what it costs to trust to those European flatteries, and to place that confidence in inveterate enemies which has been withdrawn from long tried friends.

There are many persons who, to gain their ends, extol the advantages of a republic over monarchy. I will not here undertake to examine which of these two forms of government merits the preference. I know, however, that the English nation, after having tried them both, has never found repose except in monarchy. I know, also, that in popular republics themselves, so necessary is monarchy to cement human society, it has been requisite to institute monarchical powers, . . . Nor should I here omit an observation, the truth of which appears to me incontestible—the English constitution seems to be the fruit of the experience of all anterior time, in which monarchy is so tempered that the monarch finds himself checked in his efforts to seize absolute power; and the authority of the people is so regulated that anarchy is not to be feared. But for us it is to be apprehended that, when the counterpoise of monarchy shall no longer exist, the democratic power may carry all before it and involve the whole state in confusion and ruin. Then an ambitious citizen may arise, seize the reins of power, and annihilate liberty forever; . . .

33

German Doctor's Account of War and Surgery (1777)

Britain's controversial decision to use foreign auxiliaries against the Americans caused many colonists to forsake their loyalty to the Crown. England's determination to use mercenaries made sense in London because the German troops were well-trained professionals who could be rented from cash-hungry German sovereigns for a reasonable price. The largest number of these troops came from Hesse Kassel; hence, the term Hessian *became a synonym for all German mercenaries. The author of the ensuing account was Julius F. Wasmus, an army surgeon from the German state of Brunswick. Before coming to Canada in 1776, he had served in the Seven Years' War. A member of General John Burgoyne's force as it headed south along Lake Champlain in 1777, Wasmus was captured at the Battle of Bennington. The Bennington engagement not only resulted in four years of captivity for the doctor, but it also contributed to Burgoyne's later defeat at Saratoga. Wasmus recalls the heat of the Bennington fight in the selection excerpted below.*

Questions to Consider

1. How does Julius Wasmus describe the battle?
2. How did Wasmus view his captors?
3. What seemingly surprised Wasmus about the American army?
4. Would Wasmus agree with the argument espoused in "Pennsylvania, the Poor Man's Paradise" (Document 12) and "What Is an American?" (Document 23)? How might the 1755 Pennsylvania Assembly ("Pennsylvania Assembly Comments on German Immigration," Document 20) have viewed someone like Wasmus?

J. F. Wasmus, *An Eyewitness Account of the American Revolution and New England Life: The Journal of J. F. Wasmus, German Company Surgeon, 1776–1783,* trans. Helga Doblin, ed. Mary C. Lynn (Westport, CT, 1990), 71–73. Reprinted by permission.

16th . . . The enemy is marching in force against our right wing and it appears that they want to encircle us. There is also some shooting on our right wing. After 12 o'clock, a patrol was sent out from our lines and was driven off by the enemy, who fired at them. Half an hour later, a violent volley of fire erupted against the entrenchment that was occupied by 35 dragoons. Our dragoons fired up volleys on the enemy in cold blood and with much courage, and it did not take them long to load their carbines behind the breastworks. But as soon as they rose up to take aim, bullets went through their heads. They fell backwards and no longer moved a finger. Thus, in a short time, our tallest and best dragoons were sent into eternity. The [German] cannon shot balls and grapeshot sometimes to the right, sometimes to the left and then again forward into the brush. The Savages made terrible faces and ran from one tree to the next. I had chosen a very big oak tree close behind our entrenchment, behind which I dressed the wounded. The Savages also came behind this tree and 4 or 5 of them lying down on top of me almost crushed me to death. From the enemy side, the fire became increasingly heavy and they [the enemy] pressed harder. When the Savages saw that, one of them, probably the oldest, emitted a strange cry, which cannot be described; whereupon they all ran down the mountain toward the barrage. The cannon in our entrenchment was quiet because the sergeant artificer, who commanded it, had been shot; the 8 men at the cannon were either shot or wounded. At the bridge, where our Lieut. Colonel Baum was standing, the cannon and volley fire had ceased. Capt. Dommes, who was covering our left flank and rear, was driven back with his few men and captured; we could see this quite well from our mountain. We were thus completely encircled. We too withdrew now with great speed while I was still busy dressing wounds. Then, following the regiment in a great hurry, I stumbled over a big, fallen tree about 300 paces from our entrenchment. When I got up, the enemy came rushing over our entrenchment and 3 quickly took aim and fired at me. I again fell to the ground behind the tree and the bullets were dreadful, whistling over and beyond me. I remained lying on the ground until the enemy urged me rather impolitely to get up. One grabbed me by the arm and another said he should kill me, whereupon he placed the bayonet of his gun with tightened trigger on my chest. He asked whether I was a Britisher or a Hessian. I told him I was a Braunschweig surgeon, shook hands with him, and called him my friend and brother; for what does one not do when in trouble. I was happy they understood me (Freund and Bruder) for that helped so much that he withdrew his gun. But he now took my watch, looked at it, held it to his ear and put it away [in his pocket]. After this, he made a friendly face and was so human that he urged me to take a drink from his wooden flask. He handed me over to his comrades, who started anew to search my pockets. One of them took nothing but my purse in which, however, were only 14 piasters (specie). He continued eagerly looking for money but then left, whereupon the third began searching my pockets. This one took all my small items as my knife, my paper, my lighter, but he did not find the best; they were so dumb that they did not see the pocket in my overcoat. Thus, I saved my Noble [sic] pipe. If I had put my watch and moneybag into this pocket, I would not have lost anything. . . .

When one of the enemy heard that I was a CHIRURGUS [surgeon], he led me behind our entrenchment to dress the wound of his son, who had been shot through the thigh. Now I saw what effect our cannon and musket fire had had, since the enemy had suffered great losses here. General Stark, who in attire and posture was very similar to the tailor Muller in Wolfenbut-tel, had commanded the corps of the Americans against us. As he now saw me dressing the wounds of the first, he ordered me to bandage several others of the enemy, but I hurried toward our entrenchment because there were dragoons and Hess-Hanau Artillerymen in need of my help. But the Americans did not allow me any time but pulled me along by force. We went past the trusty tree that had warded off so many bullets from me. Here I found some of my instruments and bandages etc. in a case. Putting all of it in a bag, I wanted to take it along, but my guide took it away from me and urged me to drink some strong rum with him. All the enemy were very well provided with it and I noticed that almost all of them were drunk. Each one had a wooden flask filled with rum hanging from his neck; they all were in shirt-sleeves, had nothing [to cover] their bodies but shirts, vests and long linen trousers, which reached down to their shoes; no stockings; [in addition] a powder horn, a bullet bag, a flask with rum and a gun—that was all they had on them. They all were well-shaped men of very healthy appearance and well-grown; better than the Canadians. . . . They [the Rebels] did not capture one single Savage; it is incomprehensible to me how they [the Savages] got through. The unfortunate Tories (Royalist Americans) who were not killed also fell into the hands of their countrymen. Like cattle, they were tied to each with cords and ropes and led away; it is presumed that they will be hanged. . . . These scenes cannot really be described—reading this, the best will perhaps be moved, but it is actually not possible to feel the horror of these scenes. A thought that makes your flesh creep! To see a friend or fellow creature lie bleeding on the ground who had been cruelly wounded by the murderous lead and approached his death shaking—crying for help, and then not be able, not be allowed to help him, is that not cruel?

34

Treaty of Alliance with France (1777)

American leaders understood that foreign assistance was essential in the effort to attain independence, and they looked to France for such aid. Britain's archrival was eager to weaken its traditional foe. The French had quietly encouraged colonial independence before July 1776, but they were hesitant to openly support a cause with unknown prospects for success. The American victory at Saratoga, New York, in the fall of 1777, convinced France to negotiate a treaty of alliance. On February 6, 1778, representatives of France and the United States signed two agreements: a treaty of alliance and a treaty of amity and commerce. The treaties provided the Americans with the much-needed support of a great power and transformed a small internecine struggle in North America into a major European conflict. The changing nature of the war made it increasingly difficult for the British to concentrate their forces in North America exclusively. The following selection contains excerpts from the Treaty of Alliance.

Questions to Consider

1. What are the stated purposes of this treaty?
2. Why does the treaty state that neither side may "lay down their arms" until independence had been obtained?
3. Why did France renounce claims to parts of North America?
4. What is the significance of this selection?

ART. 1.

If War should break out betwan france and Great Britain, during the continuence of the present War between the United States and England, his Majesty and the said united States, shall make it a common cause, and aid each other mutually with their good Offices, their Counsels, and their forces, according to the exigence of Conjunctures as becomes good & faithful Allies.

ART. 2.

The essential and direct End of the present defensive alliance is to maintain effectually the liberty, Sovereignty, and independence absolute and unlimited of the said united States, as well in Matters of Government as of commerce. . . .

ART. 4.

The contracting Parties agree that in case either of them should form any particular Enterprise in which the concurrence of the other may be desired, the Party whose concurrence is desired shall readily, and with good faith, join to act in concert for that Purpose, as far as circumstances and its own particular Situation will permit. . . .

Treaties and Other International Acts of the United States of America, ed. Hunter Miller, vol. 2, *1776–1818* (Washington, DC, 1931), 35–41.

ART. 5.

If the united States should think fit to attempt the Reduction of the British Power remaining in the Northern Parts of America, or the Islands of Bermudas, those Countries or Islands in case of Success, shall be confederated with or dependant upon the united States.

ART. 6.

The Most Christian King renounces for ever the possession of the Islands of Bermudas as well as of any part of the continent of North america which before the treaty of Paris in 1763 or in virtue of that Treaty, were acknowledged to belong to the Crown of Great Britain. . . .

ART. 8.

Neither of the two Parties shall conclude either Truce or Peace with Great Britain, without the formal consent of the other first obtain'd; and they mutually engage not to lay down their arms, until the Independence of the united states shall have been formally or tacitly assured by the Treaty or Treaties that shall terminate the War. . . .

35

The Battle of King's Mountain and Loyalism in the Carolinas (1780)

In the fall of 1778, the British opened up a southern theater of war when they landed at Savannah, Georgia. Convinced that the southern colonies were more valuable to Britain and sure that large numbers of Loyalists would support them, British forces quickly proved triumphant in the region. By 1780, the specter of British victory in the region had roused many local residents to resist through guerilla actions and organized battles. At King's Mountain, North Carolina, an army comprising frontier settlers confronted a force of Loyalists. The following account, written by Banastre Tarleton, describes the battle and its impact. A British cavalry officer fighting under the leadership of Lord Cornwallis, Tarleton had gained a reputation for brutality toward prisoners that led him to be called "No Quarter" Tarleton.

Questions to Consider

1. What impact did Ferguson's defeat have on Loyalists in the Carolinas?
2. What impact did Ferguson's defeat have on the British campaign in the Carolinas?
3. Why do you think Banastre Tarleton is so offended by American "insult and indignity"? What can you deduce about Tarleton from this document?
4. Why do you think the American forces at King's Mountain "exercised horrid cruelties on the prisoners"?

Near the end of September, Major Ferguson had intelligence of Clarke's having joined Sumpter, and that a swarm of backwoodsmen, by an unexpected and rapid approach to Gilbert town, now threatened his destruction. He dispatched information to Earl Cornwallis of the superior numbers to which he was opposed, and directly commenced his march to the Catawba. Notwithstanding the prudent plan of verging towards the royal army, and advertising the British general of this situation; owing to some communication, or the distance of his friends, a detachment did not march in time from Charlotte town to yield him assistance.

Colonels Campbell, Cleveland, Selby, Seveer, Williams, Brandon, and Lacy, being informed at Gilbert town, of the retreat of Ferguson by the Cherokee road, towards King's mountain, selected sixteen hundred chosen men on horseback, for a rigorous pursuit. The rapid march of this corps soon rendered an action inevitable. Major Ferguson heard of the enemy's approach at King's mountain: he occupied the most favourable position he could find, and waited the attack. The action commenced at four o'clock in the afternoon, on the 7th of October, and was disputed with great bravery near an hour, when the death of the gallant Ferguson threw his whole corps into total confusion. No effort was made after this event to resist the enemy's barbarity, or revenge the fall of their leader. By American accounts, one hundred and fifty officers and men of the provincials and loyal militias were killed, one hundred and fifty were wounded, and eight hundred were made prisoners. The mountaineers, it is reported, used every insult and indignity, after the action, towards the dead body of Major Ferguson, and exercised horrid cruelties on the prisoners that fell into their possession. . . .

The destruction of Ferguson and his corps marked the period and the extent of the first expedition into North Carolina. Added to the depression and fear it communicated to the loyalists upon the borders, and to the southward, the effect of such an important event was sensibly felt by Earl Cornwallis at Charlotte town. The weakness of his army, the extent and poverty of North Carolina, the want of knowledge of his enemy's designs, and the total ruin of his militia, presented a gloomy prospect at the commencement of the

---

Banastre Tarleton, *A History of the Campaigns of 1780 and 1781 in the Southern Provinces of North America* (Dublin, 1787), 167–169.

campaign. A farther progress by the route which he had undertaken could not possibly remove, but would undoubtedly increase his difficulties; he therefore formed a sudden determination to quit Charlotte town, and pass the Catawba river. The army was ordered to move, and expresses were dispatched to recall Lieutenant–colonel Tarleton.

36

Women's Contributions to the War Effort (1780)

The contributions of American women were essential to the success of the American Revolution. Economic boycotts of British goods before the conflict were clearly made possible by American women's willingness to produce goods in the home to replace the loss of imported items. As many American men decided to fight for independence, American women took similar steps. Esther de Berdt Reed was an early supporter of the Whig cause. The wife of prominent Philadelphia politician Joseph Reed, she organized a women's fund-raising committee in 1780 in the Philadelphia area. Her effort to create similar organizations in other colonial towns was cut short by her untimely death from dysentery in September 1780. George Washington would laud the women's support of the war effort, but he stopped short of arguing for the extension of greater legal rights or a political voice for women. The following excerpt discusses women's views toward the cause and their efforts to support the American Revolution.

Questions to Consider

1. To what audience is this document directed?
2. According to Esther de Berdt Reed, to what extent do American women share the principles of the American Revolution?
3. What can you deduce about the place of women in 18th-century America based on this essay?
4. Do you think American women of this time expected any changes in status as a result of the Revolution?

On the commencement of actual war, the Women of America manifested a firm resolution to contribute as much as could depend on them, to the deliverance of their country. Animated by the purest patriotism, they are sensible of sorrow at this day, in not offering more than barren wishes for the success of so glorious a Revolution. They aspire to render themselves more really useful; and this sentiment is universal from the north to the south of the Thirteen United States. . . .

Esther de Berdt Reed, *The Sentiments of an American Woman* (Philadelphia, 1780), 1–2.

Born for liberty, disdaining to bear the irons of a tyrannic Government, we associate ourselves to the grandeur of those Sovereign, cherished, and revered, who have held with so much splendour the scepter of the greatest States, The Batildas, the Elizabeths, the Maries, the Catharines, who have extended the empire of liberty, and contented to reign by sweetness and justice, have broken the chains of slavery, forged by tyrants in the times of ignorance and barbarity. . . .

But I must limit myself to the recollection of this small number of atchievements. Who knows if persons disposed to censure, and sometimes too severely with regard to us, may not disapprove our appearing acquainted even with the actions of which our sex boasts? We are at least certain, that he cannot be a good citizen who will not applaud our efforts for the relief of the armies which defend our lives, our possessions, our liberty? . . .

Who, amongst us, will not renounce with the highest pleasure, those vain ornaments, when she shall consider that the valiant defenders of America will be able to draw some advantage from the money which she may have laid out in these; that they will be better defended from the rigours of the seasons, that after their painful toils, they will receive some extraordinary and unexpected relief; that these presents will perhaps be valued by them at a greater price, when they will have it in their power to say: *This Is the offering of the Ladies.* The time is arrived to display the same sentiments which animated us at the beginning of the Revolution, when we renounced the use of teas, however agreeable to our taste, rather than receive them from our persecutors; when we made it appear to them that we placed former necessaries in the rank of superfluities, when our liberty was interested; when our republican and laborious hands spun the flax, prepared the linen intended for the use of our soldiers; when exiles and fugitives we supported with courage all the evils which are the concomitants of war. Let us not lose a moment; let us be engaged to offer the homage of our gratitude at the altar of military valour, and you, our brave deliverers, while mercenary slaves combat to cause you to share with them, the irons with which they are loaded, receive with a free hand our offering, the purest which can be presented to your virtue.

IDEAS, RELATIVE TO THE MANNER OF FORWARDING TO THE AMERICAN SOLDIERS, THE PRESENTS OF THE AMERICAN WOMEN

. . . 1st. All Women and Girls will be received without exception, to present their patriotic offering; and, as it is absolutely voluntary, every one will regulate it according to her ability, and her disposition. The shilling offered by the Widow or the young Girl, will be received as well as the most considerable sums presented by the Women who have the happiness to join to their patriotism, greater means to be useful.

2d. A Lady chosen by the others in each county, shall be the Treasuress; and to render her task more simple, and more easy, she will not receive but determinate sums, in a round number, from twenty hard dollars to any greater sum. The exchange forty dollars in paper for one dollar in specie.

It is hoped that there will not be one Woman who will not with pleasure charge herself with the embarrassment which will attend so honorable an operation.

3d. The Women who shall not be in a condition to send twenty dollars in specie, or above, will join in as great a number as will be necessary to make this or any greater sum, and one amongst them will carry it, or cause it to be sent to the Treasuress.

4th. The Treasuress of the county will receive the money, and will keep a register, writing the sums in her book, and causing it to be signed at the side of the whole by the person who has presented it.

5th. When several Women shall join together to make a total sum of twenty dollars or more, she amongst them who shall have the charge to carry it to the Treasuress, will make mention of all their names on the register, if her associates shall have so directed her, those whose choice it shall be, will have the liberty to remain unknown.

6th. As soon as the Treasuress of the county shall judge, that the sums which she shall have received, deserve to be sent to their destination, she will cause them to be presented with the lists, to the wife of the Governor or President of the State, who will be the Treasuress-General of the state; and she will cause it to be set down in her register, and have it sent to Mistress Washington. If the Governor or President are unmarried, all will address themselves to the wife of the Vice-President, if there is one, or of the Chief-Justice, &c.

7th. Women settled in the distant parts of the country, and not chusing for any particular reason as for the sake of greater expedition, to remit their Capital to the Treasuress, may send it directly to the wife of the Governor, or President, &c. or to Mistress Washington, who, if she shall judge necessary, will in a short answer to the sender, acquaint her with the reception of it.

8th. As Mrs. Washington may be absent from the camp when the greater part of the banks shall be sent there; the American Women considering, that General Washington is the Father and Friend of the Soldiery; that he is himself, the first Soldier of the Republic, and that their offering will be received at its destination as soon as it shall have come to his hands, they will pray him, to take the charge of receiving it, in the absence of Mrs. Washington.

9th. General Washington will dispose of this fund in the manner that he shall judge most advantageous to the Soldiery. The American Women desire only that it may not be considered as to be employed, to procure to the army, the objects of subsistence, arms or cloathing, which are due to them by the Continent. It is an extraordinary bounty intended to render the condition of the Soldier more pleasant, and not to hold place of the things which they ought to receive from the Congress, or from the States.

10th. If the General judges necessary, he will publish at the end of a certain time, an amount of that which shall have been received from each particular State.

11th. The Women who shall send their offerings, will have in their choice to conceal or to give their names; and if it shall be thought proper, on a fit occasion, to publish one day the lists, they only, who shall consent, shall be named; when with regard to the sums sent, there will be no mention made, if they so desire it.

37

The Quock Walker Decision (1783)

The Declaration of Independence may have held "that all men are created equal," but in reality this "self-evident truth" applied only to adult white males. For persons of African descent, the ideals of the American Revolution meant little; instead of liberty, the American experience meant enslavement and subjugation. But the importance of these ideals to inspire change played a major role in leading to later reforms. While slavery continued to flourish in the deep South, it withered in many northern states. In Massachusetts, slaves were legally regarded as both property and persons. This dual status made it possible for slaves to petition the courts. The following selection comes from the 1783 case of Commonwealth v. Jennison. *In this case, the third in a series that dealt with the issue, Supreme Court Justice William Cushing ruled that Quock Walker, whom Nathaniel Jennison had tried to repossess as a slave, was free under the 1780 state constitution.*

Questions to Consider

1. What rights could a slave claim under Massachusetts law in the late 18th century?

2. According to this court decision, what changes had taken place that allowed Quock Walker to be declared free?

3. How do you think Thomas Paine ("Introduction to *Common Sense*," Document 31) would have reacted to this decision?

4. To what extent do principles espoused in "John Locke on Political Society and Government" (Document 24) and "Cato's Letters" (Document 25) influence the Quock Walker decision?

AS TO THE DOCTRINE OF SLAVERY and the right of Christians to hold Africans in perpetual servitude, and sell and treat them as we do our horses and cattle, that (it is true) had been heretofore countenanced by the province laws formerly, but nowhere is it expressly enacted or established. It has been a usage—a usage which took its origin from the practice of some of the European nations, and the regulations of British government respecting the then colonies, for the benefit of trade and wealth. But whatever sentiments have formerly prevailed in this particular or slid in upon us by the example of others, a different idea has taken place with the people of America, more favorable to the natural rights of mankind, and to that natural, innate desire of liberty, which with heaven (without regard to color, complexion, or shape of noses) . . . has inspired all the human race. And upon this ground our constitution of government, by which the people of this commonwealth have solemnly bound themselves, sets out with declaring that all men are born free and equal—and that every subject is entitled to liberty, and to have it guarded by the laws, as well as life and property—and in short is totally repugnant to the idea of being born slaves. This being the case, I think the idea of slavery is inconsistent with our own conduct and constitution; and there can be no such thing as perpetual servitude of a rational creature, unless his liberty is forfeited by some criminal conduct or given up by personal consent or contract. . . .

6

Toward a New Government

As the infant United States sought its independence, it needed to create a government to replace that of Great Britain. Fearful of creating a potentially "tyrannical" government similar to the one they had revolted against, the 13 former colonies were initially bound by a loose confederation that left most power in the hands of the states. Despite the perceived weakness of the new national government, it succeeded in establishing several precedents that were later followed under the Constitution. Despite some successes, the Confederation's inability to establish a sound fiscal footing and the threat of social disorder led many to call for yet another new government. The following documents reveal the strengths and weaknesses facing the new nation, as well as the differing views of its citizens on how the government could be improved.

38

The Articles of Confederation (1777)

Even before the Continental Congress proclaimed independence, its members were contemplating how the 13 former colonies would govern themselves. In July 1775, Benjamin Franklin proposed a plan of government, but it would be more than two years before the congressional delegates agreed on the Articles of Confederation. Because the Articles required the unanimous consent of the states before going into effect, the plan of union did not begin to operate until Maryland's acceptance in 1781. The Articles provide an example of the principles for which Americans fought during the American Revolution. Essentially a continuation of the Second Continental Congress, this new central government had limited powers. The perceived weakness of the Confederation led many prominent Americans to demand that the Articles be amended and specifically that the central government be strengthened.

Questions to Consider

1. What powers were given to the Confederation government?
2. In what ways was the Confederation government weak?

3. Why might the individuals who drafted the Articles have wanted a weak central government?

4. What specific features of the Confederation government will be retained in the Constitution?

ARTICLE I. . . . this confederacy shall be The United States of America.

ARTICLE II. Each State retains its sovereignty, freedom and independence, and every power, jurisdiction and right, which is not by this confederation expressly delegated to the United States, in Congress assembled.

ARTICLE III. The said States hereby severally enter into a firm league of friendship with each other, for their common defense, the security of their liberties, and their mutual and general welfare. . . .

ARTICLE IV. . . . the free inhabitants of each of these States, paupers, vagabonds, and fugitives from justice excepted, shall be entitled to all privileges and immunities of free citizens in the several States. . . .

ARTICLE V. . . . No State shall be represented in Congress by less than two, nor by more than seven members; and no person shall be capable of being a delegate for more than three years in any term of six years. . . .

In determining questions in the United States, in Congress assembled, each State shall have one vote.

Freedom of speech and debate in Congress shall not be impeached or questioned in any court, or place out of Congress, and the members of Congress shall be protected in their persons from arrests and imprisonments, during the time of their going to and from, and attendance on Congress, except for treason, felony, or breach of the peace.

ARTICLE VI. No State without the consent of the United States in Congress assembled, shall send any embassy to, or receive any embassy from, or enter into any conference, agreement, alliance or treaty with any king prince or state. . . . No State shall engage in any war without the consent of the United States in Congress assembled, unless such State be actually invaded by enemies, . . . and the danger is so imminent as not to admit of a delay, till the United States in Congress assembled can be consulted. . . .

ARTICLE VIII. All charges of war, and all other expenses that shall be incurred for the common defense or general welfare, and allowed by the United States in Congress assembled, shall be defrayed out a common treasury, which shall be supplied by the several States, in proportion to the value of all land within each State. . . .

ARTICLE IX. The United States in Congress assembled, shall have the sole and exclusive right and power of determining on peace and war, . . . [and] entering into treaties and alliances. . . .

The United States in Congress assembled shall also be the last resort on appeal in all disputes and differences now subsisting or that hereafter may arise between two or more States concerning boundary, jurisdiction or any other cause whatever. . . .

"The Articles of Confederation," *Old South Leaflets,* no. 2 (Boston, 1896), 1–9.

The United States in Congress assembled shall also have the sole and exclusive right and power of regulating the alloy and value of coin . . . fixing the standard of weights and measures throughout the United States,—regulating the trade and managing all affairs with the Indians, not members of any of the States, provided that the legislative right of any State within its own limits be not infringed or violated—establishing and regulating post-offices from one State to another, throughout all the United States. . . .

The United States in Congress assembled shall have authority to appoint a committee, to sit in the recess of Congress, to be denominated "a committee of the States," and to consist of one delegate from each State; and to appoint such other committees and civil officers as may be necessary for managing the general affairs of the United States under their direction—to appoint one of their number to preside, provided that no person be allowed to serve in the office of president more than one year in any term of three years; to ascertain the necessary sums of money to be raised for the service of the United States, and to appropriate and apply the same for defraying the public expenses—to borrow money, or emit bills on the credit of the United States, transmitting every half year to the respective States an account of the sums of money so borrowed or emitted,—to build and equip a navy—to agree upon the number of land forces, and to make requisitions from each State for its quota, in proportion to the number of white inhabitants in such State; which requisition shall be binding, and thereupon the Legislature of each State shall appoint the regimental officers, raise the men and clothe, arm and equip them in a soldier like manner, at the expense of the United States. . . .

The United States in Congress assembled shall never engage in a war, . . . nor enter into any treaties or alliances, nor coin money, nor regulate the value thereof, nor ascertain the sums and expenses necessary for the defense and welfare of the United States, or any of them, nor emit bills, nor borrow money on the credit of the United States, nor appropriate money, nor agree upon the number of vessels of war, to be built or purchased, or the number of land or sea forces to be raised, nor appoint a commander in chief of the army or navy, unless nine States assent to the same: nor shall a question on any other point, . . . be determined, unless by the votes of a majority of the United States in Congress assembled. . . .

ARTICLE X. The committee of the States, or any nine of them, shall be authorized to execute, in the recess of Congress, such of the powers of Congress as the United States in Congress assembled, by the consent of nine states. . . .

ARTICLE XI. Canada acceding to this confederation, . . . shall be admitted into, and entitled to all the advantages of this Union. . . .

ARTICLE XII. All bills of credit emitted, monies borrowed and debts contracted by or under the authority of Congress, before the assembling of the United States, in pursuance of the present confederation, shall be deemed and considered as a charge against the United States. . . .

ARTICLE XIII. Every State shall abide by the determinations of the United States in Congress assembled, on all questions which by this confederation are submitted to them. And the articles of this confederation shall be inviolably observed by every State, and the Union shall be perpetual: nor shall any alteration at any time hereafter be made in any of them; unless such alteration be agreed to in a Congress of the United States, and be afterwards confirmed by the Legislatures of every State. . . .

39

Failure of the Continental Congress (1786)

Following the American Declaration of Independence, the Continental Congress created a permanent national government. The result was the Articles of Confederation, which passed the Congress in 1777 but was not ratified until 1781. The Articles show the extent to which a fear of centralized authority dominated American political thinking in the early 1780s. David Ramsay, a native of Pennsylvania, gained public notice as a physician in Charleston, South Carolina. His connections to the local elite led him into politics, and he was an early and outspoken supporter of independence. Captured by the British during the conquest of Charleston, he was exiled to St. Augustine, Florida, for the duration of the war. Upon his return to South Carolina, he was elected to two terms in the Confederation Congress, serving as acting president in 1785–86. In his capacity as acting president of the Confederation Congress, Ramsay sent the following letter to officials in Rhode Island, Delaware, Maryland, Virginia, North Carolina, and Georgia. It reveals some of the fundamental problems facing the government.

Questions to Consider

1. What are some of the problems facing the Continental Congress?
2. Why might many states neglect or ignore the Continental Congress?
3. Do you think David Ramsay would have been interested in supporting a stronger central government?
4. What is the historical context of this document?

THE CHAIRMAN OF CONGRESS (DAVID RAMSAY) TO CERTAIN STATES

New York January 31, 1786

Sir,

   In conformity to the resolution enclosed it becomes my duty to write to the Executives of the several States which are at present unrepresented in Congress.

"The Chairman of Congress (David Ramsay) to Certain States," January 31, 1786, *Letters of the Members of the Continental Congress,* ed. Edmund C. Burnett (Washington, DC, 1936), 8: 290–291.

Three months of the federal year are now completed and in that whole period no more than seven states have at any one time been represented. No question excepting that of adjourning from day to day can be carried without perfect unanimity. The extreme difficulty of framing resolutions against which no exception can be taken by any one State, can scarcely be conceived but by those whose unfortunate situation had led them to experience the perplexing embarrassment. Was the convenience of the present members only concerned your Excellency would not have been troubled with this letter. Sorry I am to add that the most essential interests of the United States suffer from the same cause. The languishing State of public credit is notorious both in Europe and America. What an additional wound must be given to it when it is known that no plans can be made for the payment of our debts, without the Unanimous consent of Nine States, and that only seven States have yet come forward with a representation. The disposition of our western Territory, An American Coinage, Commercial arrangements with European powers, particularly Great Britain, and a variety of other matters are of immense and pressing importance, but for want of an additional number of States nothing can be done.

I forbear to mention to your Excellency that even in private life where two persons agree to meet at a given time and place for the adjustment of their common concerns, the one who attends has a right to complain that he is not treated with common politeness by the other who breaks his appointment. I say nothing of the unequal burden imposed on the States who are present: They incur a heavy expence to maintain their delegates, and this expence is rendered inefficient, because that out of the other six no two have come forward to concur with them in dispatching the public business. Least of all would I insinuate that the present States might be justified in resolving that as they had attended three months to no purpose they would in their turn relinquish the public service, and leave the other states should they come on, to suffer a similar mortification to what they have long experienced of meeting and adjourning from day to day without having it in their power to enter on the most important and pressing national business.

The remissness of the States in keeping up a representation in Congress naturally tends to annihilate our Confederation. That once dissolved our State establishments would be of short duration. Anarchy, or intestine wars would follow till some future Caesar seized our Liberties, or we would be the sport of European politics, and perhaps parcelled out as appendages to their several Governments.

In behalf of Congress in the chair of which I at present have the honor to sit I beseech your Excellency by the regard you have for our federal Government to use your utmost endeavours to induce the delegates of your State to give their immediate attendance in Congress.

I have the honor to be Your Excellency's
Most obedient and most humble Servant,

—David Ramsay.

40

The Northwest Ordinance (1787)

Two of the most pressing issues facing the Confederation government were western lands and the need to raise revenue. Conflicting claims between the various states had delayed the ratification of the Articles for four years. But after several states abandoned their claims to territory north of the Ohio, the national government devised a method to dispose of the lands, thus raising much needed funds. In 1785, Congress passed an ordinance that provided for the orderly disposal of lands in the Old Northwest (the present states of Ohio, Indiana, Illinois, Michigan, Wisconsin, and part of Minnesota). Two years later, a lobbyist representing land speculators spurred Congress into passing the Northwest Ordinance, which is excerpted below. The plan, which borrowed from an earlier proposal offered by Thomas Jefferson, described the process by which territories were to become states.

Questions to Consider

1. What are the steps in forming a government in new territory?
2. What must the territorial government provide its citizens?
3. What role does the federal government play in the formation of western states?
4. To what extent is the role of the federal government described different than the role envisioned in the "Articles of Confederation" (Document 38)? Why do you think this change occurred?

. . . Be it ordained by the authority aforesaid, That there shall be appointed, from time to time, by Congress, a governor, whose commission shall continue in force for the term of three years, unless sooner revoked by Congress; he shall reside in the district, and have a freehold estate therein in 1000 acres of land, while in the exercise of his office.

There shall be appointed, from time to time, by Congress a secretary, whose commission shall continue in force for four years unless sooner revoked; . . . There shall also be appointed a court to consist of three judges, any two of whom to form a court, who shall have a common law jurisdiction, and reside in the district. . . .

The governor and judges, or a majority of them, shall adopt and publish in the district such laws of the original States, criminal and civil, as may be necessary and best suited to the circumstances of the district, and report them to Congress from time to time. . . .

"The Ordinance of 1787," *Old South Leaflets*, no. 13 (Boston, 1896), 1–7.

Previous to the organization of the General Assembly, the governor shall appoint such magistrates and other civil officers. . . .

So soon as there shall be 5000 free male inhabitants of full age in the district, upon giving proof thereof to the governor, they shall receive authority, with time and place, to elect representatives from their counties or townships to represent them in the General Assembly: Provided, That, for every 500 free male inhabitants, there shall be one representative, and so on progressively with the number of free male inhabitants, shall the right of representation increase, until the number of representatives shall amount to 25; after which, the number and proportion of representatives shall be regulated by the legislature: Provided, That no person be eligible or qualified to act as a representative unless he shall have been a citizen of one of the United States three years, and be a resident in the district, or unless he shall have resided in the district three years; and, in either case, shall likewise hold in his own right, in fee simple, 500 acres of land within the same: Provided, also, That a freehold in 50 acres of land in the district, having been a citizen of one of the States, and being resident in the district, or the like freehold and two years residence in the district, shall be necessary to qualify a man as an elector of a representative.

The representatives thus elected, shall serve for the term of two years. . . .

Art. 1st. No person, demeaning himself in a peaceable and orderly manner, shall ever be molested on account of his mode [of] worship or religious sentiments, in the said territory.

Art. 2d. The inhabitants of the said territory shall always be entitled to the benefits of the writ of habeas corpus, and of the trial by jury; of a proportionate representation of the people in the legislature; and of judicial proceedings according to the course of the common law. . . .

Art. 3d. Religion, morality, and knowledge, being necessary to good government and the happiness of mankind, schools and the means of education shall forever be encouraged. The utmost good faith shall always be observed towards the Indians; their lands and property shall never be taken from them without their consent; and, in their property, rights, and liberty, they shall never be invaded or disturbed, unless in just and lawful wars authorized by Congress; but laws founded in justice and humanity, shall, from time to time, be made for preventing wrongs being done to them, and for preserving peace and friendship with them.

Art. 4th. The said territory, and the States which may be formed therein, shall forever remain a part of this confederacy of the United States of America, subject to the Articles of Confederation, and to such alterations therein as shall be constitutionally made; and to all the acts and ordinances of the United States in Congress assembled, conformable thereto. . . .

Art. 5th. There shall be formed in the said territory, not less than three nor more than five States; and the boundaries of the States, as soon as Virginia shall alter her act of cession, and consent to the same, shall become fixed and established. . . . Provided, however, and it is further understood and declared, that the boundaries of these three States shall be subject so far to be altered, that, if Congress shall hereafter find it expedient, they shall have authority to form one or two States in that part of the said territory which lies North of an East and West line drawn through the Southerly bend or extreme of lake Michigan. And, whenever any of the said States shall have 60,000 free inhabitants therein, such State shall be admitted, by its delegates, into the Congress of the United States, on an equal footing with the original States in all respects whatever, and shall be at liberty to form a permanent constitution and State government: Provided, the constitution and government so to be formed, shall be republican, and in conformity to the principles contained in these articles; and, so far as it can be consistent with the general interest of the confederacy, such admission shall be allowed at an earlier period, and when there may be a less number of free inhabitants in the State than 60,000.

Art. 6th. There shall be neither slavery nor involuntary servitude in the said territory, otherwise than in the punishment of crimes, whereof the party shall have been duly convicted. . . .

41

Grievances of the Shays Rebels (1786)

Whig concepts of liberty and proclamations of "No taxation without representation" did not die away after the American Revolution. Some inhabitants of the nation's back-country believed that their respective state governments, dominated by Eastern elites, ignored the problems of the interior. Feeling underrepresented and overtaxed, many balked at what they considered the overbearing control of a distant and unresponsive government. By the mid-1780s, the situation was particularly acute in western Massachusetts, where traditional resentment of Eastern control was exacerbated by an economic depression. High taxes were more than just a nuisance; many local farmers thought the taxes threatened the farmers' ability to continue owning their land. Popular unrest broke out in August 1786, when citizens in Northampton disrupted a meeting of the court of common pleas. Daniel Shays, a revolutionary war hero and leader in the poor upland community of Pelham, soon emerged as the leader of the Regulators. The Shaysites succeeded in shutting down state courts in the interior, but the movement soon collapsed in the face of an aggressive military campaign mounted by state officials. The specter of Shays' Rebellion specifically—and agrarian unrest more generally—was a catalyst in the drafting of a stronger central government in 1787. The following document is part of a petition to the governor of Massachusetts that outlines rebel grievances.

Questions to Consider

1. What is the intended audience of this document?
2. Why do the rebels believe their liberty is under attack?
3. What similarities does the petition draw from the principles of the American Revolution?
4. Do you think the individuals who drafted "The Northwest Ordinance" (Document 40) supported the Shaysites? Why or why not?

To his Excellency James BOWDOIN, Esq; Governour and Commander in Chief of said Commonwealth, and to the Honourable COUNCIL, convened at *Boston* in *December,* 1786.

The PETITION *of a Committee from several Towns in the County of* Worcester; *together with a Committee from a BODY of MEN, from the Counties of* Worcester, Hampshire *and* Berkshire, *all convened at* Worcester, *under the Command of Captain* SHAYS *and Captain* WHEELER, *who, on the 4th instant, did obstruct the sitting of the* COURT *of* COMMON PLEAS,

HUMBLY SHEWETH,

THAT the people first assembled, seeking a redress of public grievances, which they supposed in a great measure to be derived from the great expences and abuses of said Court, together with the General Sessions of the Peace, and from many other burthens, with which your Petitioners conceive the yeomanry unproportionably burthened: Notwithstanding, your Petitioners would have dutifully submitted, and waited for relief from the wisdom of the Hon. General Court, as they gratefully acknowledge the attention of that Body, in some instances, respecting their grievances, in the last session of the General Court:

Your Petitioners beg leave to mention their horrour of the suspension of the privilege of the writ of Habeas Corpus, that your Excellency and your Honours may be convinced your Petitioners are not of the wicked, dissolute and abandoned, as it is not confined to a factious few, but extended to towns and counties, and almost every individual who derives his living from the labour of his hands or an income of a farm. That the suspension of said privilege your Petitioners view as dangerous, if not absolutely destructive to a Republican Government. That under the cover of the suspension of said privilege, your Petitioners have been informed that the eyes and breasts of women and children have been wounded, if not destroyed; the house of the innocent broken open, their limbs mangled, their friends conveyed to gaol in another country, and now languishing (if alive) under their wounds.

In vindication of our liberties, your Petitioners beg leave to point to your Excellency and your Honours the arguments used by our virtuous asserters of liberty against the act of the British Parliament, in conveying our countrymen from county to county, and even beyond the sea for trial.

Likewise the inhuman murder of Maverick and others, from mercenary principles under the ostensible right of government.

Your Petitioners, induced from a supreme love to peace, liberty and good order,

Humbly pray,

THAT your Excellency and your Honours would be graciously pleased to grant, That our friends that are under confinement out of the counties to which they belong, may have the favour of the Act of Indemnity, with your Petitioners, and that so long as they and your Petitioners shall behave orderly,

---

"*The* PETITION *of a Committee from several Towns in the County of Worcester,*" (Boston) *Independent Chronicle and the Universal Advertiser,* December 15, 1786.

both they and we may be safe in our persons and properties, and if consistent with your wisdom, that there may be an adjournment of the Courts of Common Pleas and General Sessions of the Peace, in the three Counties of *Berkshire, Hampshire,* and *Worcester,* until after the next May session of the Hon. General Court of this Commonwealth.

Your Petitioners, for themselves and party, engage to return to their respective homes, and conduct themselves as good and faithful subjects.

With the greatest uprightness, your petitioners assure your Excellency and Honours, that they were not induced to rise from a . . . to the Commonwealth, or instigated by British Emissaries, but from those sufferings which disenabled them to provide for their wives and children, or to discharge their honest debts, tho' in possession of the lands of their country.

Your petitioners are not induced to petition in this way, from the mean fear of death, as they esteem one moment of liberty, to be worth an eternity of bondage; or from the uncertainty of war, the injuries of hunger, cold, nakedness, or the infamous name of rebel; as under all those disadvantages they once before engaged, and through the blessing of God have come off victorious. To that God they now appeal, conscious of the innocence of their intentions, expecting direction from that Being who is able to strengthen the counsels of the weak, and to turn the wisdom of the wise into foolishness; but from a love to the people, and a horror of the thoughts of the cruelties and devastations of a civil war. For the prevention of so great an evil, your petitioners *humbly pray* for the love, candour and interposition of your Excellency and Honours, in releasing our unfortunate and suffering friends from gaol, your petitioners engaging for their good conduct as well as their own; waiting for a redress of grievances from your wisdom, both at the present time, and in all future elections.—And as in duty bound, shall ever pray.

42

Pennsylvania Dissent to the Ratification of the Constitution (1787)

The constitutional convention that met in Philadelphia during the summer of 1787 did its work in secrecy. When it presented the Constitution for ratification, supporters of the new government had the benefit of organization on their side. Pennsylvania quickly assented to the new pact, but not without opposition. Yeoman farmers in the state's interior bitterly opposed the new Constitution, believing that it instituted a form of tyranny similar to that previously exercised by Britain. The Constitution's opponents (known as Anti-Federalists) wanted stronger guarantees for individual liberties and state power; Federalists who supported the new government argued that the states enjoyed enough power and that state constitutions were sufficient to guarantee individual liberties. The following document, which appeared in Philadelphia's Pennsylvania Packet and Daily Advertiser, *records the dissent of Pennsylvania's Anti-Federalists and amendments proposed to improve the Constitution.*

Questions to Consider

1. For what reasons do the Anti-Federalists dissent about the Constitution?
2. How do you think the authors of this document reacted to Shays' Rebellion?
3. What additions to the Constitution are proposed by this document?
4. Which "propositions" eventually become parts of the Constitution?

The convention met, and the same disposition was soon manifested in considering the proposed constitution that had been exhibited in every other stage of the business. We were prohibited by an express vote of the convention from taking any question on the separate articles of the plan, and reduced to the necessity of adopting or rejecting *in toto*. It is true the majority permitted us to debate on each article, but restrained us from proposing amendments. They also determined not to permit us to enter on the minutes our reasons of dissent against any of the articles, nor even on the final question our reasons of dissent against the whole. Thus situated we entered on the examination of the proposed system of government, and found it to be such as we could not adopt without, as we conceived, surrendering up your dearest rights. We offered our objections to the convention, . . . and closed our arguments by offering the following propositions to the convention.

1. The right of conscience shall be held inviolable, and neither the legislative, executive nor judicial powers of the United States shall have authority to alter, abrogate, or infringe any part of the constitution of the several states which provide for the preservation of liberty in matters of religion.

2. That in controversies respecting property, and in suits between man and man, trial by jury shall remain as heretofore, as well in the federal courts, as in those of the several states.

3. That in all capital and criminal prosecutions, a man has a right to demand the cause and nature of his accusation, as well in the federal courts, as in those of the several states; to be heard by himself and his counsel; to be confronted with the accusers and witnesses; to call for evidence in his favor, and a speedy trial by an impartial jury of his vicinage, without whose unanimous consent, he cannot be found guilty, nor can he be compelled to give evidence against himself; and that no man be deprived of his liberty, except by the law of the land or the judgment of his peers.

4. That excessive bail ought not to be required, nor excessive fines imposed, nor cruel nor unusual punishments inflicted.

5. That warrants unsupported by evidence, whereby any officer or messenger may be commanded or required to search suspected places, or to

---

"Address and Reason of Dissent of the Minority of the Convention of Pennsylvania," (Philadelphia) *Pennsylvania Packet and Daily Advertiser*, December 18, 1787.

seize any person or persons, his or their property, not particularly described, are grievous and oppressive, and shall not be granted either by the magistrates of the federal government or others.

6. That the people have a right to the freedom of speech, of writing and publishing their sentiments. Therefore, the freedom of the press shall not be restrained by any law of the United States.

7. That the people have a right to bear arms for the defense of themselves and their own state, or the United States, or for the purpose of killing game; and no law shall be passed for disarming the people or any of them, unless for crimes committed, or real danger of public injury from individuals; and as standing armies in the time of peace are dangerous to liberty, they ought not to be kept up; and that the military shall be kept under strict subordination to and be governed by the civil powers.

8. The inhabitants of the several states shall have liberty to fowl and hunt in seasonable times, on the lands they hold, and on all other lands in the United States not enclosed, and in like manner to fish in all navigable waters, and others not private property, . . .

9. That no law shall be passed to restrain the legislatures of the several states from enacting laws for imposing taxes, except imposts and duties on goods imported or exported, and that no taxes, except imposts and duties upon goods imported and duties upon goods imported and exported, and postage on letters shall be levied by the authority of Congress.

10. That the house of representatives be properly increased in number; that elections shall remain free; that the several states shall have power to regulate the elections for senators and representatives, without . . . any interference on the part of the Congress; and that elections of representatives be annual.

11. That the power of organizing, arming, and disciplining the militia . . . remain with the individual states, and that Congress shall not have authority to call or march any of the militia out of their own state, without the consent of such state, and for such length of time only as such state shall agree.

    That the sovereignty, freedom and independence of the several states shall be retained, and every power, jurisdiction and right which is not by this constitution expressly delegated to the United States in Congress assembled.

12. That the legislative, executive, and judicial powers be kept separate; and to this end that a constitutional council be appointed, to advise and assist the president, who shall be responsible for the advice they give, thereby the senators would be relieved from almost constant attendance; and also that the judges be made completely independent.

13. That no treaty which shall be directly opposed to the existing laws of the United States in Congress assembled, shall be valid until such laws shall be repealed, or made conformable to such treaty; neither shall any

treaties be valid which are in contradiction to the constitution of the United States, or the constitutions of the several states.

14. That the judiciary power of the United States shall be confined to cases affecting ambassadors, other public ministers and consuls; to cases of admiralty and maritime jurisdiction; to controversies to which the United States shall be a party; to controversies between two or more states; between a state and citizens of different states; between citizens claiming lands under grants of different states; and between a state or the citizen thereof and foreign states, and in criminal cases, to such only as are expressly enumerated in the constitution, and that the United States in Congress assembled, shall not have power to enact laws, which shall alter the laws of descents and distribution of the effects of deceased persons, the titles of lands or goods, or the regulation of contracts in the individual states. . . .

43

Federalist Number 10 (1788)

As the states deliberated about whether to agree to the Constitution, it became increasingly clear that ratification by New York and Virginia would be essential to the new government's success. During the hard-fought ratification debate in New York, Alexander Hamilton, James Madison, and John Jay wrote a series of essays under the pseudonym Publius *in support of the Constitution. Known collectively as* The Federalist, *the essays have become classic expressions of Federalist thought and are among the most significant contributions to American political theory. The following excerpt is from "Federalist 10," the most important of the essays. The author of the selection, James Madison, had a keen interest in the subject. He had helped his home state of Virginia draft a new constitution in 1776, and he was an early advocate of reforming or replacing the Articles with a stronger central government. Few individuals had a better understanding of the Constitution than Madison, one of the document's principal creators.*

Questions to Consider

1. What is significant about the historical context of this document?
2. According to James Madison, what are the problems with "factions"?
3. What are Madison's views on democracy?
4. Does the Constitution seem to be a radical document or a conservative one?

. . . By a faction, I understand a number of citizens, whether amounting to a majority or minority of the whole, who are united and actuated by some common impulse of passion, or of interest, adverse to the rights of other citizens, or to the permanent and aggregate interests of the community.

There are two methods of curing the mischiefs of faction: the one, by removing its causes; the other, by controlling its effects.

There are again two methods of removing the causes of faction: the one, by destroying the liberty which is essential to its existence; the other, by giving to every citizen the same opinions, the same passions, and the same interests.

It could never be more truly said than of the first remedy that it was worse than the disease. Liberty is to faction what air is to fire, an aliment without which it instantly expires. But it could not be less folly to abolish liberty, which is essential to political life, because it nourishes faction, than it would be to wish the annihilation of air, which is essential to animal life. . . .

The second expedient is as impracticable as the first would be unwise. As long as the reason of man continues fallible, and he is at liberty to exercise it, different opinions will be formed. . . . The diversity in the faculties of men, from which the rights of property originate, is not less an insuperable obstacle to a uniformity of interests. The protection of these faculties is the first object of government. . . .

The latent causes of faction are thus sown in the nature of man; and we see them everywhere brought into different degrees of activity, according to the different circumstances of civil society. . . . But the most common and durable source of factions has been the various and unequal distribution of property.

Those who hold and those who are without property have ever formed distinct interests in society. Those who are creditors and those who are debtors fall under a like discrimination. A landed interest, a manufacturing interest, a mercantile interest, a moneyed interest, with many lesser interests, grow up of necessity in civilized nations and divide them into different classes, actuated by different sentiments and views. The regulation of these various and interfering interests forms the principal task of modern legislation and involves the spirit of party and faction in the necessary and ordinary operations of the government. . . .

It is in vain to say that enlightened statesmen will be able to adjust these clashing interests and render them all subservient to the public good. Enlightened statesmen will not always be at the helm. Nor, in many cases, can such an adjustment be made at all without taking into view indirect and remote considerations, which will rarely prevail over the immediate interest which one party may find in disregarding the rights of another or the good of the whole.

The inference to which we are brought is that the causes of faction cannot be removed and that relief is only to be sought in the means of controlling its effects.

"The Numerous Advantages of the Union," *The Federalist* (New York, 1901), 44–51.

If a faction consists of less than a majority, relief is supplied by the republican principle, which enables the majority to defeat its sinister views by regular vote. . . . When a majority is included in a faction, the form of popular government, on the other hand, enables it to sacrifice to its ruling passion or interest both the public good and the rights of other citizens. To secure the public good and private rights against the danger of such a faction, and at the same time to preserve the spirit and the form of popular government, is then the great object to which our inquiries are directed. . . .

From this view of the subject it may be concluded that a pure democracy, by which I mean a society consisting of a small number of citizens who assemble and administer the government in person, can admit of no cure for the mischiefs of faction. A common passion or interest will, in almost every case, be felt by a majority of the whole; a communication and concert result from the form of government itself; and there is nothing to check the inducements to sacrifice the weaker party or an obnoxious individual. Hence it is that such democracies have ever been spectacles of turbulence and contention; have ever been found incompatible with personal security or the rights of property; and have in general been as short in their lives as they have been violent in their deaths. Theoretic politicians, who have patronized this species of government, have erroneously supposed that by reducing mankind to a perfect equality in their political rights, they would, at the same time, be perfectly equalized and assimilated in their possessions, their opinions, and their passions.

A republic, by which I mean a government in which the scheme of representation takes place, opens a different prospect and promises the cure for which we are seeking. . . .

The two great points of difference between a democracy and a republic are: first, the delegation of the government, in the latter, to a small number of citizens elected by the rest; secondly, the greater number of citizens, and greater sphere of country, over which the latter may be extended.

The effect of the first difference is, on the one hand, to refine and enlarge the public views by passing them through the medium of a chosen body of citizens, whose wisdom may best discern the true interest of their country, and whose patriotism and love of justice will be least likely to sacrifice it to temporary or partial considerations. . . . Men of factious tempers, of local prejudices, or of sinister designs may, by intrigue, by corruption, or by other means, first obtain the suffrages, and then betray the interests of the people. The question resulting is, whether small or extensive republics are more favorable to the election of proper guardians of the public weal; and it is clearly decided in favor of the latter by two obvious considerations:

In the first place, it is to be remarked that, however small the republic may be, the representatives must be raised to a certain number, in order to guard against the cabals of a few; and that; however large it may be, they must be limited to a certain number, in order to guard against the confusion of a multitude. . . .

In the next place, as each representative will be chosen by a greater number of citizens in the large than in the small republic, it will be more difficult for unworthy candidates to practice with success the vicious arts by which elections are too often carried; and the suffrages of the people being more free, will be more likely to center in men who possess the most attractive merit and the most diffusive and established character.

. . . By enlarging too much the number of electors, you render the representative too little acquainted with all their local circumstances and lesser interests; as by reducing it too much, you render him unduly attached to these and too little fit to comprehend and pursue great and national objects. The federal Constitution forms a happy combination in this respect: the great and aggregate interests being referred to the national, the local and particular to the state legislatures.

The other point of difference is the greater number of citizens and extent of territory which may be brought within the compass of republican than of democratic government; and it is this circumstance principally which renders factious combinations less to be dreaded in the former than in the latter. The smaller the society, the fewer probably will be the distinct parties and interests composing it; . . . the more easily will they concert and execute their plans of oppression. Extend the sphere and you take in a greater variety of parties and interests; you make it less probable that a majority of the whole will have a common motive to invade the rights of other citizens; or if such a common motive exists, it will be more difficult for all who feel it to discover their own strength and to act in unison with each other. . . .

Hence, it clearly appears that the same advantage which a republic has over a democracy, in controlling the effects of factions, is enjoyed by a large over a small republic—is enjoyed by the Union over the states composing it. . . .

In the extent, and proper structure of the Union, therefore, we behold a republican remedy for the diseases most incident to republican government. And according to the degree of pleasure and pride we feel in being republicans, ought to be our zeal in cherishing the spirit and supporting the character of Federalists.

44

Mercy Otis Warren
and the New Constitution (1788)

The document that resulted from the meeting of the Constitutional Convention in the summer of 1787 was considerably different from the Articles of Confederation. The Constitution gave the new national government much greater power than what had existed under the Articles. The creation of a powerful executive branch and a Senate further removed control of the government from the hands of the people. Many praised the new document as one that could bring stability to the country while resolving differences among states. Others saw the government of the Constitution as a threat to liberty. Mercy Otis Warren was among the critics of the new government. Sister of the revolutionary leader James Otis, she played a considerable role in the prerevolutionary resistance to Britain. In 1772, Warren began to write a series of satirical sketches dripping with Whig propaganda and would continue to write plays and poems supporting the patriot cause during the war. Following the Revolution, she grew increasingly distrustful of the calls for order in Massachusetts. In the following selection, she analyzes some of the potential perils in the government proposed by the Constitution.

Questions to Consider

1. What problems does Mercy Otis Warren see in the new Constitution?
2. How do some of her views compare with those expressed by John Locke (Document 24), "Cato's Letters" (Document 25), and Thomas Paine (Document 31)?
3. To what extent might Warren's gender have influenced her views?
4. Does Warren consider the Constitution to be consistent with the principles of the American Revolution?

1. [T]he best political writers have supported the principles of annual elections with a precision that cannot be confuted, though they may be darkened by the sophistical arguments that have been thrown out with design, to undermine all the barriers of freedom.
2. There is no security in the profered system, either for the rights of conscience, or the liberty of the press. . . .
3. There are no well defined limits of the judiciary powers, they seem to be left as a boundless ocean, that has broken over the chart of the supreme lawgiver, *"thus far shalt thou go and no farther,"* . . .
4. The executive and the legislative are so dangerously blended as to give just cause of alarm, and every thing relative thereto, is couched in such ambiguous terms—in such vague and indefinite expressions, as is a sufficient ground without any other objection, for the reprobation of a system, that the authors dare not hazard to a clear investigation.
5. The abolition of trial by jury in civil causes.—This mode of trial, the learned judge Blackstone observes, "has been coeval with the first rudiments of civil government, that property, liberty and life, depend on maintaining in its legal force the constitutional trial by jury." . . .
6. Though it has been said by Mr. *Wilson,* and many others, that a standing army is necessary for the dignity and safety of America, yet freedom revolts at the idea, when the Divan, or the despot, may draw out his dragoons to suppress the murmurs of a few, who may yet cherish those

Mercy Otis Warren, "A Columbian Patriot," *Observations on the New Constitution and on the Federal and State Conventions* (Boston, 1788), 8–14.

sublime principles which call forth the exertions, and lead to the best improvement of the human mind. It is hoped this country may yet be governed by milder methods than are usually displayed beneath the bannerets of military law. Standing armies have been the nursery of vice and the bane of liberty, . . . By the edicts of authority vested in the sovereign power by the proposed constitution, the militia of the country, the bulwark of defence, and the security of national liberty, is no longer under the controul of civil authority; but at the rescript of the monarch, or the aristocracy, they may either be employed to extort the enormous sums that will be necessary to support the civil list—to maintain the regalia of power—and the splendour of the most useless part of the community, or they may be sent into foreign countries for the fulfilment of treaties, stipulated by the president and two thirds of the senate.

7. Notwithstanding the delusory promise to guarantee a republican form of government to every state in the union—if the most discerning eye could discover any meaning at all in the engagement, there are no resources left for the support of internal government, or the liquidation of the debts of the state. Every source of revenue is in the monopoly of Congress, . . .

8. As the new Congress are impowered to determine their own salaries, the requisitions for this purpose may not be very moderate, and the drain for public monies will probably rise past all calculation; . . .

9. There is no provision for a rotation, nor any thing to prevent the perpetuity of office in the same hands for life; which by a little well timed bribery, will probably be done, to the exclusion of men of the best abilities from their share in the offices of government.—By this neglect we lose the advantages of that check to the overbearing insolence of office, which by rendering him ineligible at certain periods, keeps the mind of man in equilibrio, and teaches him the feelings of the governed, and better qualifies him to govern in his turn.

10. The inhabitants of the United States, are liable to be dragged from the vicinity of their own county, or state, to answer to the litigious or unjust suit of an adversary, on the most distant borders of the continent: In short, the appellate jurisdiction of the supreme federal court, includes an unwarrantable stretch of power over the liberty, life, and property of the subject, through the wide continent of America.

11. One representative to thirty thousand inhabitants is a very inadequate representation; and every man who is not lost to all sense of freedom to his country, must reprobate the idea of Congress altering by law, or on any pretence whatever interfering with any regulations for the time, places, and manner of choosing our own representatives.

12. If the sovereignty of America is designed to be elective, the circumscribing the votes to only ten electors in this state, and the same proportion in all the others, is nearly tantamount to the exclusion of the voice of the people in the choice of their first magistrate. It is vesting the choice

solely in an aristocratic junto, who may easily combine in each state to place at the head of the union the most convenient instrument for despotic sway.

13. A senate chosen for six years, will in most instances, be an appointment for life, as the influence of such a body over the minds of the people, will be coeval to the extensive powers with which they are vested, and they will not only forget, but be forgotten by their constituents; a branch of the supreme legislature thus set beyond all responsibility, is totally repugnant to every principle of a free government.

14. There is no provision by a bill of rights to guard against the dangerous encroachments of power in too many instances to be named: . . .

15. The difficulty, if not impracticability, of exercising the equal and equitable powers of government by a single legislature over an extent of territory that reaches from the Missisippi to the western lakes, and from them to the Atlantic ocean, is an insuperable objection to the adoption of the new system. . . .

16. It is an indisputed fact, that not one legislature in the United States had the most distant idea when they first appointed members for a convention, entirely commercial, or when they afterwards authorised them to consider on some amendments of the federal union, that they would, without any warrant from their constituents, presume on so bold and daring a stride, as ultimately to destroy the state governments, and offer a *consolidated system* . . .

17. The first appearance of the article which declares the ratification of nine states sufficient for the establishment of the new system, wears the face of dissention, is a subversion of the union of the confederated states, and tends to the introduction of anarchy and civil convulsions,—and may be a means of involving the whole country in blood.

18. The mode in which this constitution is recommended to the people to judge without either the advice of Congress, or the legislatures of the several states, is very reprehensible. . . .

. . . But it is needless to enumerate other instances, in which the proposed constitution appears contradictory to the first principles which ought to govern mankind; and it is equally so to enquire into the motives that induced to so bold a step as the annihilation of the independence and sovereignty of the thirteen states.—They are but too obvious through the whole progress of the business, from the first shutting up the doors of the Federal Convention, and resolving that no member should correspond with gentlemen in the different states on the subject under discussion . . .

7

Defining the New Nation

The ratification of the Constitution inaugurated a new government for the United States, but ambiguities over the limits of state and national power left many questions concerning its power unanswered. Shortly after the government had been created, political factions emerged that soon crystallized into parties. These groups differed over various issues, including the future of America's economy, the franchise, foreign policy, and the limits of federal authority. Despite these differences, all agreed that participation in the early republic should be limited to adult white males. The ensuing documents reveal some of the constitutional ambiguities facing the new government and varying opinions on how the Constitution should be interpreted.

45

Voting Qualifications in Virginia (1779)

During the American Revolution, every state adopted a written constitution that embraced the principles of republicanism. Because republicanism checked tyranny through the consent of the governed as expressed by their elected representatives, the franchise was considered a key component to maintaining liberty. But while the Founders may have espoused republican forms of government, they were not democrats. Not only was democracy viewed as an unstable political form that tended toward manipulation by demagogues and ultimately led to anarchy, but most Revolutionary-era leaders also did not believe that all individuals were fit to vote. The ensuing account describes the franchise as it existed in late 18th-century Virginia.

Questions to Consider

1. Who is excluded from voting? Why?
2. What happens if a qualified voter fails to vote?
3. What are the requirements for holding political office?
4. How do you think those participating in either Shays' Rebellion (Document 41) or the Whiskey Rebellion (Document 49) would view property qualifications for voting?

Every male citizen (other than free negroes or mulattos) of this commonwealth, aged twenty-one years, or such as have refused to give assurance of fidelity to the commonwealth, being possessed, or whose tenant for years, at will, or at sufferance, is possessed of twenty-five acres of land, with a house, the superficial content of the foundation whereof is twelve feet square, or equal to that quantity, and a plantation thereon, or fifty acres of unimproved land, or a lot or part of a lot of land in a city or town established by act of general with a house thereon, of the like superficial content or quantity, having in such land an estate of freehold at the least, and unless the title shall have come to him by descent, devise, marriage, or marriage-settlement, having been so possessed six months, and no other person shall be qualified to vote for delegates to serve in general assembly, for the country, city, or borough respectively, in which the land lieth. If the fifty acres of land being one entire parcel, lie in several counties, the holders shall vote in that county wherein the greater part of the land lieth only; and if the twenty-five acres of land, being one entire parcel, be in several counties, the holder shall vote in that county wherein the house standeth only. In right of land holden by parceners, joint-tenants, or tenants in common, but one vote shall be given by all the holders capable of voting, who shall be present, and agree to vote for the same candidate or candidates, unless the quantity of land, in case partition had been made thereof, be sufficient to entitle every holder present to vote separately, or unless some one or more of the holders may lawfully vote in right of another estate or estates in the same county, in which case the others may vote, if holding solely, they might have voted. . . .

Every person having such a freehold in the city of Williamsburg or borough of Norfolk, as will qualify him to vote for delegates to represent the county, and also every freeman, except as before excepted, aged twenty-one years, being a citizen of the commonwealth, and not having refused to give assurance of fidelity, who shall be a house keeper, and shall have resided for six months in the said city or borough, and shall be possessed of a visible estate of the value of fifty pounds at least, or shall actually have served as an apprentice to some trade within the said city or borough, and no other, shall be qualified to vote for a delegate to represent the said city or borough respectively in general assembly. Every person qualified as aforesaid to vote for delegates, shall be capable of being elected a delegate for the county, city, or borough, or senator for the district in which he resides. No person who shall have served as a member of the legislature for seven years in the whole, shall be afterwards compellable to serve therein. Any elector qualified according to this act, failing to attend any annual election of delegates or of a senator, and if a poll be taken, to give or offer to such levies and taxes as shall be assessed and levied in his county the ensuing year: And for discovering such defaulters, the sheriff or other officer taking the poll, shall with ten days after the said election, deliver to the clerk of the county or corporation court, as the

"An act concerning election of members of the general assembly," *The Statutes at Large,* ed. William W. Hening (Richmond, 1823), 12: 121–122.

case may be, a copy of the poll by him taken, to be kept in his office, who shall suffer any candidate or elector to take a copy thereof, and the said clerk is hereby directed to cause a copy of the same to be delivered to the next grand-jury to be sworn for the county or corporation, who shall be charged by the presiding magistrate to make presentment of all such persons qualified to vote residing in the said county or corporation, who shall have failed to have given their votes at the said election agreeable to law. . . . Upon the election of a senator, and also of a delegate, or delegates cannot be determined by view, the sheriff, or in his absence the under sheriff of the county, or the mayor of the city or borough, shall in presence of the candidates, or their agents, cause the poll to be taken in the court-house or if that be in a town infected with any contagious disease, or be in danger of an attack from a public enemy, at some other place. . . .

46

How Revolutionary Was the American Revolution?

The American Revolution had been fought to secure liberty. Most members of the founding generation believed that a republican form of government that rested on the consent of the governed was the best means for securing this liberty. Before the Revolution, liberty was the preserve of adult, white male property owners, because they were the only ones who possessed the franchise. But the Revolution had required sacrifice from all strata of society. In the aftermath of independence, democratic pressures began to build to extend voting rights beyond adult, white male property owners. The first image that follows is a depiction of the Constitutional Convention in Philadelphia. The painter has to employ imagination to depict this scene because the proceedings were secret. The second image is a satire of the women of Edenton, North Carolina, pledging their support for the boycott of British goods in 1774. Despite women's support and participation in the Revolution, they were not recognized by the new Constitution.

Questions to Consider

1. What can you deduce about later 18th-century attitudes concerning wealth and gender from these two images?

2. Does the first image portray consensus or conflict in the drafting of the Constitution? Based on what you know about the Constitutional Convention, how accurate is this depiction?

3. What attitudes does the creator of the second image seem to have toward women? What might you deduce about the status of women from this image?

4. How revolutionary was the American Revolution?

Library of Congress, Prints and Photographs Division, LC-USA7-34630

"Scene at signing of the Constitution of the United States"

Library of Congress, Prints and Photographs Division, LC-USZ62-12711

"A society of patriotic ladies, at Edenton in North Carolina"

47

Benjamin Banneker to Thomas Jefferson, Blacks and Liberty in the New Nation (1791)

Although many Founders struggled over the paradox of slavery's existence in a free society, most remained convinced that individuals of African descent were intellectually inferior to whites. Because of these attitudes, it became virtually impossible for even free African Americans to enjoy basic rights and work at anything more than the most menial tasks. Benjamin Banneker, a free black from Maryland, managed to escape the fate of most freemen, as he learned to read at an early age and later mastered mathematics. An astronomer of note, Banneker had expert surveying skills that enabled him to participate in laying out the Federal District in 1791. In the following selection, Benjamin Banneker responds to Thomas Jefferson's observations on African-American inferiority and comments on the issue of blacks and liberty.

Questions to Consider

1. Why is Benjamin Banneker writing to Thomas Jefferson?
2. What can we deduce from this document about Thomas Jefferson's views on race?
3. What is the basis of Banneker's argument that African Americans and whites are equal?
4. Why does Banneker point out the inconsistency between the ideals of the Declaration of Independence and the reality in the United States?

Maryland, Baltimore County,
August 19, 1791

I am fully sensible of the greatness of that freedom, which I take with you on the present occasion; a liberty which seemed to me scarcely allowable, when I reflected on that distinguished and dignified station in which you stand, and the almost general prejudice and prepossession, which is so prevalent in the world against those of my complexion.

I suppose it is a truth too well attested to you, to need a proof here, that we are a race of beings, who have long labored under the abuse and censure of the world; that we have long been looked upon with an eye of contempt; and that we have long been considered rather as brutish than human, and scarcely capable of mental endowments.

Sir, I hope I may safely admit, in consequence of that report which hath reached me, that you are a man less inflexible in sentiments of this nature, than many others; that you are measureably friendly, and well disposed towards us; and that you are willing and ready to lend your aid and assistance to our relief, from those many distresses, and numerous calamaties, to which we are reduced.

Now Sir, if this is founded in truth, I apprehend you will embrace every opportunity, to eradicate that train of absurd and false ideas and opinions, which so generally prevails with respect to us; and that your sentiments are concurrent with mine, which are, that one universal Father hath given being

---

"Benjamin Banneker to Thomas Jefferson, Blacks and Liberty in the New Nation," *Great Documents in Black American History*, ed. C. Eric Lincoln (New York, 1970), 22–27. Reprinted by permission.

to us all; and that he hath not only made us all of one flesh, but that he hath also, without partiality, afforded us all the same sensations and endowed us all with the same faculties; and that however variable we may be in society or religion, however diversified in situation or color, we are all of the same family, and stand in the same relation to him.

Sir, if these are sentiments of which you are fully persuaded, I hope you cannot but acknowledge, that it is the indispensable duty of those, who maintain for themselves the rights of human nature, and who possess the obligations of Christianity, to extend their power and influence to the relief of every part of the human race, from whatever burden or oppression they may unjustly labor under; . . .

Sir, I have long been convinced, that if your love for yourselves, and for those inestimable laws, which preserved to you the rights of human nature, was founded on sincerity, you could not but be solicitous, that every individual, of whatever rank or distinction, might with you equally enjoy the blessings thereof; neither could you rest satisfied short of the most active effusion of your exertions, in order to their promotion from any state of degradation, to which the unjustifiable cruelty and barbarism of men may have reduced them.

Sir, I freely and cheerfully acknowledge, that I am of the African race, and in the color which is natural to them of the deepest dye; and it is under a sense of the most profound gratitude to the Supreme Ruler of the Universe, that I now confess to you, that I am not under that state of tyrannical thraldom, and inhuman captivity, to which too many of my brethren are doomed, but that I have abundantly tasted of the fruition of those blessings, which proceed from that free and unequalled liberty with which you are favored; and which, I hope, you will willingly allow you have mercifully received, from the immediate have of that Being, from whom proceedeth every good and perfect Gift.

Sir, suffer me to recall to your mind that time, in which the arms and tyranny of the British crown were exerted, with every powerful effort, in order to reduce you to a state of servitude: look back, I entreat you, on the variety of dangers to which you were exposed; reflect on that time, in which every human aid appeared unavailable, and in which even hope and fortitude wore the aspect of inability to the conflict, and you cannot but be led to a serious and grateful sense of your miraculous and providential preservation; . . .

This sir, was a time when you clearly saw into the injustice of a state of slavery, and in which you had just apprehensions of the horrors of its condition. It was now that your abhorrence thereof was so excited, that you publicly held forth this true and invaluable doctrine, which is worthy to be recorded, and remembered in all succeeding ages: "We hold these truths to be self-evident, that all men are created equal; that they are endowed by their Creator with certain unalienable rights, and that among these are life, liberty, and the pursuit of happiness."

Here was a time, in which your tender feelings for yourselves had engaged you thus to declare, you were then impressed with proper ideas of the great violation of liberty, and the free possession of those blessings, to which you were entitled by nature; but, Sir, how pitiable is it to reflect, . . . that you should at the same time counteract his [God's] mercies, in detaining by fraud and violence so numerous a part of my brethren, under groaning captivity and cruel oppression, that you should at the same time be found guilty of that most criminal act, which you professedly detested in others, with respect to yourselves.

I suppose that your knowledge of the situation of my brethren, is too extensive to need a recital here; neither shall I presume to prescribe methods by which they may be relieved, otherwise than by recommending to you and all others, to wean yourselves from those narrow prejudices which you have imbibed with respect to them, and as Job proposed to his friends, "put your soul in their souls' stead;" thus shall your hearts be enlarged with kindness and benevolence towards them; and thus shall you need neither the direction of myself or others, in what manner to proceed herein.

. . . I ardently hope, that your candor and generosity will plead with you in my behalf, when I make known to you, that it was not originally my design; but having taken up my pen in order to direct to you, as a present, a copy of an Almanac, which I have calculated for the succeeding year, I was unexpectedly and unavoidably led thereto. . . .

And now, Sir, I shall conclude, and subscribe myself, with the most profound respect,

Your most obedient and humble servant,
Benjamin Banneker

48

Alexander Hamilton Speaks in Favor of the National Bank (1791)

Fiscal instability and the weakness of the central government were two of the major criticisms leveled against the Articles of Confederation. Although the Constitution clearly provided the new government with powers in these areas, the extent to which these powers would be exercised remained open to debate. Alexander Hamilton believed that a strong central government was essential to the survival of the new government. A native of the British West Indian island of Nevis, Hamilton rose to prominence as a protégé of George Washington during the Revolution and as a leading figure in New York City politics in its aftermath. He established his conservative credentials at the Constitutional Convention by questioning whether the new government should be republican. Convinced of the need for a strong central government supported by the nation's leading creditors, Hamilton offered a financial plan that expanded national power at the expense of the states. In the following document, the United States' first secretary of the treasury argues that the Constitution could be interpreted to permit the establishment of the Bank of the United States.

Questions to Consider

1. To whom is this document addressed?

2. Why does Alexander Hamilton support a "loose construction" of the Constitution?

3. How do you suppose an 18th-century financier would have responded to this document?

4. How do you think Mercy Otis Warren (Document 44) responded to Hamilton's views of "loose construction"?

. . . In entering upon the argument, it ought to be premised that the objections of the secretary of state and attorney general are founded on a general denial of the authority of the United States to erect anything in the bill which is not warranted by the Constitution, it is the clause of incorporation.

Now it appears to the Secretary of the Treasury that this *general principle* is *inherent* in the very *definition* of government and *essential* to every step of the progress to be made by that of the United States, namely: that every power vested in a government is in its nature *sovereign* and includes, by *force* of the term, a right to employ all the *means* requisite and fairly applicable to the attainment of the *ends* of such power, and which are not precluded by restrictions and exceptions specified in the Constitution, or not immoral, or contrary to the *essential ends* of political society. . . .

The circumstance that the powers of sovereignty are in this country divided between the National and State governments does not afford the distinction required. It does not follow from this, that each of the portion of *powers* delegated to the one or to the other, is not sovereign with *regard to its proper objects*. It will only *follow* from it, that each has sovereign power as to *certain things,* and not as to other things. To deny that the government of the United States has sovereign power, as to its declared purposes and trusts, because its power does not extend to all cases, would be equally to deny that the State governments have sovereign power in any case, because their power does not extend to every case. The tenth section of the first article of the Constitution exhibits a long list of very important things which they may not do. And thus the United States would furnish the singular spectacle of a *political* society without *sovereignty,* or of a *people governed* without *government.* . . .

. . . the foundation of the Constitution is laid on this ground: "That all powers not delegated to the United States by the Constitution, nor prohibited to it by the states, are reserved for the States, or to the people." Whence it is meant to be inferred that Congress can in no case exercise any power not included in those not enumerated in the Constitution. And it is affirmed that the power of erecting a corporation is not included in any of the enumerated powers. . . .

"Hamilton to Washington: Opinion as to the Constitutionality of the Bank of the United States," February 23, 1791, *Works of Alexander Hamilton,* ed. Henry Cabot Lodge (New York, 1904), 4: 104–138.

It is not denied that there are *implied* as well as *express powers* and that the *former* are as effectually delegated as the *latter*. . . .

Then it follows that as a power of erecting a corporation may as well be *implied* as any other thing, it may as well be employed as an *instrument* or mean of carrying into execution any of the specified powers as any other *instrument* or *mean* whatever. The only question must be, in this, as in every other case, whether the mean to be employed or, in this instance, the corporation to be erected, has a natural relation to any of the acknowledged objects or lawful ends of the government. Thus a corporation may not be erected by Congress for superintending the police of the city of Philadelphia, because they are not authorized to *regulate* the *police* of that city. But one may be erected in relation. . . to a general *sovereign* or *legislative* power to regulate a thing, to employ all the means which relate to its regulation to the best and greatest advantage. . . .

Through this mode of reasoning respecting the right of employing all the means requisite to the execution of the specified powers of the government, it is objected that none but necessary and proper means are to be employed; and the Secretary of the State maintains that no means are to be considered as *necessary* but those without which the grant of the power would be *nugatory*. Nay, so far does he go in his restrictive interpretation of the *word* as even to make the case of the *necessity* which shall warrant the constitutional exercise of the power to depend on *casual* and *temporary* circumstances; an idea which alone refutes the construction. The *expediency* of exercising a particular power at a particular time, must, indeed, depend on circumstances; but the constitutional right of exercising it must be uniform and invariable, the same today as tomorrow.

All the arguments, therefore, against the constitutionality of the bill derived from the accidental existence of certain State banks, institutions which happen to exist today and, for aught that concerns the government of the United States, may disappear tomorrow—must not only be rejected as fallacious but must be viewed as demonstrative that there is a *radical* source of error in the reasoning. . . .

. . . *necessary* often means no more than *needful, requisite, incidental, usefull,* or *conductive to.* It is a common mode of expression to say that it is *necessary* for a government or a person to do this or that thing, when nothing more is intended or understood than that the interests of the government or person require, or will be promoted by, the doing this or that thing. . . .

To understand the word as the secretary of state does would be to depart from its obvious and popular sense and to give it a restrictive operation, an idea never before entertained. . . .

It may be truly said of every government, as well as that of the United States, that it has only a right to pass such laws as are necessary and a right to do *merely what it pleases.* . . . Hence, by a process of reasoning similar to that of the Secretary of State, it might be proved that neither of the State governments has a right to incorporate a bank. It might be shown that all the public business of the state could be performed without a bank, and inferring thence it was unnecessary, it might be argued that it could not be done, because it is against the rule which has been just mentioned. A like mode of reasoning would prove that there was no power to incorporate the inhabitants of a town, with a view to a more perfect police. . . .

This restrictive interpretation of the word *necessary* is also contrary to this maxim of construction; namely, that the powers contained in a constitution of government, especially those which concern the general administration of the affairs of a country, its finances, trade, defense, etc., ought to be construed liberally in advancement of the public good. . . . The means by which national exigencies are to be provided for, national inconveniences obviated, national prosperity promoted, are of such infinite variety, extent, and complexity that there must of necessity be great latitude of discretion in the selection and application of those means. Hence, consequently, the necessity and propriety of exercising the authorities intrusted to a government on principles of liberal construction. . . .

The truth is that difficulties on this point are inherent in the nature of the Federal Constitution; they result inevitably from a division of the legislative power. The consequence of this division is that there will be cases clearly within the power of the national government; others, clearly without its powers; and a third class which will leave room for controvers. . . .

But the doctrine which is contended for is not chargeable with the consequences imputed to it. It does not affirm that the national government is sovereign in all respects, but that it is sovereign to a certain extent; that is, to the extent of the objects of its specified powers.

It leaves, therefore, a criterion of what is constitutional and of what is not so. This criterion is the *end* to which the measure relates as a *mean*. If the *end* be clearly comprehended within any of the specified powers, and if the measure have an obvious relation to that *end,* and is not forbidden by a particular provision of the Constitution, it may safely be deemed to come within the compass of the national authority. . . .

To establish such a right, it remains to show the relation of such an institution to one or more of the specified powers of the government. Accordingly, it is affirmed that it has a relation, more or less direct, to the power of collecting taxes, to that of borrowing money, to that of regulating trade between the states, and to those of raising and maintaining fleets and armies. To the two former the relation may be said to be immediate; and in the last place it will be argued that it is clearly within the provision which authorizes the making of all needful rules and regulations concerning the property of the United States, as the same has been practised upon by the government. . . .

A hope is entertained that it has, by this time, been made to appear, to the satisfaction of the President, that a bank has a natural relation to the power of collecting taxes—to that of regulating trade—to that of providing for the common defense—and that, as the bill under consideration contemplates the government in the light of a joint proprietor of the stock of the bank, it brings the case within the provision of the clause of the Constitution which immediately respects the property of the United States.

Under a conviction that such a relation subsists, the Secretary of the Treasury, with all defence, conceives that it will result as a necessary consequence from the position that all the specified powers of government are sovereign, as to the proper objects; that the incorporation of a bank is a constitutional measure; and that the objections taken to the bill, in this respect, are ill-founded. . . .

49

Opposing Views of the Whiskey Rebellion (1794)

Secretary of the Treasury Alexander Hamilton wasted little time in attempting to raise money for the new government. Eager to placate seaboard merchants, Hamilton successfully pressed for an excise tax on whiskey despite opposition to similar taxes during the Confederation period. Western Pennsylvania farmers quickly protested the new duty, arguing that they were being taxed unfairly and that the excise would prove ruinous to farmers who depended on the sale of whiskey to make a living. The Whiskey Rebellion was an early test for the federal government. Could it quell back-country unrest, and how would it do so? The ensuing document from the Pennsylvania Gazette *reveals differing perspectives of the excise. Governor Thomas Mifflin, the leading political figure in Pennsylvania during the 1790s, supported action against the rebels only after President Washington officially declared the region in rebellion. The second part of this document reveals how western Pennsylvanians organized to resist the excise.*

Questions to Consider

1. Why is the governor of Pennsylvania determined to put down the rebellion? What threat do the rebels appear to pose?

2. In what ways are the inhabitants of Pittsburgh resisting the excise?

3. What similarities do the citizens of Pittsburgh share with the sentiments expressed in "Grievances of the Shays Rebels" (Document 41)?

4. In what ways do you think the legacy of the American Revolution shapes the governor of Pennsylvania's response? The citizens of Pittsburgh?

In the name, and by the authority of the Commonwealth of Pennsylvania, by
THOMAS MIFFLIN, Governor of the said Commonwealth,
A PROCLAMATION.

WHEREAS information has been received, that several lawless bodies of armed men have, at sundry times, assembled in the county of Allegheny,

(Philadelphia) *The Pennsylvania Gazette,* August 13, 1794.

within the commonwealth of Pennsylvania, and being so assembled, have committed various cruel and aggravated acts of riot and arson; and more particularly, that on the 17th ultimo, one of the said lawless bodies of armed men attacked the dwelling house of John Nevill, Esq; Inspector of the Revenue for the fourth survey of the district of Pennsylvania; and after firing upon, and wounding sundry persons employed in protecting and defending the said dwelling-house, set fire to, and totally burned and destroyed the same, together with the furniture and effects therein, and the barns, stables, and other buildings thereto adjoining and appurtenant:

And whereas it appears from the Proclamation of the President of the United States, bearing date this day as well as from other evidence, that the outrages and criminal proceedings aforesaid, have been undertaken and prosecuted by certain unlawful combinations of persons, who thereby design to obstruct and have actually obstructed the execution of the laws of the United States; and that by reason thereof, in pursuance of the authority in him vested, he has resolved to call forth the militia, for the purpose of supressing the said unlawful combinations, and of enforcing the execution of the laws so obstructed as aforesaid.

And whereas every good and enlightened citizen must perceive how unworthy it is thus riotously to oppose the constitution and laws of our country, (the government and laws of the state being herein as much affected as the government and laws of the United States) which were formed by the deliberate will of the people, and which (by the same legitimate authority) can, in a regular course, be peaceably amended or altered. How incompatible it is with the principles of a republican government, and dangerous in point of precedent, that a minority should attempt to controul the majority, or a part of the community undertake to prescribe to the whole! how indispensible, though painful an obligation, is imposed upon the officers of government, to employ the public force for the purpose of subduing and punishing such unwarrantable proceedings, when the judiciary authority has proved incompetent to the task: And how necessary it is, that the deluded rioters aforesaid should forthwith be brought to a just sense of their duty, as a longer deviation from it must inevitably be destructive to their own happiness, as well as injurious to the reputation and prosperity of their country.

AND WHEREAS, entertaining a just sense of my federal obligations, and feeling a perfect conviction of the necessity of pursuing immediate measures to suppress the spirit of insurrection, which has appeared as aforesaid, and to restore tranquillity and order—I have heretofore given instructions to the proper officers of the commonwealth, to investigate the circumstances of the said riots, to ascertain the names of the rioters, and to institute the regular process of the law, for bringing offenders to justice.

NOW THEREFORE, I have deemed it expedient also to issue this Proclamation, hereby publicly announcing my determination, by all lawful means, to cause to be prosecuted and punished, all persons whomever, that have engaged, or shall engage, in any of the unlawful combinations or proceedings aforesaid:

AND FURTHER DECLARING, that whatever requisition the President of the United States shall make, or whatever duty he shall impose in pursuance of his constitutional and legal powers, for the purpose of maintaining the authority, and executing the laws of the United States—will, on my part, be promptly undertaken and faithfully discharged: And all judges, justices, sheriffs, coroners, constables, and other officers of the commonwealth, according to the duties of their respective stations, are hereby required and enjoined to employ all lawful means for discovering, apprehending, securing, trying and bringing to justice, each and every person concerned in the said riots and unlawful proceedings.

Given under my hand, and the great seal of the state, at Philadelphia, this seventh day of August, in the year of our Lord, one thousand seven hundred and ninety-four, and of the commonwealth the nineteenth.
THOMAS MIFFLIN.
By the Governor,
A. J. DALLAS,
Secretary of the Commonwealth.

The following is the Copy of a hand bill, printed at Pittsburgh. The Post rider left that place without any letters or Newspapers—
AT A MEETING OF THE INHABITANTS OF PITTSBURGH. On Thursday Evening, July 31, 1794, to take into consideration the present situation of Affairs, and declare their sentiments on this delicate Crisis.

A GREAT majority, almost the whole of the inhabitants of the town, assembled. It being announced to the meeting, that certain gentlemen from the town of Washington, had arrived, and had signified that they were instructed with a message to the inhabitants of the town, relative to present affairs; a committee of three persons were appointed to confer with them, and report the message to the meeting; the persons appointed were George Wallace, H. H. Brackenridge, and John Wilkins, junr. these gentlemen made report to the meeting, to wit.

That in consequence of certain letters sent by the last mail, certain persons were discovered as advocates of the Excise Law, and enemies to the interests of the country; and that a certain Edward Day, James Brison, and Abraham Kirkpatrick, were particularly obnoxious, and that it was expected of the country should be dismissed from the town without delay; whereupon, it was resolved, that it should be so done, and a committee of twenty-one were appointed to see the resolution carried in effect, to wit. George Wallace, H. H. Brackenridge, Peter Audrain, John Scull, John McMasters, John Wilkins, Sen. Andrew McIntire, George Robinson, John Irwin, merchant, Andrew Watson, George Adams, David Evans, Josiah Tannehill, Matthew Ernest, William Farls, Alexander McNickle, Col. John Irwin, James Clow, William Gormly, Nathaniel Irish, A. Tannehill.

Also, That whereas it is a part of the message from the gentlemen of Washington that a great body of the people of the country will meet to morrow at Bradock's fields, in order to carry into effect measures that may seem to them adviseable with respect to the Excise Law and the advocates of it, Resolved, That the above committee shall, at an early hour, wait upon the people on the ground, and assure the people that the above resolution, with respect to the proscribed persons, has been carried into effect.

Resolved, also, That the inhabitants of the town shall march out, and join the people on Braddock's Field, as brethren, to carry into effect with them any measure that may seem adviseable to the common cause.

Resolved, also, That we shall be watchful among ourselves of all characters, that by word or act may be unfriendly to the common cause, and when discovered, will not suffer them to live amongst us, but they shall instantly depart the town.

Resolved, also, That the above committee shall exist as a committee of information and correspondence, as an organ of our sentiments, until our next town meeting.

And that whereas a general meeting of delegates from the townships of the country on the west of the mountains, will be held at Parkinson's ferry, on the Monongahela, on the 14th of August next, Resolved, That delegates shall be appointed to that meeting, and that the 9th of August next be appointed for a town meeting, to elect such delegates.

Resolved also, That a number of handbills be struck off, at the expence of the committee, and distributed among the inhabitants of the town, that they may conduct themselves accordingly.

50

George Washington's "Farewell Address" (1796)

The ratification of the Constitution was, in part, made possible by the understanding that George Washington would be the nation's first president. During his eight-year tenure, Washington presided over a government riddled by factionalism. One of the most divisive issues was how to respond to events in Europe, where revolutionary France toppled the monarchy, created a republic, and engaged in a series of wars with many of its neighbors. The events in France horrified many conservative Americans; eventually, they became supporters of the Federalist party. The Democratic Republicans supported France and urged the government to honor its treaty commitments to America's wartime ally. In his farewell, President Washington addressed the nation on what he saw as potential problems for the United States. In this selection, he advises the nation on its future approach to dealing with the European powers.

Questions to Consider

1. What is Washington's warning about foreign relations?
2. What did Washington see as the main purpose of American foreign policy? Why?

3. How was American politics affected by foreign affairs?

4. To what extent have Washington's views on foreign relations been a guide for American foreign policy in the 19th century? The 20th?

. . . Against the insidious wiles of foreign influence (I conjure you to believe me, fellow-citizens,) the jealousy of a free people ought to be constantly awake; since history and experience prove, that foreign influence is one of the baneful foes of Republican Government. But that jealousy, to be useful, must be impartial; else it becomes the instrument of the very influence to be avoided, instead of a defense against it. Excessive partiality for one nation, and excessive dislike of another, cause those whom they actuate to see danger only on one side, and serve to veil and even second the arts of influence on the other. Real patriots, who may resist the intrigues of the favorite, are liable to become suspected and odious; while its tools and dupes usurp the applause and confidence of the people, to surrender their interests.

The great rule of conduct for us, in regard to foreign nations is, extending our commercial relations, to have with them as little political connection as possible. So far as we have already formed engagements, let them be fulfilled with perfect good faith. Here let us stop.

Europe has her own set of primary interests, which to us have none, or a very remote relation. Hence she must be engaged in frequent controversies, the causes of which are essentially foreign to our concerns. Hence, therefore, it must be unwise in us to implicate ourselves, by artificial ties, in the ordinary vicissitudes of her politics, or the ordinary combinations and collusions of her friendships or enmities.

Our detached and distant situation invites and enables us to pursue a different course. If we remain one free people, under an efficient government, the period is not far off, when we may defy material injury from external annoyance; when we may take such an attitude as will cause the neutrality, we may at any time resolve upon, to be scrupulously respected; when belligerent nations, under the impossibility of making acquisitions upon us, will not lightly hazard the giving us provocation; when we may choose peace or war, as our interest, guided by justice, shall counsel.

Why forego the advantages of so peculiar a situation? Why quit our own to stand upon foreign ground? Why, by interweaving our destiny with that of any part of Europe, entangle our peace and prosperity in the toils of European ambition, rivalship, interest, humor, or caprice?

It is our true policy to steer clear of permanent alliances with any portion of the foreign world; so far, I mean, as we are now at liberty to do it; for let me not be understood as capable of patronizing infidelity to existing engagements. I hold the maxim no less applicable to public than to private affairs, that honesty is always the best policy. I repeat it, therefore, let those engagements be observed in their genuine sense. But, in my opinion, it is unnecessary and would be unwise to extend them.

George Washington, "Farewell Address," *A Compilation of the Messages and Papers of the Presidents,* ed. James D. Richardson (Washington, DC, 1903), 1: 213–224.

Taking care always to keep ourselves, by suitable establishments, on a respectable defensive posture, we may safely trust to temporary alliances in extraordinary emergencies.

Harmony, liberal intercourse with all nations, are recommended by policy, humanity, and interest. But even our commercial policy should hold an equal and impartial hand; neither seeking nor granting exclusive favors or preferences; consulting the natural course of things; diffusing and diversifying by gentle means the streams of commerce, but forcing nothing; establishing, with powers so disposed, in order to give trade a stable course, to define the rights of our merchants, and to enable the government to support them, conventional rules of intercourse, the best the present circumstances and mutual opinion will permit, but temporary, and liable to be from time to time abandoned or varied, as experience and circumstances shall dictate; constantly keeping in view, that it is folly in one nation to look for disinterested favors from another; that it must pay with a portion of its independence for whatever it may accept under that character; that, by such acceptance, it may place itself in the condition of having given equivalents for nominal favors, and yet of being reproached with ingratitude for not giving more. There can be no greater error than to expect or calculate upon real favors from nation to nation. It is an illusion, which experience must cure, which a just pride ought to discard. . . .

51

The Virginia Resolutions (1798)

The political divisions that emerged during the Washington administration became more heated during the presidency of John Adams. America's entry into an undeclared "quasi-war" with France in 1798 caused the Federalist-dominated Congress to respond by passing the Alien and Sedition Acts. Inspired by fears of Republican treachery and French intrigue, the acts made naturalization requirements more stringent and squelched dissent. In response, Thomas Jefferson, vice president but no friend of the administration, and former Democratic Republican congressional leader James Madison, temporarily retired from public life, respectively authored the Kentucky and Virginia Resolutions. The Democratic Republican–controlled legislature of each state accepted and passed the resolutions. The Virginia Resolutions, an excerpt of which follows, were among the first theoretical arguments for states' rights under the new federal system.

Questions to Consider

1. Why do the Virginia Resolutions protest against the Alien and Sedition Acts?

2. Upon what basis did the Virginia Resolutions declare these laws to be illegal?

3. According to the Virginia Resolutions, who is the final decision maker in the federal government?

4. Are the ideas espoused in the Virginia Resolutions consistent with those found in *Federalist Number 10* (Document 43)? How might you account for any differences?

RESOLUTIONS OF VIRGINIA
OF DECEMBER 21, 1798

1. Resolved, That the General Assembly of Virginia doth unequivocally express a firm resolution to maintain and defend the Constitution of the United States, and the Constitution of this State, against every aggression either foreign or domestic; and that they will support the Government of the United States in all measures warranted by the former.

2. That this Assembly most solemnly declares a warm attachment to the Union of the States, to maintain which it pledges all its powers; and that, for this end, it is their duty to watch over and oppose every infraction of those principles which constitute the only basis of that Union, because a faithful observance of them can alone secure its existence and the public happiness.

3. That this Assembly doth explicitly and peremptorily declare that it views the powers of the Federal Government as resulting from the compact to which the States are parties, as limited by the plain sense and intention of the instrument constituting that compact; as not further valid than they are authorized by the grants enumerated in that compact; and that, in case of a deliberate, palpable, and dangerous exercise of other powers not granted by the said compact, the States, who are parties thereto, have the right and are in duty bound to interpose for arresting the progress of the evil, and for maintaining within their respective limits the authorities, rights, and liberties appertaining to them.

4. That the General Assembly doth also express its deep regret, that a spirit has in sundry instances been manifested by the Federal Government to enlarge its powers by forced constructions of the constitutional charter which defines them; and that indications have appeared of a design to expound certain general phrases (which, having been copied from the very limited grant of powers in the former Articles of Confederation, were the less liable to be misconstrued) so as to destroy the meaning and effect of the particular enumeration which necessarily explains and limits the general phrases; and so as to consolidate the States, by degrees, into one sovereignty, the obvious tendency and inevitable result of

"Resolutions of Virginia," *The Virginia Report of 1799–1800* (Richmond, 1850), 22–23.

which would be to transform the present republican system of the United States into an absolute, or, at best, a mixed monarchy.

5. That the General Assembly doth particularly protest against the palpable and alarming infractions of the Constitution in the two late cases of the "Alien and Sedition Acts," passed at the last session of Congress; the first of which exercises a power nowhere delegated to the Federal Government and which, by uniting legislative and judicial powers to those of [the] executive, subverts the general principles of free government, as well as the particular organization and positive provisions of the federal Constitution; and the other of which acts exercises, in like manner, a power not delegated by the Constitution, but, on the contrary, expressly and positively forbidden by one of the amendments thereto,—a power which more than any other, ought to produce universal alarm, because it is levelled against the right of freely examining public characters and measures, and of free communication among the people thereon, which has ever been justly deemed the only effectual guardian of every other right.

6. That this state having by its convention which ratified the federal Constitution expressly declared, "that among other essential rights, the liberty of conscience and of the press cannot be cancelled, abridged, restrained, or modified by any authority of the United States," and from its extreme anxiety to guard these rights from every possible attack of sophistry or ambition, having, with other States, recommended an amendment for that purpose, which amendment was in due time annexed to the Constitution,—it would mark a reproachful inconsistency and criminal degeneracy, if an indifference were now shown to the palpable violation of one of the rights thus declared and secured, and to the establishment of a precedent which may be fatal to the other.

7. That the good people of this commonwealth, having ever felt and continuing to feel the most sincere affection to their brethren of the other States, the truest anxiety for establishing and perpetuating the union of all and the most scrupulous fidelity to that Constitution, which is the pledge of mutual friendship, and the instrument of mutual happiness, the General Assembly doth solemnly appeal to the like dispositions of the other States, in confidence that they will concur with this commonwealth in declaring, as it does hereby declare, that the acts aforesaid are unconstitutional, and that the necessary and proper measure[s] will be taken by each for co-operating with this State, in maintaining unimpaired the authorities, rights, and liberties reserved to the States respectively, or to the people.

8. That the Governor be desired to transmit a copy of the foregoing resolutions to the Executive authority of each of the other States, with a request that the same may be communicated to the legislature thereof. And that a copy be furnished to each of the Senators and Representatives representing this State in the Congress of the United States.

52

Marbury v. Madison (1803)

By 1800, even the federal judiciary had become politicized. During the late 1790s, Federalist-controlled federal courts used their power for political ends against their Democratic Republican enemies. When Jefferson became president in 1801, he sought to settle old scores while reducing Federalist influence in the courts. One of his first actions was to instruct Secretary of State James Madison to withhold several of the "midnight appointments," which outgoing President Adams had made shortly before leaving office. William Marbury, Adams' selection to serve as the District of Columbia's justice of peace, filed a writ of mandamus demanding delivery of his commission. Chief Justice John Marshall, a Virginia Federalist, issued the response excerpted as follows, which helped establish the precedent of judicial review.

Questions to Consider

1. What is John Marshall's decision about William Marbury's appointment?
2. What powers does Marshall determine are the Supreme Court's? What is the basis of this decision?
3. How might partisan politics have influenced the Court's decision?
4. Why is this Court case so significant?

... In the order in which the court has viewed this subject, the following questions have been considered and decided.

1st. Has the applicant a right to the commission he demands?

2d. If he has a right, and that right has been violated, do the laws of his country afford him a remedy?

3d. If they do afford him a remedy, is it a mandamus issuing from this court? The first object of inquiry is,

1st. Has the applicant a right to the commission he demands? ...

It appears, from the affidavits, that in compliance with this law, a commission for William Marbury, as a justice of the peace for the county of Washington, was signed by John Adams, then President of the United States; after which the seal of the United States was affixed to it; but the commission has never reached the person for whom it was made out. ...

It is, therefore, decidedly the opinion of the court, that when a commission had been signed by the President, the appointment is made; and that the

---

"*Marbury v. Madison*," *The Constitutional Decisions of John Marshall*, ed. Joseph P. Cotton, Jr. (New York, 1905), 1: 7–43.

commission is complete when the seal of the United States has been affixed to it by the Secretary of State. . . .

Mr. Marbury, then, since his commission was signed by the President, and sealed by the Secretary of State, was appointed; and as the law creating the office, gave the officer a right to hold for five years, independent of the executive, the appointment was not revocable, but vested in the officer legal rights, which are protected by the laws of his country.

To withhold his commission, therefore, is an act deemed by the court not warranted by law, but violative of a vested legal right.

This brings us to the second inquiry; which is,

2d. If he has a right, and that right has been violated, do the laws of his country afford him a remedy?. . .

It is, then, the opinion of the Court, . . .

That, having this legal title to the office, he has a consequent right to the commission; a refusal to deliver which is a plain violation of that right, for which the laws of his country afford him a remedy.

It remains to be inquired whether,

3d. he is entitled to the remedy for which he applies. This depends on,

1st. The nature of the writ applied for; and,

2d. The power of this court.

1st. The nature of the writ. . . .

It is true that the mandamus, now moved for, is not for the performance of an act expressly enjoined by statute.

It is to deliver a commission; on which subject the acts of congress are silent. This difference is not considered as affecting the case. It has already been stated that the applicant has, to that commission, a vested legal right, of which the executive cannot deprive him. He has been appointed to an office, from which he is not removable at the will of the executive; and being so appointed, he has a right to the commission which the secretary has received from the President for his use. The act of congress does not indeed order the Secretary of State to send it to him, but it is placed in his hands for the person entitled to it; and cannot be more lawfully withheld by him than by any other person. . . .

In the distribution of this power it is declared that "the Supreme Court shall have original jurisdiction in all cases affecting ambassadors, other public ministers and consuls, and those in which a state shall be a party. In all other cases, the Supreme Court shall have appellate jurisdiction.". . .

To enable this court, then, to issue mandamus, it must be shown to be an exercise of appellate jurisdiction, or to be necessary to enable them to exercise appellate jurisdiction.

It has been stated at the bar that the appellate jurisdiction may be exercised in a variety of forms, and that if it be the will of the legislature that a mandamus should be used for that purpose, that will must be obeyed. This is true, yet the jurisdiction must be appellate, not original.

It is the essential criterion of appellate jurisdiction, that it revises and corrects the proceedings in a cause already instituted, and does not create that cause. Although, therefore, a mandamus may be directed to courts, yet to issue such a writ to an officer for the delivery of a paper, is in effect the same as to sustain an original action for that paper, and, therefore, seems not to belong to appellate, but to original jurisdiction. Neither is it necessary in such a case as this, to enable the court to exercise its appellate jurisdiction.

The authority, therefore, given to the Supreme Court, by the act establishing the judicial courts of the United States, to issue writs of mandamus to public officers, appears not to be warranted by the constitution; and it becomes necessary to inquire whether a jurisdiction so conferred can be exercised.

The question, whether an act, repugnant to the constitution, can become the law of the land, is a question deeply interesting to the United States. . . .

The constitution is either a superior paramount law, unchangeable by ordinary means, or it is on a level with ordinary legislative acts, and, like other acts, is alterable when the legislature shall please to alter it.

If the former part of the alternative be true, then a legislative act contrary to the constitution is not law: if the latter part be true, then written constitutions are absurd attempts, on the part of the people, to limit a power in its own nature illimitable.

Certainly all those who have framed written constitutions contemplate them as forming the fundamental and paramount law of the nation, and, consequently, the theory of every such government must be, that an act of the legislature, repugnant to the constitution, is void.

This theory is essentially attached to a written constitution, and, is consequently, to be considered, by this court, as one of the fundamental principles of our society. It is not therefore to be lost sight of in the further consideration of this subject. . . .

Thus, the particular phraseology of the constitution of the United States confirms and strengthens the principle, supposed to be essential to all written constitutions, that a law repugnant to the constitution is void; and that courts, as well as other departments, are bound by that instrument.

The rule must be discharged.

8

The New Nation and Its Place in the World

In addition to having to work out the details of how the new government would operate, the United States also had to establish a pattern of relations with foreign states. During much of this period, the United States attempted to remain neutral, while keeping the Europeans from meddling in America's affairs. With the European flank covered, the young nation remained free to acquire land in the West and more than doubled its territorial size during the first quarter of the 19th century. Westward expansion often involved foreign relations of another sort—negotiating with Native Americans. The following documents demonstrate the American policy of neutrality and territorial acquisition, as well as the opposition to these policies.

53

Jefferson's Instructions to Robert Livingston, Minister to France (1802)

Large numbers of settlers migrated to the area beyond the Appalachians after the American Revolution. By 1800, Kentucky and Tennessee had achieved statehood. Westerners considered the right to navigate the Mississippi River and to deposit goods at New Orleans as necessities. Thomas Jefferson, who counted on the West for political support, was eager to preserve these privileges. American access to the "Father of Waters" seemed threatened in October 1802, when Spain transferred the Louisiana Territory to the more militarily powerful French and suspended the right of American traders to deposit goods in New Orleans. Americans, many of whom believed that Napoleon had ordered the revocation of the right of deposit, feared the establishment of a French empire in the Mississippi Valley. In the following dispatch, President Thomas Jefferson provides Robert E. Livingston, the American minister to France, with instructions for negotiating the issue.

Questions to Consider

1. Why does Thomas Jefferson believe that French control of Louisiana "works most sorely on the United States"?

2. How do Jefferson's views on territorial expansion get reconciled with the views expressed in "The Virginia Resolutions" (Document 51)?

3. Why are events in St. Domingo important to American interests? Does Livingston complete Jefferson's instructions?

4. To what extent do Jefferson's remarks anticipate the ideas espoused by "The Monroe Doctrine" (Document 60)?

. . . The cession of Louisiana and the Floridas by Spain to France, works most sorely on the United States. On this subject the Secretary of State has written to you fully, yet I cannot forbear recurring to it personally, so deep is the impression it makes on my mind. It completely reverses all the political relations of the United States, and will form a new epoch in our political course. Of all nations of any consideration, France is the one which, hitherto, has offered the fewest points on which we could have any conflict of right, and the most points of a communion of interests. From these causes, we have ever looked to her as our natural friend, as one with which we never could have an occasion of difference. Her growth, therefore, we viewed as our own, her misfortunes ours. There is on the globe one single spot, the possessor of which is our natural and habitual enemy. It is New Orleans, through which the produce of three-eighths of our territory must pass to market, and from its fertility it will ere long yield more than half of our whole produce, and contain more than half of our inhabitants. France, placing herself in that door, assumes to us the attitude of defiance. Spain might have retained it quietly for years. Her pacific dispositions, her feeble state, would induce her to increase our facilities there, so that her possession of the place would be hardly felt by us, and it would not, perhaps, be very long before some circumstance might arise, which might make the cession of it to us the price of something of more worth to her. Not soon can it ever be in the hands of France: the impetuosity of her temper, the energy and restlessness of her character, placed in a point of eternal friction with us, and our character, which though quiet and loving peace and the pursuit of wealth, is high-minded, despising wealth in competition with insult or injury, enterprising and energetic as any nation on earth; these circumstances render it impossible that France and the United States can continue long friends, when they meet in so irritable a position. They, as well as we, must be blind if they do not see this; and we must be very improvident if we do not begin to make arrangements on that hypothesis. The day that France takes possession of New Orleans, fixes the sentence which is to restrain her forever within her low-water

"To the United States (Robert E. Livingston) Minister to France," *The Works of Thomas Jefferson*, ed. Paul Leicester Ford (New York, 1905), 9: 363–368.

mark. It seals the union of two nations, who, in conjunction, can maintain exclusive possession of the ocean. From that moment, we must marry ourselves to the British fleet and nation. We must turn all our attention to a maritime force, for which our resources place us on very high ground; and having formed and connected together a power which may render reinforcement of her settlements here impossible to France, make the first cannon which shall be fired in Europe the signal for the tearing up any settlement she may have made, and for holding the two continents of America in sequestration for the common purposes of the United British and American nations. This is not a state of things we seek or desire. . . .

If France considers Louisiana, however, as indispensable for her views, she might perhaps be willing to look about for arrangements which might reconcile it to our interests. If anything could do this, it would be the ceding to us the island of New Orleans and the Floridas. This would certainly, in a great degree, remove the causes of jarring and irritation between us, and perhaps for such a length of time, as might produce other means of making the measure permanently conciliatory to our interests and friendships. It would, at any rate, relieve us from the necessity of taking immediate measures for counter-vailing such an operation by arrangements in another quarter. But still we should consider New Orleans and the Floridas as no equivalent for the risk of a quarrel with France, produced by her vicinage. . . .

The idea here is, that the troops sent to St. Domingo, were to proceed to Louisiana after finishing their work in that island. If this were the arrangement, it will give you time to return again and again to the charge. For the conquest of St. Domingo will not be a short work. It will take considerable time, and wear down a great number of soldiers. Every eye in the United States is now fixed on the affairs of Louisiana. Perhaps nothing since the revolutionary war, has produced more uneasy sensations through the body of the nation. . . .

54

―――――――――

Heading West with Lewis and Clark (1804)

Thomas Jefferson's intense curiosity in the West predated his presidency. Once elected to the office, he wasted little time in planning an expedition to travel up the Missouri River to the Pacific Ocean. Meriwether Lewis and William Clark, both acquaintances of Jefferson, would lead the mission. Their task was enormous: to make their way into unmarked territory with little hope of outside support in an effort to report on prospects for trade, to collect scientific data on the region's flora and fauna, and to map their route. The purchase of Louisiana shortly before their debarkation from St. Louis did little to simplify the mission. The following account by Patrick Gass describes their winter quarters among the Mandan Indians near modern-day Bismarck, North Dakota. A Pennsylvania native, Gass had served in the army before joining the expedition, where his construction skills were useful in building winter shelter. The Mandan had long had friendly relations with French traders, but in 1837, a smallpox epidemic virtually wiped out the tribe. Gass's account of the expedition first appeared in 1807.

Questions to Consider

1. What are the author's attitudes toward native life?

2. Compare and contrast Gass's view of Native Americans with those of Tecumseh ("Tecumseh on White Encroachment," Document 56). How do you account for these differences?

3. In what ways does weather appear to affect the expedition?

SATURDAY 27TH. The morning was clear and pleasant and we set out early. At half past seven we arrived at the first village of the Mandans and halted about two hours. This village contains 40 or 50 lodges built in the manner of those of the Rickarees. These Indians have better complexions than most other Indians, and some of the children have fair hair. We passed a bluff on the south side with a stratum of black resembling coal. There is a bottom on the north side, where the second Mandan village is situated. We went about a mile above it, and encamped in the same bottom, for the purpose of holding a council with the natives. This place is 1610 miles from the mouth of the river du Bois, where we first embarked to proceed on the expedition. There are about the same number of lodges, and people, in this village as in the first. These people do not bury their dead, but place the body on a scaffold, wrapped in a buffaloe robe, where it lies exposed. . . .

FRIDAY 2ND. Captain Lewis, myself and some of the men, went up to the first village of the Mandans, who gave us some corn. Captain Clarke and the rest of our party, having dropt half a mile lower down the river, began to clear a place for a camp and fort. We pitched our tents and laid the foundation of our line of huts.

SATURDAY 3RD. A clear day; we continued building, and six men went down the river in a periogue to hunt. They will perhaps have to go 30 or 40 miles before they come to good hunting ground.—The following is the manner in which our huts and fort were built. The huts were in two rows, containing four rooms each, and joined at one end forming an angle. When raised about 7 feet high a floor of puncheons or split plank were laid, and covered with grass and clay; which made a warm loft. The upper part projected a foot over and the roofs were made shed-fashion, rising from the inner side, and making the outer wall about 18 feet high. The part not enclosed by the huts we intend to picket. In the angle formed by the two rows of huts we built two rooms, for holding our provisions and stores. . . .

THURSDAY 29TH. This day was clear, but cold. We went to unrig the boat, and by an accident one of the sergeants had his shoulder dislocated. The 30th the weather continued the same. Early in the morning of this day we saw an Indian on the opposite side of the river, and brought him over. He informed us, that a few days ago, eight of his nation were out hunting, and were attacked by a party of the Sioux tribe, who killed one and wounded two more; and also carried off their horses. Captain Clarke and twenty-three men

---

Patrick Gass, *Journal of the Lewis and Clark Expedition* (Chicago, 1904, reprint of 1811 ed.), 54–61.

immediately set out with an intention of pursuing the murderers. They went up to the first village of the Mandans, but their warriors did not seem disposed to turn out. They suggested the coldness of the weather; that the Sioux were too far gone to be overtaken: and put off the expedition to the spring of the year. Captain Clarke and his party returned the same evening to the fort. We have been daily visited by the Indians since we came here. Our fort is called Fort Mandan, and by observation is in N. latitude 47.21.33.8.

SATURDAY 1ST DECEMBER, 1804. The day was pleasant, and we began to cut and carry pickets to complete our fort. One of the traders from the North West Company came to the fort, and related that the Indians had been troublesome in his way through. An Indian came down from the first Mandan village, and told us that a great number of the Chien or Dog nation had arrived near the village. . . .

FRIDAY 7TH. A clear cold morning. At 9 o'clock, the Bigwhite head chief, of the first village of the Mandans, came to our garrison and told us that the buffaloe were in the prairie coming into the bottom. Captain Lewis and eleven more of us went out immediately, and saw the prairie covered with buffaloe and the Indians on horseback killing them. They shoot them with bows and arrows, and have their horses so trained that they will advance very near and suddenly wheel and fly off in case the wounded buffaloe attempt an attack. . . .

MONDAY 10TH. After breakfasting on marrow bones, Captain Lewis and four of us set out for the fort. Four hunters and another man to keep camp remained out. On our return we met one of our men, who said that a party had gone down with the horses for more meat. This day was very cold: an experiment was made with proof spirits, which in fifteen minutes froze into hard ice. In the evening two of our hunters came in with the horses, but had killed nothing. Five encamped out. . . .

SUNDAY 16TH. A clear cold day; I went up with some of the men to the 1st and 2nd village of the Mandans, and we were treated with much kindness. Three of the traders from the N.W. Company came to our fort, and brought a letter to our commanding officers. They remained with us all night. The object of the visits we received from the N.W. Company, was to ascertain our motives for visiting that country, and to gain information with respect to the change of government. . . .

55

A Frontier View of the *Chesapeake* Affair (1807)

The new nation sought to reap the benefits of neutrality as Great Britain and France engaged in the Napoleonic Wars. Utterly dependent on its navy for security, Britain found large numbers of sailors deserting to the better pay and conditions of the U.S. merchant marine and navy. Desperate to maintain manpower, the British resorted to impressment, stopping American ships and forcibly removing those sailors they believed to be deserters. In 1807, the H.M.S. Leopard attacked the U.S.S. Chesapeake off Norfolk, Virginia, resulting in the death of three American seamen and the removal of four others. The incident, coupled with British seizure of American ships trading with archenemy France, nearly led to war. In this document, citizens living on the southwestern frontier pledge their support in the face of perceived British tyranny.

Questions to Consider

1. Why are the inhabitants of Washington county so angry about the *Chesapeake* affair?

2. What can you deduce about America's place in the world at this time based on this document?

3. In what ways are the inhabitants of Washington county influenced by the ideology of the American Revolution?

4. Why do you think the inhabitants of Washington county are so willing to sacrifice their lives over this issue?

COMMUNICATED TO THE SENATE

OF THE 27TH OCTOBER, 1807.

At a meeting to the inhabitants of Washington county, Mississippi Territory, at the court-house in the town of Wakefield, on the 8th of September, 1807, in consequence of the attack by the British ship of war *Leopard* on the United States frigate *Chesapeake,* the following declaration of the sentiments of the meeting was unanimously adopted:

Situated in a remote corner of the territory of the United States, and unconnected with every other body of American citizens, the people inhabiting the county lying on the waters of the Mobile have at length heard of the outrage which has been committed on our national rights by the arrogant representatives of British despotism. We think and feel on the occasion as every American thinks and feels. We despise the bully and the coward who, as captain of the *Leopard,* was the instrument of exhibiting the enormous extent of the claims of the pretended Mistress of the Ocean. But our attention is in instant drawn from him to ourselves and our own situation. Is national independence a dream? Shall Great Britain or any other nation come at pleasure into our territory and lay hold of whomsoever she pleases, under the pretence that this man is her subject and that man in her employ: that here there is a felon, and there a deserter? Our national ships are our territory, in whatever quarter of the world they are found; much more so, then, when

---

The Declarations of the American Citizens on the Mobile, with Relation to British Aggressions (1807).

within our own acknowledged limits and jurisdiction. We care not who the men were that were demanded from the *Chesapeake;* we care not whence they came, where they were from Europe stained with blood, no foreign force had a right to invade our territory; no foreign officer, civil or military, had a right to exercise his functions within our limits, or to transport the supposed offender to the precincts of a distant tribunal.

If there be a mutual convention between two nations reciprocally to deliver up felons, it is well; but no one nation has a right to force another into such a stipulation. And shall the plea, not of a treason, not of a murder, not of a felony having been committed, but the mere plea of desertion from a service, the tyranny and enormities of which are now arming the whole civilized world against it—shall such a plea be ground sufficient for us to stifle our jealously of national rights, or to surrender our claims to perfect and unqualified independence?

England may count upon our divisions. She is mistaken. The violence of her conduct had united all America. We judge not only from what we hear, but from what we see among ourselves. Our own settlement originally consisted, and still in a great degree consists, of those who adhered to England in the revolutionary war. They were led by principle; their elders taught them that resistance was sinful; and they imbibed from their infancy a deep veneration for their King. But the delusion lasts no longer. We have since seen that King engaged in almost incessant wars on the liberty and happiness of man; whilst the Government which has succeeded his in America has preserved us in peace with all the world, and been pre-eminently occupied in promoting our national prosperity. Old factions are forgotten; we all view with the same sensibility any outrage on the honor of our common country; and old whigs and old tories will cordially united in devoting their lives and fortunes to avenge the wounded dignity of America against the insults and oppressions of any Government upon earth. What may be the immediate issue of an appeal to arms we know not. That knowledge is confined to the Lord of Host; and on him, trusting to the justice of our cause, we rely with humble confidence.

But, though the operations and events of war are always uncertain, we can calculate with some confidence that a five years' state of non-intercourse with Great Britain will establish the manufactures of America on a foundation which no return of peace will ever shake. It will render us forever after in a high degree independent of the British manufacturers of wool, and still more so of those of cotton. Our planters, too, will hereafter find their market at home; and the British navy, if Britain and her navy should continue to exist, will at length find that her tyranny on the ocean has given *commercial independence* to those confederated States which British tyranny on the land first led to *political independence*. . . .

As to ourselves and our own local concerns, it is true we have sometimes feared that we were overlooked in the council of the nation. Our population is small; we are surrounded, except on the Spanish side, by the most powerful tribes of Indians existing within the original limits of the United States. The want of land cuts off from us the prospect of having our strength increased.

We had hoped that a treaty entered into with the Choctaws, which, by making a valuable addition to our land, would have invited population, and placed us in a state of greater security and respectability, would have been ratified. But we have been disappointed. Yet, few as we are, we consider ourselves as an advanced guard, destined to defend the immense tract of valuable territory which lies between the settlements on the Mobile and the State of Tennessee. We may *perish* at our posts, but we shall not *slumber* there. . . .

The charter of that independence was drawn up in '76; it was ratified by the peace of '83; but it still cries out for the blood of American citizens to seal it and to give it practical validity. Our blood shall be mingled with that of other Americans in offering the solemn sacrifice.

Resolve, unanimously. That the chairman of this meeting forward to the President of the United States a copy of this declaration, and that he give it such other circulation as he may deem necessary.

56

Tecumseh on White Encroachment (1810)

The wave of settlement that swept over the Appalachians after the Revolution threatened Native Americans in the region. Earlier Indian leaders had attempted to create an alliance to resist white encroachment, but these efforts proved difficult given traditional animosities and conflicting political agendas among the various tribes. The Shawnee warrior Tecumseh, who had grown up near white settlers and was familiar with American society, attempted to create such an alliance with the assistance of his brother Tenskwatawa. While Tenskwatawa preached a religious message, Tecumseh sought to create a military alliance with British support. In the excerpted speech, Tecumseh summarizes many of the grievances the natives had concerning their treatment at the hands of the Euro-Americans.

Questions to Consider

1. According to Tecumseh, what are the reasons for Native American opposition to the whites?

2. What does Tecumseh hope to accomplish?

3. How do you think white American contemporaries would react to this document?

4. Compare Tecumseh's views on white encroachment with those found in "The Pontiac Manuscript" (Document 22). What similarities do you note? Differences?

... You ought to know that after we agreed to bury the Tomahawk at Greenville we then found their new fathers in the Americans who told us they would treat us well, not like the British who gave us but a small piece of pork every day. I want now to remind you of the promises of the white people. . . .

Brother. Since the peace was made you have kill'd some of the Shawanese, Winebagoes Delawares and Miamies and you have taken our lands from us and I do not see how we can remain at peace with you if you continue to do so. You have given goods to the Kickapoos for the sale of their lands to you which has been the cause of many deaths amongst them. You have promised us assistance but I do not see that you have given us any.

You try to force the red people to do some injury. It is you that is pushing them on to do mischief. You endeavour to make destructions, you wish to prevent the Indians to do as we wish them to unite and let them consider their land as the common property of the whole you take tribes aside and advise them not to come into this measure and untill our design is accomplished we do not wish to accept of your invitation to go and visit the President.

The reason I tell you this is—You want by your distinctions of Indian tribes in allotting to each a particular track of land to make them to war with each other. You never see an Indian come and endeavour to make the white people do so. You are continually driving the red people when at last you will drive them into the great lake where they can't either stand or work.

Brother. You ought to know what you are doing with the Indians. Perhaps it is by direction of the President to make those distinctions. It is a very bad thing and we do not like it. Since my residence at Tippecanoe we have endeavoured to level all distinctions to destroy village chiefs by whom all mischief is done; it is they who sell our land to the Americans our object is to let all our affairs be transacted by Warriors.

Brother. This land that was sold and the goods that was given for it was only done by a few. The treaty was afterwards brought here and the Weas were induced to give their consent because of their small numbers. The treaty at Fort Wayne was made through the threats of Winamac but in future we are prepared to punish those chiefs who may come forward to propose to sell their land. If you continue to purchase of them it will produce war among the different tribes and at last I do not know what will be the consequences to the white people.

Brother. I was glad to hear your speech you said if we could show that the land was sold by persons that had no right to sell you would restore it. . . . These tribes set up a claim but the tribes with me will not agree to their claim, if the land is not restored to us you will soon see when we return to our homes how it will be settled. We shall have a great council at which all the tribes shall be present when we will show to those who sold that they had no right to see the claim they set up and we will know what will be done with those Chiefs that did sell the land to you. I am not alone

"Speech of Tecumseh," *Governors Messages and Papers,* ed. Logan B. Esarey, Indiana Historical Society, *Collections* (Indianapolis, 1922), 7: 463–467.

in this determination it is the determination of all the warriors and red people that listen to me.

I now wish you to listen to me. If you do not it will appear as if you wished me to kill all the chiefs that sold you this land. I tell you so because I am authorised by all the tribes to do so. I am at the head of them all. I am a Warrior and all the Warriors will meet together in two or three moons from this. Then I will call for those chiefs that sold you that land and shall know what to do with them. If you do not restore the land you will have a hand in killing them.

Brother. Do not believe that I came here to get presents from you if you offer us anything we will not take it. By taking goods from you you will hereafter say that with them you purchased another piece of land from us. If we want anything we are able to buy it, from your traders. Since the land was sold to you no traders come among us. I now wish you would clear all the roads and let the traders come among us. Then perhaps some of our young men will occasionally call upon you to get their guns repaired. This is all the assistance we ask of you. . . .

Brother. It has been the object of both myself and brother from the beginning to prevent the lands being sold should you not return the land, it will occasion us to call a great council that will meet at the Huron Village where the council fire has already been lighted. At which those who sold the land shall be call'd and shall suffer for their conduct.

Brother. I wish you would take pity on all the red people and do what I have requested. If you will not give up the land and do cross the boundary of your present settlement it will be very hard and produce great troubles among us. How can we have confidence in the white people when Jesus Christ came upon the earth you kill'd and nail'd him on a cross, you thought he was dead but you were mistaken. You have shaken among you and you laugh and make light of their worship. . . .

57

Dolley Madison on British Invasion of Washington (1814)

Freedom of the seas, western land hunger, and an assertion of national rights were among the factors that led the United States into the War of 1812. The nation managed to survive the conflict, but the British campaigns of 1814 placed such a result in doubt. In the following account, First Lady Dolley Madison waits at the President's Mansion while her husband directs the American defense at Bladensburg, Maryland, just east of the District of Columbia. Following the collapse of the American defense, Dolley fled just before British forces arrived and set fire to the mansion. Whitewash was later used to cover the burn marks, giving the building its familiar name, the White House. Britain's ability to take the American capital underscored the young nation's weakness.

Questions to Consider

1. What are Dolley Madison's responsibilities if the British advanced on Washington?
2. How does she describe American defense forces?
3. What does Madison remove from the presidential mansion before the British arrive? Why?
4. What can we deduce from this document about women's roles in the early 19th century?

Tuesday Augt 23d 1814.

Dear Sister,—My husband left me yesterday morning to join Gen. Winder. He inquired anxiously whether I had courage, or firmness to remain in the President's house until his return, on the morrow, or succeeding day and on my assurance that I had no fear but for him and the success of our army, he left me, beseeching me to take care of myself, and of the cabinet papers, public and private. I have since received two despatches from him written with a pencil; the last is alarming, because he desires I should be ready at a moment's warning to enter my carriage and leave the city; that the enemy seemed stronger than had been reported, and that it might happen they would reach the city, with intention to destroy it. . . . I am accordingly ready; I have pressed as many cabinet papers into trunks to fill one carriage; our private property must be sacrificed, as it is impossible to procure wagons for its transportation. I am determined not to go myself until I see Mr. Madison safe, and he can accompany me. . . .

Wednesday morning twelve o'clock,—Since sunrise I have been turning my spy glass in every direction and watching with unwearied anxiety, hoping to discover the approach of my dear husband and his friends; but, alas, I can descry only groups of military wandering in all directions, as if there was a lack of arms, or of spirit to fight for their own firesides.

Three o'clock.—Will you believe it, my sister? We have had a battle, or skirmish near Bladensburg, and I am still here within sound of the cannon! Mr. Madison comes not; may God protect him! Two messengers, covered with dust, come to bid me fly; but I wait for him. . . . At this late hour, a wagon has been procured; I have had it filled with the plate and most valuable portable articles belonging to the house; whether it will reach its destination, the Bank of Maryland, or fall into the hands of British soldiery, events must determine.

Our kind friend, Mr. Carroll, has come to hasten my departure, and is in a very bad humor with me because I insist on waiting until the large picture

---

Life and Letters of Dolly Madison, ed. Allen C. Clark (Washington, DC, 1914), 164–167.

of Gen. Washington is secured, and it requires to be unscrewed from the wall. This process was found too tedious for these perilous moments; I have ordered the frame to be broken, and the canvass taken out; it is done,—and the precious portrait placed in the hands of two gentlemen of New York, for safe keeping. And now, dear sister, I must leave this house, or the retreating army will make me a prisoner in it, by filling up the road I am directed to take. When I shall again write to you, or where I shall be tomorrow, I cannot tell!! —Doll[e]y.

58

Resolutions of the Hartford Convention (1815)

Federalist-dominated New England had opposed "Mr. Madison's War" from the start. The center of the American mercantile trade was New England, whose shippers had struggled economically since Jefferson's embargo of 1807. In addition, the region contained a rump of arch-Federalists who contemplated disunion. The British sought to take advantage of the region's hostility to the war by conducting a hands-off policy in 1812–13. By 1814, however, British operations increasingly focused on the New England coast. Shipping interests faced with mounting losses combined with local disunionists to demand changes in the federal compact that would protect minority interests. New England Federalists issued the document excerpted as follows from their meeting at Hartford, Connecticut.

Questions to Consider

1. What is the historical context of this document?
2. How does the Hartford Convention justify its proposed changes to the Constitution?
3. Why do they want two-thirds majorities of both houses of Congress to determine actions?
4. What do you think President Madison thought when he saw this document?

. . . Resolved, That it be and hereby is recommended to the said Legislatures, to authorize an immediate and earnest application to be made to the government of the United States, requesting their consent to some arrangement, whereby the said states may, separately or in concert, be empowered to assume upon themselves the defense of their territory against the enemy; and a reasonable portion of the taxes, collected within said States, may be paid

Theodore Dwight, *History of the Hartford Convention* (New York, 1833), 376–379.

into the respective treasuries thereof, and appropriated to the payment of the balance due said states, and to the future defense of the same. The amount so paid into the said treasuries to be credited, and the disbursements made as aforesaid to be charged to the United States.

Resolved, That it be and hereby is recommended to the legislatures of the aforesaid states, to pass laws (where it has not already been done) authorizing the governors or commanders-in-chief of their militia to make detachments from the same, or to form voluntary corps, as shall be most convenient and conformable to their constitutions, and to cause the same to be well armed, equipped, and disciplined, and held in readiness for service; and upon the request of the governor of either of the other states to employ the whole of such detachment or corps, as well as the regular forces of the state, or such part thereof as may be required and can be spared consistently with the safety of the state, in assisting the state, making such request to repel any invasion thereof which shall be made or attempted by the public enemy.

Resolved, That the following amendments of the constitution of the United States be recommended to the states represented as aforesaid, to be proposed by them for adoption by the state legislatures, and in such cases as may be deemed expedient by a convention chosen by the people of each state. . . .

First. Representatives and direct taxes shall be apportioned among the several states which may be included within this Union, according to their respective numbers of free persons, including those bound to serve for a term of years, and excluding Indians not taxed, and all other persons.

Second. No new state shall be admitted into the Union by Congress, in virtue of the power granted by the constitution, without the concurrence of two thirds of both houses.

Third. Congress shall not have power to lay any embargo on the ships or vessels of the citizens of the United States, in the ports or harbors thereof, for more than sixty days.

Fourth. Congress shall not have power, without the concurrence of two thirds of both houses, to interdict the commercial intercourse between the United States and any foreign nation, or the dependencies thereof.

Fifth. Congress shall not make or declare war, or authorize acts of hostility against any foreign nation, without the concurrence of two thirds of both houses, except such acts of hostility be in defense of the territories of the United States when actually invaded.

Sixth. No person who shall hereafter be naturalized, shall be eligible as a member of the senate or house of representatives of the United States, nor capable of holding any civil office under the authority of the United States.

Seventh. The same person shall not be elected president of the United States a second time nor shall the president be elected from the same state two terms in succession.

Resolved, That if the application of these states to the government of the United States, recommended in a foregoing resolution, should be unsuccessful, and peace should not be concluded, and the defense of these states should be neglected, as it has been since the commencement of the war, it will, in the opinion of this convention, be expedient for the legislatures of the several states to appoint delegates to another convention, to meet at Boston in the state of Massachusetts, on the third Thursday of June next, with such powers and instructions as the exigency of a crisis so momentous may require. . . .

59

Tennessee Expansionists on the Adams–Onís Treaty (1819)

As new settlers began to displace Native Americans in the Old Southwest, it became increasingly important for American policy makers to safeguard U.S. interests in the region. As a result, negotiations with the Spanish over Florida and the Texas–Louisiana border were of great importance. Among those who were eager to secure an American presence in the West was Secretary of State John Quincy Adams, an experienced diplomat and ardent nationalist. Andrew Jackson's controversial invasion of Florida in 1818 provided Adams with an opportunity in his negotiations with the Spanish. By exposing Spain's weakness in Florida, Adams successfully forced Spain to relinquish Florida and to abandon its claim to territory north and east of the Sabine River in the Adams–Onís (or Transcontinental) Treaty. The following selection from the (Nashville) Clarion & Tennessee State Gazette *reveals the attitude of expansion-minded Tenesseeans toward the secretary of state's negotiations on the Texas border.*

Questions to Consider

1. Compare this document with John O'Sullivan's "Annexation" (Document 87). What similarities do you note? Differences?
2. Why does the Tennessee newspaper oppose the boundary line between Spain and the United States?
3. What is the newspaper's view on the land west of the boundary?
4. What can you deduce from this selection about American attitudes?

When we first heard the outlines of this treaty we were astonished; what we hear every day confirms our displeasure—at first we had no anticipation that the line of boundary crossed Red river—this it does, and gives Spain a territory four times as large as the state of Tennessee, besides what we believed ceded—a territory as necessary to us as any part of Upper Louisiana. In a late New York paper, there is published a communication from Wm. Darby, who

---

"Spanish Treaty," (Nashville) *The Clarion & Tennessee State Gazette,* April 6, 1819, p. 3.

surveyed the western part of Louisiana, and is probably better acquainted with the country than any man living. He says,

> Let any person view a good map of that part of this continent over which the new line of demarcation, between Spain and the United . . . States, is to pass; and compare it with the Louisiana in the real extent of the term, will perceive that if the treaty is ratified, we have relinquished a territory of upwards 240,000 square miles of surface. . . .
>
> I remember when the regions now included in the states of Indiana, Missouri, the Arkansas territory, the states of Mississippi, Louisiana and Alabama, were considered relatively and remote, as at present Texas, from the Atlantic border of the United States; but the irresistible impulse of our augmenting population has brought these former expansive territories to view.
>
> Let no man deceive himself with the main expectation that artificial lines will operate to stem the torrent of western emigration. The laws of nature will be neither arrested nor thwarted by a roll of parchment though the names of the king of Spain and his minister are both attached to its margin. The increasing and wrestless men of the west, will follow the courses of the rivers that flow into the Mississippi and Gulf of Mexico, regardless of future consequences . . . to prevent the flow of emigration is beyond human power. . . .
>
> Texas is filled with Indian tribes, some are settled in fixed residence, but most are wandering hordes, who subsist by hunting and who are in almost perpetual war. As the settlements upon the Arkansaw and Red Rivers advance, the whites will come to contact with the native inhabitants; and as our former system of treating savage bands is perpetuated, savage war will continue and those savages be finally destroyed.
>
> The positive authority of Spain exists no more in America. It is worse than folly to legislate upon a state of things which has ceased to exist—and can never again be restored. Why the United States should relinquish a part of its domain, a part, itself the extent of an Empire, I cannot see; and still less can I see the sense or policy of adopting an order of things which must inevitably produce a repetition of events so much to be deprecated.

It is possible that some future event may put it in the power of some more enlightened statesman to correct blunders of the late treaty.

60

The Monroe Doctrine (1823)

The preeminent expression of America's postwar diplomatic nationalism was the 1823 Monroe Doctrine. The genesis of the document came as a response to the developing alliance system of Europe. Of particular worry was the so-called Holy Alliance, which implied that European powers might forcibly restore Spain's recently independent

American states to their former owner. The British, who were eager to exploit trade with the new countries, requested that a joint Anglo-American statement be issued opposing European intervention in American affairs. Secretary of State John Quincy Adams rebuffed the British, reportedly stating that the United States should not "come in a cock boat in the wake of the British man-of-war." President James Monroe delivered America's unilateral position on European–American relations in his December 2 address to Congress.

Questions to Consider

1. What is the thesis of this document?
2. How powerful is the United States at this time in comparison with major European powers?
3. How does the United States view the newly independent nations of Latin America?
4. Why are European interests in the Western Hemisphere a danger to the United States?

. . . The citizens of the United States cherish sentiments the most friendly in favor of the liberty and happiness of their fellow-men on that side of the Atlantic. In the wars of the European powers in matters relating to themselves we have never taken any part, nor does it comport with our policy so to do. It is only when our rights are invaded or seriously menaced that we resent injuries or make preparation for our defense. With the movements in this hemisphere we are of necessity more immediately connected, and by causes which must be obvious to all enlightened and impartial observers. The political system of the allied powers is essentially different in this respect from that of America. This difference proceeds from that which exists in their respective Governments; and to the defense of our own, which has been achieved by the loss of so much blood and treasure, and matured by the wisdom of their most enlightened citizens, and under which we have enjoyed unexampled felicity, this whole nation is devoted. We owe it, therefore, to candor and to the amicable relations existing between the United States and those powers to declare that we should consider any attempt on their part to extend their system to any portion of this hemisphere as dangerous to our peace and safety. With the existing colonies or dependencies of any European power we have not interfered and shall not interfere. But with the Governments who have declared their independence and maintained it, and whose independence we have, on great consideration and on just principles, acknowledged, we could not view any interposition for the purpose of oppressing them, or controlling in any other manner their destiny, by any European power in any

James Monroe, *"Seventh Annual Message," A Compilation of the Messages and Papers of the Presidents,* ed. James D. Richardson (Washington, DC, 1903), 2: 218–219.

other light than as the manifestation of an unfriendly disposition toward the United States. In the war between those new Governments and Spain we declared our neutrality at the time of their recognition, and to this we have adhered, and shall continue to adhere, provided no change shall occur which, in the judgment of the competent authorities of this Government, shall make a corresponding change on the part of the United States indispensable to their security.

The late events in Spain and Portugal show that Europe is still unsettled. . . . Our policy in regard to Europe, which was adopted at an early stage of the wars which have so long agitated that quarter of the globe, nevertheless remains the same, which is, not to interfere in the internal concerns of any of its powers; to consider the government de facto as the legitimate government for us; to cultivate friendly relations with it, and to preserve those relations by a frank, firm, and manly policy, meeting in all instances the just claims of every power, submitting to injuries from none. But in regard to those continents circumstances are eminently and conspicuously different. It is impossible that the allied powers should extend their political system to any portion of either continent without endangering our peace and happiness; nor can anyone believe that our southern brethren, if left to themselves, would adopt it of their own accord. It is equally impossible, therefore, that we should behold such interposition in any form with indifference. If we look to the comparative strength and resources of Spain and those new Governments, and their distance from each other, it must be obvious that she can never subdue them. It is still the true policy of the United States to leave the parties to themselves, in the hope that other powers will pursue the same course.

9

The Democratic Republic

Following the War of 1812, the United States experienced a wave of nationalist euphoria. While newspaper editors hailed the end of the divisiveness that had marked the first quarter-century of the republic, thousands of Americans moved into the recently opened lands of the trans-Appalachian West. The Panic of 1819, precipitated in part by declining cotton prices, initiated a shift in mood that was quickly followed by a new set of problems. By the 1820s, differences over the spread of slavery and the power of the federal government began to dominate the political debate, creating rifts along regional lines. The following documents provide glimpses of the differing views over national and state power.

61

Richmond Enquirer on *McCulloch* v. *Maryland* (1819)

One of the most important items on the postwar nationalist agenda was the charter of a national bank. The first bank's charter had expired before the war, but the Republican Congress passed John C. Calhoun's bill chartering the Second Bank of the United States in 1816. The new bank was not without its opponents; Maryland passed a law in 1818 taxing all banks not established by its authority. The case of McCulloch v. Maryland *came before the Supreme Court during the first phase of the Panic of 1819, an economic debacle that many Americans blamed on the Second Bank's policies. John Marshall, a Hamiltonian Federalist, led the court in ruling that the state could not tax a federally chartered institution. The following editorial is excerpted from Thomas Ritchie's* Richmond Enquirer, *one of the nation's most influential Republican newspapers.*

Questions to Consider

1. How does Thomas Ritchie support the position that the Constitution is a "compact" of the states?
2. Why does Ritchie believe that the Supreme Court's decision endangers states' rights?
3. What does Ritchie fear could ultimately result from this decision?
4. What is the long-term significance of this decision?

SIR—I have read with considerable attention the opinion pronounced by the Chief Justice of the U.S. in the case of McCulloch against the state of Maryland. In that opinion we are informed, 1st. That it is [the] unanimous and decided opinion of the Supreme Court, that the act to incorporate the Bank of the U.S. is a law made to pursuance of the Constitution, and . . . part of the supreme law of the land. . . . That the Court is also unanimously of opinion that the law of Maryland imposing a tax on the Bank of Maryland, is unconstitutional and void. . . .

I confess, that as a citizen, I should have been better pleased to have seen the separate opinions of the judges. . . . On this great constitutional question, affecting very much the rights of the several states composing our confederacy, the decision of which abrogated the law of one state, and is supposed to have formed a rule for the future conduct of other states, the people had surely a right to expect that each judge should assign his own reasons for the vote which he gave. The court seems to have thought that it was sitting as an umpire to decide between the conflicting claims of a sovereign state on the one hand, and the whole United States on the other, and yet the judges decline the expression of the principles on which they have separately formed their judgments! Having thus declined the declaration of their separate opinions, we are driven, however reluctantly, to the conclusion that each judge approves of each argument and position advanced by the chief justice. . . .

There are two principles advocated and decided on by the supreme court, which appear to me to endanger the very existence of state rights. The first is the denial that the powers of the federal government was delegated by the states: and the second is, that the grant of powers to that government, and particularly the grant of powers "necessary and proper" to carry the other powers into effect, ought to be construed into a liberal, rather than a restricted sense. Both of these principles tend directly to consolidation of the states, and to strip them of some of the most important attributes of their sovereignty. If the Congress of the United States should think proper to legislate to the full extent, upon the principles now adjudicated by the supreme court it is difficult to say how small would be the remnant of power left in the hands of the state authorities.

"On the Opinion of the Supreme Court," *Richmond Enquirer,* March 30, 1819, p. 3.

The first position, that the powers of the federal government are not delegated by the states, or in other words that the states are not parties to the compact, is untenable in itself, and fatal in its consequences. . . .

The several states did delegate to the federal government its powers, and they are parties to the compact. Who gave birth to the constitution? The history of the times, and the instrument itself furnish the ready answer to the question. The federal convention of 1787 was composed of delegates appointed by the respective state legislatures; and who voted by states; the constitution was submitted on their recommendation, to conventions elected by the people of the several states, that is to say, to the states themselves by their highest political, and sovereign authority; by those separate conventions representing not the whole mass of the population of the United States, but the people only within the limits of the respective sovereign states, the constitution was adopted and brought into existence. The individuality of the several states was still kept up when they assembled in convention: their sovereignty was still preserved, and the only effect of the adoption of the constitution was to take from one set of their agents and servants, to wit, the state governments, a certain portion of specified powers, and to delegate that same portion to another set of servants and agents, then, namely, the federal government. . . .

The states not only gave birth to the constitution, but its life depends upon the existence of the state governments.—The Senate derives its being from them. The President is elected by persons who are as to numbers partly chosen on the federal principle. Destroy the state governments, and you by the same blow destroy the Senate, and with it the constitution. Again, how may this constitution be amended and reformed? By the legislatures of three-fourths of the states, or by conventions of the same number of states in the manner provided by the 5th article.—The states then gave birth to the constitution; they support its existence and they alone are capable of reforming or of changing its form and substance, and yet we are informed by a solemn adjudication that its powers are not derived from that source, and consequently that they are not parties to it!! . . .

The doctrine, if admitted to be true, would be of fatal consequence to the rights and freedom of the people of the states. If the states are not parties to the compact, the legislatures of the several states, who annually bring together the feelings, the wishes, and the opinions of the people within their respective limits, would not have a right to canvass the public measures of the Congress, or of the President, nor to remonstrate against the encroachments of power, nor to resist the advances of usurpation, tyranny and oppression. They would no longer be hailed as the centinels of the public liberty, nor as the protectors of their own rights. Every government, which has ever yet been established, feels a disposition to increase its own powers. Without the restraints which are imposed by an enlightened public opinion, this tendency will inevitably conduct the freest government to the exercise of tyrannic power. If the right of resistance be denied, or taken away, despotism inevitably follows. . . .

62

Fanny Wright on Equality (1830)

For reform-minded Europeans in the 1820s and 1830s, America's democratic political system, cheap available land, and lack of tradition seemed to offer an opportunity to shape a better tomorrow. One of the most renowned of these visitors was Scottish-born Frances "Fanny" Wright, who arrived in the United States in 1818 and fell in love with the country. Her behavior over the next decade would make her name a household word for radicalism. Rumors abounded that her friendship with the Marquis de Lafayette was more than platonic and that her utopian community at Nashoba was an experiment in free love and miscegenation. Her radical critique of American life drew large crowds and incited riots in some cities. By 1830, she had settled in New York's Bowery, where this lecture took place. There, the Market Revolution had transformed the manufacturing workplace from small shops of upwardly mobile skilled craftsmen into low-paid, semi-skilled workers. Her name became synonymous with the working-men's movement.

Questions to Consider

1. What is the basis of Wright's argument for equality?
2. Based on your reading of this document, why do you think Fanny Wright was so controversial?
3. How do you think a contemporary businessman would have reacted to her views?
4. Compare and contrast Fanny Wright's views with those expressed in "Sarah Grimké Argues for Gender Equality" (Document 84). What similarities and differences do you see?

. . . Our object, however reviled by false ambition, odious to knavery, offensive to vanity, or misconceived of by error, will ever be recognised by the great mass of this people as consistent with their national institutions, and as requisite for the practical development of the truths set forth in their declaration of independence. No! we shall not be driven to deny, nor seduced to qualify, the object, to which, as to the ultimate goal of reform, we, as Americans, are constitutionally pledged to aspire. That object—that ultimate goal is, as I have said, PRACTICAL EQUALITY, OF, THE UNIVERSAL AND EQUAL IMPROVEMENT OF THE CONDITION OF ALL, UNTIL, BY THE GRADUAL CHANGE IN THE VIEWS AND HABITS OF MEN, AND THE CHANGE CONSEQUENT UPON THE SAME, IN THE WHOLE SOCIAL ARRANGEMENTS OF THE BODY POLITIC, THE AMERI-

Frances Wright, *Parting Address as [d]elivered in the Bowery Theatre to the People of New York, June 1830* (New York, 1830).

CAN PEOPLE SHALL PRESENT, IN ANOTHER GENERATION, BUT ONE CLASS, AND, AS IT WERE, BUT ONE FAMILY—EACH INDEPENDENT IN HIS AND HER OWN THOUGHTS, ACTIONS, RIGHTS, PERSON, AND POSSESSIONS, AND ALL CO-OPERATING, ACCORDING TO THEIR INDIVIDUAL TASTE AND ABILITY, TO THE PROMOTION OF THE COMMON WEAL.

Taking this comprehensive view of all that is embraced in our *ultimate* object, every intelligent mind will distinguish that it is not attainable in this generation, and that all we can do, (though this *all* is immense,) is to exercise our own minds, and school our own feelings, in and by its contemplation, to correct such abuses as more immediately tend to exalt, at the present time, individuals or bodies of men at the expense of the mass of the community, and, first and last, and above all, to prepare the way for the entire fulfillment of what I conceive to constitute the one great constitutional duty of Americans—namely, the equal promotion of the happiness of all, by laying the foundation of a plan of education in unison with nature, with reason, with justice, and with THIS INSTRUMENT.

Such then is our ultimate object, and let us boldly declare it; such are the means—gradual and constitutional, but sure and radical, by which we propose that object to be attained. Such is our ultimate object, and let those who challenge it forego the name, even as they have forsworn the feelings of Americans. Such are the means we stand ready to adopt, and let those who blaspheme them forego the title even as they have forsworn the principles of honest man. Here—in our design or in the mode laid down for effecting that design, there is nothing to conceal, and nothing to *concede* or *extenuate*. I will take on me to speak, in this matter, in the name of my fellow citizens—constitutional is our object, righteous our means, and *determined our resolve*. We have no fear, no doubt, no hesitation, and no concealment. Why should we have? Thought here is free, speech is free, and all action free, which has in view our own benefit, combined with the benefit of our fellow man.

Behold, we have every advantage with us, which, as honest citizens, or as reasonable beings, we could ambition—a righteous object, a constitutional object, and an object feasible without violence to any, and with certain benefit to all. In Europe, the reformer, how expanded soever his mind, or generous his heart, may indeed hesitate to express the fulness of his desire. *Liberty and equality* there, is a cry whose very thought is treason, and its utterance death; but here, treason lies only in its challenge. How then should there be a point at issue with American reformers? All true and honest citizens *must,* upon reflection, have the same object—for, behold! It is engraven on their national escutcheon—it is engraven in never dying letters, in this Holy Bible of their country's faith, their country's hope, their country's love. To commence the practical illustration of the truths proclaimed to the world by the fathers of this nation's liberties, is what we ask at this day—no more could human philanthropy desire, no less could American patriotism demand.

For myself, I feel proud to declare, that no less perfect and entire is the democracy of my views and principles, than what by this charter is demanded of an American citizen; and, had I felt it otherwise, I had not claimed the noble title. I would see the righteous declaration here penned by Jefferson, signed by sages, sealed with the blood of the fathers of this nation, and solemnly sworn to by their sons on each anniversary of its birth.—I would—what shall I say? *See* its realization? That cannot be. But see such measures adopted as shall secure its realization for posterity, to the fullest extent ever conceived or conceivable by the human mind. Yes! My democracy has no reservations; my yearnings for the liberty of man acknowledge no exceptions, no prejudices, no predilections. Equal rights, equal privileges, equal enjoyments—I would see them shared by every man, by every woman, by every nation, by every race on the face of the globe. But, as I distinguish that equal condition must originate in equal knowledge, and that sound knowledge; in similar habits, and those good habits; in brotherly sympathies, and those fostered from youth up under a system of RATIONAL AND NATIONAL REPUBLICAN EDUCATION.

63

Daniel Webster's Second Reply to Robert Y. Hayne (1830)

The publication of John C. Calhoun's "Exposition and Protest" advancing the doctrine of nullification highlighted different views over the division of powers between the state and federal governments. The issue emerged in the halls of Congress late in 1829 when Senator Samuel A. Foot of Connecticut pressed for the temporary restriction of western land sales. The debate soon became an argument over national and states' rights when South Carolina Senator Robert Y. Hayne linked the issues the following January. Massachusetts Senator Daniel Webster responded with a blistering attack on the "Exposition and Protest." Perhaps the nation's best trial lawyer, having won several cases before the Supreme Court (including McCulloch v. Maryland, the Dartmouth College case, and Gibbons v. Ogden), Webster contended that South Carolina's problems resulted from its slave economy, not the tariff of 1828. Following Hayne's response came Webster's final oration, excerpted as follows, which contained the essence of nationalism as it had begun to develop in the antebellum North.

Questions to Consider

1. How does Daniel Webster attack states' rights?
2. Why is the federal union "most dear" to Webster?
3. According to Webster, what is the basis of the federal union?

4. Compare the views contained in this document with those found in "South Carolina Nullifies the Tariff" (Document 64). In what ways do they differ?

. . . I profess, Sir, in my career hitherto, to have kept steadily in view the prosperity and honor of the whole country, and the preservation of our Federal Union. It is to that Union we owe our safety at home, and our consideration and dignity abroad. It is to that Union that we are chiefly indebted for whatever makes us most proud of our country. That Union we reached only by the discipline of our virtues in the severe school of adversity. It had its origin in the necessities of disordered finance, prostrate commerce, and ruined credit. Under its benign influences, these great interests immediately awoke, as from the dead, and sprang forth with newness of life. Every year of its duration has teemed with fresh proofs of its utility and its blessings; and although our territory has stretched out wider and wider, and our population spread farther and farther, they have not outrun its protection or its benefits. It has been to us all a copious fountain of national, social, and personal happiness.

I have not allowed myself, Sir, to look beyond the Union, to see what might lie hidden in the dark recess behind. I have not coolly weighed the chances of preserving liberty when the bonds that unite us together shall be broken asunder. I have not accustomed myself to hang over the precipice of disunion, to see whether, with my short sight, I can fathom the depth of the abyss below; nor could I regard him as a safe counsellor in the affairs of this government, whose thoughts should be mainly bent on considering, not how the Union may be best preserved, but how tolerable might be the condition of the people when it should be broken up and destroyed. While the Union lasts we have high, exciting, gratifying prospects spread out before us, for us and our children. Beyond that I seek not to penetrate the veil. God grant that in my day, at least, that curtain may not rise! God grant that on my vision never may be opened what lies behind! When my eyes shall be turned to behold for the last time the sun in heaven, may I not see him shining on the broken and dishonored fragments of a once glorious Union; on States dissevered, discordant, belligerent; on a land rent with civil feuds, or drenched, it may be, in fraternal blood! Let their last feeble and lingering glance rather behold the gorgeous ensign of the republic, now known and honored throughout the earth, still full high advanced, its arms and trophies streaming in their original lustre, not a stripe erased or polluted, nor a single star obscured, bearing for its motto, no such miserable interrogatory as "What is all this worth?" nor those words of delusion and folly, "Liberty first and Union afterwards"; but everywhere, spread all over in characters of living light, blazing on all its ample folds, as they float over the sea and over the land, and in every wind under the whole heavens, that other sentiment, dear to every true American heart,—Liberty and Union, now and for ever, one and inseparable!

"Second Speech on Foot's Resolution," *The Writings and Speeches of Daniel Webster* (Boston, 1903), 6: 3–75.

64

South Carolina Nullifies the Tariff (1832)

During the 1820s, a new system of party alignments changed American politics, while a revolution in market patterns, transportation, and industry transformed the economy. These issues converged in the 1828 "Tariff of Abominations," which raised levies on various foreign goods. Several southern politicians despised the new tariff's high duties, believing that it favored northern manufacturers at the South's expense. Such sentiments were especially strong in South Carolina, where agricultural depression had eroded the local economy. In response, Vice President John C. Calhoun articulated the theory of nullification in 1828. When Congress failed to lower the tariff on cotton textiles in 1832, South Carolina invoked the doctrine. An excerpt from the nullification ordinance appears as follows.

Questions to Consider

1. What is the historical context of this document?
2. What appears to be South Carolina's view of the relationship of federal and state power?
3. Why does South Carolina seem so fearful of the federal government?
4. Compare the views contained in this document with those found in "Daniel Webster's Second Reply to Robert Y. Hayne" (Document 63). In what ways do they differ?

. . . We, therefore; the People of the State of South Carolina in Convention assembled, do declare and ordain, and it is hereby declared and ordained, that the several Acts and parts of Acts of the Congress of the United States, purporting to be laws for the imposing of duties and imposts on the importation of foreign commodities, and now having actual operation and effect within the U. States, and more especially an act entitled "an act in alteration of the several acts imposing duties on imports," approved on the nineteenth day of May, one thousand eight hundred and twenty-eight, and also an act entitled "an act to alter and amend the several acts imposing duties on imports," approved on the fourteenth day of July, one thousand eight hundred and thirty-two, are unauthorized by the Constitution of the U. States, and violate the true meaning and intent thereof, and are Null, Void, and no Law, nor binding upon this State, its officers or Citizens; and all promises, contracts, obligations made or entered into or to be made or entered into the purpose to secure the duties imposed by the said acts, and all judicial proceedings which shall be hereafter had in affirmance thereof, are and shall be held utterly Null and Void:

"An Ordinance to Nullify Certain Acts of Congress of the United States," *Charleston Mercury*, November 29, 1832, p. 2.

And it is further ordained, That it shall not be lawful for any of the constituted authorities, whether of this State or of the United States, to enforce the payment of duties imposed by the said Acts within the limits of this State; but that it shall be the duty of the legislature to adopt such measures and pass such acts as may be necessary to give full effect to this Ordinance, and to prevent the enforcement and arrest the operation of the said acts and parts of acts of the Congress of the United States, within the limits of this State, from and after the 1st day of February next, and the duty of the other constituted authorities, and of all persons residing or being within the limits of this State and they are hereby required and joined to obey and give effect to this Ordinance and such acts and measures of the Legislature as may be passed or adopted in obedience thereto. . . .

And we, the People of South Carolina, to the end, that it may be fully understood by the Government of the United States, and the People of the co-States, that we are determined to maintain this, our Ordinance and Declaration, at every hazard, do further declare, that we will not submit to the application of force, on the part of the Federal Government, to reduce this State to obedience; but that we will consider the passage by Congress, of any act, authorizing the employment of a military or naval force against the State of South Carolina, her constituted authorities or citizens; or any act, abolishing or closing the ports of this State, or any of them, or otherwise obstructing the free ingress and egress of vessels, to and from the said ports; or any other act on the part of the Federal Government, to coerce the State, shut up her ports, destroy or harrass her commerce, or to enforce the acts hereby declared to be null and void, otherwise than through the civil tribunals of the country, as inconsistent with the longer continuance of South Carolina in the Union: and that the people of this State will thenceforth hold themselves absolved from all further obligation to maintain or preserve their political connexion with the people of the other States, and will forthwith proceed to organize a separate Government, and do all other acts and things, which sovereign and independent States may of right do.

65

The American System (1832)

The economic changes that emerged in the aftermath of the War of 1812 demanded a political response. Some insisted on trying to protect citizens from the uncertainties of the new economy. Others believed that the issue should be left to state governments and private enterprise, while some argued that the federal government should play a role in shaping these changes. More nationally minded Republicans had begun to advance an agenda that came to be known as the American System. It called for a national bank to provide fiscal stability, a tariff to protect key industries and raise revenues, and federally funded internal improvements to develop a national transportation infrastructure. Henry Clay's name would become synonymous with the American System.

A native of Virginia, he built a spectacular political career in Kentucky. Elected as speaker of the House in his first term, he was a prominent member of the Republican pro-war faction who demanded American entry into the War of 1812. After helping to negotiate the treaty ending the war, he served as President John Quincy Adams' secretary of state before returning to the U.S. Senate in 1831. The following excerpt contains his defense of the American System.

Questions to Consider

1. According to Henry Clay, what impact has the American System had on the United States?
2. What appear to be the major criticisms of the American System?
3. How do you think Andrew Jackson ("Bank Veto Message," Document 66) responded to Clay's American System? Why?

. . . On a general survey, we behold cultivation extended, the arts flourishing, the face of the country improved, our people fully and profitably employed, and the public countenance exhibiting tranquillity, contentment, and happiness. And if we descend into particulars, we have the agreeable contemplation of a people out of debt; land rising slowly in value, but in a secure and salutary degree; a ready though not extravagant market for all the surplus productions of our industry; innumerable flocks and herds browsing and gamboling on ten thousand hills and plains, covered with rich and verdant grasses; our cities expanded, and whole villages springing up, as it were, by enchantment; our exports and imports increased and increasing; our tonnage, foreign and coastwise, swelling and fully occupied; the rivers of our interior animated by the perpetual thunder and lightning of countless steamboats; the currency sound and abundant; the public debt of two wars nearly redeemed; and, to crown all, the public treasury overflowing, embarrassing Congress, not to find subjects of taxation, but to select the objects which shall be liberated from the impost. *If the term of seven years were to be selected, of the greatest prosperity which this people have enjoyed since the establishment of their present Constitution, it would be exactly that period of seven years which immediately followed the passage of the tariff of 1824.*

This transformation of the condition of the country from gloom and distress to brightness and prosperity, has been mainly the work of American legislation, fostering American industry, instead of allowing it to be controlled by foreign legislation, cherishing foreign industry. The foes of the American system, in 1824, with great boldness and confidence, predicted, first, the ruin of the public revenue, and the creation of a necessity to resort to direct taxation; the gentleman from South Carolina (General Hayne), I believe, thought

---

"On the American System," 2, 3, & 6 February 1832, *Works of Henry Clay,* ed. Calvin Colton (New York, 1904), 7: 437–444.

that the tariff of 1824 would operate a reduction of revenue to the large amount of eight millions of dollars; secondly the destruction of our navigation; thirdly, the desolation of commercial cities; and, fourthly, the augmentation of the price of objects of consumption, and further decline in that of the articles of our exports. Every prediction which they made has failed, utterly failed. Instead of the ruin of the public revenue, with which they then sought to deter us from the adoption of the American system, we are now threatened with its subversion, by the vast amount of the public revenue produced by that system. . . .

While we thus behold the entire failure of all that was foretold against the system, it is a subject of just felicitation to its friends, that all their anticipations of its benefits have been fulfilled, or are in progress of fulfillment. The Honorable gentleman from South Carolina has made an allusion to a speech made by me, in 1824, in the other House, in support of the tariff, and to which, otherwise, I should not have particularly referred. But I would ask any one, who can now command the courage to peruse that long production, what principle there laid down is not true? What prediction then made has been falsified by practical experience?

It is now proposed to abolish the system, to which we owe so much of the public prosperity, and it is urged that the arrival of the period of the redemption of the public debt has been confidently looked to as presenting a suitable occasion to rid the country of the evils with which the system is alleged to be fraught. . . . But the people of the United States have not coupled the payment of their public debt with the destruction of the protection of their industry against foreign laws and foreign industry. They have been accustomed to regard the extinction of the public debt as relief from a burden, and not as the infliction of a curse. If it is to be attended or followed by the subversion of the American system, and an exposure of our establishments and our productions to the unguarded consequences of the selfish policy of foreign powers, the payment of the public debt will be the bitterest of curses. . . .

If the system of protection be founded on principles erroneous in theory, pernicious in practice, above all, if it be unconstitutional, as is alleged, it ought to be forthwith abolished, and not a vestige of it suffered to remain. But before we sanction this sweeping denunciation, let us look a little at this system, its magnitude, its ramifications, its duration, and the high authorities which have sustained it. We shall see that its foes will have accomplished comparatively nothing, after having achieved their present aim of breaking down our iron-founderies, our woolen, cotton, and hemp manufactories, and our sugar plantations. The destruction of these would, undoubtedly, lead to the sacrifice of immense capital, the ruin of many thousands of our fellow-citizens, and incalculable loss to the whole community. . . . Why, sir, there is scarcely an interest, scarcely a vocation in society, which is not embraced by the beneficence of this system. . . . We might well pause and contemplate, if human imagination could conceive the extent of mischief and ruin from its total overthrow, before we proceed to the work of destruction. . . .

66

Andrew Jackson's Bank Veto Message (1832)

By 1832, the Second Bank of the United States had become one of the most contro-versial issues in American politics. To many, the institution was important for fiscal management in a rapidly changing economy. But to Andrew Jackson and his supporters, the Bank represented the emergence of a moneyed aristocracy that would use it to deprive the common man of liberty and the ability to improve his economic lot. Jackson also had political reasons for opposing the Bank. Bank President Nicholas Biddle had championed cautious fiscal policies, which alienated many of Jackson's supporters in the South and Southwest, who wanted greater access to credit. Biddle also had close associ-ations with many of Jackson's leading opponents. Henry Clay, Jackson's opponent for the presidency in 1832, was a Bank supporter who had pushed a recharter bill through Congress in order to force Jackson's hand on a controversial issue during an election year. Jackson's veto dominated the fall election campaign, which Jackson won. The veto galvanized his opponents, who created the Whig party two years later.

Questions to Consider

1. What is Andrew Jackson's perspective in this document?
2. Why does Jackson veto the Bank recharter bill?
3. Whom does Jackson identify as a threat to American liberty?
4. How do you suppose the failure to recharter the Bank affected the American economy?

Washington, July 10, 1832

To the Senate:

The bill "to modify and continue" the act entitled "An act to incorporate the subscribers to the Bank of the United States" was presented to me on the 4th July instant. Having considered it with that solemn regard to the princi-ples of the Constitution which the day was calculated to inspire, and come to the conclusion that it ought not to become a law, I herewith return it to the Senate, in which it originated, with my objections.

A bank of the United States is in many respects convenient for the Gov-ernment and useful to the people. Entertaining this opinion, and deeply impressed with the belief that some of the powers and privileges possessed by

---

Andrew Jackson, "Veto Message," *A Compilation of the Messages and Papers of the Presidents*, ed. James D. Richardson (Washington, DC, 1903), 2: 576–581.

the existing bank are unauthorized by the Constitution, subversive of the rights of the States, and dangerous to the liberties of the people, I felt it my duty at an early period of my Administration to call the attention of Congress to the practicability of organizing an institution combining all its advantages and obviating these objections. I sincerely regret that in the act before me I can perceive none of those modifications of the bank charter which are necessary, in my opinion, to make it compatible with justice, with sound policy, or with the Constitution of our country.

The present corporate body, denominated the president, directors, and company of the Bank of the United States, will have existed at the time this act is intended to take effect twenty years. It enjoys an exclusive privilege of banking under the authority of the General Government, a monopoly of its favor and support, and, as a necessary consequence, almost a monopoly of the foreign and domestic exchange. The powers, privileges, and favors bestowed upon it in the original charter, by increasing the value of the stock far above its par value, operated as a gratuity of many millions to the stockholders.

An apology may be found for the failure to guard against this result in the consideration that the effect of the original act of incorporation could not be certainly foreseen at its time of [its] passage. The act before me proposes another gratuity to the holders of the same stock, and in many cases to the same men, of at least seven millions more. This donation finds no apology in any uncertainty as to the effect of the act. On all hands it is conceded that its passage will increase at least 20 or 30 per cent more the market price of the stock, subject to the payment of annuity of $200,000 per year secured by the act, thus adding in a moment one-fourth to its par value. It is not our own citizens only who are to receive the bounty of our Government. More than eight millions of the stock of this bank are held by foreigners. By this act the American Republic proposes virtually to make them a present of some millions of dollars. For these gratuities to foreigners and to some of our own opulent citizens the act secures no equivalent whatever. They are the certain gains of the present stockholders under the operation of this act, after making full allowance for the payment of the bonus.

Every monopoly and all exclusive privileges are granted at the expense of the public, which ought to receive a fair equivalent. The many millions which this act proposes to bestow on the stockholders of this existing bank must come directly or indirectly out of the earnings of the American people. It is due to them, therefore, if their Government sell monopolies and exclusive privileges, that they should at least exact for them as much as they are worth in open market. The value of monopoly in this case may be correctly ascertained. The twenty-eight millions of stock would probably be at an advance of 50 per cent, and command in market at least $42,000,000, subject to the payment of the present bonus. The present value of the monopoly, therefore, is $17,000,000, and this act proposes to sell for three millions, payable in fifteen annual installments of $200,000 each.

It is not conceivable how the present stockholders can have any claim to the special favor of the Government. The present corporation has enjoyed its monopoly during the period stipulated in the original contract. If we must have such a corporation, why should not the Government sell out the whole stock and thus secure to the people the full market value of the privileges granted? Why should not Congress create and sell twenty-eight millions of stock, incorporating the purchasers with all the powers and privileges secured in this act and putting the premium upon the sales into the Treasury?

But this act does not permit competition in the purchase of this monopoly. It seems to be predicated on the erroneous idea that the present stockholders have a prescriptive right not only to the favor but to the bounty of the Government. It appears that more than a fourth part of the stock is held by foreigners and the residue is held by a few hundred of our own citizens, chiefly of the richest class. . . .

67

Opposing Perspectives of the Jackson Presidency

Andrew Jackson was one of the most controversial presidents in American history. His decisive actions on issues such as nullification, Indian removal, and the Second Bank of the United States made him a hero to many Americans and a villain to others. The first image depicts Jackson's decision to remove federal money from the Second Bank of the United States and place it with state-chartered banks across the country. Jackson's supporters hailed his veto of the bill to recharter the Second Bank in 1832 and his subsequent removal of federal money as a bold stroke for the common people against the "moneyed interest" and foreigners. But his opponents saw it as an abuse of power and a threat to the republic. The second image, which depicts Jackson as a king, captures these fears. Jackson's opponents would soon form a new opposition party, choosing the name Whigs in reference to those who had fought for liberty in the English and American Revolutions.

Questions to Consider

1. Based on what you see in these images, how politically polarized was the United States in the 1830s?

2. What differences do you see in the way Andrew Jackson is portrayed? What seem to be the chief threats to liberty?

3. How does the symbolism in each of these images depict threats to liberty?

4. Compare and contrast the sentiments in these images with those found in "Andrew Jackson's Bank Veto Message" (Document 66) and "Spirit of Jacksonism" (Document 70).

"The Downfall of Mother Bank"

"King Andrew I" as depicted by his political enemies

68
_____

The *Cherokee Phoenix* on Georgia Policy Toward the Cherokee (1832)

Territorial expansion was a key element in Jacksonian ideology. To provide land in the West, it was necessary to extinguish native title. Many argued that Native Americans should be removed and resettled west of the Mississippi. Such a policy would not only provide farmsteads for thousands of white settlers, but it would also save America's original inhabitants from the pressures of Euro-American society while providing the tribes the time to acclimate to white culture. The Cherokee, who lived in the southern Appalachians, had already adopted many aspects of Euro-American culture, including similar farming techniques, slavery, a newspaper, a constitution, and evangelical Protestantism. Despite these reforms, land hunger, coupled with gold discoveries, led Georgia's political leaders to put increasing pressure on the Cherokee. The issue of Indian removal divided the nation. Jackson's supporters, especially in the South, were eager to remove the Native Americans, whereas many northern evangelicals and reformers believed the Cherokee provided evidence that nonwhites could adjust to American culture. Excerpted as follows is an editorial from the Cherokee Phoenix *that analyzes the policies of states' rights governor Wilson Lumpkin.*

Questions to Consider

1. What does Georgia propose for the Cherokee?
2. What does the *Cherokee Phoenix* advocate for the Cherokee?
3. Compare the sentiments expressed in this document with those found in "Benjamin Banneker to Thomas Jefferson, Blacks and Liberty in the New Nation" (Document 47). What comparisons can you draw between white views of African Americans and Native Americans?
4. What can you deduce from this document about who can be considered American in the 1830s?

. . . From the message [Governor Lumpkin of Georgia], it can be no longer doubted, that the occupancy of the vacant lands of the Cherokees, by the state of Georgia, will now soon be attempted; we deem it therefore necessary to say a word to the effects of this forcible occupation of our lands, in the event of the non–interference of the federal government. His Excellency has called the attention of the legislature to the serious deliberation of the condition of the Cherokees: Special and appropriate legislation he deems necessary to secure in them their rights of property. If each Indian had five hundred bushels of corn, and the Governor was to take by force four hundred of it, would it not be a mockery of justice to deliberate seriously . . . to secure

(New Echota, CT) *Cherokee Phoenix*, November 24, 1832 (n.p.).

what was left? Such an act we have no doubt would be pronounced outrageous and atrocious. But the hardships arising out of the land case are much greater. . . . Shall we go to Arkansas? But it is said, there no wood is to be found.—Shall we go to Milledgeville [capital of Georgia]? It is said there justice & precepts have parted. The grave deliberations of the legislature recommended by his Excellency will be productive of enormous injustice to the Cherokees, and their endless sufferings. To this confiscation of our property, we will not submit, we would choose to be placed in the silent regions of death, and be gathered to our fathers, than to remain depressed by Georgia oppression.

The Guard of Governor Lumpkin at the Sixes Gold Mine has again spilt Cherokee blood. A Cherokee by the name of Nicojack was discovered digging for gold, when one of the guard fired, and severely wounded the Indian in the arm and leg.—He has nearly recovered.

69

Commentary on Elections in Jacksonian America (1832)

Of the several foreign visitors who described American life in the antebellum period, few were more critical than Frances Trollope. The novelist visited America between 1827 and 1831, spending most of her time in Cincinnati, but also touring much of the rest of the country. Upon her return to Great Britain, she wrote Domestic Manners of the Americans, *which appeared in 1832. Her American experience undoubtedly colored her views: On her trip to the United States, the English radical Frances Wright convinced the Trollopes to invest in a Cincinnati business venture, which failed. Her humorous observations of American society depict a rough, egalitarian country that offended her bourgeois sensibilities. American reviewers vilified Mrs. Trollope for her criticisms of their democratic experiment. In the following selection, Mrs. Trollope wittily observes the popular nature of American politics and, in the process, questions the sincerity of American political convictions.*

Questions to Consider

1. What is the thesis of this document?
2. What does Frances Trollope consider so contradictory about American politics?
3. Why does she question the sincerity of American politicians?
4. How do you think an American contemporary would respond to this account?

. . . When a candidate for any office starts, his party endow him with every virtue, and with all the talents. They are all ready to peck out the eyes of those who oppose him, and in the warm and mettlesome south-western states, do literally often perform this operation; but as soon as he succeeds, his virtues and his talents vanish, and, excepting those holding office under his appointment, every man Jonathan of them sets off again full gallop to elect his successor. When I first arrived in America Mr. John Quincy Adams was president, and it was impossible to doubt, even from the statement of his enemies, that he was every way calculated to do honor to the office. All I ever heard against him was, that "he was too much of a gentleman"; but a new candidate must be set up, and Mr. Adams was out-voted for no other reason, that I could learn, but because it was "best to change." "Jackson for ever!" was, therefore, screamed from the mouths, both drunk and sober, till he was elected; but no sooner in his place, than the same ceaseless operation went on again, with "Clay for ever" for its war-whoop.

I was one morning paying a visit, when a party of gentlemen arrived at the same house, on horseback. The one whose air proclaimed him the chief of his party, left us not long in doubt as to his business, for he said, almost in entering,

"Mr. P——, I come to ask for your vote."

"Who are you for, sir?" was the reply.

"Clay for ever!" the rejoinder; and the vote was promised.

This gentleman was candidate for a place in the state representation, whose members have a vote in the presidential election.

I was introduced to him as an Englishwoman: he addressed me with: "Well, madam, you see we do these things openly and above-board here; you mince such matters more, I expect."

After his departure his history and standing were discussed. "Mr. M. is highly respectable, and of very good standing; there can be no doubt of his election if he is a thorough-going Clay-man," said my host.

I asked what his station was.

The lady of the house told me that his father had been a merchant, and when this future legislator was a young man, he had been sent to some port in the Mediterranean as his supercargo. The youth, being a free-born high-spirited youth, appropriated the proceeds to his own uses, traded with great success upon the fund thus obtained, and returned, after an absence of twelve years, a gentleman of fortune and excellent standing. I expressed some little disapprobation of this proceeding, but was assured that Mr. M. was considered by every one as a very "honorable man."

Were I to relate one-tenth part of the dishonest transactions recounted to me by Americans, of their fellow-citizens and friends, I am confident that no English reader would give me credit for veracity; it would, therefore, be very unwise to repeat them, but I cannot refrain from expressing the opinion that nearly four years of attentive observation impressed on me, namely, that the moral sense is on every point blunter than with us. Make an American believe that his next door neighbor is a very worthless fellow, and I dare say (if he were quite sure he could make nothing by him) he would drop the

Frances Trollope, *Domestic Manners of the Americans* (New York, 1832), 206–208.

acquaintance; but as to what constitutes a worthless fellow, people differ on the opposite sides of the Atlantic, almost by the whole decalogue [a fundamental set of rules]. There is, as it appeared to me, an obtusity on all points of honorable feeling. . . .

70

"Spirit of Jacksonism" (1832)

Although the American electorate enthusiastically sent Andrew Jackson to the White House in 1828 and 1832, a growing number of individuals became increasingly critical of his policies. Jackson's veto of the Bank of the United States as well as his stand on various other issues alarmed his opponents, who feared that he was a demagogue who manipulated the people only to abuse his power. Such attacks led Jackson's foes to label him as King Andrew and caused them to adopt the name Whigs, thereby associating themselves with those who had opposed executive tyranny in both the English and American revolutions. Alexander H. Everett, author of The Conduct of the Administration, *from which this excerpt was taken, personified much of Jackson's opposition. A native of Boston and protégé of John Quincy Adams, he served as American minister to Spain from 1825 until 1829. In 1830, he succeeded Jared Sparks as editor of the* North American Review, *one of New England's leading journals. He used this position to champion the anti-Jackson cause. In 1835, Everett had a change of heart and abandoned the Whigs in favor of the Democrats.*

Questions to Consider

1. According to Alexander Everett, what is the "spirit of Jacksonism"?
2. What evidence does Everett provide to support his case that Jacksonism was spreading?
3. What contradictions does Everett see in Jackson's supporters?
4. To what extent does Everett use the language found in "Cato's Letters" (Document 25) and "Introduction to *Common Sense*" (Document 31)? How do you account for these similarities?

SPIRIT OF JACKSONISM—CONCLUSION

In the preceding chapters, we have rapidly reviewed the measures by which the present Administration rose to power, and have exposed in detail the unconstitutional character and ruinous tendency of their principal measures. At

Alexander H. Everett, "Spirit of Jacksonism," *The Conduct of the Administration* (Boston, 1832), 74–78.

the close of our last essay, we stated that since the dissolution of the Van Buren cabinet, the effective power of the government had been lodged in the hands of a secret and irresponsible cabal, sometimes denominated the Kitchen Cabinet, and the "Cabinet improper." We propose to notice, in conclusion, the general spirit of the Administration as now constituted, and of the party which it represents, with the means which they employ to perpetuate their influence.

The spirit of Jacksonism, the most remarkable exhibitions of which we have separately examined and characterized, which has been distinctly perceptible ever since the formation of the Jackson party, and has become, from day to day, more and more apparent, especially since the organization of the "improper Cabinet," is the same that prevailed in France at the worst period of the Revolution, and was then known by the name of JACOBINISM. As it then existed in France, and as it now exists in this country, it may be described as a spirit which aims at the subversion of social order and the regular and wholesome authority of law, for the purpose of concentrating the whole power of the country in the hands of a single ruler. Its Alpha is ANARCHY, and its Omega DESPOTISM. It addresses itself to the worst passions of the least informed portion of the people;—denounces the most valuable and salutary institutions as intolerably oppressive, reviles the possessors of property, talents, virtue, every thing that gives distinction and influence in society, as tyrants and aristocrats;—and when by these delusive and maddening appeals it has brought the people to acts of open violence, and broken down the existing forms of government, it erects upon their ruins a throne for the boldest pretender, commonly some daring and reckless military chieftain, who happens to be at hand at the proper moment to take possession of it. . . .

In this political disease, wherever it has occurred, there have been, as we have said, two distinct tendencies—one towards disorganization and anarchy, the other towards despotism and a concentration of the whole power of society in the hands of a single ruler. The former is generally more observable in the earlier and the latter in the later stages of the malady, but they exist together, and develop themselves as circumstances happen to furnish occasion. Both these tendencies have been distinctly visible in the operations of Jacksonism. We have seen it encouraging the encroachments of the States on the Federal Government, denying the National Legislature all their most important powers, openly defying the authority of the Supreme Court, and encouraging the States to do the same; endeavoring, in a word, to bring back the present Constitution to the imbecility of the Old Confederation. We have seen it attempting to array the poor against the rich, denouncing the possession of property, talents, distinction of any kind, under the name of aristocracy, as an unpardonable crime, and straining every nerve to place the whole political influence in the hands of those, who for want of education and good moral qualities, are the least qualified to exercise it. Such are the proofs of the disorganizing and anarchical tendency of Jacksonism. On the other hand, we see but too plainly in the violent and arbitrary conduct of the chief, and in the servile complaisance—the insane man-worship of his flatter-ers—the evidences of a tendency to strengthen the Executive branch of the Government, which, if appearances were in other respects less favorable than they are, would justly excite the most serious alarm for the permanence of our institutions.

. . . He [Jackson] openly claims the right of executing or not executing, at discretion, the very laws which he has himself approved. He declares himself, in terms, entirely independent of the Supreme Court. He nullifies of his own mere motion a whole series of solemn treaties concluded with the Indian tribes, and the Intercourse Law, which makes it his duty to sustain these treaties, if necessary, by military force. He does in fact substantially what his own caprice happens to suggest, without the slightest regard to the letter or spirit of the constitution.

In the mean time, what is the language of the partisan prints? Are the soi-disant champions of State Rights and democracy alarmed at these undis-guised and almost avowed usurpations of power by the Federal Executive? Quite the contrary. The persons who are clamoring most loudly against the encroachments of the Federal Government, and the influence of Aristocracy, are the same who justify and applaud every act of General Jackson. These same persons are constantly loading him with the grossest and most fulsome flattery. Napoleon at the height of greatness did not receive more abject adu-lation than is daily lavished upon the imbecile automaton who is now the nominal head of our Government. The *Globe* tells us that he was BORN TO COMMAND. The *Indiana Times* assures us that he takes great interest in the welfare of his SUBJECTS. Mr. Van Buren thinks that the GLORY of acting under his orders, is enough to satisfy the most extravagant ambition. Finally, a late Ohio paper, after inveighing severely against the two opposition parties for having had the temerity to form a coalition in that State, as they have done elsewhere against a common enemy, remarks that "a republican form of government is quite too mild and lenient" for such offenders, and that "the despotic laws of a CROMWELL and a ROBESPIERRE would mete out no more than justice to such a combination of men!!!"

The meaning of this seems to be clear. We understand it to be, that if the party cannot retain the SPOILS OF VICTORY in any other way, they will be fully justified in abolishing the present republican form of government, and investing the man who was BORN TO COMMAND, with the dictato-rial authority of a CROMWELL or a ROBESPIERRE. . . .

10

Diversifying Society and Economy

The first half of the 19th century was characterized by a Market Revolution that transformed American life. Improvements in transportation, communication, manufacturing, and finance integrated disparate segments of the United States economy into an emerging world system. By 1860, the new economy had displaced much of the old. This profound alteration contributed to enormous social change. In many areas, new arrangements displaced centuries of social tradition, affecting ideology, class structure, gender roles, and race relations. The documents that follow reveal some of the forces that contributed to this metamorphosis and their impact on society.

71

Description of a Conversion Experience at Cane Ridge, KY (1801)

By the dawn of the 19th century, growing numbers of Americans felt alienated from their well-educated, rational-minded clergy. This factor, coupled with a rapidly expanding frontier population and a shortage of ordained ministers, led some churches (especially the Baptists and Methodists) to ordain ministers who had less formal education. These individuals used revivals to appeal emotionally to their converts. Revivals, which became a hallmark of the Second Great Awakening, began on the frontier, but they ultimately spread throughout much of the country. Not only did converts develop closer community bonds, but with the new religion's emphasis on emotion and a personal approach to God, they also helped democratize American Christianity. The following selection contains an excerpt from the writings of James B. Finley, who describes his experiences immediately after attending the great Cane Ridge, Kentucky, revival in 1801.

Questions to Consider

1. What is the historical context of this document?
2. Why was James B. Finley curious about the revival at Cane Ridge?
3. What happened to Finley at Cane Ridge?

4. What impact would revivals such as Cane Ridge have on religion in America?

. . . About this time a great revival of religion broke out in the state of Kentucky. It was attended with such peculiar circumstances as to produce great alarm all over the country. It was reported that hundreds who attended the meetings were suddenly struck down, and would lie for hours and, sometimes, for days, in a state of insensibility; and that when they recovered and came out of that state, they would commence praising God for his pardoning mercy and redeeming love. This exercise was accompanied with that strange and unaccountable phenomenon denominated the jerks, in which hundreds of men and women would commence jerking backward and forward with great rapidity and violence, so much so that their bodies would bend so as to bring their heads near to the floor, and the hair of the women would crack like the lash of a driver's whip. This was not confined to any particular class of individuals, but saint, seeker, and sinner were alike subject to these wonderful phenomena.

The excitement created by these reports, was of the most intense and astonishing character. Some thought that the world was coming to an end; others that some dreadful calamity was coming upon the country as a judgment of God on the nation; others still, that it was the work of the devil, who had been unchained for a season, and assuming the garments of an angel of light, was permitted to deceive the ministers of religion and the very elect themselves. Many of the preachers spent whole Sabbaths in laboring to show that it was the work of the devil, and nothing but the wildest fanaticism, produced through the means of an overheated and distempered imagination. . . .

In the month of August, 1801, I learned that there was to be a great meeting at Cane Ridge, in my father's old congregation. Feeling a great desire to see the wonderful things which had come to my ears, and having been solicited by some of my old schoolmates to go over into Kentucky for the purpose of revisiting the scenes of my boyhood, I resolved to go. . . . We arrived upon the ground, and here a scene presented itself to my mind not only novel and unaccountable, but awful beyond description. A vast crowd, supposed by some to have amounted to twenty-five thousand, was collected together. The noise was like the roar of Niagara. The vast sea of human beings seemed to be agitated as if by a storm. I counted seven ministers, all preaching at one time, some on stumps, others in wagons, and one—the Rev. William Burke, now of Cincinnati—was standing on a tree which had, in falling, lodged against another. Some of the people were singing, others praying, some crying for mercy in the most piteous accents, while others were shouting most vociferously. While witnessing these scenes, a peculiarly-strange sensation, such as I had never felt before, came over me. My heart beat tumultuously, my knees trembled, my lip quivered, and I felt as though I must fall to the ground. A strange supernatural power seemed to pervade the

Autobiography of the Reverend James B. Finley, ed. W. P. Strickland (Cincinnati, 1854), 165–170.

entire mass of mind there collected. I became so weak and powerless that I found it necessary to sit down. Soon after I left and went into the woods, and there I strove to rally and man up my courage. I tried to philosophize in regard to these wonderful exhibitions, resolving them into mere sympathetic excitement—a kind of religious enthusiasm, inspired by songs and eloquent harangues. My pride was wounded, for I had supposed that my mental and physical strength and vigor could most successfully resist these influences.

After some time I returned to the scene of excitement, the waves of which, if possible, had risen still higher. The same awfulness of feeling came over me. I stepped up on to a log where I could have a better view of the surging sea of humanity. The scene that then presented itself to my mind was indescribable. At one time I saw at least five hundred swept down in a moment, as if a battery of a thousand guns had been opened upon them, and then, immediately followed shrieks and shouts that rent the very heavens. My hair rose up on my head, my whole frame trembled, the blood ran cold in my veins, and I fled for the woods a second time, and wished I had stayed at home. While I remained here my feelings became intense and insupportable. A sense of suffocation and blindness seemed to come over me, and I thought I was going to die. . . . In this state I wandered about from place to place, in and around the encampment. At times it seemed as if all the sins I had ever committed in my life were vividly brought up in array before my terrified imagination, and under their pressure I felt that I must die if I did not get relief. Then it was that I saw clearly through the thin vail of Universalism, and this refuge of lies was swept away by the Spirit of God. Then fell the scales from my sin-blinded eyes, and I realized, in all its force and power, the awful truth, that if I died in my sins I was a lost man forever. . . .

As soon as day broke I went to the woods to pray, and no sooner had my knees touched the ground than I cried aloud for mercy and salvation and fell prostrate. My cries were so loud that they attracted the attention of the neighbors, many of whom gathered around me. Among the number was a German from Switzerland, who had experienced religion. He, understanding fully, my condition, had me carried to his house and laid on a bed. The old Dutch saint directed me to look right away to the Savior. He then kneeled at the bedside and prayed for my salvation most fervently, in Dutch and broken English. He then rose and sung in the same manner, and continued singing and praying alternately till nine o'clock, when suddenly my load was gone, my guilt removed, and presently the direct witness from heaven shone full upon my soul. . . .

72

Promoting the Erie Canal (1818)

As the United States expanded westward, demands for internal improvements became an increasingly important issue. Congress passed a bill to fund road construction after the War of 1812, but President James Madison vetoed it, arguing that a constitutional amendment would be necessary for such legislation. As a result, internal improvements became the prerogative of the individual states. The most important of these transportation projects was New York's Erie Canal. Championed by Governor De Witt Clinton, the waterway was to connect the Great Lakes with the Atlantic by way of the Mohawk River system. By 1825, the canal opened and was an immediate success. Charles G. Haines was one of the canal's leading proponents. A native of New Hampshire, the young law student had just begun to serve as private secretary to Governor Clinton when he wrote the following excerpt.

Questions to Consider

1. What does Charles Haines believe the Erie Canal can do for the nation?
2. What advantages will the canal bring to the Great Lakes region and upstate New York?
3. According to Haines, in what ways will New York City will be affected?
4. How accurate is Haines in assessing the positive impact of the canal on New York?

. . . The people of this state early perceived the benefits of Internal Trade, and previous to the late war with England, the Grand Canal from the Hudson to Lake Erie was contemplated. Such an undertaking was alone suitable to a state of peace. It was accordingly postponed to that period when more favorable auspices should await its prosecution. That period arrived, when De Witt Clinton was unanimously called to the chief magistracy of the state. The eyes of the people were fixed upon him, with an expectation that the Great Western Canal would be vigorously prosecuted to its final completion. The work will be prosecuted and triumphantly finished. . . .

The length of the canal, from the Hudson to the Lakes, is calculated at three hundred and fifty-three miles, according to the report of the commissioners appointed by the New-York Legislature, on the 17th April, 1816. They observed, that in their opinion, "the dimensions of the Western or Erie Canal and Locks, should be as follows, viz.:—width on the water surface, forty feet; at the bottom, twenty-eight feet, and depth of water, four feet; the length of a lock ninety feet, and its width, twelve feet in the clear. Vessels carrying one hundred tons may navigate a canal of this size—and all the lumber produced in the country, and required for the market, may be transported upon it." The aggregate rise and fall is in feet 661 35, and the elevation of Lake Erie above the Hudson, is calculated to be in feet 564 85.—The number of locks will be seventy-seven. The canal has been divided into three great sections. The western section reaches from Lake Erie to Seneca River; the middle section leads from Seneca River to Rome, and the eastern, from Rome to Hudson. . . .

Charles G. Haines, *Considerations on the Great Western Canal, from the Hudson to Lake Erie* (Brooklyn, NY, 1818), 4–5, 7–12, 28.

We have before taken a view of the principal advantages that must result to our union, and to our republican institutions, by attaching the various sections of the country more immediately together, by means of internal communication. Our Great canal, in this respect, will produce a train of exclusive and permanent benefits, which could not, from local causes, pertain to any similar undertakings within the scope of ourselves or of the nation. When you connect the Hudson with the Lakes, by such a communication, you virtually place the Atlantic seaboard and the great western interior by the side of each other. From the ocean, you can pass through this whole chain of inland seas, navigable to vessels of the largest burthen. Nor should we stop here—New-York and New-Orleans could be brought, in point of intercourse, near each other. At trifling expense, and with no great effort of labor, you could open a communication by water, through which a vast commerce could be carried on from Lake Michigan to the Illinois River, which empties into the Mississippi above St. Louis, and traverses nearly the whole extent of that rising and fertile territory, which will soon be admitted as a state among the other sisters of the union. Even in high waters, there is now a navigation for small craft, between the waters of the Illinois and the southern extremity of Lake Michigan through Chenango Creek. . . .

Pause for a moment, and consider the mighty population which will yet cluster on the shores of this chain of Lakes, and the unnumbered streams which roll their tributary bounties into their bosoms! The great western world which reposes upon their wide-stretched shores, needs no description of ours, to enhance its value in the estimation of the American people. It will yet contain a population, unequalled by any in the world for industry, enterprize and independence; a population bound together by those ties of union and interest, created and fortified by a grand system of internal improvements, of which the Great western canal will be the bulwark. In the animating spectacle here presented in perspective, we see a great republican community, cemented by the strongest considerations that ever influenced a political body—assimilated in manners, laws, sentiments and maxims, with their eyes fixed on their connection with the seaboard, as the life and support of their prosperity and happiness.—Yes, in this noble race of citizens, we see the cradle of liberty, laws, and the arts; we see the hallowed light of our liberal institutions beaming in its native purity, blended with the mild lustre of virtue, magnanimity and intelligence. . . .

While referring to the advantages resulting to the nation, and to the state, from the Western Canal, we ought not to forget its effects on the prosperity of our own city. New-York is now, and ever must be, the great depot of that vast trade circulating between the country bordering on the Lakes, and the Atlantic seaboard. Would the increase of this trade to ten times its present extent be of no consequence to her interests? Does New-York forget that she is yet to contend with New-Orleans, for the character of the first commercial city of the new world? We shall not here draw a comparison between the natural advantages of the two places; but we do say, that without the Western Canal, the competition will be fearful, before the lapse of half a century. It is by drawing to her control the trade of the west and the north; it is by aiding the State Government, in every liberal undertaking, for the promotion of internal commerce, that New-York is to stand, without a rival on this side [of] the ocean. The Canal will render her a commercial emporium, second to none on the globe. It will pour into her bosom a tide of commerce, which must leave its bounties by the way, to enrich and adorn, like the floods of the Nile. In trade, in wealth, and in arts, it will render her the London of America. . . .

73

Charles G. Finney Describes the Rochester Revival (1830–31)

The Second Great Awakening was one of the most important cultural movements of the early 19th century. The waves of emotionally charged religious reform were so intense that upstate New York became known as the "Burned-Over District." One of the most "Burned-Over" areas was Rochester, New York. Located on Lake Ontario, Rochester had been a frontier village before the completion of the Erie Canal. The waterway brought access to distant markets and immediately transformed the community into one of America's most dynamic cities. But rapid change brought community stress, as hordes of newcomers sought a niche in a community with no firmly established structures. Charles Grandison Finney's visit in 1830 would change all of that. A religious experience caused him to leave the legal profession in 1821, and by the mid-1820s, his vivid sermons demanded that sinners in the audience repent or face eternal damnation. In his memoirs, excerpted as follows, Finney describes the techniques he used to win converts.

Questions to Consider

1. What is the author's perspective toward Rochester and its need for conversion?

2. Why does Charles G. Finney seem so eager to convert Rochester's leading citizens?

3. How did the author use social pressure to gain converts?

4. Compare and contrast the portrayal of religion found in this document with that contained in "Description of a Conversion Experience at Cane Ridge, KY" (Document 71). How do you account for the differences?

. . . I had never, I believe, except in rare instances, until I went to Rochester, used as a means of promoting revivals, what has since been called "the anxious seat." I had sometimes asked persons in the congregation to stand up; but this I had not frequently done. However, in studying upon the subject, I had often felt the necessity of some measure that would bring sinners to a stand. From my own experience and observation I had found, that with the higher classes especially, the greatest obstacle to be overcome was their fear of being known as anxious inquirers. They were too proud to take any position that would reveal them to others as anxious for their souls.

I had found also that something was needed, to make the impression on them that they were expected at once to give up their hearts; something that would call them to act, and act as publicly before the world, as they had in their sins; something that would commit them publicly to the service of Christ. When I had called them simply to stand up in the public congregation, I found that this had a very good effect; and so far as it went, it answered the purpose for which it was intended. But after all, I had felt for some time, that something more was necessary to bring them out from among the mass of the ungodly, to a public renunciation of their sinful ways, and a public committal of themselves to God.

At Rochester, if I recollect right, I first introduced this measure. . . . I made a call, I think for the first time, upon all that class of persons whose convictions were so ripe that they were willing to renounce their sins and give themselves to God, to come forward to certain seats which I requested to be vacated, and offer themselves up to God, while we made them subjects of prayer. A much larger number came forward than I expected, and among them was another prominent lady; and several others of her acquaintance, and belonging to the same circle of society, came forward. This increased the interest among that class of people; and it was soon seen that the Lord was aiming at the conversion of the highest classes of society. My meetings soon became thronged with that class. The Lawyers, physicians, merchants, and indeed all the most intelligent people, became more and more interested, and more and more easily influenced.

Very soon the work took effect, extensively, among the lawyers in that city. There has always been a large number of the leading lawyers of the state, resident at Rochester. The work soon got hold of numbers of these. They became very anxious, and came freely to our meetings of inquiry; and numbers of them came forward to the anxious seat, as it has since been called, and publicly gave their hearts to God. . . .

This revival made a great change in the moral state and subsequent history of Rochester. The great majority of the leading men and women in the city, were converted.

Memoirs of Rev. Charles G. Finney (New York, 1876), 288–290.

74

"Americans on the Move" (1835)

Numerous foreign travelers came to the United States during the antebellum period eager to report on the progress of the American experiment. None of these visitors has become better known for his sage observations of 1830s America than French nobleman Alexis de Tocqueville. Tocqueville came to America with his associate M. Gustave de Beaumont in 1831 to study American prisons and remained until the following year. During his short stay, Tocqueville had the opportunity to travel extensively and met with luminaries such as Albert Gallatin and Edward Livingston. His observations of the young nation gained great notoriety in both Europe and the United States. In Democracy in America, *Tocqueville described a people who, despite their differences, shared strong religious values, believed in their nation's special mission, and who, most noticeably, were fervently egalitarian. In this selection, Tocqueville describes Americans as "venturous conservatives" engaged in a restless quest to make money.*

Questions to Consider

1. Why are Americans in "constant motion"?
2. How would Tocqueville describe the typical American?
3. Why does he believe Americans are eager to make money?
4. Does Tocqueville's description of Americans seem consistent with the description found in Crèvecouer's "What Is an American?" (Document 23)? Does it seem consistent with traits described by Frances Trollope in "Commentary on Elections in Jacksonian America" (Document 69)?

Nothing tends to materialize man, and to deprive his work of the faintest trace of mind, more than extreme division of labor. In a country like America, where men devoted to special occupations are rare, a long apprenticeship cannot be required from anyone who embraces a profession. The Americans, therefore, change their means of gauging a livelihood very readily; and they suit their occupations to the exigencies of the moment, in the manner most profitable to themselves. Men are to be met with who have successively been barristers, farmers, merchants, ministers of the gospel, and physicians. If the American be less perfect in each craft than the European, at least there is scarcely any trade with which he is utterly unacquainted. His capacity is more general, and the circle of his intelligence is enlarged.

The inhabitants of the United States are never fettered by the axioms of their profession; they escape from all the prejudices of their present station; they are not more attached to one line of operation than to another; they are not more prone to employ an old method than a new one; they have no

Alexis de Tocqueville, *Democracy in America,* trans. Henry Reeve (New York, 1900), 1: 432–434.

rooted habits, and they easily shake off the influence which the habits of other nations might exercise upon their minds from conviction that their country is unlike any other, and that its situation is without a precedent in the world. America is a land of wonders, in which everything is in constant motion, and every movement seems an improvement. The idea of novelty is there indissolubly connected with the idea of amelioration. No natural boundary seems to be set to the efforts of man: and what is not yet done is only what he has not yet attempted to do.

This perpetual change which goes on in the United States, these frequent vicissitudes of fortune, accompanied by such unforeseen fluctuations in private and in public wealth, serve to keep the minds of citizens in a perpetual state of feverish agitation, which admirably invigorates their exertions, and keeps them in a state of excitement above the ordinary level of mankind. The whole life of an American is passed like a game of chance, a revolutionary crisis, or a battle. As the same causes are continually in operation throughout the country, they ultimately impart an irresistible impulse to the national character. The American, taken as a chance specimen of his countrymen, must then be a man of singular warmth in his desires; enterprising, fond of adventure, and above all, of innovation. The same bent is manifest in all that he does; he introduces it into his political laws, his religious doctrines, his theories of social economy, and his domestic occupations; he bears it with him in the depths of the backwoods, as well as in the business of the city. It is this same passion, applied to maritime commerce, which makes him the cheapest and the quickest trader in the world.

As long as the sailors of the United States retain these inspiriting advantages, and the practical superiority which they derive from them, they will not only continue to supply the wants of the producers and consumers of their own country, but they will tend more and more to become, like the English, the factors of all other peoples. This prediction has already begun to be realized; we perceive that the American traders are introducing themselves as intermediate agents in the commerce of several European nations; and America will offer a still wider field to their enterprise. . . .

It is unquestionable that the Americans of the North will one day supply the wants of the Americans of the South. Nature has placed them in contiguity, and has furnished the former with every means of establishing a permanent connection with those States, and of gradually filling their markets. The merchants of the United States could only forfeit these natural advantages if he were very inferior to the merchant of Europe; to whom he is, on the contrary, superior in several respects. The Americans of the United States already exercise a very considerable moral influence upon all the peoples of the New World. They are the source of intelligence, and all the nations which inhabit the same continent are already accustomed to consider them as the most enlightened, the most powerful, and the most wealthy members of the great American family. All eyes are therefore turned towards the Union; and the States of which the body is composed are the models which the other communities try to imitate to the best of their power; it is from the United States that they borrow their political principles and their laws. . . .

75

An Optimistic View of the Promise of the Marketplace

The Market Revolution that swept over many parts of the nation in the first half of the 19th century brought dramatic change. In the 18th century, most Americans lived in tiny rural communities where they produced most goods for home or local consumption. However, changes in transportation, communication, finance, and manufacturing pulled many rural Americans into a system of exchange that enabled them to produce goods for distant markets at substantial profit. The first image is of Lockport, New York, a town created by the best-known transportation improvement of the era, the Erie Canal. Another outgrowth of market change can be found in the second image: The Market Revolution's contribution to class development redefined gender roles. The second image offers a depiction of ideal gender types in the new middle class.

Questions to Consider

1. What conclusions can be drawn about the Erie Canal's impact from the first image?

2. Does the first image seem to be a "real" or "romanticized" version of what Lockport looked like? Why?

3. What can you deduce about women's roles from the second image? The role of husbands? What can you deduce about middle-class attitudes in general?

Library of Congress, Prints and Photographs Division, LC-USZ62-49239

"View of the Upper Village of Lockport, Niagara Co. N.Y."

Library of Congress, Prints and Photographs Division, LC-USZ62-92903

"Look at Papa"

76

American Mania for Railroads (1834)

The invention of the railroad was one of the most significant transportation develop-ments in human history. A primary symbol of the Industrial Revolution, the locomo-tive freed people from their reliance on water transportation while expediting long-dis-tance movement. In this selection from Society, Manners and Politics in the United States, *Michel Chevalier, a French visitor who toured the United States from 1833 to 1835, observed some of the United States' earliest rail projects. Chevalier's interest in America and its railroads grew out of his belief that America held the key to under-standing the future. He argued that the nation's "most visible emblem" was the loco-motive. The developing rail network that attracted Chevalier's attention did indeed herald the American future, as it shifted patterns of trade and accelerated regional economic specialization.*

Questions to Consider

1. Why is Michel Chevalier so enthusiastic about railroad development in the United States?

2. What are some problems with the Boston to New Orleans route Cheva-lier described?

3. Compare and contrast the views expressed in this document with those contained in Haines' "Promoting the Erie Canal" (Document 72)? Why are internal improvements so important to America?

4. What does the support for internal improvements say about antebellum America?

. . . The distance from Boston to New Orleans is 1600 miles, or twice the distance from Havre to Marseilles. It is highly probable, that within a few years this immense line will be covered by a series of railroads stretching from bay to bay, from river to river, and offering to the ever-impatient Americans the service of their rapid cars at the points where the steamboats leave their passengers. This is not a castle in the air, like so many of those grand schemes which are projected amidst the fogs of the Seine, the Loire, and the Garonne; it is already half completed. The railroad from Boston to Providence is in active progress; the work goes on a l'Americaine, that is to say, rapidly. From New York to Philadelphia, there will soon be not only one open to travel, but two in competition with each other, the one on the right, the other on the left bank of the Delaware; the passage between the two cities will be made in seven hours, five hours on the railroad, and two in the steamboat, in the beautiful Hudson and the magnificent Bay of New York, which the Americans, who are not afflicted by modesty, compare with the Bay of Naples. From Philadelphia, travellers go to Baltimore by the Delaware and Chesapeake, and by the Newcastle and Frenchtown railroad, in eight hours; from Baltimore to Washington, a railroad has been resolved upon, a company chartered, the shares taken, and the work begun, all within the space of a few months. Between Washington and Blakely, in North Carolina, 60 miles of railroad are completed, from Blakely northwards. A company has just been chartered to complete the remaining space, that is, from Richmond to the Potomac, a distance of 70 miles, and the Potomac bears you to the Federal city by Mt. Vernon, a delightful spot, the patrimony of George Washington, where he passed his honored old age, and where his body now reposes in a modest tomb. Between Washington and Blakely, those who prefer the steamboats, may take another route; by descending the Chesapeake to Norfolk, they will find another railroad, 70 miles in length, of which two thirds are now finished, and which carries them to Blakely, and even beyond. Blakely is a new town, which you will not find on any map, born of yesterday; it is the eldest, and as yet the only daughter of the Petersburg and Blakely railroad. From Blakely to Charleston the distance is great, but the Americans are enterprising, and there is no region in the world in which railroads can be constructed so easily and so cheaply; the surface has been graded by nature, and the vast forests which cover it, will furnish the wood of which the railroad will be made; for here most of these works have a wooden superstructure. From Charleston, a railroad 137 miles in length, as

Michel Chevalier, *Society, Manners and Politics in the United States*, trans. from 3rd ed. by Thomas G. Bradford (Boston, 1839), 83–87.

yet the longest in the world, extends to Augusta, whence to Montgomery, Alabama, there is a long interval to be supplied. From this last town steamboats descend the River Alabama to Mobile, and those who do not wish to pay their respects to the Gulf of Mexico, on their way to New Orleans, will soon find a railroad which will spare them the necessity of offering this act of homage to the memory of the great Cortez.

Within ten years this whole line will be completed, and traversed by locomotive engines, provided the present crisis terminates promptly and happily, as I hope it will. Ten years is a long time in these days, and a plan, whose execution requires ten years, seems like a romance or a dream. But in respect to railroads, the Americans have already something to show. Pennsylvania, which by the last census, in 1830, contained only 1,348,000 inhabitants, has 325 miles of railroads actually completed, or which will be so within the year, without reckoning 76 miles which the capitalists of Philadelphia have constructed in the little States of New Jersey and Delaware. The total length of all the railroads in France is 95 miles, that is, a little more than what the citizens of Philadelphia, in their liberality, have given to their poor neighbors. In the State of New York, whose population is the most adventurous and the most successful in their speculations, there are at present only four or five short railroads, but if the sixth part of those which are projected and authorized by the legislature, are executed, New York will not be behind Pennsylvania in this respect. The merchants of Baltimore, which at the time of the Declaration of Independence contained 6,000 inhabitants, and which now numbers 100,000, have taken it into their heads to make a railroad between their city and the Ohio, a distance of above 300 miles. They have begun it with great spirit, and have now finished about one third of the whole road. In almost every section east of the Ohio and the Mississippi, there are railroads projected, in progress, or completed, and on most of them locomotive steam-engines are employed. There are some in the Alleghenies, whose inclined planes are really terrific, from their great inclination; these were originally designed only for the transportation of goods, but passenger-cars have been set up on them, at the risk of breaking the necks of travellers. . . .

77

Urban Riots (1835)

By the 1830s, New York City had begun to feel the full effects of market change. The Market Revolution offered opportunity to some, but skilled artisans began to discover that they could not compete with the emerging factory system. The new economy demanded huge quantities of cheap labor, much of which came from abroad, particularly Ireland. By the mid-1830s, immigrants crowded the Five Points neighborhood of lower Manhattan. But in the eyes of middle-class New Yorkers, Five Points was the most notorious slum in America. Newspapers printed lurid accounts of the dangers that lurked in that neighborhood. The following selection from the Niles Weekly Register *depicts a series of riots in 1834 and 1835, which it claims was the work of the Irish immigrants in the neighborhood.*

Questions to Consider

1. Does the author of this selection consider the Irish to be "real Americans"? What does this say about antebellum attitudes toward ethnicity?

2. Why do mobs seem so threatening to Americans in the 1830s when they had been so important to the success of the American Revolutionary movement? What had changed?

3. What does the author recommend as a solution to the problem?

4. Why do you suppose the riots took place? Why in Five Points?

And—the New York "Evening Star," with reference to these matters say—

"The riots at the spring election of 1834 were the boldest attacks on the liberties of the people ever known in this country. An organized force, armed with deadly weapons, was brought into the field to overawe the freedom of election and foreigners beat our citizens at the polls; beat the mayor, knocked down and maltreated the watch, and for a time, the peace and safety of the whole city was menaced. The ringleaders were richly rewarded by the Albany regency, and a number of the conspicuous rioters were arrested and bailed by their friends, since which time nothing had been heard of them—nothing done with them. In the following July, the abolition riots took place: the accused were tried, convicted, and sent to the penitentiary. Justice overtook them speedily, because they were *Americans;* but the Irishman engaged in the worst and most dangerous riots of the preceding spring remained untouched and are still allowed to be free." . . .

There was an outrageous riot in New York, on Sunday last—but the mayor and police succeeded in quieting it, after great exertions, capturing some of the ringleaders—which the "Commercial Advertiser" in the "mirth of sorrow," advises shall be immediately dismissed to save expenses!

Other riots, or indeed, a succession of them, have happened in New York; at and about the "Five Points" in the famous 6th ward—in which a physician was killed, who was attending a patient in the neighborhood, a Dr. McCaffrey, and many others very seriously—justice Lowndes being among the wounded. The mayor and police had severe duties to perform, but they arrested many persons such as "Patrick O'Rourke, Patrick Mulooney, Tom Sullivan, Barney McCanan,"—the police office was filled with them. It was proposed to organize a regiment of these, to be called the "*O'Connell guards!*" Several public houses were attacked during those affrays—and the city was in a most unfortunate condition.

(Baltimore) *Niles Weekly Register,* June 27, 1835, 48: 289–290.

The "Herald" speaking of these things says—

Such proceedings are truly disgraceful in the city. Our constitution guarantees to all men equal protection, no matter to what nation they belong. These desperate attacks upon public property call loudly for immediate municipal interference. The leaders of this disgraceful transaction ought to be discovered, and a warning example made of them. Under such a state of things, no individual can consider his life was properly safe. Why didn't the police do their duty? Have we none? or were they asleep?

These riots we believe began with the Irish of the Five Points on Sunday afternoon. That neighborhood and the contiguous streets have been a scene of demoralizations ever since. The violent inhabitants of the city are prowling about every night. We have hitherto defended the Irish from the attacks of their foes—but we will not countenance any riotous proceedings in them or any others. We shall hold their clergy—from the bishop down to the sexton, responsible for the morals of their disciples. We must examine this matter seriously. Let the whole militia of the city turn out under the authority of the corporation, and put down at once, this riotous disposition. If the Irish or others will not be quiet by mild words, other means must be [tried].

And the "*Commercial Advertiser*" observes—

As was expected, or rather feared, the tranquility of the city was again disturbed last [or Monday] evening by mobs composed partly of Irishmen and partly of Americans, between whom it was apparent that a hostile feeling existed. We are too heartily sick and disgusted with these miserable evidences of our unsound and unsafe condition, with such elements of discord and violence raving among us, and but too many who ought to know and to do better, ready to excite them into fearful activity, to go into the details; it is enough to say that crowds assembled in various places—that angry words were spoken and soon followed by blows—that the watchmen and the police had great difficulty in restoring peace—that the mayor and other officers were present and did their duty; and that several of the rioters were arrested—but not until some property had been destroyed, and that personal injury sustained by several individuals.

It is probably that the idea of forming an *Irish* regiment, of *American* citizens, has chiefly caused the excitement.

78

Women Workers Protest "Lowell Wage Slavery" (1847)

In 1822, the Boston Associates created a cotton mill complex at the falls of the Merrimack River in northeastern Massachusetts that they named Lowell. These mills soon attracted laborers from nearby rural New England, most of whom were young women. Although some came to Lowell to escape rural boredom, more worked in the mills because of declining economic opportunities in the countryside. Lowell's founders com-

pared the dreary conditions of England's industrial towns with the Lowell system, which sought to contribute to the moral, spiritual, and intellectual improvement of the "Lowell girls." As such, Lowell was part finishing school and part industrial employer. Countless visitors came to marvel at the idyllic industrial village. The following account, however, reveals that the Lowell experience also had another side.

Questions to Consider

1. What is the difference between the "romance" and the "reality" for the "Lowell girls"?
2. Why are the factory girls unable to appreciate lectures and the books that are available?
3. In what ways does this article characterize the effects of working in Lowell?
4. How do you suppose Charles Haines, author of "Promoting the Erie Canal" (Document 72), would respond to this document?

Aristocratic strangers, in broad cloths and silks, with their imaginations excited by the wonderful stories—romances of Factory Life—which they have heard, have paid hasty visits to Lowell, or Manchester, and have gone away to praise, in prose and verse, the beauty of our "Factory Queens," and the comfort, elegance and almost perfection, of the arrangements by which the very fatherly care of Agents, Superintendents, Overseers, &c., has surrounded them. To these nice visitors everything in and around a Lowell Cotton Mill is bathed in an atmosphere of rose-colored light. . . .

These lovers of the Romance of Labor—they don't like the reality very well—see not the pale and emaciated ones. They see not those who wear Consumption's hectic flush. They think little of the weariness and pain of those fair forms, as they stand there, at the loom and spindle, thirteen long hours, each day! They know not how long these hours of toil seem to them, as they look out upon the fields, and hills, and woods, which lie beyond the Merrimack, steeped in golden sunlight and radiant with beauty. . . . Six days shalt thou labor and do all thy work, and on the seventh thou shalt go to church, is the Commandment as improved by the mammon worshiping Christianity of modern Civilization. The factory girl is required to go to meeting on Sunday, where long, and too often unmeaning, word-prayers are repeated, and dull prosey sermons "delivered," and where God is worshiped, according to law, by pious Agents and Overseers, while the poor Irishman is blasting rocks for them in the Corporation's canal, that the mills may not be stopped on Monday.

There are lectures of various kinds, some of them free, and others requiring only a trifling fee to secure admission, to all who wish it. Then there are also libraries of well selected books, to which all can have access.

"Factory Life—Romance and Reality," (Boston) *Voice of Industry,* December 3, 1847, p. 2.

Those who recollect the fable of Tantalus in the old Mythology, will be able to appreciate the position of a large portion of the population with respect to these exalted privileges. . . . The unremitted toil of thirteen long hours, drains off the vital energy and unfits for study or reflection. They need amusement, relaxation, rest, and not mental exertion of any kind. A really sound and instructive lecture cannot, under such circumstances, be appreciated, and the lecturer fails, to a great extent, in making an impression.—"Jim Crow" performances are much better patronized than scientific lectures, and the trashy, milk-and-water sentimentalities of the *Lady's Book* and *Olive Branch,* are more read than the works of Gibbon, or Goldsmith, or Bancroft.

If each factory girl could suspend her labors in the Mill for a few months each year, for the purpose of availing herself of the advantages for intellectual culture by which she is surrounded, much good might be derived. . . . But day by day they feel their over-tasked systems give way.—A dizziness in the head or a pain in the side, or the shoulders or the back, admonishes them to return to their country homes before it is too late. But too often these friendly monitions are unheeded. They resolve to toil a little longer.—But nature cannot be cheated, and the poor victim of a false system of Industrial Oppression is carried home—to die. . . . There are now in our very midst hundreds of these loving, self-sacrificing martyr-spirits. They will die unhonored and unsung, but not unwept; for the poor factory girl has a home and loved ones, and dark will be that home, and sad those loved ones when the light of her smile shines on them no more.

79

"On Irish Emigration" (1852)

The economic transformation of antebellum America also brought sweeping demographic changes. The demands of early industrialism created a huge need for unskilled labor, which was often filled by immigrants. The majority who arrived before 1850 came from Ireland, their numbers further swelled by the potato famine of 1845–48. The enormous quantity of immigrants who poured into America elicited a variety of responses, ranging from nativism to the creation of an immigration bureaucracy to process the newly arrived. In the following account, Edward Everett Hale discusses this bureaucracy. Hale, a Unitarian minister, was a frequent contributor to local newspapers who espoused a New Civilization, which envisioned an improvement of all human relationships. Hale's original letters first appeared in the Boston Daily Advertiser, *a newspaper edited by his father, and later were reprinted as* Letters on Irish Emigration.

Questions to Consider

1. Why are shippers so interested in transporting Irish immigrants to America?

2. Why were immigrants examined?

3. What can you deduce about the U.S. economy from this selection?

4. Compare and contrast the views of Irishmen contained in this document with those found in "Urban Riots" (Document 77). How do you account for the similarities? Differences?

. . . The competition between different lines of packets and different shipping houses, had been enough to scatter through the most barbarous parts of Ireland full information as to the means of passage to America. The most remote villages receive the advertisements of different lines, just as we find in our most remote villages the inducements which the same lines scatter to Irishmen to send out remittances and passage tickets for their friends.

The correspondence from this country carries a great deal of detailed information, and at present it is the principal means of supply for the expenses of the voyage. An emigrant who has succeeded here, sends out for his friends, and sends money enough to bring them. Or, which amounts to the same thing, he buys here passage tickets which he sends to them. . . .

The importance of this business to ship owners will readily be seen. Ships of large accommodations for freighting, which carry out our bulky raw produce, and bring back the more condensed manufactures of England, have just the room to spare, which is made into accommodations for these passengers. In Mr. Robert B. Minturn's testimony before the "Lords' Committee" June 20, 1848, he says that the amounts paid for the passage of emigrants go very far towards paying the expense of voyages of ships from America to Europe and back.

By far the larger number of these emigrants collect at Liverpool therefore,—the large commerce of the port offering all the facilities for the cheapest passage. Of 223,078 who sailed from the United Kingdom to the United States in 1850, 165,828 were from Liverpool, 31,297 were from Irish ports, and 11,448 from Scotch ports. The ease of passage from Ireland to Liverpool carries most of the Irish emigration that way. The English Commissioners suppose that almost all the Liverpool emigration is Irish; certainly much more than nine-tenths of it. Our own returns at New York confirm this supposition.

Vessels engaged in this trade, are now subject to a double inspection. In Great Britain they are examined by English Officers, that it may be known that they comply with the British statute,—and here, that they may comply with ours. The experience of the awful suffering of emigrants in 1847, when of 90,000 who embarked for Canada in British vessels, 15,000 died on the way, or after arrival, called the attention of the English Government to the necessity of a more stringent law for passenger vessels. . . .

THREE-FOURTHS at least of the emigrants arriving in this country land at the port of New York. . . . [T]he subsequent inspection, though rapid, is complete enough to prevent much danger of deception. The Captain is bound to report, within twenty-four hours of his arrival, to the Mayor of the

Edward E. Hale, *Letters on Irish Emigration* (Boston, 1852), 6–10, 24–26. Published letters in the *Boston Daily Advertiser*.

city, the number of his passengers who are citizens, and the number who, being foreigners, have never been bonded, their place of birth, last residence, age, name and occupation. He shows this report to the Health officer. The officer then questions him and the ship's physician as to the health of the passengers, whether any of them are lunatic, idiot, deaf, dumb, blind or infirm, if so whether they are accompanied by relatives who can take care of them; and again with regard to the deaths on the passage. All these particulars the Captain is bound to specify in his report to the Mayor, and if he fail to specify them correctly, the Commissioners of emigration on the report of their Health Officer would prosecute him for the penalty provided. Such penalties, when recovered, are a part of their available funds.

While the Health Officer obtains the details of the Captain's report, the emigrants are mustered on deck for his personal examination. He then goes below with his men,—examines the emigrant decks, that he may see those who are not well enough to go on deck,—and satisfy himself that no persons are concealed on board, so far as such an examination will satisfy him. This visit enables him to observe, in a measure, whether the United States statute regarding the treatment of emigrants on board any vessel has been violated. This statute applies to all vessels arriving here; the examination made in England having been made, of course, with reference to the provisions of the English laws. Any violation of the American statute would be reported by the Emigrant Commissioners to the United States Attorney.

This examination finished, he goes on deck, with his men, to inspect those reported as in health who are assembled there. You know that in some instances there have been more than a thousand on a single vessel. The inspection is rapid indeed. A rope is drawn across the vessel, leaving a passage between the Health Officer and one of his boatmen, wide enough for one emigrant at a time to pass through. They pass quickly through, from the throng where they are assembled, and are counted as they go. If the quick eye of the Health Officer detects a blind, deaf, dumb or idiotic person,—or one who has any aspect of sickness, he stops him, questions him,—and if he do not pass such questioning satisfactorily, he is reported. The main object of this personal examination, however, with that made below, is to obtain evidence that the ship has not brought more than the number of passengers allowed by law.

At this same visit the Health Officer and his men distribute among the emigrants papers of simple advice, which are prepared by the Commissioners in different languages.

If, now, among those ascertained to be sick, there are any suffering under diseases classed as contagious, they are landed at the Quarantine Hospital. The whole vessel and passengers, of course, are subjected to the Quarantine arrangements of the Port. If there be other sick passengers, unable to provide for themselves, the Commissioners of emigration are at once notified of the fact, and on the arrival of the vessel at New York, these persons are removed to the emigrant hospital at Ward's Island, of which I shall speak hereafter. . . .

11

Social Reform

T he economic and social changes that swept antebellum America were accompanied by a reform crusade that sought to morally revitalize the republic. Influenced by such diverse elements as the Second Great Awakening, republican ideas of liberty, and the perceived decline of revolutionary values, reformers strove to perfect American society and institutions. Although reformers could be found throughout America, the movement was centered in the northern states. There, a small but vocal minority agitated for an end to slavery, expanded political rights for women, reform of the penal system, and free public education for the masses, often in the face of a hostile audience. The following documents illustrate some of the reformers', and their opponents', methods and goals.

80

"Appeal to the Coloured Citizens of the World" (1829)

West Indian and southern slave insurrections of the late 18th and early 19th centuries made clear that large numbers of African Americans resisted their position. The following document contains a selection from Walker's Appeal . . . to the Coloured Citizens of the World. *Author David Walker, a free black born in North Carolina, had traveled widely in the South and was well read, especially in the classics. In 1827, he left the South to settle in Boston, where he opened a clothing business and became active in the Massachusetts General Colored Association. In 1829, he produced this antislavery pamphlet. The* Appeal *not only refuted widely held myths of the happy slave and the ignorant African American, but it also demanded that African Americans respond to their oppression. Walker's appeal alarmed many in both the North and South; the state legislatures of Georgia, Virginia, and North Carolina held secret sessions to consider the pamphlet, while Boston mayor Harrison Gray Otis condemned Walker's views. Walker's work, which he reissued shortly before his mysterious death in 1830, prompted northern abolitionists to adopt a more aggressive stance against slavery.*

Questions to Consider

1. How does David Walker describe slavery?

2. What is Walker's appeal to slaves?

3. How do Walker's views differ from those of his white contemporaries?

4. Compare and contrast the views contained in this document with those expressed in "Mexican View of U.S. Occupation" (Document 90). What conclusions can you draw concerning mid-19th-century white Americans' views toward people of other races and cultures?

. . . [A]ll the inhabitants of the earth, (except, however, the sons of Africa) are called men, and of course are, and ought to be free. But we, (colored people) and our children are brutes!! and of course are, and ought to be SLAVES to the American people and their children forever!! to dig their mines and work their farms; and thus go on enriching them, from one generation to another with our blood and our tears!!!!

. . . we, (colored people of these United States of America) are the most wretched, degraded and abject set of beings that ever lived since the world began, and that the white Americans having reduced us to the wretched state of slavery, treat us in that condition more cruel (they being an enlightened and Christian people,) than any heathen nation did any people whom it had reduced to our condition. These affirmations are so well confirmed in the minds of all unprejudiced men, who have taken the trouble to read histories, that they need no elucidation from me. . . .

Do they not institute laws to prohibit us from marrying among the whites? I would wish, candidly, however, before the Lord, to be understood, that I would not give a pinch of snuff to be married to any white person I ever saw in all the days of my life. And I do say it, that the black man, or man of color, who will leave his own color (provided he can get one, who is good for any thing) and marry a white woman, to be a double slave to her, just because she is white, ought to be treated by her as he surely will be. . . .

. . . show me a page of history, either sacred or profane, on which a verse can be found, which maintains, that the Egyptians heaped the insupportable insult upon the children of Israel, by telling them that they were not of the human family. Can the whites deny the charge? Have they not, after having reduced us to the deplorable condition of slaves under their feet, held us as descending originally from the tribes of Monkeys or Orangutans? . . . So far, my brethren, were the Egyptians from heaping those insults upon their slaves, that the Pharaoh's daughter took Moses, a son of Israel for her own. . . .

They think because they hold us in their infernal chains of slavery, that we wish to be white, or of their color—but they are dreadfully deceived—we wish to be just as it pleased our Creator to have made us, and no avaricious

---

David Walker, *Walker's Appeal, in Four Articles: Together with a Preamble to Coloured Citizens of the World* (Boston, 1830), 11–87.

and unmerciful wretches, have any business to make slaves of, or hold us in slavery. How would they like for us to make slaves of, and hold them in cruel slavery, and murder them as they do to us? . . .

Fear not the number and education of our enemies, against whom we shall have to contend for our lawful light; guaranteed to us by our Maker; for why should we be afraid, when God is, and will continue, (if we continue humble) to be on our side?

The man who would not fight under our Lord and Master Jesus Christ, in the Glorious and heavenly cause of freedom and of God—to be delivered from the most wretched, abject and servile slavery, that ever a people was afflicted with since the foundation of the world, to the present day—ought to be kept with all of his children or family, in slavery, or in chains, to be butchered by his *cruel enemies*. . . .

I have been for years troubling the pages of historians, to find out what our fathers have done to the white Christians of America, to merit such condign punishment as they have inflicted upon them, and do continue to inflict upon us their children. But I must aver, that my researches have hitherto been to no effect. I have therefore, come to the immoveable conclusion, that they (Americans) have, and do continue to punish us for nothing else, but for enriching them and their country. For I cannot conceive of anything else. Nor will I ever believe otherwise, until the Lord shall convince me. . . .

We, and the world wish to see the charges of Mr. Jefferson refuted by the blacks themselves, . . . I know well, that there are some talents and learning among the colored people of this country, which we have not a chance to develop, in consequence of oppression; but our oppression ought not to hinder us from acquiring all we can. For we will have a chance to develop them by and by. God will not suffer us, always to be oppressed. Our sufferings will come to an end, in spite of all the Americans this side of eternity. Then we will want all the learning and talents among ourselves, and perhaps more, to govern ourselves.—"Every dog must have its day," the American's is coming to an end.

But let us review Mr. Jefferson's remarks respecting us some further. Comparing our miserable fathers, with the learned philosophers of Greece, he says: . . . "Epictetus, Terence and Phaedrus, were slaves,—but they were of the race of whites. It is not their condition, then, but nature, which has produced the distinction." . . . I am after those who know and feel, that we are MEN, as well as other people; to them, I say, that unless we try to refute Mr. Jefferson's arguments respecting us, we will only establish them.

. . . Are we MEN!!—I ask you, O my brethren! are we MEN? Did our creator make us to be slaves to dust and ashes like ourselves? Are they not dying worms as well as we? Have they not to make their appearance before the tribunal of Heaven, to answer for the deeds done in the body, as well as we? Have we any other Master but Jesus Christ alone? Is he not their Master as well as ours?—What right then, have we to obey and call any other Master, but Himself? How we could be so submissive to a gang of men, whom we cannot tell whether they are as good as ourselves or not, I never could conceive. However, this is shut up with the Lord, and we cannot precisely tell—but I declare, we judge men by their works.

The whites have always been an unjust, jealous, unmerciful, avaricious and blood-thirsty set of beings, always seeking after power and authority. . . .

81

William Lloyd Garrison on Slavery (1831)

William Lloyd Garrison's name remains synonymous with the abolitionist movement. A native of Newburyport, Massachusetts, Garrison bounced from printing job to printing job before working for Quaker abolitionist Benjamin Lundy on the Genius of Universal Emancipation *in Baltimore. By 1830, Garrison had left Lundy because of philosophical differences over emancipation and set out to publish his own newspaper. The following selection comes from Garrison's first issue of* The Liberator, *published in January 1831. In it, Garrison makes clear his uncompromising views toward slavery. Two years later, Garrison was instrumental in creating the New England Anti-Slavery Society. Garrison's views brought him approbation in both the North and the South; in 1835, Boston officials requested that he soften his public statements. When he refused, a mob threatened his life and local officials jailed him for his own safety. Despite these setbacks, he remained resolute in his convictions. His support for female membership in the society led to a split among American abolitionists in the early 1840s.*

Questions to Consider

1. Why does William Lloyd Garrison advocate emancipation and enfranchisement of slaves?
2. Why will he be uncompromising on the issue?
3. Why would Garrison's views be seen as controversial in the 1830s?
4. Would Garrison agree with David Walker (Document 80) about the status of African Americans?

During my recent tour for the purpose of exciting the minds of the people by a series of discourses on the subject of slavery, every place that I visited gave fresh evidence of the fact that a greater revolution in public sentiment was to be effected in the free states—and particularly in New England—than at the south. I found contempt more bitter, opposition more active, detraction more relentless, prejudice more stubborn, and apathy more frozen, than among slave owners themselves. Of course, there were individual exceptions to the contrary. This state of things afflicted, but did not dishearten me. I determined, at every hazard, to lift up the standard of emancipation in the

"To the Public," (Boston) *The Liberator*, January 1, 1831, p. 1.

eyes of the nation, within sight of Bunker Hill and in the birth place of liberty. That standard is now unfurled; and long may it float, unhurt by the spoliations of time or the missiles of a desperate foe—yea, till every chain be broken, and every bondman set free! Let southern oppressors tremble—let their secret abettors tremble—let their northern apologists tremble—let all the enemies of the persecuted blacks tremble.

. . . Assenting to the 'self-evident truth' maintained in the American Declaration of Independence, 'that all men are created equal, and endowed by their Creator with certain inalienable rights—among which are life, liberty and the pursuit of happiness,' I shall strenuously contend for the immediate enfranchisement of our slave population. . . .

I am aware, that many object to the severity of my language; but is there not cause for severity? I will be as harsh as truth, and as uncompromising as justice. On this subject, I do not wish to think, or speak, or write, with moderation. No! no! Tell a man whose house is on fire, to give a moderate alarm; tell him to moderately rescue his wife from the hands of the ravisher; tell the mother to gradually extricate her babe from the fire into which it has fallen;—but urge me not to use moderation in a cause like the present. I am in earnest—I will not equivocate—I will not excuse—I will not retreat a single inch—AND I WILL BE HEARD. The apathy of the people is enough to make every statue leap from its pedestal, and to hasten the resurrection of the dead.

It is pretended, that I am retarding the cause of emancipation by the coarseness of my invective, and the precipitancy of my measure. The charge is not true. On this question my influence,—humble as it is,—is felt at this moment to a considerable extent, and shall be felt in coming years—not perniciously, but beneficially—not as a curse, but as a blessing; and posterity will bear testimony that I was right. I desire to thank God, that he enables me to disregard 'the fear of man which bringeth a snare,' and to speak this truth in its simplicity and power.

And here I close with this fresh dedication:

Oppression! I have seen thee, face to face,
  And met thy cruel eye and cloudy brow;
  But thy soul-withering glance I fear not now—
  For dread to prouder feelings doth give place
  Of deep abhorrence! Scorning the disgrace
  Of slavish knees that at thy footstool bow,
  I also kneel—but with far other bow
  Do hail thee and thy herd of hirelings base:—
  I swear, while life-blood warms my throbbing veins,
  Still to oppose and thwart, with heart and hand,
  Thy brutalizing sway—till Afric's chains
  Are burst, and Freedom rules the rescued land,—
  Trampling Oppression and his iron rod:
  Such is the vow I take—So HELP ME GOD!'
                        William Lloyd Garrison.
                        Boston, January 1, 1831.

82
―――――――

Horace Mann on Educational Reform (1840)

Free public education appealed to reformers, who believed in the individual's capability for improvement while arguing that education provided opportunity and helped social- ize the masses. Horace Mann was the best known of the early reformers. Trained as a lawyer, Mann served in both houses of the Massachusetts legislature before becoming Senate president in 1836. Under his leadership, the legislature created a state board of education in 1837 to oversee the Massachusetts public school system. Mann aban- doned his promising political career to oversee the state's educational reforms. Under his leadership, Massachusetts became a model for other reform-minded states, as Mann increased the number of free public schools and regularized teacher training and cur- riculum. He remained board secretary until 1848, when he resigned to serve in the U.S. House of Representatives. In 1852, he made an unsuccessful bid to become gov- ernor. The following selection is a letter that Mann included in his 1839 annual report to the state legislature.

Questions to Consider

1. Why does the railroad contractor prefer literate workers?
2. According to the contractor, how are the literate people better citizens?
3. Why was teacher education important?
4. Compare the view of immigrants contained in this document with those expressed in "Urban Riots" (Document 77).

EXTRACTS FROM A LETTER OF JONATHAN CRANE, ESQ., FOR SEVERAL YEARS A LARGE CONTRACTOR ON THE RAILROADS IN MASSACHUSETTS. My principal business, for about ten years past, has been grading railroads. During that time, the num- ber of men employed has varied from fifty to three hundred and fifty, nearly all Irishmen, with the exception of superintendents. Some facts have been so apparent, that my superintendents and myself could not but notice them: these I will freely give you. I should say that not less than three thousand dif- ferent men have been, more or less, in my employment during the before- mentioned period, and the number that could read and write intelligibly was about one to eight. Independently of their natural endowments, those who could read and write, and had some knowledge of the first principles of arithmetic, have almost invariably manifested a readiness to apprehend what

―――――――
Horace Mann, "Report for 1839," *Annual Reports on Education* (Boston, 1868), 8–10.

was required of them, and skill in performing it, and have more readily and frequently devised new modes by which the same amount of work could be better done. Some of these men we have selected for superintendents, and they are now contractors. With regard to the morals of the two classes, we have seen very little difference; but the better-educated class are more cleanly in their persons and their households, and generally discover more refinement in their manners, and practice a more economical mode in their living. Their families are better brought up, and they are more anxious to send their children to school. In regard to their standing and respectability among co-laborers, neighbors, and fellow-citizens, the more educated are much more respected; and in settling minor controversies, they are more commonly applied to as arbitrators. With regard to the morals of the two classes before mentioned, permit me to remark, that it furnishes an illustration of the truth of a common saying, that merely cultivating the understanding, without improving the heart, does not make a man better. The more extensively knowledge and virtue prevail in our country, the greater security have we that our institutions will not be overthrown. Our common-school system, connected as it is, or ought to be, with the inculcation of sound and practical morality, is the most vigilant and efficient police for the protection of persons, property, and character, that could be devised; and is it not gratifying that men of wealth are beginning to see, that, if they would protect their property and persons, a portion of that property should be expended for the education of the poorer classes? Merely selfish considerations would lead any man of wealth to do this, if he would only view the subject in its true light. Nowhere is this subject better understood than in Massachusetts; and the free discussions which have of late been held, in county and town meetings, have had the effect to call the attention of the public to it; and I trust the time is not far distant, when, at least in Massachusetts, the common-school system will accomplish all the good which it is capable of producing. Why do we not in these United States have a revolution, almost annually, as in the republics of South America? Ignorance and vice always have invited, and always will invite, such characters as Shakespeare's Jack Cade to rule over them. And may we not feel an assurance, that in proportion as the nation shall recover from the baneful influence of intemperance, so will its attention be directed pre-eminently to the promotion of virtue and knowledge, and nowhere in our country will an incompetent or intemperate common-school teacher be entrusted with the education of our children?

83

Lyman Beecher on Intemperance (1825)

One of the most important reforms championed by members of America's Benevolent Empire was the temperance movement. In the late 18th and early 19th centuries, the

Americans consumed considerable quantities of alcohol. By the 1820s and 1830s, grow-
ing numbers of reformers became concerned that such consumption was ruinous to health,
destructive of family life, contributed to vice, and undermined the drinker's ability to
compete in the rapidly changing market economy. One of the leading proponents of
temperance was Lyman Beecher. A protégé of Yale President Timothy Dwight, Beecher
left school to become a Presbyterian minister. During the 1820s, he used revivals to
attract converts and was a pioneer in creating voluntary societies to promote the gospel.
His Six Sermons on . . . Intemperance, *excerpted below, established him in the*
vanguard of the movement.

Questions to Consider

1. Why does Lyman Beecher believe alcohol consumption is harmful?
2. How would you describe the author's opinion on the United States' systems of economy and government?
3. How can Beecher's views be reconciled with concepts of individual liberty as understood by 19th-century Americans?

In the preceding discourses we have illustrated THE NATURE, THE OCCASIONS, AND THE SYMPTOMS OF INTEMPERANCE.

In this discourse we propose to illustrate the evils of intemperance.

This physical and moral influence of this sin upon its victims, has of necessity been disclosed in giving an account of the causes and symptoms of this criminal disease. We shall therefore take a more comprehensive view of the subject, and consider the effect of intemperance upon national prosperity. To this view of the subject the text leads us. It announces the general principle, that communities which rise by a violation of the laws of humanity and society, shall not prosper, . . . by promoting intemperance, will bring upon the community intemperance, and poverty, and shame as providential retribution.

1. The effects of intemperance upon the health and physical energies of a nation, are not to be overlooked or lightly esteemed. . . .

   The duration of human life, and the relative amount of health or disease, will manifestly vary according to the amount of ardent spirits consumed in the land. Even now, no small proportion of the deaths which annually make up our national bills of mortality, are cases of those who have been brought to an untimely end, and who have, directly or indirectly, fallen victims to the deleterious influence of ardent spirits; fulfilling, with fearful accuracy, the prediction, "the wicked shall not live out half their days." . . .

Lyman Beecher, *Six Sermons on the Nature, Occasions, Signs, and Evils and Remedy of Intemperance,* 10th ed. (New York, 1843), 47–59.

2. The injurious influence of general intemperance upon national intellect, is equally certain, and not less to be deprecated. . . .

3. The effect of intemperance upon the military prowess of a nation, cannot but be great and evil. The mortality in the seasoning of recruits, already half destroyed by intemperance, will be double to that experienced among hardy and temperate men. If in the early wars of our country the mortality of the camp had been as great as it has been since intemperance has facilitated the raising of recruits, New England would have been depopulated, . . . An army, whose energy in conflict depends on the excitement of ardent spirits, cannot possess the coolness nor sustain the shock of a powerful onset, like an army of determined, temperate men; . . .

4. The effect of intemperance upon the patriotism of a nation is neither obscure nor doubtful. When excess has despoiled the man of the natural affections of husband, father, brother, and friend, and thrust him down to the condition of an animal; we are not to expect of him comprehensive views, and a disinterested regard for his country. . . .

5. Upon the national conscience or moral principle the effects of intemperance are deadly.

     It obliterates the fear of the Lord, and a sense of accountability, paralyses the power of conscience, and hardens the heart, and turns out upon society a sordid, selfish, ferocious animal.

6. Upon national industry the effects of intemperance are manifest and mischievous.

The results of national industry depend on the amount of well-directed intellectual and physical power. But intemperance paralyses and prevents both these springs of human action.

In the inventory of national loss by intemperance, may be set down—the labor prevented by Indolence, by debility, by sickness, by quarrels and litigation, by gambling and idleness, by mistakes and misdirected effort, by improvidence and wastefulness, and by the shortened date of human life and activity. Little wastes in great establishments constantly occurring may defeat the energies of a mighty capital. . . . Thus is the insatiable destroyer of industry marching through the land, rearing poor-houses, and augmenting taxation: night and day, with sleepless activity, squandering property, cutting the sinews of industry, undermining vigor, engendering disease, paralysing intellect, impairing moral principle, cutting short the date of life, and rolling up a national debt, invisible, but real and terrific as the debt of England continually transferring larger and larger bodies of men, from the class of contributors to the national income, to the class of worthless consumers.

Add the loss sustained by the subtraction of labor, and the shortened date of life, to the expense of sustaining the poor, created by intemperance; and the nation is now taxed annually more than the expense which would be requisite for the maintenance of government, and for the support of all our schools and colleges, and all the religious instruction of the nation. Already a portion of the entire capital of the nation is mortgaged for the support of drunkards. . . .

The effects of intemperance upon civil liberty may not be lightly passed over.

It is admitted that intelligence and virtue are the pillars of republican institutions, and that the illumination of schools, and the moral power of religious institutions, are indispensable to produce this intelligence and virtue. . . . Almost the entire amount of national ignorance and crime is the offspring of intemperance. Throughout the land, the intemperate are hewing down the pillars, and undermining the foundations of our national edifice. . . .

Should the evil advance as it has done, the day is not far distant when the great body of the laboring classes of the community, the bones and sinews of the nation, will be contaminated; and when this is accomplished, the right of suffrage becomes the engine of self-destruction. . . . As intemperance increases, the power of taxation will come more and more into the hands of men of intemperate habits and desperate fortunes; of course the laws gradually will become subservient to the debtor, and less efficacious in protecting the rights of property. This will be a vital stab to liberty—to the security of which property is indispensable. . . .

We boast of our liberties, and rejoice in our prospective instrumentality in disenthralling the world. But our own foundations rest on the heaving sides of a burning mountain, through which, in thousands of places, the fire has burst out, and is blazing around us. If they cannot be extinguished, we are undone. Our sun is fast setting, and the darkness of an endless night is closing in upon us. . . .

84

Sarah Grimké Argues for Gender Equality (1837)

The passion to perfect society that was so much a part of the Second Great Awakening not only spurred the rise of abolitionism in the North, but when female representatives were denied positions of influence, it also helped ignite demands for women's rights. One of the earliest proponents of women's rights was Sarah Grimké. A native of South Carolina, by the 1820s she and her younger sister Angelina had moved to Philadelphia, where they emerged as outspoken critics of slavery. Both sisters soon became deeply involved in the movement by writing antislavery tracts, and in defiance of accepted convention, as public speakers. By the late 1830s, Sarah had begun to shift her attention to demanding greater rights for women. The following selection is from her Letters on the Equality of the Sexes, *which were addressed to fellow abolitionist Mary Parker.*

Questions to Consider

1. In what ways might Grimké seek greater equality for women?
2. How might men of the time react to this document?
3. How might Sarah Grimké respond to the views contained in "Eliza Lucas, A Modern Women" (Document 16)? What changes seem to have occurred in women's status from the early 18th century to mid-19th century?

. . . During the early part of my life, my lot was cast among the butterflies of the *fashionable* world; and of this class of women, I am constrained to say, both from experience and observation, that their education is miserably deficient; that they are taught to regard marriage as the one thing needful, the only avenue to distinction; hence to attract the notice and win the attentions of men, by their external charms, is the chief business of fashionable girls. They seldom think that men will be allured by intellectual acquirements, because they find, that where any mental superiority exists, a woman is generally shunned and regarded as stepping out of her 'appropriate sphere,' which, in their view, is to dress, to dance, to set out to the best possible advantage her person, to read the novels which inundate the press, and which do more to destroy her character as a rational creature, than any thing else. Fashionable women regard themselves, and are regarded by men, as pretty toys or as mere instruments of pleasure; and the vacuity of mind, the heartlessness, the frivolity which is the necessary result of this false and debasing estimate of women, can only be fully understood by those who have mingled in the folly and wickedness of fashionable life; and who have been called from such pursuits by the voice of the Lord Jesus, inviting their weary and heavy laden souls to come unto Him and learn of Him, that they may find something worthy of their immortal spirit, and their intellectual powers; that they may learn the high and holy purposes of their creation, and consecrate themselves unto the service of God; and not as is now the case, to the pleasure of man.

There is another and much more numerous class in this country, who are withdrawn by education or circumstances from the circle of fashionable amusements, but who are brought up with the dangerous and absurd idea, that *marriage* is a kind of preferment; and that to be able to keep their husband's house, and render his situation comfortable, is the end of her being. Much that she does and says and thinks is done in reference to this situation; and to be married is too often held up to the view of girls as the sine qua non of human happiness and human existence. For this purpose more than for any other, I verily believe the majority of girls are trained. This is demonstrated by the imperfect education which is bestowed upon them, and the little pains

Sarah M. Grimké, "Letter VIII: On the Condition of Women in the United States, 1837," *Letters on the Equality of the Sexes and the Condition of Woman* (Boston, 1838), 46–55.

taken to cultivate their minds, after they leave school, by the little time allowed them for reading and by the idea being constantly inculcated, that although all household concerns should be attended to with scrupulous punctuality at particular seasons, the improvement of their intellectual capacities is only a secondary consideration, and may serve as an occupation to fill up the odds and ends of time. . . .

Let no one think, from these remarks, that I regard a knowledge of housewifery as beneath the acquisition of women. Far from it: I believe that a complete knowledge of household affairs is an indispensable requisite in a woman's education,—that by the mistress of a family, whether married or single, doing her duty thoroughly and *understandingly,* the happiness of the family is increased to an incalculable degree, as well as a vast amount of time and money saved. All I complain of is, that our education consists so almost exclusively in culinary and other manual operations. . . .

The influence of women over the minds and character of *children* of both sexes, is allowed to be far greater than that of men. This being the case by the very ordering of nature, women should be prepared by education for the per-formance of their sacred duties as mothers and as sisters. . . .

There is another way in which the general opinion, that women are infe-rior to men, is manifested, that bears with tremendous effect on the laboring class, and indeed on almost all who are obliged to earn a subsistence, whether it be by mental or physical exertion—I allude to the disproportionate value set on the time and labor of men and of women. A man who is engaged in teaching, can always, I believe, command a higher price for tuition than a woman—even when he teaches the same branches, and is not in any respect superior to the woman. This I know is the case in boarding and other schools with which I have been acquainted, and it is so in every occupation in which the sexes engage indiscriminately. As for example, in tailoring, a man has twice, or three times as much for making a waistcoat or pantaloons as a woman, although the work done by each may be equally good. In those employments which are peculiar to women, their time is estimated at only half the value of that of men. A woman who goes out to wash, works as hard in proportion as a wood sawyer, or a coal heaver, but she is not generally able to make more than half as much by a day's work. The low remuneration which women receive for their work, has claimed the attention of a few philanthro-pists, and I hope it will continue to do so until some remedy is applied for this enormous evil. I have known a widow, left with four or five children, to provide for, unable to leave home because her helpless babes demand her atten-tion, compelled to earn a scanty subsistence, by making coarse shirts at 12 1-2 cents a piece, or by taking in washing, for which she was paid by some wealthy persons 12 1-2 cents per dozen. All these things evince the low esti-mation in which woman is held. There is yet another and more disastrous consequence arising from this unscriptual notion—women being educated, from earliest childhood, to regard themselves as inferior creatures, have not that self-respect which conscious equality would engender, and hence when their virtue is assailed, they yield to temptation with facility, under the idea that it rather exalts than debases them to be connected with a superior being. . . .

I cannot close this letter, without saying a few words on the benefits to be derived by men, as well as women, from the opinions I advocate relative to the equality of the sexes. Many women are now supported, in idleness and extravagance, by the industry of their husbands, fathers, or brothers, who are compelled to toil out their existence, at the counting house, or in the printing office, or some other laborious occupation, while the wife and daughters and sisters take no part in the support of the family, and appear to think that their sole business is to spend the hard bought earnings of their male friends. I deeply regret such a state of things, because I believe that if women felt their responsibility, for the support of themselves, or their families it would add strength and dignity to their characters, and teach them more true sympathy for their husbands, than is now generally manifested,—a sympathy which would be exhibited by actions as well as words. Our brethren may reject my doctrine, because it runs counter to common opinions, and because it wounds their pride; but I believe they would be 'partakers of the benefit' resulting from the Equality of the Sexes, and would find that woman, as their equal, was unspeakably more valuable than woman as their inferior, both as a moral and an intellectual being.

Thine in the bonds of womanhood,
SARAH M. GRIMKÉ.

85

"Declaration of Sentiments," Seneca Falls Convention (1848)

The women's rights movement had its roots in abolitionism, which attracted a large number of female supporters from the outset. By the late 1830s, female abolitionists horrified gender-integrated audiences with their accounts of the treatment of slaves. Congregational clergy and conservative abolitionist criticisms of such practices had led Sarah Grimké to proclaim the equality of the sexes. The World Anti-Slavery Convention in London brought the issue to a head when convention organizers refused to allow delegates Lucretia Mott and Elizabeth Cady Stanton to participate. Seven years later in 1848, Stanton and Mott organized the Seneca Falls Convention. The following selection is taken from the convention "Declaration of Sentiments." Many of those present at Seneca Falls remained active in the movement throughout the rest of the 19th century.

Questions to Consider

1. Why does the Seneca Falls Convention use the Declaration of Independence as the framework for its "Sentiments"?
2. What is the evidence that man has denied woman her rights?
3. What does the declaration advocate for women?
4. For what reasons would some women who advocated the "Declaration of Sentiments" also have supported William Lloyd Garrison in the abolitionist movement ("William Lloyd Garrison on Slavery," Document 81)?

When, in the course of human events, it becomes necessary for one portion of the family of man to assume among the people of the earth a position different from that which they have hitherto occupied, but one to which the laws of nature and of nature's God entitle them, a decent respect to the opinions of mankind requires that they should declare the causes that impel them to such a course.

We hold these truths to be self-evident: that all men and women are created equal; that they are endowed by their Creator with certain inalienable rights; that among these are life, liberty, and the pursuit of happiness; that to secure these rights governments are instituted, deriving their just powers from the consent of the governed. Whenever any form of government becomes destructive of these ends, it is the right of those who suffer from it to refuse allegiance to it, and to insist upon the institution of a new government, laying its foundation on such principles, and organizing its powers in such form, as to them shall seem most likely to effect their safety and happiness. Prudence, indeed, will dictate that governments long established should not be changed for light and transient causes; and accordingly all experience hath shown that mankind are more disposed to suffer, while evils are sufferable, than to right themselves by abolishing forms to which they were accustomed. But a long train of abuses and usurpations, pursuing invariably the same object evinces a design to reduce them under absolute despotism, it is their duty to throw off such government, and to provide new guards for their future security. Such has been the patient sufferance of the women under this government, and such is now the necessity which constrains them to demand the equal station to which they are entitled.

The history of mankind is a history of repeated injuries and usurpations on the part of man toward woman, having in direct object the establishment of an absolute tyranny over her. To prove this, let facts be submitted to a candid world.

He has never permitted her to exercise her inalienable right to the elective franchise.

"Declaration of Sentiments," *History of Woman Suffrage,* eds. Susan B. Anthony, Elizabeth Cady Stanton, and Matilda Joslyn Gage (New York, 1881), 1: 70–73.

He has compelled her to submit to laws, in the formation of which she had no voice.

He has withheld from her rights which are given to the most ignorant and degraded men—both natives and foreigners.

Having deprived her of this first right of a citizen, the elective franchise, thereby leaving her without representation in the halls of legislation, he has oppressed her on all sides.

He has made her, if married, in the eye of the law, civilly dead.

He has taken from her all right in property, even to the wages she earns.

He has made her, morally, an irresponsible being, as she can commit many crimes with impunity, provided they be done in the presence of her husband. In the covenant of marriage, she is compelled to promise obedience to her husband, he becoming, to all intents and purposes, her master—the law giving him power to deprive her of all liberty, and to administer chastisement.

He has so framed the laws of divorce, as to what shall be the proper causes, and in case of separation, to whom the guardianship of the children shall be given, as to be wholly regardless of the happiness of women—the law, in all cases, going upon a false supposition of the supremacy of man, and giving all power into his hands.

After depriving her of all her rights as a married woman, if single, and the owner of property, he has taxed her to support a government which recognizes her only when her property can be made profitable to it.

He has monopolized nearly all the profitable employments, and from those she is permitted to follow, she receives but a scanty remuneration. He closes against her all the avenues to wealth and distinction which he considers most honorable to himself. As a teacher of theology, medicine, or law, she is not known.

He has denied her the facilities for obtaining a thorough education, all colleges being closed against her.

He allows her in Church, as well as State, but a subordinate position, claiming Apostolic authority for her exclusion from the ministry, and, with some exceptions, from any public participation in the affairs of the Church.

He has created a false public sentiment by giving to the world a different code of morals for men and women, by which moral delinquencies which exclude women from society, are not only tolerated, but deemed of little account in man.

He has usurped the prerogative of Jehovah himself, claiming it as his right to assign for her a sphere of action, when that belongs to her conscience and to her God.

He has endeavored, in every way that he could, to destroy her confidence in her own powers, to lessen her self-respect, and to make her willing to lead a dependent and abject life.

Now, in view of this entire disfranchisement of one-half the people of this country, their social and religious degradation—in view of the unjust laws above mentioned, and because women do feel themselves aggrieved, oppressed, and fraudulently deprived of their most sacred rights, we insist that they have immediate admission to all the rights and privileges which belong to them as citizens of the United States.

In entering upon the great work before us, we anticipate no small amount of misconception, misrepresentation, and ridicule; but we shall use every instrumentality within our power to effect our object. We shall employ agents, circulate tracts, petition the State and National legislatures, and endeavor to enlist the pulpit and the press in our behalf. We hope this Convention will be followed by a series of Conventions embracing every part of the country.

12

Manifest Destiny
and American Expansion

In the first half of the 19th century, the United States had expanded from a collection of states with a tenuous hold over territories west of the Appalachians to an increasingly self-confident colossus stretching from the Atlantic to the Pacific. By the 1840s, the mentality that supported such expansion had been labeled "manifest destiny." According to this belief, America possessed a special purpose that legitimized its westward expansion. Supporters of the doctrine argued that the acquisition of new lands did more than provide opportunity for white Americans; it replaced "backward" and "savage" customs with "superior" American institutions. Opponents argued that America needed to first perfect its institutions within its existing borders. The following selections reveal the sentiments of the expansionists and their opponents.

86

Mid-19th-Century Images of Race and Nation

One of the defining characteristics of the American experience has been the contact between white and nonwhite culture. Throughout history, American intellectuals grappled with how to come to terms with these cultural differences. By the mid-19th century, early social scientific beliefs on cultural evolution occurring in progressive stages combined with emerging American nationalism's emphasis on the superiority of American institutions. The results justified white Americans' sense of ethnic and racial superiority and legitimized the conquest and subjugation of nonwhite peoples and their land. The first set of images depicts an early view of racial hierarchy as depicted in Josiah Nott's text Types of Mankind. *Nott, a southern physician and early anthropologist, sought to "prove" the separate origins of human races in this book. The next image is a mid-19th-century romantic painting of America's triumphant march across the continent. Both sets of images clearly demonstrate the sense of "progress" inherent in mid-19th-century American thought and depict the white American sense of superiority.*

Questions to Consider

1. What can you deduce from the first set of images about white attitudes toward Africans and African Americans?
2. How do you think the first set of images might be used to justify slavery? Or the subjugation of Native Americans?
3. What symbols of progress are depicted in the romantic painting?
4. What can you deduce about American nationalism from this set of images?

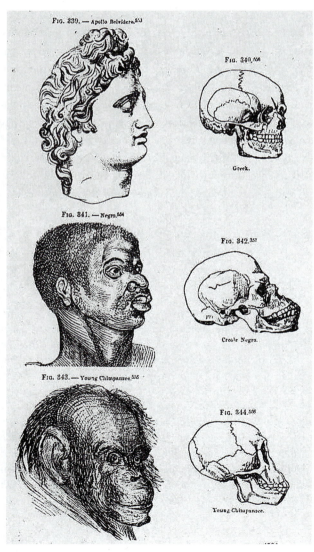

From J.C. Nott and George R. Gliddon, *Types of mankind: or, Ethnological researches* (1845)

"Types of Mankind"

"American Progress"

87

Texas and California Annexation (1845)

Territorial expansion had been a virtual act of faith for many Americans since the arrival of the first settlers. By the 1840s, the sense of a special mission shared by many Americans, coupled with economic depression, led to renewed calls for expansion. The issue divided the parties: Democrats argued in favor of expansion, while the Whigs opposed the acquisition of added territories. The following selection first appeared in the New York–based United States Magazine and Democratic Review *in the summer of 1845. Its author, John L. O'Sullivan, trumpets his view of America's "manifest destiny" and captures the boisterous spirit of the expansionists. O'Sullivan established the* Review *in 1837 to foster America's "democratic genius." By the mid-1840s, he also served as editor of the* New York Morning News, *which he had founded with future Democratic presidential candidate Samuel J. Tilden. Territorial expansion became the leading issue in the 1844 election campaign, and differences over the annexation of Texas fueled sectional tensions.*

Questions to Consider

1. How does John O'Sullivan define "manifest destiny"?

2. According to O'Sullivan, why was Texas acquired?

3. What does America offer the unsettled regions, especially California?

4. How do you suppose O'Sullivan would respond to the views expressed in "Tecumseh on White Encroachment" (Document 56) or "Appeal to the Coloured Citizens of the World" (Document 80)?

IT IS TIME NOW for opposition to the annexation of Texas to cease . . . Texas is now ours. Already, before these words are written, her convention has undoubtedly ratified the acceptance, by her congress, of our proffered invitation into the Union; and made the requisite changes in her already republican form of constitution to adapt it to its future federal relations. Her star and her stripe may already be said to have taken their place in the glorious blazon of our common nationality; and the sweep of our eagle's wing already includes within its circuit the wide extent of her fair and fertile land. . . .

Why, were other reasoning wanting, in favor of now elevating this question of the reception of Texas into the Union, out of the lower region of our past party dissensions, up to its proper level of a high and broad nationality, it surely is to be found, found abundantly, in the manner in which other nations have undertaken to intrude themselves into it, between us and the proper parties to the case, in a spirit of hostile interference against us, for the avowed object of thwarting our policy and hampering our power, limiting our greatness and checking the fulfillment of our manifest destiny to overspread the continent allotted by Providence for the free development of our yearly multiplying millions. . . .

The independence of Texas was complete and absolute. It was an independence, not only in fact, but of right. No obligation of duty toward Mexico tended in the least degree to restrain our right to effect the desired recovery of the fair province. . . . If Texas became peopled with an American population, it was by no contrivance of our government, but on the express invitation of that of Mexico herself; accompanied with such guaranties of state independence, and the maintenance of a federal system analogous to our own, as constituted a compact fully justifying the strongest measures of redress on the part of those afterward deceived in this guaranty, and sought to be enslaved under the yoke imposed by its violation.

She was released, rightfully and absolutely released, from all Mexican allegiance, or duty of cohesion to the Mexican political body, by the acts and fault of Mexico herself, and Mexico alone. There never was a clearer case. It was not revolution; it was resistance to revolution. . . .

Nor is there any just foundation for the charge that annexation is a great pro-slavery measure—calculated to increase and perpetuate that institution.

Slavery had nothing to do with it. Opinions were and are greatly divided, both at the North and South, as to the influence to be exerted by it on slavery and the slave states. That it will tend to facilitate the disappearance of slavery from all the northern tier of the present slave states, cannot surely admit of serious question. The greater value in Texas of the slave labor now employed in those states, must soon produce the effect of draining off that labor southwardly, by the same unvarying law that bids water descend the slope that invites it. . . .

The Spanish-Indian-American population of Mexico, Central America, and South America, afford the only receptacle capable of absorbing that race whenever we shall be prepared to slough it off—to emancipate it from slavery, and (simultaneously necessary) to remove it from the midst of our own. Themselves already of mixed and confused blood, and free from the "prejudices" which among us so insuperably forbid the social amalgamation which can alone elevate the Negro race out of a virtually servile degradation. . . .

California will, probably, next fall away from the loose adhesion which, in such a country as Mexico, holds a remote province in a slight equivocal kind of dependence on the metropolis. Imbecile and distracted, Mexico never can exert any real government authority over such a country. . . .

The Anglo-Saxon foot is already on its borders. Already the advance guard of the irresistible army of Anglo-Saxon emigration has begun to pour down upon it, armed with the plough and the rifle, and marking its trail with schools and colleges, courts and representative halls, mills and meetinghouses. A population will soon be in actual occupation of California, over which it will be idle for Mexico to dream of dominion. They will necessarily become independent. . . .

Their right to independence will be the natural right of self-government belonging to any community strong enough to maintain—distinct in position, origin and character, and free from any mutual obligations of membership of a common political body, binding it to others by the duty of loyalty and compact of public faith. This will be their title to independence; and by this title, there can be no doubt that the population now fast streaming down upon California will both assert and maintain that independence.

Whether they will then attach themselves to our Union or not, is not to be predicted with any certainty. Unless the projected railroad across the continent to the Pacific be carried into effect, perhaps they may not; though even in that case, the day is not distant when the empires of the Atlantic and Pacific would again flow together into one, as soon as their inland border should approach each other. But that great work, colossal as appears the plan on its first suggestion, cannot remain long unbuilt.

Its necessity for this very purpose of binding and holding together in its iron clasp our fast-settling Pacific region with that of the Mississippi Valley. . . . these considerations give assurance that the day cannot be distant which shall witness the conveyance of the representatives from Oregon and California to Washington within less time than a few years ago was devoted to a similar journey by those from Ohio; while the magnetic telegraph will enable the editors of the *San Francisco Union,* the *Astoria Evening Post,* or the *Nootka Morning News,* to set up in type the first half of the President's inaugural before the echoes of the latter half shall have died away beneath the lofty porch of the Capitol, as spoken from his lips. . . .

88

American Description of Mexican Women in Santa Fe (1845)

The expansion-minded spirit of manifest destiny that characterized the United States in the 1830s and 1840s contributed to growing interest in the Southwest and the Pacific Coast. American interest in New Mexico was primarily economic. Traders followed the roughly 900-mile Santa Fe Trail from Independence, Missouri, to the remote Mexican town of Santa Fe, where the exchange of goods brought enormous profits. The arrival of American merchants contributed to the increasingly multiethnic community there. George W. Kendall was one of those who made the trip to Santa Fe. A newspaper editor and journalist, who had worked on many of the nation's leading newspapers, Kendall had moved in 1837 to New Orleans, where he established the Times–Picayune. *In 1841, he joined a Republic of Texas–sanctioned expedition to Santa Fe. The following selection offers Kendall's observations on Mexican women. He would later report the Mexican-American War back to the* Picayune, *becoming one of America's first war correspondents.*

Questions to Consider

1. What is the historical context of this account?

2. What can you deduce from this document about 19th-century sexual mores? How do they differ from those expressed by Cotton Mather in "The Evils of 'Self-Pollution'" (Document 14)?

3. What does this document tell you about 19th-century attitudes concerning ethnicity and gender?

. . . The dress worn by the females of Northern Mexico, in fact all over the country, is a cotton or linen chemise and a blue or red short woollen petticoat—frequently, among the more wealthy, the latter is made of a gaudy, figured merino, imported expressly for the purpose. These simple articles of raiment are usually made with no little degree of neatness, the chemise, in particular, being in many cases elaborately worked with flowers and different conceits, while the edges are tastefully decorated with ruffles or laces, if it lies

---

G. W. Kendall, *Narrative of the Texan Santa Fe Expedition* (Bristol, England, 1845), 233–236.

within the power of the wearer to procure them. On first entering the country, the Anglo-Saxon traveller, who has been used to see the gentler sex of his native land in more full, and perhaps I should say more becoming costume, feels not a little astonished at the Eve-like and scanty garments of the females he meets; he thinks that they are but half-dressed, and wonders how they can have the indelicacy, or, as he would deem it at home, brazen impudence, to appear before him in dishabille so immodest. But he soon learns that it is the custom and fashion of the country—that, to use a common Yankee expression, the women "don't know any better." He soon looks, with an eye of some leniency, at such little deficiencies of dress as the absence of a gown, and is not long in coming to the honest conclusion, as the eye becomes more weaned from the fastidiousness of early habit and association, that a pretty girl is quite as pretty without as with that garment. By-and-by, he is even led to think that the dress of the women, among whom fate, business, or a desire to see the world may have thrown him, is really graceful, easy—aye, becoming: he next wonders how the females of his native land can press and confine, can twist and contort themselves out of all proportion, causing the most gracefully-curving lines of beauty to become straight and rigid, the exquisite undulations of the natural form to become flat or angular, or conical, or jutting, and all in homage to a fickle and capricious goddess—a heathen goddess, whose worshippers are Christians! He looks around him, he compares, he deliberates—the result is altogether in favour of his new-found friends.

Among the Mexican women, young and old, corsets are unknown, and by a majority of them, probably unheard of. I travelled nearly seven hundred miles through the country, without seeing a single gown—all the females were dressed in the same style, with the same *abandon*. The consequence any one may readily imagine: the forms of the gentler sex obtain a roundness, a fulness which the divinity of tight lacing never allows her votaries. The Mexican belles certainly have studied, too, their personal comfort in the costume they have adopted, and it is impossible to see the prettier of the dark-eyed *senoras* of the northern departments without acknowledging that their personal appearance and attractions are materially enhanced by the *negligé* style. Moore's beautiful lines to Nora Creina appear to apply especially to the Mexican girls, for their dress certainly leaves

—every beauty free
To sink or swell as Heaven pleases.

But by all this the reader must not understand that the traveller sees no full-dressed ladies in Mexico. In the great city of the Montezumas, in fact in all the larger towns where foreigners and French milliners have settled, he sees them habited after the fashion of his own land, although he cannot but notice that a large portion of those so attired feel constrained and ill at ease under the infliction. I have seen, in one of the larger cities, a lady with the body and sleeves of a fashionable frock hanging dangling at her back, without even attempting to conceal what many would call a gross departure from all rules and reasons.

Bonnets are never worn, either by rich or poor, high or low; but in their stead the *mantilla* and *reboso,* more especially the latter, are in general use among all classes. The latter is a species of long, narrow scarf, made of cotton, and in a majority of cases figured with two colours only, blue and white. These indispensable articles in the toilet of the Mexican female serve not only the uses of parasol and bonnet, but also of shawl, veil, and workbag. The manner of wearing them is extremely graceful—sometimes upon the head, at others over the shoulders, and again round the waist, with the ends hanging across the arms; in the streets they are worn almost invariably over the head, and so archly and coquettishly does the fair Mexican draw the reboso around her face, that the inquisitive beholder is frequently repaid with no other than the sight of a dark and lustrous eye peering out from amid its folds.

The ends of the reboso are frequently used as an apron, to carry any little articles that cannot be held in the hands, and seldom is a female seen without one of them, from the extreme north of Mexico to its southern-most boundaries. From childhood it is worn, and long habit has so accustomed them to its use that it is not laid aside when engaged in common household labour. . . .

89

Mob Violence against Mormons (1846)

While many Americans joined reform movements during the turbulent 1830s, others sought refuge in new religions. One of the most prominent of these new faiths was the Church of Jesus Christ of Latter-day Saints. Founded by Joseph Smith in the Burned-Over District of New York, the faith followed the teaching found in the Book of Mormon. The Mormons, as they came to be known, established a tight-knit community structure that emphasized hard work and loyalty to the faith. While the Mormons prospered, their sense of exclusiveness alienated many of their contemporaries. Driven from Ohio and then Missouri, in 1839 they established a model religious community along the Mississippi River in Nauvoo, Illinois. William Clayton, a British immigrant, was serving as personal secretary to founder Joseph Smith when the Mormons began to practice polygamy in 1843. This action increased tensions with surrounding neighbors. The following selection from William Clayton's Journal *discusses the violence directed against the Mormons at Nauvoo. Clayton and the rest of the Saints ultimately fled to the present-day state of Utah.*

Questions to Consider

1. What is William Clayton's perspective in this document?
2. How would you describe the Mormons' relations with their neighbors?
3. What can you deduce about mid-19th-century American views toward alternative religious practices?

4. How tolerant is mainstream society toward religious, ethnic, and racial minorities during this period?

. . . THURSDAY, 24th. Very cold all day. I did not feel so well. I have been told that Daniel H. Wells and William Cutler have arrived in camp and brought a report that there has been a battle fought in Nauvoo and some of the brethren killed.

FRIDAY, 25th. I learned today that the mob had made it known that they were coming to drive out the "Mormons." The Governor sent an officer to raise volunteers to disperse the mob, but the mob learning this they came sooner than they had calculated. The brethren being apprised of the intentions of the mob prepared to meet them as well as their circumstances would permit. Some of the new citizens also made preparations to join the brethren. They made five cannon shot of an old steam boat shaft. They also filled some barrels with powder, old iron, etc., which were buried in the pass to the city which could be fired by slow match but this was of no avail as some traitors informed the mob of it, hence they did not come into the settled part of the city. On Saturday the 12 inst., the mob made their appearance being about twelve hundred in number. The brethren and some of the new citizens in the whole about one hundred and sixty went to give them battle, but many of the new citizens and some of the brethren when they saw the numbers of the mob fled and left about one hundred, nearly all brethren to fight the enemy. The mob had pieces of cannon. They met near Boscow's store on Winchester street. The cannon of the mob fired a number of times into Barlow's old barn expecting many of the brethren were concealed there but in this they were disappointed, the brethren chiefly lying down on the ground behind some shelter and fired in that position. They fought one hour and twenty minutes when the mob offered terms of compromise which were these, that all the "Mormons" should leave the city within five days leaving ten families to finish the unsettled business. The brethren consented to this inasmuch as they had been well informed that 1500 more were coming to join the mob and they had nothing to expect from the authorities of the state. Lyman Johnson, one of the twelve, headed a party of the mob from Keokuk, Iowa territory. Three of the brethren were killed, viz. William Anderson, his son, and Norris, a blacksmith. Three others wounded. The mob would not own to any of their party being killed but one person saw them put sixteen men into one wagon and handled them more like dead persons than wounded. The ground where they stood was pretty much covered with blood, so that there is no doubt they had many slain or wounded. They had 150 baggage wagons. Esquire Wells took command of the brethren and rode to and fro during the whole battle without receiving injury, although the balls whistled by him on every side. Amos Davis fought bravely. While running across a plowed field he stumbled and fell on his left arm which formed a triangle with his head. As he fell a cannon ball passed through the angle of his arm between that and his head. Hiram Kimball received a slight wound with a musket ball on the forehead. The mob fired sixty-two shots with the cannon and ten rounds with the muskets making 12,000 musket balls only killing three and wounding three. The brethren did not fire so much in proportion but did much more execution. Truly, the Lord fights the battles of his saints. The cannon of the brethren was not of much service, they would not carry more than a quarter of a mile, whereas those of the mob would hold well a half a mile. They shot nine balls through a small smith shop, one through Wells' barn and one at his house but the ball struck the ground in front of his house and glanced through the well curb. The mayor of Quincy watched the battle from the tower of the temple and owned that history never afforded a parallel. The brethren then began to get their families and effects over the river where they remain in a suffering and destitute condition until wagons and means are sent from the saints to their relief. On the Thursday following, the mob 1200 strong, entered the city. 'Tis said from good authority that such is the distress and sufferings of the saints as actually to draw tears from this mob. . . .

90

Mexican View of U.S. Occupation (1847)

American expansion created conflict with Mexico during the 1830s and 1840s. A newly independent Mexico encouraged American immigrants to settle in Texas during the 1820s, but sought to curtail further settlement in the ensuing decade as the number of North American immigrants threatened to overwhelm the province. This policy, along with the Mexican government's attempt to exert greater control over its northern province, caused Texans of both Anglo and Mexican origin to successfully revolt in 1836. The Republic of Texas remained independent until annexed by the United States in 1845, just days before James K. Polk, a fervent expansionist from Tennessee, became president. The ensuing war, instigated by the new American administration's eagerness to add California and the Southwest to the nation, ended with American armies occupying Mexico City in 1847. In the ensuing selection, José Fernando Ramirez, a leading political and intellectual figure of mid-19th-century Mexico, describes the Mexican response to the Yankee conquerors' behavior.

Questions to Consider

1. How does José Fernando Ramirez characterize the American occupation of Mexico City?

2. How did the Mexicans resist?

3. How do you think Ramirez would respond to the sentiments found in John O'Sullivan's views on "Texas and California Annexation" (Document 87)?

4. Whom does Ramirez blame for the city's occupation?

Mexico City, September 30, 1847

My dear friend:

I have not received any word from you to which I can reply, because, since the unfortunate inhabitants of this city are being treated as enemies, there has been no opportunity to get mail in from the outside. Where it is being held heaven only knows. We have hopes that the mail will eventually be permitted to come in, and then I shall know what I have to reply to.

What shall I tell you? Well, to be frank, nothing because this city is no longer the center of political life. According to reports, the center has been transferred to many other centers that will exhaust whatever political life is left to us by our enemy who is oppressing and humiliating us. How I would like to bring home this lesson to certain politicians who have talked incessantly about despotism, etc! Here they would see and get a taste of what it means to live without guarantees! It is all so frightful. I must say that those who have conquered us, brutally savage as they are, have conducted themselves in a manner different from that of European armies belonging to nations that bear the standard of civilization. This does not mean that they do not commit countless excesses every day. But we have here a phenomenon consisting of mingled barbarism and restraint. This has been the situation for several days, and there is no way to account for it.

Open fighting ceased the third day after the city was occupied; but the undercover struggle goes on, and it is assuming a fearful aspect. The enemy's forces are growing weaker day by day because of assassinations, and it is impossible to discover who the assassins are. Anyone who takes a walk through the streets or goes a short distance away from the center of the city is a dead man. I have been told that a small cemetery has been found in a pulque tavern where deadly liquor was dispensed for the purpose of assuring an increasing number of victims. Seven corpses were discovered inside the establishment, but the tavern keeper could not be found. I am also told that the number of those who have been taken off this way amounts to 300, without counting those dying of sickness and wounds. Five days ago a funeral cortege with the bodies of four officers passed by my residence. The plague has begun to show its signs, and the monuments that those filthy soldiers have scattered along the streets of their quarters unmistakably testify to the fact that dysentery is destroying them. I have never before seen such sodden drunkenness, nor any more scandalous or impudent than the drunkenness that holds these men in its grip. Nor have I ever seen more unrestrained appetites. Every hour of the day, except during the evenings, when they are all drunk, one can find them eating everything they see.

The Palace and almost all public buildings have been savagely ransacked and destroyed. I think it only right to say, however, that our disgraceful rabble were the ones who began it all. When the enemy's troops entered the Palace, the doors had already been broken down and the building had been plundered.

Reprinted from *Mexico During the War with the United States,* edited by Walter V. Scholes, trans. Elliott B. Scherr, by permission of the University of Missouri Press. Copyright © 1970 by Ms. Marie V. Scholes.

Three days later the embroidered velvet canopy was sold for four pesos at the Palace entrance. The Government records and other items were sold for two reales. The infamous and eternally accursed Santa Anna abandoned us all, both individuals and property, to the mercy of the enemy and did not leave even one sentinel to defend us.

In Durango you probably know more of what is going on than I do, and you no doubt can see how horrible our future is. I am forwarding to you some documents, two of which I want you to keep as testimony of the iniquitous and shameful rule that the Americans have imposed upon us. The sad thing about all this is that the punishment has been deserved.

Forward the enclosed letters and tell the members of my family that we are all in good health. Do not forget your friend, who holds you in great esteem.

91

San Francisco and the California Gold Rush (1848)

The Spanish first colonized California in the 18th century, extending missions and settlements up the coast to protect the northern approaches to Mexico. By the early 19th century, a small but profitable ranching community had emerged, supplying Yankee traders with tallow and skins for the China trade. Such opportunities attracted a small American community to the area. The war with Mexico escalated American interest in the region, but it was the 1848 discovery of gold in the American River Valley near Sacramento that rapidly transformed California. E. Gould Buffum was among those who witnessed the gold rush's beginnings. He first came to the San Francisco area in March 1846 as a lieutenant of the 7th Regiment of New York State volunteers. Just two years later, he, like so many others, headed to the gold fields to seek a fortune that few realized. The following account, from Buffum's Six Months in the Gold Mines, *describes San Franciscans' response to the news of gold discoveries. News of the strikes quickly made its way east. By the end of 1849, almost 100,000 people lived in California, most of them recent arrivals.*

Questions to Consider

1. How was gold discovered in California?

2. What effect did the discovery have on people in California?

3. Does this document seem consistent with the views of American behavior expressed by Alexis de Tocqueville in "Americans on the Move" (Document 74)?

E. Gould Buffum, *Six Months in the Gold Mines* (Philadelphia, 1850), 67–69, 89–91.

During the month of January, 1848, two men, named Marshall and Bennett, were engaged in the erection of a saw-mill located by John A. Sutter on the South Fork of the American River, at a point, where oak, pine, cypress, and cedar trees covered the surrounding hills, and where Indian labor was to be procured at a mere nominal price. These were the motives that prompted Sutter to establish a mill and trading post in this, then unknown, region. Little did he imagine to foresee that, in the hands of an overruling Providence, he was to be the instrument to disclose to mankind riches of which the most sanguine day-dreamer never dreamt, and open caves in which the wonderful lamp of Aladdin would have been dimmed by the surrounding brightness.

One morning Marshall, while examining the tail-race of the mill, discovered, much to his astonishment, some small shining particles in the sand at the bottom of the race, which upon examination he became satisfied were gold. Not content, however, with his own investigations, some specimens which were found throughout the whole race were sent to San Francisco by Bennett, where an assayer removed all doubt of their nature and purity. The discovery was kept a profound secret while Bennett proceeded to Monterey and tried to obtain a grant of the land on which the gold had been found from Colonel Mason, then Governor of the Territory. Colonel Mason informed him, however, that he had no authority to make any such conveyance, and Bennett returned to San Francisco, where he exhibited his specimens to Sam. Brannan, Mr. Hastings, and several others. A number of persons immediately visited the spot, and satisfied their curiosity. Captain Sutter himself came to San Francisco, and confirmed the statements of Bennett, and about the 1st of April, the story became public property. Of course, the news spread like wild fire, and in less than one week after the news reached Monterey, one thousand people were on their way to the gold region. The more staid and sensible citizens affected to view it as an illusion, and cautioned the people against the fearful reaction that would inevitably ensue. Yet many a man who one day boldly pronounced the discovery a humbug, and the gold-hunters little better than maniacs, was seen on the morrow stealthily wending his way, with a tin pan and shovel concealed beneath his cloak or serape, to a launch about proceeding up the golden Sacramento. Before the middle of July, the whole lower country was depopulated. Rancheros left their herds to revel in delightful liberty upon the hills of their ranchos; merchants closed their stores, lawyers left their clients, doctors their patients, soldiers took "French leave." Colonel Mason, then Governor of California, was himself seized with the "mania," and taking his adjutant and an escort, started for the mines, "in order to be better able to make a report to the Government." The alcalde of San Francisco stopped the wheels of justice, and went also. Every idler in the country, who could purchase, beg, or steal, a horse, was off, and ere the first time of August the principal towns were entirely deserted.

In San Francisco, the very headquarters of all the business in California, there were, at this time, but seven male inhabitants, and but one store open. In the mean time the most extravagant stories were in circulation. Hundreds and sometimes even thousands of dollars were spoken of as the reward of a day's labor. Indians were said to pay readily a hundred dollars for a blanket, sixteen for a bottle of grog, and everything else in proportion. In the mean time, new discoveries had been made at Mormon Island, as far north as the Yuba River, and as far south as the Stanislaus; and the mining population had swelled to about three thousand. The stories that had been put in circulation in regard to the richness of the placers were in the main true. A few months after their discovery I saw men, in whom I placed the utmost confidence, who assured me that for days in succession they had dug from the bowels of the earth over five hundred dollars a day. . . .

92

"Civil Disobedience" (1849)

The Mexican War was one of America's most unpopular foreign ventures. Ostensibly begun because of Mexico's invasion of Texas, the war was primarily the result of America's desire to acquire territory. Opposition to the war was particularly strong in New England, where many viewed the conflict as an unjust expansion of slavery. Henry David Thoreau was among those prominent in his opposition to the war. Like his fellow Transcendentalists, he eschewed rationalism, believing that the material world could be transcended and a higher form of reality realized through intuition. Thoreau's philosophy led him to live as a semi-hermit at Walden Pond outside of Concord, Massachusetts. The declaration of the Mexican War, however, demanded a response. In July 1846, Thoreau protested the war by refusing to pay his taxes, an act that briefly landed him in jail. Three years later, he commented at length on "passive resistance" in "Civil Disobedience." His suggestions, some of which are found in the following selection, became a model for later leaders such as India's Mohandas Gandhi and civil rights advocate Martin Luther King, Jr.

Questions to Consider

1. What kind of peaceful revolution does Thoreau advocate?
2. Why is Thoreau wary of the rich when it comes to righteous causes?
3. According to Thoreau, why do people need government?
4. Based on this document, what are Thoreau's views toward American democracy?

. . . Under a government which imprisons any unjustly, the true place for a just man is also a prison. The proper place to-day, the only place which

Henry David Thoreau, "Civil Disobedience," *The Writings of Henry David Thoreau*, vol. 4, *Cape Cod and Miscellanies* (New York, 1968; reprint edition of 1906 ed.), 356–387.

Massachusetts has provided for her freer and less desponding spirits, is in her prisons, to be put out and locked out of the State by her own act, as they have already put themselves out by their principles. It is there that the fugitive slave, and the Mexican prisoner on parole, and the Indian come to plead the wrongs of his race should find them; on that separate, but more free and honorable, ground, where the State places those who are not with her, but against her,—the only house in a slave State in which a free man can abide with honor. If any think that their influence would be lost there, and their voices no longer afflict the ear of the State, that they would not be as an enemy within its walls, they do not know by how much truth is stronger than error, nor how much more eloquently and effectively he can combat injustice who has experienced a little in his own person. Cast your whole vote, not a strip of paper merely, but your whole influence. A minority is powerless while it conforms to the majority; it is not even a minority then; but it is irresistible when it clogs by its whole weight. If the alternative is to keep all just men in prison, or give up war and slavery, the State will not hesitate which to choose. If a thousand men were not to pay their tax-bills this year, that would not be a violent and bloody measure, as it would be to pay them, and enable the State to commit violence and shed innocent blood. This is, in fact, the definition of a peaceable revolution, if any such is possible. If the tax-gatherer, or any other public officer, asks me, as one has done, "But what shall I do?" my answer is, "If you really wish to do anything, resign your office." When the subject has refused allegiance, and the officer has resigned his office, then the revolution is accomplished. But even suppose blood should flow. Is there not a sort of blood shed when the conscience is wounded? Through this would a man's real manhood and immortality flow out, and he bleeds to an everlasting death. I see this blood flowing now.

I have contemplated the imprisonment of the offender, rather than the seizure of his goods,—though both will serve the same purpose,—because they who assert the purest right, and consequently are most dangerous to a corrupt State, commonly have not spent much time in accumulating property. To such the State renders comparatively small service, and a slight tax is wont to appear exorbitant, particularly if they are obliged to earn it by special labor with their hands. If there were one who lived wholly without the use of money, the State itself would hesitate to demand it of him. But the rich man—not to make any invidious comparison—is always sold to the institution which makes him rich. Absolutely speaking, the more money, the less virtue; for money comes between a man and his objects, and obtains them for him; and it was certainly no great virtue to obtain it. It puts to rest many questions which he would otherwise be taxed to answer; while the only new question which it puts is the hard but superfluous one, how to spend it. Thus his moral ground is taken from under his feet. The opportunities of living are diminished in proportion as what are called the "means" are increased. The best thing a man can do for his culture when he is rich is to endeavor to carry out those schemes which he entertained when he was poor. Christ answered the Herodians according to their condition. "Show me the tribute-money," said he;—and one took a penny out of his pocket;—if you use money which has the image of Caesar on it, and which he has made current and valuable, that is, if you are men of the State, and gladly enjoy the advantages of Caesar's government, then pay him back some of his own when he demands it. "Render therefore to Caesar that which is Caesar's, and to God those things which are God's,"—leaving them no wiser than before as to which was which; for they did not wish to know.

When I converse with the freest of my neighbors, I perceive that, whatever they may say about the magnitude and seriousness of the question, and their regard for the public tranquility, the long and the short of the matter is, that they cannot spare the protection of the existing government, and they dread the consequences to their property and families of disobedience to it. For my own part, I should not like to think that I ever rely on the protection of the State. But, if I deny the authority of the State when it presents its tax-bill, it will soon take and waste all my property, and so harass me and my children without end. This is hard. This makes it impossible for a man to live honestly, and at the same time comfortably, in outward respects. It will not be worth the while to accumulate property; that would be sure to go again. You must hire or squat somewhere, and raise but a small crop, and eat that soon. You must live within yourself, and depend upon yourself always tucked up and ready for a start, and not have many affairs. . . .

93

A Chinese American at Yale (1850)

The concept of "manifest destiny" conjures images of a muscular nationalism and the desire for territorial expansion based on white American beliefs in the superiority of their political, social, economic, and religious institutions. Such beliefs, now seen as racist and ethnocentric, predominated during the mid-19th century; however, not all Americans embraced these views. Many missionaries were sincere in their desire to convert non-Christians to Christianity and formed close relationships with converts, suggesting a belief in racial equality that was unusual in the 19th century. The following document, written by Yale's first Chinese graduate, suggests a different view of the era of Manifest Destiny. Yung Ming had received a Western education at a missionary school in southeastern China (Guangdong Province). He came to the United States, attended a preparatory school, and eventually attended Yale University.

Questions to Consider

1. Did Yung Ming seem to enjoy his experience at Yale?
2. Who is supporting Yung Ming's efforts to receive an education? Why?

3. How would John L. O'Sullivan, author of "Texas and California Annexation" (Document 87), respond to Yung Ming's presence at Yale? How do you account for such different views on race and ethnicity during this period?

4. How does Yung Ming's life as a student seem similar to yours? How does it seem different?

During the summer of 1850, it seems that Brown who had been making a visit in the South to see his sister, while there had occasion to call on some of the members of "The Ladies' Association" in Savannah, Ga., to whom he mentioned my case. He returned home in the nick of time, just after I had the interview with the board of trustees of the academy. I told him of the outcome, when, as stated above, he approved my position, and told me what he had done. He said that the members of the association agreed to help me in college. On the strength of that I gathered fresh courage, and went down to New Haven to pass my examination for entrance. How I got in, I do not know, as I had had only fifteen months of Latin and twelve months of Greek, and ten months of mathematics. My preparation had been interrupted because the academy had been broken up by the Palmer & New London R.R. that was being built close by. As compared with the college preparation of nine-tenths of my class-mates, I was far behind. However, I passed without condition. But I was convinced I was not sufficiently prepared as my recitations in the class-room clearly proved. Between the struggle of how to make ends meet financially and how to keep up with the class in my studies, I had a pretty tough time of it. I used to sweat over my studies till twelve o'clock every night the whole Freshman year. I took little or no exercise and my health and strength began to fail and I was obliged to ask for a leave of absence of a week. I went to East Windsor to get rested and came back refreshed.

In the Sophomore year, from my utter aversion to mathematics especially to differential and integral calculus, which I abhorred and detested, and which did me little or no good in the way of mental discipline, I used to . . . flunk so often that I really thought I was going to be dropped from the class, or dismissed from college. But for some unexplained reasons I was saved from such a catastrophe, and I squeezed through the second year in college with so low a mark that I was afraid to ask my division tutor, who happened to be Tutor Blodget, who had me in Greek, about it. The only redeeming feature that saved me as a student in the class of 1854, was the fortunate circumstance that I happened to be a successful competitor on two occasions in English composition in my division. I was awarded the first prize in the second term, and the first prize in the third term of the year. These prizes gave me quite an eclat in the college as well as in the outside world, but I was not at all elated over them on account of my poor scholarship which I felt keenly through the whole college course.

Yung Ming, *My Life in China and America* (New York, 1909), 36–40.

Before the close of my second year, I succeeded in securing the steward-ship of a boarding club consisting of sophomores and juniors. There were altogether twenty members. I did all the marketing and served at the table. In this way, I earned my board through the latter half of my college course. In money matters, I was supplied with remittances from "The Ladies Associa-tion" in Savannah, and also contributions from the Olyphant Brothers of New York. In addition to these sources of supply, I was paid for being an assistant librarian to the "Brothers of Unity," which was one of the two col-lege debating societies that owned a library, and of which I was a member.

In my senior year I was again elected librarian to the same Society and got $30.00. These combined sums were large enough to meet all my cash bills, since my wants had to be finely trimmed to suit the cloth. If most of the country parsons of that period could get along with a salary of $200 or $300 a year (supplemented, of course, with an annual donation party, which sometimes carried away more than it donated), having as a general thing a large family to look after, I certainly ought to have been able to get through college with gifts of nearly a like amount, supplemented with donations of shirts and stockings from ladies who took an interest in my education.

The class of 1854, to which I had the honor and the good fortune to belong, graduated ninety-eight all told. Being the first Chinaman who had ever been known to go through a first-class American college, I naturally attracted considerable attention; and from the fact that I was librarian for one of the college debating societies (Linonia was the other) for two years, I was known by members of three classes above, and members of the three classes below me. This fact had contributed towards familiarizing me with the college world at large, and my nationality, of course, added piquancy to my popularity.

As an undergraduate, I had already acquired a factitious reputation within the walls of Yale. But that was ephemeral and soon passed out of existence after graduation.

13

Slavery and the Old South

The republic's founders envisioned a nation of liberty, assuming that slavery would gradually wither away. Economic forces, however, conspired to make slavery profitable in the South. By the 1830s, many southerners argued that the "peculiar institution" was essential to their way of life. The persistence of slavery made the region increasingly distinct from the North and brought condemnation from reformers on both sides of the Atlantic. White southerners responded to these attacks by portraying their culture as an idyllic society to be emulated, not maligned. Individuals of African descent provided a much different view of southern society. The following excerpts include these varying viewpoints about the Old South.

94

Olaudah Equiano Describes the "Middle Passage" (1789)

The first Africans arrived in the English colonies in 1619, when a Dutch vessel brought a group to Jamestown, Virginia. The status of the Africans was initially murky, but by the end of the 17th century, Africans were legally classified as slaves who filled European demands for cheap labor. The African slave trade, which predated the arrival of the Europeans in Africa, became an enormous business in which traders became rich through the sale of human beings. The slave trade created a cycle of violence in West Africa that devastated many groups and virtually depopulated certain regions. The following account by Olaudah Equiano (Gustavus Vassa) vividly describes the horrors of the trade.

Questions to Consider

1. What was Equiano's initial reaction to contact with the white slave traders?
2. What were conditions like on the slave ship crossing the Atlantic?
3. What was Equiano's attitude toward the "middle passage"?

Olaudah Equiano, *The Life of Olaudah Equiano, or Gustavus Vassa, the African* (Boston, 1837), 43–52.

The first object which saluted my eyes when I arrived on the coast was the sea, and a slave ship, which was then riding at anchor, and waiting for its cargo. These filled me with astonishment, which was soon converted into terror when I was carried on board. I was immediately handled and tossed up to see if I were sound by some of the crew; and I was now persuaded that I had gotten into a world of bad spirits, and that they were going to kill me. Their complexions, too, differing so much from ours, their long hair, and the language they spoke, (which was very different from any I had ever heard) united to confirm me in this belief. Indeed such were the horrors of my views and fears at the moment, that, if ten thousand worlds had been my own, I would have freely parted with them all to have exchanged my condition with that of the meanest slave in my own country. When I looked round the ship too, and saw a large furnace of copper boiling, and a multitude of black people of every description chained together, every one of their countenances expressing dejection and sorrow, I no longer doubted my fate; and, quite overpowered with horror and anguish, I fell motionless on the deck and fainted. When I recovered a little I found some black people about me, who I believe were some of those who brought me on board, and had been receiving their pay; they talked to me in order to cheer me, but all in vain. I asked them if we were not to be eaten by those white men with horrible looks, red faces, and loose hair. They told me I was not. . . .

I now saw myself deprived of all chance of returning to my native country, or even the least glimpse of hope of gaining the shore, which I now considered as friendly; and I even wished for my former slavery in preference to my present situation. . . . I was soon put down under the decks, and there I received such a salutation in my nostrils as I had never experienced in my life: so that, with the loathsomeness of the stench, and crying together, I became so sick and low that I was not able to eat, nor had I the least desire to taste any thing. I now wished for the last friend, death, to relieve me; but soon, to my grief, two of the white men offered me eatables; and, on my refusing to eat, one of them held me fast by the hands, and laid me across I think the windlass, and tied my feet, while the other flogged me severely. . . . In a little time after, amongst the poor chained men, I found some of my own nation, which in a small degree gave ease to my mind. I inquired of these what was to be done with us; they gave me to understand we were to be carried to these white people's country to work for them. I then was a little revived, and thought, if it were no worse than working, my situation was not so desperate: but still I feared I should be put to death, the white people looked and acted, as I thought, in so savage a manner; for I had never seen among any people such instances of brutal cruelty; and this not only shown towards us blacks, but also to some of the whites themselves. . . . The stench of the hold while we were on the coast was so intolerably loathsome, that it was dangerous to remain there for any time, and some of us had been permitted to stay on the deck for the fresh air; but now that the whole ship's cargo were confined together; it became absolutely pestilential. The closeness of the place, and the heat of the climate, added to the number in the ship, which was so crowded that each had scarcely room to turn himself, almost suffocated us. This produced copious perspirations, so that the air soon became unfit for respiration, from a variety of loathsome smells, and brought on a sickness among the slaves, of which many died, thus falling victims to the improvident avarice, as I may call it, of their purchasers. The wretched situation was again aggravated by the galling of the chains, now become insupportable; and the filth of the necessary tubs, into which the children often fell, and were almost suffocated. The shrieks of the women, and the groans of the dying, rendered the whole scene of horror almost inconceivable. Happily perhaps for myself, I was soon reduced so low here that it was thought necessary to keep me almost always on deck; and from my extreme youth I was not put in fetters. . . .

One day, when we had a smooth sea and moderate wind, two of my wearied countrymen who were chained together (I was near them at the time), preferring death to such a life of misery, somehow made through the nettings and jumped into the sea: immediately another quite dejected fellow . . . followed their example. . . .

At last we came in sight of the island of Barbados, at which the whites on board gave a great shout, and made many signs of joy to us. . . . Many merchants and planters now came on board, though it was evening. They put us in separate parcels, and examined us attentively. They also made us jump, and pointed to the land, signifying we were to go there. . . . We were not many days in the merchant's custody before we were sold after their usual manner, which is this:—On a signal given, (as the beat of a drum) the buyers rush at once into the yard where the slaves are confined, and make a choice of that parcel they like best. The noise and clamor with which this is attended, and the eagerness visible in the countenances of the buyers, serve not a little to increase the apprehensions of the terrified Africans, who may well be supposed to consider them as the ministers of that destruction to which they think themselves devoted. In this manner, without scruple, are relations and friends separated, most of them never to see each other again. . . .

95

Perspectives on Slavery

The South's dependence on slave labor helped fuel the booming cotton kingdom, but slavery became an increasingly divisive issue in American life. As the debate over slavery intensified during the decades before the Civil War, opponents and proponents of the "peculiar institution" went to great lengths to make their case. The first set of images that follows compares the status of Africans in Africa with those in the United States. Supporters of slavery, arguing from a perspective similar to the proponents of Manifest Destiny, believed that African-American contact with "superior" white culture improved the quality of the slaves' lives. But abolitionists, both white and black, told a different story of exploitation and humiliation. The first pair of images depicts the purported improvement offered by contact with American society. The third image shows slaves picking cotton.

Questions to Consider

1. Why do you suppose white Americans might wish to believe the views offered in the first set of images?
2. In what ways is the ideology depicted in the first set of images similar to the views expressed by the supporters of Manifest Destiny?
3. What can you deduce from the image about the use of black labor on southern plantations?
4. What can you deduce from the image about the black family?

"The Negro in His Own Country"

"The Negro in America"

Library of Congress, Prints and Photographs Division, LC-USZ62-76385

"Picking cotton on a Georgia plantation"

96

The Trial of Denmark Vesey (1822)

The Old South's dependence on slave labor provided opportunity for wealth among its white inhabitants, but at the expense of the African-American slaves who toiled on their behalf. White southerners chose to believe that their slaves were content with their status, but the slaveowners' anxiety over the possibility of a slave insurrection belied underlying fears. Slave insurrections had been infrequent in America, but the success of the revolt on St. Domingue in the 1790s was an example of what could happen. Before the discovery of the Vesey plot in 1822, many white citizens in Charleston, South Carolina, chose to ignore the potential for revolt. Denmark Vesey was probably born in Africa and arrived in Charleston in 1783. Having purchased his freedom with winnings from a local lottery, Vesey found that his freedom and wealth still left him without status in race-conscious Charleston. Vesey, other free blacks in the city, and an undetermined number of slaves responded by plotting to launch an insurrection on July 14, 1822. White authorities uncovered the plot in late May and arrested Vesey on June 22. The following account is from his trial transcript. He and 34 fellow conspirators were later executed.

Questions to Consider

1. What can you deduce from this account about white attitudes toward African Americans?

2. Why do you think an account of the Denmark Vesey trial was published?

3. Why do you think the transcript is so clear in describing Vesey as a "free black man"?

4. Are the attitudes expressed in this document consistent with what David Walker said about white American society in "Appeal to the Coloured Citizens of the World" (Document 80)?

THE TRIAL OF DENMARK VESEY, A FREE BLACK MAN—COL. G.W. CROSS ATTENDING AS HIS COUNSEL

EVIDENCE.

William, the slave of Mr. Paul, testified as follows:—Mingo Harth told me *that Denmark Vesey was the chiefest man, and more concerned than any one else*— Denmark Vesey is an old man in whose yard my master's negro woman Sarah cooks—he was her father in law, having married her mother Beck, and though they have been parted some tome, yet he visited her at her house near the Indendant's, (Major Hamilton) where I have often heard him speak of the rising—*He said he would not like to have a white man in his presence—that he had a great hatred for the whites,* and that if all were like him they would resist the whites—he studies all he can to put it into the heads of the blacks to have a rising against the whites, and tried to induce me to join—he tries to induce all his acquaintances—this has been his chief study and delight for a considerable time—my last conversation with him was in April—he studies the Bible a great deal and tries to prove from it that slavery and bondage is against the Bible. I am persuaded that Denmark Vesey was chiefly concerned in business. . . .

Frank, Mrs. Ferguson's slave gave the following evidence—I know Denmark Vesey and have been to his house—I have heard him say that the negroe's situation was so bad he did not know how they could endure it, and was astonished they did not rise and fend for themselves, and he advised me to join and rise—he said he was going about to see different people, and mentioned the names of Ned Bennett and Peter Poyas as concerned with him—

"The Trial of Denmark Vesey, a Free Black Man," *An Official Report of the Trials of Sundry Negroes charged with an Attempt to Raise an Insurrection in the State of South Carolina,* comp. Lionel H. Kennedy and Thomas Parker (Charleston, 1822), 85–90.

that he had spoken to Ned and Peter on this subject; and that they were to go about and tell the blacks that they were free, and must rise and *fight for themselves*—that they would take the Magazines and Guard-Houses, and the city and be free—that he was going to send *into the country* to inform the people there too—he said he wanted me to join them—I said I could not answer— he said if I would not go into the country for him he could get others—he said himself, Ned Bennett, Peter Poyas and Monday Gell were the principals men and himself the head man. He said they were the principal men to go about and inform the people and fix them, &c. that *one party would land on South-Bay, one about Wappoo, and about the farms*—that the party which was to land on South-Bay was to take the Guard-House and get arms and then they would be able to go on—that the attack was to commence about 12 o'clock at night—*that great numbers would come from all about,* and it must succeed as so many were engaged in it—that they would kill all the whites—that they would leave their master's houses and assemble together near the lines, march down and meet the party which would land on South-Bay—. . .

The court *unanimously* found Denmark Vesey GUILTY, and passed upon him the sentence of DEATH. After his conviction, a good deal of testimony was given against him during the succeeding trials.—

97

The Alabama Frontier (1821)

The War of 1812 proved disastrous for the Native Americans of the trans-Appalachian West. Andrew Jackson's victory against the Creeks at Horseshoe Bend in March 1814 opened Alabama to white settlement. Following the war, settlers who were eager to obtain rich lands in the expanding cotton kingdom swarmed to areas such as north Alabama's Tennessee River Valley. By 1819, Alabama had attracted enough people to become a state. Although most of the settlers came in search of farmland, many of the newcomers clustered together in towns that emerged from the wilderness virtually overnight. One of the boom towns on the South's urban frontier was Florence, Alabama. In the following letter, Anne Royal boosts the prospects of her new community and conveys the optimism shared by many early settlers.

Questions to Consider

1. To what audience is this document directed?
2. What natural advantages does Florence, Alabama, possess?
3. How does Anne Royal suggest that the town still retains a sense of rugged frontier individualism?
4. What can you deduce about frontier attitudes from this document?

. . . Florence is one of the new towns of this beautiful and rapid rising state. It is happily situated for commerce at the head of steamboat navigation, on the north side of Tennessee river, in the county of Lauderdale, five miles below the port of the Muscle Shoals, and ten miles from the line of the state of Tennessee.

Florence is to be the great emporium of the northern part of this state. I do not see why it should not; it has a great capital and is patronized by the wealthiest gentlemen in the state. It has a great state at its back; another in front, and a noble river on all sides, the steamboats pouring every necessary and every luxury into its lap. Its citizens, bold, enterprising, and industrious— much more so than any I have seen in the state.

Many large and elegant brick buildings are already built here, (although it was sold out, but two years since,) and frame houses are putting up daily. It is not uncommon to see a framed building begun in the morning and finished by night.

Several respectable mercantile houses are established here, and much business is done on commission also. The site of the town is beautifully situated on an eminence, commanding an extensive view of the surrounding country, and Tennessee River, from which it is three quarters of a mile distant. It has two springs of excellent and never failing water. Florence has communication by water with Mississippi, Missouri, Louisiana, Indiana, Illinois, Ohio, Kentucky, West Pennsylvania, West Virginia, and East Tennessee, and very shortly will communicate with the Eastern States, through the great canal!!! The great Military road that leads from Nashville to New Orleans, by way of Lake Ponchartrain, passes through this town, and the number of people who travel through it, and the numerous droves of horses for the lower country, for market, are incredible. Florence contains one printing press, and publishes a paper weekly called the *Florence Gazette;* it is ably patronized, and edited by one of our first men, and said to be the best paper in the state. Florence is inhabited by people from almost all parts of Europe and the United States; here are English, Irish, Welsh, Scotch, French, Dutch, Germans, and Grecians. The first Greek I ever saw was in this town. I conversed with him on the subject of his country, but found him grossly ignorant. He butchers for the town, and has taken to his arms a mulatto woman for a wife. He very often takes an airing on horseback of a Sunday afternoon, with his wife riding by his side, and both arrayed in shining costume.

The river at Florence is upwards of five-hundred yards wide; it is ferried in a large boat worked by four horses, and crosses in a few minutes.

There are two large and well kept taverns in Florence, and several Doggeries. A Doggery is a place where spirituous liquors are sold; and where men get drunk, quarrel, and fight, as often as they choose, but where there is

---

Anne Royal to her sister, 10 July 1821, Letter 45, Anne Royal, *Letters from Alabama on Various Subjects* (Washington, DC, 1830), 144–146.

nothing to eat for man or beast. Did you ever hear any thing better named. "I sware!" said a Yankee peddlar, one day, with both his eyes bunged up, "that are Doggery, be rightly named. Never seed the like on't. If I get to hum agin it 'il be a nice man 'il catch me in these here parts. Awfullest place one could be at." It appeared the inmates of the Doggery enticed him under pretence of buying his wares, and forced him to drink; and then forced him to fight; but the poor little Yankee was sadly beaten. Not content with blacking up his eyes, they over-turned his tin-cart, and scattered his tins to the four winds; frightened his horse, and tormented his very soul out about lasses, &c. He was a laughable object—but to hear his dialect in laying off the law, was a complete farce, particularly when Pat came to invite him into the same Doggery to drink friends—"I ben't a dog to go into that are dog house."

The people, you see, know a thing or two, here; they call things by their right names. But to proceed—there may be about one hundred dwelling houses and stores, a court house, and several warehouses in Florence. The latter are however on the river. One of the longest buildings I ever saw, is in Florence. It was built by a company of gentlemen, and is said to have cost $90,000, and is not yet finished. The proprietors, being of this place, are men of immense wealth, and are pushing their capital with great foresight and activity. For industry and activity, Florence outstrips all the northern towns in the state. More people travel this road than all our western roads put together. . . .

98

A Reaction to the Nat Turner Revolt (1831)

In the antebellum South, slave revolts occurred with enough frequency to alarm whites who lived in areas with large slave populations. The bloody uprising on St. Domingue (Haiti) between 1792 and 1802, followed by the Gabriel Prosser revolt in Virginia (1800) and the Vesey plot in South Carolina (1822), inflamed these fears. But the insurrection that had the greatest impact occurred in the summer of 1831 in South-hampton County, Virginia. The revolt's leader, Nat Turner, was instrumental in organizing the slaves' attempt to gain their freedom. An extraordinary individual who had learned to read at a young age, Turner sought refuge from his bondage in the Bible. Convinced that he had a divine mission, he hatched his plot in August 1831. The revolt failed after the insurgents had killed more than 60 whites; at least 120 African Americans would be killed in retribution. Turner and many of his co-conspirators subsequently paid with their lives. The insurrection, which many southern whites blamed on abolitionist agitation, caused southern leaders to become increasingly defensive of the institution. The following selection from the Norfolk and Portsmouth Herald *indicates the white response to news of the revolt.*

Questions to Consider

1. How does the newspaper describe the insurrection?

2. Why does the paper believe the revolt would fail?

3. Why do you think the newspaper is so graphic in its descriptions of the murders?

4. Why is Nat Turner's revolt significant?

. . .An express arrived from Jerusalem this morning, reports sixty four killed and several missing;—the Blacks in a state of confusion and closely pursued, and when overtaken shown to quarters.

Among the killed, are Mrs. Catharine White, head, 5 daughters, 1 son and 1 Grandson; Mr. Levi Waller's family, 14 in number, himself the only one that escaped; Mr. Travis and family 5; Mr. William and family 5; Mr. Jacob Williams and family 4; Mr. Vaughan, sister and family 5; Mr. Barrow and Wife 2; Mr. Reesse and family 4;—together with others not recollected, sufficient to make the above number, 64.

The information from Suffolk received yesterday, states that the troops under Col. Worth and Com. Elliot, on their arrival at Suffolk, passed rapidly on to Southampton.

No disaffections had taken place on any of the plantations, as far as was known, since Monday. The number of the brigands is supposed to be from 100 to 150, chiefly on horseback, and armed with fowling pieces, but they have never shown themselves in a body of more than 40,—the rest being divided into small marauding parties. A number of them have been shot down in the roads, and their carcasses strew the highways. As there are probably by this time upwards of 3000 troops in pursuit of them, there is little doubt of their being soon hemmed in and captured.

We have intimated that this insurrection was not the result of concert to any extent, nor rested on any combination to give it the least chance of success. This is evident from the small number of adherents which the ringleaders with all their threats and persuasions were able to enlist in their cause. The slaves throughout the country are generally well affected, and even faithful to their employers.—A pleasing instance of this is said to have occurred while the black demons of slaughter were executing their horrid work. Before they had received any considerable increase, and in the early stage of their butcheries, they approached the dwelling of Dr. Blount, with the fell purpose of murdering him and his family, when they were met by the doctor's own servants, who resolutely opposed their entrance, declaring that they would lose every drop of blood in defense of their master and his family. The brigands still persisting a battle ensued in which they were finally routed, leaving one of

"Insurrection in Southampton County," *Norfolk and Portsmouth Herald*, August 26, 1831, p. 2

their party and two horses behind them. We give the story as it was related to us; if true, great indeed will be the desert of these noble hearted Africans.

Extract of a letter to the Editor of the Herald, dated
    WINTON, (N.C.) Aug. 24.
We are all in a state of confusion here. There has been an insurrection among the negroes in Southampton, Va. in the neighborhood of the Cross Keys, about 30 miles from this place. From the best information we have had, three white men and four slaves of a gentleman near the Cross Keys, rose upon him about an hour before day on Monday morning and killed him and all his white family. They then proceeded to Mrs. Catherine Whitehead's and murdered the whole of the white family, consisting of 7 persons. This took place about day light. Mr. Williams, a near neighbor to Mrs. W. hearing their cries, ran over, and found Mrs. W. butchered with an axe, her son (a minister of the Gospel) with his head severed from his body, and a young lady lying dead in the fire place of her chamber. Mr. Williams immediately returned to his own dwellings, when he was met by one of his own negro boys with the terrible tidings that his wife and children had been murdered in his absence. After pressing all the slaves they fell in with, under the penalty of death for refusal, they had accumulated from 100 to 200, and in their progress have murdered the families of Sir Geo Vaughan, Mr. Thomas Barrow, and many others whose names are not recollected. . . .

99

The Plantation Labor Force (1838–39)

Plantation slaves performed a variety of tasks. While a handful of slaves worked in the "big house" and some others worked as artisans, most toiled in the fields. Male and female field hands were subject to a highly organized hierarchy that carefully governed their work patterns. Generally organized into gangs or assigned to complete specific tasks, they were carefully watched by either white overseers or slave drivers. The following selection describes the power that overseers and drivers had over the slaves. Author Fanny Kemble was among the most intriguing characters of the antebellum period. A member of one of the leading acting families in British history, she was one of the first great actresses to appear on American stages and was also an accomplished poet and playwright. Her marriage to slave owner Pierce Butler brought her to his Georgia plantation and provided her with a first-hand view of slavery. She and Butler divorced in 1849. Having given up the stage, she continued her writing, finally publishing Journal of a Residence on a Georgian Plantation in 1838–39 *in 1863. An excerpt from the work appears as follows.*

Questions to Consider

1. What does Fanny Kemble find disturbing about slavery?
2. How is the slave workforce organized?
3. How would southern white slaveholders respond to this document?
4. In what ways might Kemble's gender have influenced her views toward slavery?

At the upper end of the row of houses, and nearest to our overseer's residence, is the hut of the head driver. Let me explain, by the way, his office. The negroes, as I before told you, are divided into troops or gangs, as they are called; at the head of each gang is a driver, who stands over them, whip in hand, while they perform their daily task, who renders an account of each individual slave and his work every evening to the overseer, and receives from him directions for their next day's tasks. Each driver is allowed to inflict a dozen lashes upon any refractory slave in the field, and at the time of the offense; they may not, however, extend the chastisement, and if it is found ineffectual, their remedy lies in reporting the unmanageable individual either to the head driver or the overseer, the former of whom has power to inflict three dozen lashes at his own discretion, and the latter as many as he himself sees fit, within the number of fifty; which limit, however, I must tell you, is an arbitrary one on this plantation, appointed by the founder of the estate, Major——, Mr.——'s grandfather, many of whose regulations, indeed I believe most of them, are still observed in the government of the plantation. Limits of this sort, however, to the power of either driver, head driver, or overseer, may or may not exist elsewhere; they are, to a certain degree, a check upon the power of these individuals; but in the absence of the master, the overseer may confine himself within the limit or not, as he chooses; and as for the master himself, where is his limit? He may, if he likes, flog a slave to death, for the laws which pretend that he may not are a mere pretense, inasmuch as the testimony of a black is never taken against a white; and upon this plantation of ours, and a thousand more, the overseer is the *only* white man, so whence should come the testimony to any crime of his? With regard to the oft-repeated statement that it is not the owner's interest to destroy his human property, it answers nothing; the instances in which men, to gratify the immediate impulse of passion, sacrifice not only their eternal, but their evident, palpable, positive worldly interest, are infinite. Nothing is commoner than for a man under the transient influence of anger to disregard his worldly advantage; and the black slave, whose preservation is indeed supposed to be his owner's interest, may be, will be, and is occasionally sacrificed to the blind impulse of passion. . . .

In considering the whole condition of the people on this plantation, it appears to me that the principal hardships fall to the lot of the women—that

Frances Anne Kemble, *Journal of a Residence on a Georgian Plantation in 1838–1839* (New York, 1863), 42–43, 263.

is, the principal physical hardships. The very young members of the community are of course idle and neglected; the very, very, old, idle and neglected too; the middle-aged men do not appear to me overworked, and lead a mere animal existence, in itself not peculiarly cruel or distressing, but involving a constant element of fear and uncertainty, and the trifling evils of unrequited labor, ignorance the most profound (to which they are condemned by law), and the unutterable injustice which precludes them from all the merits and all the benefits of voluntary exertion, and the progress that results from it. . . .

100

Martin Delany and African-American Nationalism (1852)

The sense of nationalism that was so pervasive in mid-19th-century America was exclusively white. Americans of African descent, subject to widespread and dehumanizing discrimination yet affected by many of the same intellectual currents as whites, would develop their own form of nationalism. The leading Black Nationalist of the time was Martin Delany. A free black from Virginia, Delany settled in Pittsburgh to apprentice as a medical doctor. He eventually won acceptance to Harvard Medical School in 1850, but left following student protests against his presence. By this time he had already begun publishing material for abolitionist presses and briefly co-edited Frederick Douglass's North Star. *Often considered the father of Black Nationalism, he published the following account in 1852. After a brief time in Canada and an exploration of the Niger Valley of West Africa, Delany returned to serve in the Civil War. Following the war, he moved to Charleston, South Carolina, where he became involved in local Republican politics and was an outspoken advocate of African-American self-reliance.*

Questions to Consider

1. Compare and contrast the nationalism expressed by Martin Delany with that of John O'Sullivan ("Texas and California Annexation," Document 87).

2. How does Martin Delany plan to promote Black Nationalism?

3. How might white Americans of the mid-19th century have responded to this proposal?

4. To what extent have African Americans adopted views of race and nation that parallel those expressed by white contemporaries?

Martin R. Delany, *The Condition, Emigration, and Destiny of the Colored People of the United States, Politically Considered* (Philadelphia, 1852), 209–214.

APPENDIX

A PROJECT FOR AN EXPEDITION OF ADVENTURE, TO THE EASTERN COAST OF AFRICA

Every people should be the originators of their own designs, the projector of their own schemes, and creators of the events that lead to their destiny—the consummations of their desires.

Situated as we are, in the United States, many, and almost insurmountable obstacles present themselves. We are four-and-a-half millions in numbers, free and bond; six hundred thousand free, and three-and-a-half millions bond.

We have native hearts and virtues, just as other nations; which in their pristine purity are noble, potent, and worthy of example. We are a nation within a nation;—as the Poles in Russia, the Hungarians in Austria, the Welsh, Irish, and Scotch in the British dominions.

But we have been, by our oppressors, despoiled of our purity, and corrupted in our native characteristics, so that we have inherited their vices, and but few of their virtues, leaving us in character, really a *broken people.*

Being distinguished by complexion, we are still singled out—although having merged in the habits and customs of our oppressors—as a distinct nation of people; as the Poles, Hungarians, Irish, and others, who still retain their native peculiarities, of language, habits, and various other traits. The claims of no people, according to established policy and usage, are respected by any nation, until they are presented in a national capacity.

To accomplish so great and desirable an end, there should be held, a great representative gathering of the colored people of the United States; not what is termed a national Convention, represented en masse, such as have been, for the last few years, held at various times and places; but a true representation of the intelligence and wisdom of the colored freemen; because it will be futile and an utter failure, to attempt such a project without the highest grade of intelligence.

No great project was ever devised without the consultation of the most mature intelligence, and discreet discernment and precaution.

To effect this, and prevent intrusion and improper representation, there should be a CONFIDENTIAL COUNCIL held; and circulars issued, only to such persons as shall be *known* to the projectors to be equal to the desired object. . . .

By this Council to be appointed, a Board of Commissioners, to consist of three, five, or such reasonable number as may be decided upon, one of whom shall be chosen as Principal or Conductor of the Board, whose duty and business shall be, to go on an expedition to the EASTERN COAST of Africa, to make researches for a suitable location on that section of the coast, for the settlement of colored adventurers from the United States, and elsewhere. Their mission should be to all such places as might meet the approbation of the people; as South America, Mexico, the West Indies, &c. . . .

The Council shall appoint a permanent Board of Directors, to manage and supervise the doings of the Commissioners, and to whom they shall be amenable for their doings, who shall hold their office until successors shall be appointed.

A National Confidential Council, to be held once in three years; and sooner, if necessity or emergency should demand it; the Board of Directors giving at least three months' notice, by circulars and newspapers. . . .

MANNER OF RAISING FUNDS

The National Council shall appoint one or two Special Commissioners, to England and France, to solicit, in the name of the Representatives of a Broken Nation, of four-and-a-half millions, the necessary outfit and support, for any period not exceeding three years, of such an expedition. Certainly, what England and France would do, for a little nation—mere nominal nation, of five thousand civilized Liberians, they would be willing and ready to do, for five millions; if they be but authentically represented, in a national capacity. What was due to Greece, enveloped by Turkey, should be due to us, enveloped by the United States; and we believe would be respected, if properly presented. To England and France, we should look for sustenance, and the people of those two nations—as they would have everything to gain from such an adventure and eventual settlement on the Eastern Coast of Africa—the opening of an immense trade being the consequence. The whole Continent is rich in minerals, and the most precious metals, as but a superficial notice of the topographical and geological reports from that country, plainly show to any mind versed in the least, in the science of the earth. . . .

101

A Slave Describes Sugar Cultivation (1853)

Cotton production dominated the economy of the Old South, but large numbers of slaves also labored to bring in cash crops such as sugar. In the following account, Solomon Northup describes the sugar harvest and production during his days of bondage. Born free in Minerva, New York, Northup lived a relatively uneventful life until he was kidnapped not far from his home and sold into slavery in March 1841. Following an unsuccessful attempt to commandeer the slave ship on which he traveled, he spent 12 years working for several different masters in Louisiana. In January 1853, Northup returned to New York after a prominent member of the family that had once owned his father secured the kidnapped slave's freedom. Northup returned to Glens Falls, New York, and published his account later that year, an excerpt of which follows.

Questions to Consider

1. According to Solomon Northup, what did the slaves do to plant and harvest sugar cane?
2. What is gang labor?
3. Was it common to sell the services of a slave to others?
4. What is the significance of this excerpt?

. . . In consequence of my inability in cotton-picking, Epps was in the habit of hiring me out on sugar plantations during the season of cane-cutting and sugar-making. He received for my services a dollar a day, with the money supplying my place on his cotton plantation. Cutting cane was an employment that suited me, and for three successive years I held the lead row at Hawkins', leading a gang of from fifty to an hundred hands. . . .

The ground is prepared in beds, the same as it is prepared for the reception of the cotton seed, except it is ploughed deeper. Drills are made in the same manner. Planting commences in January, and continues until April. It is necessary to plant a sugar field only once in three years. Three crops are taken before the seed or plant is exhausted.

Three gangs are employed in the operation. One draws the cane from the rick, or stack, cutting the top and flags from the stalk, leaving only that part which is sound and healthy. Each joint of the cane has an eye, like the eye of a potato, which sends forth a sprout when buried in the soil. Another gang lays the cane in the drill, placing two stalks side by side in such manner that joints will occur once in four or six inches. The third gang follows with hoes, drawing earth upon the stalks, and covering them to the depth of three inches.

In four weeks, at the farthest, the sprouts appear above the ground, and from this time forward grow with great rapidity. A sugar field is hoed three times, the same as cotton, save that a greater quantity of earth is drawn to the roots. By the first of August hoeing is usually over. About the middle of September, whatever is required for seed is cut and stacked in ricks, as they are termed. In October it is ready for the mill or sugar-house, and then the general cutting begins. The blade of a cane-knife is fifteen inches long, three inches wide in the middle, and tapering towards the point and handle. The blade is thin, and in order to be at all serviceable must be kept very sharp. Every third hand takes the lead of two others, one of whom is on each side of him. The lead hand, in the first place, with a blow of his knife shears the flags from the stalk. He next cuts off the top down as far as it is green. He must be careful to sever all the green from the ripe part, inasmuch as the juice of the former sours the molasses, and renders it unsalable. Then he severs the stalk at the root, and lays it directly behind him. His right and left hand companions lay their stalks when cut in the same manner, upon his. To

Solomon Northup, *Twelve Years a Slave* (Auburn, NY, 1853), 208–211.

every three hands there is a cart, which follows, and the stalks are thrown into it by the younger slaves, when it is drawn to the sugar-house and ground. . . .

In the month of January the slaves enter the field again to prepare for another crop. The ground is now strewn with the tops, and flags cut from the past year's cane. On a dry day fire is set to this combustible refuse, which sweeps over the field, leaving it bare and clean, and ready for the hoes. The earth is loosened about the roots of the old stubble, and in process of time another crop springs up from the last year's seed. It is the same the year following; but the third year the seed has exhausted its strength, and the field must be ploughed and planted again. The second year the cane is sweeter and yields more than the first, and the third year more than the second. . . .

102

A Defense of Southern Society (1854)

As northern and European reformers increasingly criticized the institution of slavery, southerners grew more defensive of their society and its "peculiar institution." The discomfort that southerners such as Thomas Jefferson felt about the institution was replaced by the ideas of people like Thomas R. Dew, who argued that slavery was a "positive good." George Fitzhugh was among the most effective defenders of southern society during the years immediately preceding the Civil War. Trained in the law, he served in the attorney general's office during the Buchanan administration, but he became well-known for his comparative essays on northern and southern economies and society. An 1856 trip to the North brought him to the home of Gerrit Smith, a relative and staunch abolitionist. While there, he also met Harriet Beecher Stowe, the author of Uncle Tom's Cabin. *The visit made the Virginia native a more aggressive defender of southern civilization. In the following selection from* The Sociology for the South, *Fitzhugh compared the laissez-faire economy of the North with southern paternalism.*

Questions to Consider

1. According to George Fitzhugh, why does the South have the better way of life?

2. Why is the South's economy so strong in comparison to the North's?

3. Why is the South's society better than the North's?

4. How might a northerner respond to this document?

George Fitzhugh, *The Sociology for the South; Or, The Failure of Free Society* (Richmond, VA, 1854), 253–255.

. . . At the slaveholding South all is peace, quiet, plenty and contentment. We have no mobs, no trades unions, no strikes for higher wages, no armed resistance to the law, but little jealousy of the rich by the poor. We have but few in our jails, and fewer in our poor houses. We produce enough of the comforts and necessaries of life for a population three or four times as numerous as ours. We are wholly exempt from the torrent of pauperism, crime, agrarianism, and infidelity which Europe is pouring from her jails and alms houses on the already crowded North. Population increases slowly, wealth rapidly. In the tide water region of Eastern Virginia, as far as our experience extends, the crops have doubled in fifteen years, whilst the population has been almost stationary. In the same period in the lands, owing to improvements of the soil and the many fine houses erected in the country, have nearly doubled in value. This ratio of improvement has been approximated or exceeded wherever in the South slaves are numerous. We have enough for the present, and no Malthusian spectres frightening us for the future. Wealth is more equally distributed than at the North, where a few millionaires own most of the property of the country. (These millionaires are men of cold hearts and weak minds; they know how to make money, but not how to use it, either for the benefit of themselves or of others.) High intellectual and moral attainments, refinement of head and heart, give standing to a man in the South, however poor he may be. Money is, with few exceptions, the only thing that ennobles at the North. We have poor among us, but none who are over-worked and under-fed. We do not crowd cities because lands are abundant and their owners kind, merciful and hospitable. The poor are as hospitable as the rich, the negro as the white man. Nobody dreams of turning a friend, a relative, or a stranger from his door. The very negro who deems it no crime to steal, would scorn to sell his hospitality. We have no loafers, because the poor relative or friend who borrows our horse, or spends a week under our roof, is a welcome guest. The loose economy, the wasteful mode of living at the South, is a blessing when rightly considered; it keeps want, scarcity and famine at a distance, because it leaves room for retrenchment. The nice, accurate economy of France, England and New England, keeps society always on the verge of famine, because it leaves no room to retrench, that is to live on a part only of what they now consume. Our society exhibits no appearance of precocity, no symptoms of decay. A long course of continuing improvement is in prospect before us, with no limits which human foresight can descry. Actual liberty and equality with our white population has been approached much nearer than in the free States. Few of our whites ever work as day laborers, none as cooks, scullions, ostlers, body servants, or in other menial capacities. One free citizen does not lord it over another; hence that feeling of independence and equality that distinguishes us; hence that pride of character, that self-respect, that give us ascendence when we come in contact with Northerners. It is a distinction to be a Southerner, as it once was to be a Roman citizen. . . .

103

The Southern Yeomen (1860)

The Old South has been commonly stereotyped as a land of planters, plantation mistresses, and slaves. Most antebellum white southerners, however, were not slave owners. In Social Relations in Our Southern States, *Daniel R. Hundley sought to dispel the traditional myths about southern society and emphasize the role that the yeomen played in the South. An Alabama native who grew up on the family plantation, Hundley attended a variety of educational institutions before receiving a law degree from Harvard in 1853. After his graduation, he moved to Chicago, where he dabbled in a wide variety of business ventures. The widespread unemployment and financial ruin created by the Panic of 1857 led Hundley to champion a "charity fund" to relieve increasing urban poverty. Despite his Chicago career, Hundley retained his southern contacts, wintering each year in his native state. Hundley never expressed serious interest in politics before 1860 and remained committed to the Union until the election of Lincoln, an event that he believed doomed the nation. In the following document, Hundley describes the southern yeomanry who formed the bulk of the region's white population.*

Questions to Consider

1. Why does Daniel Hundley marvel at the yeoman farmer?
2. Why does he distinguish between the yeoman and "poor White Trash"?
3. Why do the distinctions between master and slave blur when the yeoman owns slaves?
4. How do you think a slave would respond to this excerpt?

. . . For while princes, presidents, and governors may boast of their castles and lands, their silken gowns and robes of ceremony—all which can be made the sport of fortune, and do often vanish away in a moment, leaving their sometime owners poor indeed—the COMMON PEOPLE, as the masses are called, possess in and of themselves a far richer inheritance, which is the ability and the will to earn an honest livelihood (not by the tricks of trade and the lying spirit of barter, nor yet by trampling on any man's rights, but) by the toilsome sweat of their own brows, delving patiently and trustingly in old mother earth, who under the blessing of God, never deceives or disappoints those who put their trust in her generous bosom. And of all the hardy sons of toil, in all free lands the Yeomen are most deserving of our esteem. . . .

Daniel R. Hundley, *Social Relations in Our Southern States* (New York, 1860), 192–198.

But you have no Yeoman in the South, my dear Sir? Beg your pardon, our dear Sir, but we have hosts of them. I thought you had only poor White Trash? . . .

Know, then, that the Poor Whites of the South constitute a separate class to themselves; the Southern Yeomen are as distinct from them as the Southern Gentleman is from the Cotton Snob. Certainly the Southern Yeomen are nearly always poor, at least so far as this world's goods are to be taken into the account. As a general thing they own no slaves; and even in case they do, the wealthiest of them rarely possess more than from ten to fifteen. But even when they are slaveholders, they seem to exercise but few of the rights of ownership over their human chattels, making so little distinction between master and man, that their negroes invariably become spoiled, like so many frequently see black and white, slave and freeman, camping out together, living sometimes in the same tent or temporary pine-pole cabin; drinking . . . out of the same tin dipper or long-handled gourd their home-distilled apple brandy; dining on the same homely but substantial fare, and sharing one bed in common, videlicet, the cabin floor.

Again should you go among the hardy yeomanry of Tennessee, Kentucky, or Missouri, whenever or wherever they own slaves (which in these States is not often the case) you will invariably see the negroes and their masters ploughing side by side in the fields; or bared to the waist, and with old-fashioned scythe vying with one another who can cut down the broadest swath of yellow wheat, or of the waving timothy; or bearing the tall stalks of maize and packing them into the stout-built barn, with ear and fodder on, ready for the winter's husking. . . .

And yet, notwithstanding the Southern Yeoman allows his slaves so much freedom of speech and action, is not offended when they call him familiarly by his Christian name, and hardly makes them work enough to earn their salt, still he is very proud of being a slaveholder; and when he is not such, his greatest ambition is to make money enough to buy a negro. . . .

14

Origins of the Civil War

D espite social, cultural, and economic differences, the North and South had managed to negotiate their disputes successfully during the first half-century of the nation's existence. After the Mexican War, this spirit of compromise quickly disintegrated into an increasingly hostile exchange. Northerners, alarmed by the spread of slavery, became vocal in their criticism of the South, while southerners decried attempts to undermine their way of life. The events of the 1850s exacerbated these differences. As the political middle collapsed, politicians from both sections championed more radical solutions to the issues that divided the nation, deepening the cleavage between the sections. The following excerpts shed light on these issues and the hostility they generated.

104

An African-American Minister Responds to the Fugitive Slave Law (1851)

The Compromise of 1850 sought to defuse sectional tensions by addressing all of the major issues that divided North and South and meeting at least some of each section's demands. Southern slaveholders demanded a stronger fugitive slave law. As part of the compromise, the federal government pledged to support the recovery of runaway slaves. The resulting law provided financial incentives for judges to find African Americans as fugitive slaves, denied alleged runaways from testifying on their own behalf, and imposed penalties on anyone who assisted fugitives. The law and its subsequent enforcement brought a howl of protest from many northerners while threatening the freedom of northern blacks. Samuel R. Ward was among those in jeopardy. Escaping slavery at an early age, Ward had little memory of the institution. Licensed to preach in 1839, he served primarily white congregations in upstate New York. Active in anti-slavery circles as a writer and speaker, he placed himself at great jeopardy by publicly speaking against the law. Fearful for his safety, he fled to Canada in 1851. The following selection from his autobiography details his decision to do so.

Questions to Consider

1. What effect did the Fugitive Slave Law have on free blacks in the North?
2. What can you discern about northern racism from this document?
3. How do you think William Lloyd Garrison (Document 81) would respond to this document?
4. How would those who supported the prosecution of Denmark Vesey ("The Trial of Denmark Vesey," Document 96) respond to this document?

. . . In the summer of 1851, business called me to travel in various parts of the country. I visited numerous districts of New York, Pennsylvania, Ohio, Illinois, Wisconsin, Michigan, and Indiana, as well as Connecticut, Rhode Island, Massachusetts, and New Hampshire. Smarting as we were under the recently passed Fugitive Law—and these irritations being inflamed and aggravated by the dragging of some poor victim of it from some Northern town to the South and to slavery, every month or so—of course this law became *the theme* of most I said and wrote. In October, Mrs. Ward accompanied me in a tour through Ohio. We were about finishing that tour, when we saw in the papers an account of the Gorsuch case, in Christiana, Pennsylvania. That was a case in which the Reverend Mr. Gorsuch went armed to the house of a Negro, in the suburbs of the town named, in search of a slave who had escaped from him. The owner of the house denied him admittance. Several Negroes, armed, stood ready inside the house to defend it against the *reverend* slave-catcher and his party—the latter declaring his slave was in that house, avowing his determination to have him, if he went to h—ll after him; and, intending to intimidate the Negroes, fired upon the house with a rifle. Fortunately none of the besieged party were killed; but, they returned Mr. Gorsuch's fire, and *he* dropped a corpse!

The authorities arraigned these poor Negroes for murder. They seemed determined to have their blood. Upon reading this, I handed the paper containing the account to my wife; and we concluded that resistance was fruitless, that the country was hopelessly given to the execution of this barbarous enactment, and that it were vain to hope for the reformation of such a country. At the same time, my secular prospects became exceedingly involved and embarrassed; and willing as I might be to be one of a forlorn hope in the assault upon slavery's citadel, I had no reasonable prospect of doing so, consistently with my duty to my family. The anti-slavery cause does not, cannot, find bread and education for one's children. We then jointly determined to wind up our affairs, and go to Canada; and, with the remnant of what might be left to us, purchase a little hut and garden, and pass the remainder of our days in peace, in a free British country. . . .

Samuel R. Ward, *Autobiography of a Fugitive Negro* (London, 1855), 115–117.

105

Southern Review of *Uncle Tom's Cabin* (1852)

During the decade preceding the Civil War, long-standing differences between North and South became more pronounced and increasingly difficult to compromise. Slavery proved the most divisive of these issues. The publication of Harriet Beecher Stowe's Uncle Tom's Cabin *in 1852 further inflamed regional discord. Stowe grew up in New England before moving in 1832 with her family to Cincinnati, where her father, Congregationalist minister Lyman Beecher, had accepted the leadership of Lane Theological Seminary. While living in Cincinnati, she had the opportunity to observe the institution of slavery more closely, while also embarking on a writing career. The Fugitive Slave Law of 1850 intensified her opposition to slavery. In 1852, she produced* Uncle Tom's Cabin, *a fictional account of the "peculiar institution" as seen through slaves' eyes. The following selection is a review of Stowe's work that appeared in the* Southern Literary Messenger. *Formerly edited by Edgar Allan Poe, the Richmond, Virginia–based journal was the South's leading literary periodical.*

Questions to Consider

1. Why does the *Southern Literary Messenger* point out that a "female writer" authored Uncle Tom's Cabin?
2. How is the book characterized in the review?
3. Why is the author of the review fearful of the book's influence?
4. What is the significance of *Uncle Tom's Cabin?*

. . . [W]e beg to make a distinction between lady writers and female writers. We could not find it in our hearts to visit the dullness or ignorance of a well-meaning lady with the rigorous discipline which it is necessary to inflict upon male dunces and blockheads. But where a writer of the softer sex manifests, in her productions, a shameless disregard of truth and of those amenities which so peculiarly belong to her sphere of life, we hold that she has forfeited the claim to be considered a lady, and with that claim all exemption from the utmost stringency of critical punishment. . . .

. . . [Mrs. Stowe] wished, by the work now under consideration, to persuade us of the horrible guilt of Slavery, and with the kindest feelings for us as brethren, to teach us that our constitution and laws are repugnant to every sentiment of humanity. We know that among other novel doctrines in vogue in the land of Mrs. Stowe's nativity—the pleasant land of New England—which we are old-fashioned enough to condemn, is one which would place woman on a footing of political equality with man, and causing her to look beyond the office for which she was created—the high and holy place of maternity—would engage her in the administration of public affairs; thus handing over the State to the perilous protection of diaper diplomatists and wet-nurse politicians. Mrs. Stowe, we believe, belongs to this school of Woman's Rights, and on this ground she may assert her prerogative to teach us how wicked are we ourselves and the Constitution under which we live. . . .

But whatever her designs may have been, it is very certain that she has shockingly traduced the slaveholding society of the United States, and we desire to be understood as acting entirely on the defensive, when we proceed to expose the miserable misrepresentations of her story. . . .

. . . many of the allegations of cruelty towards the slaves, brought forward by Mrs. Stowe, are absolutely and unqualifiedly false. . . . We are of opinion too that heart-rending separations [of families] are much less frequent under the institution of slavery than in countries where poverty rules the working classes with despotic sway. . . .

But let it be borne in mind that this slanderous work has found its way to every section of our country and has crossed the water to Great Britain, filling the minds of all who know nothing of slavery with hatred for that institution and those who uphold it. Justice to ourselves would seem to demand that it should not be suffered to circulate longer without the brand of falsehood upon it. Let it be recollected, too, that the importance Mrs. Stowe will derive from Southern criticism will be one of infamy. Indeed she is only entitled to criticism at all, as the mouthpiece of a large and dangerous faction which if we do not put down with the pen, we may be compelled one day (God grant that day may never come!) to repel with the bayonet. There are questions that underlie the story of "Uncle Tom's Cabin" of far deeper significance than any mere false coloring of Southern society, and our readers will probably see the work discussed, in other points of view, in the next number of the *Messenger,* by a far abler and more scholar-like hand than our own. Our editorial task is now ended, and in dismissing the disagreeable subject, we beg to make a single suggestion to Mrs. Stowe—that, as she is fond of referring to the Bible, she will turn over, before writing her next work of fiction, to the twentieth chapter of Exodus and there read these words—"THOU SHALT NOT BEAR FALSE WITNESS AGAINST THY NEIGHBOR."

106

Charles Sumner on "Bleeding Kansas" (1856)

The 1850s brought a new, less compromising generation of politicians to prominence in both the North and South. Among this new group was Charles Sumner of Massachusetts. Holding undergraduate and law degrees from Harvard, Sumner spent the years immediately after his education touring Europe, where he met many of the leading statesmen and learned to speak French, German, and Italian. Sumner's involvement in politics began with his vigorous denunciations of the Mexican War. By 1848, he was condemning many of Massachusetts' leading textile magnates for their comfortable association with the "slaveocracy." A coalition of Free Soilers and Democrats sent him to the Senate in 1851. A brilliant orator, he hurled his initial attacks at the Compromise of 1850. The passage of the Kansas-Nebraska Act led him to join the Republican party. In the spring of 1856, he delivered his "Crime of Kansas" speech, which is excerpted as follows. Within weeks, 1 million copies had been printed in the North. South Carolina Congressman Preston Brooks responded to the verbal attack against his relative, A. Pierce Butler, by assaulting Sumner, who sat helpless at his Senate desk. The assault further polarized the sections.

Questions to Consider

1. Why does Sumner link slavery and the southern way of life to South Carolina's Senator Pierce Butler?
2. Why does Sumner appeal to Kansas residents to vote?
3. Does Sumner envision a resolution to the growing sectional division within the country?
4. Why does Sumner use the imagery of sexual exploitation in his speech? What does this say about contemporary views of race? Sex?

Before entering upon the argument, I must say something of a general character, particularly in response to what has fallen from senators who have raised themselves to eminence on this floor in the championship of human wrong: I mean the senator from South Carolina [Mr. Butler] and the senator from Illinois [Mr. Douglas], who though unlike as Don Quixote and Sancho Panza, yet, like this couple, sally forth together in the same adventure, I regret much to miss the elder senator from his seat; but the cause against which he has run a tilt, with such ebullition of animosity, demands that the opportunity of exposing him should not be lost; and it is for the cause that I speak. The senator from South Carolina has read many books of chivalry and believes himself a chivalrous knight, with sentiments of honor and courage. Of course he has chosen a mistress to whom he has made his vows and who, though ugly to others, is always lovely to him; though polluted in the sight of the world, is chaste in his sight. I mean the harlot Slavery. To her his tongue is always profuse in words. Let her be impeached in character, or any proposition be made from the extension of her wantonness, and no extravagance of manner or hardihood of assertion is then too great for this senator. The frenzy of Don Quixote in behalf of his wench . . . is all surpassed. The

"Speech on Kansas," *Memoirs and Letters of Charles Sumner,* ed. Edward L. Pierce (London, 1893), 3: 446–452.

asserted rights of slavery which shock equality of all kinds, are cloaked by a fantastic claim of equality. If the slave States cannot enjoy what, in mockery of the great fathers of the republic, he misnames equality under the Constitution,—in other words the full power in the national territories to compel fellowmen to unpaid toil, separate husband and wife, and to sell little children at the auction-block, then, sir, the chivalric senator will conduct the State of South Carolina out of the Union! Heroic knight! exalted senator! a second Moses come for the second exodus!

Not content with this poor menace, . . . the senator, in the unrestrained chivalry of his nature, has undertaken to apply opprobrious words to those who differ from him . . . He calls them "sectional and fanatical;" and resistance to the usurpation of Kansas he denounces as "an uncalculating fanaticism." To be sure, these charges lack all grace of originality and all sentiment of truth; but the adventurous senator does not hesitate. He is the uncompromising, unblushing representative on this floor of a flagrant sectionalism now domineering over the republic; and yet with a ludicrous ignorance of his own position, unable to see himself as others see him, or with an effrontery which even his white head ought not to protect from rebuke, he applies to those here who resist his sectionalism the very epithet which designates himself. The men who strive to bring back the government to its original policy, when freedom and not slavery was national, while slavery and not freedom was sectional, he arraigns as sectional. This will not do; it involves too great a perversion of terms. I tell that senator that it is to himself, and to the "organization" of which he is the "committed advocate," that this epithet belongs. I now fasten it upon them. For myself, . . . I affirm that the Republican party of the Union is in no just sense sectional, but, more than any other party, national; and that it now goes forth to dislodge from the high places that tyrannical sectionalism of which the senator from South Carolina is one of the maddest zealots.

. . . the senator from South Carolina [Mr. Butler], who, omnipresent in this debate, overflows with rage at the simple suggestion that Kansas has applied for admission as a State, and with incoherent phrase discharges the loose expectoration of his speech, now upon her representative, and the upon her people. . . . the senator touches nothing which he does not disfigure with error,—sometimes of principle, sometimes of fact. He shows an incapacity of accuracy, whether in stating the Constitution or in stating the law, whether in details of statistics or diversions of scholarship. He cannot open his mouth but out here flies another blunder. . . .

But it is against the people of Kansas that the sensibilities of the senator are particularly aroused. Coming, as he announces, "from a State,"—ay, sir, from South Carolina,—he turns his lordly disgust from this newly formed community, which he will not recognize even as "a member of the body politic." Pray, sir, by what title does he indulge in this egotism? Has he read the history of the "State" which he represents? . . . He cannot forget its wretched persistence in the slave trade, as the very apple of its eye, and the condition of its participation in the Union. He cannot forget its constitution, which is republican only in name, confirming power in the hands of the few, ...Were the whole history of South Carolina blotted out of existence, ... civilization might lose—I do not say how little, but surely less than it has already gained by the example of Kansas in that valiant struggle against oppression. ...

The contest which, beginning in Kansas, reaches us, will be transferred soon from Congress to that broader stage, where every citizen is not only spectator but actor; and to their judgment I confidently turn. To the people about to exercise the electoral franchise in choosing a chief magistrate of the republic, I appeal to vindicate the electoral franchise in Kansas. Let the ballot-box of the Union with multitudinous might protect the ballot-box in that Territory. Let the voters everywhere, while rejoicing in their own rights, help guard the equal rights of distant fellow-citizens, that the shrines of popular institutions now desecrated may be sanctified anew; ... In just regard for free labor, ... in Christian sympathy with the slave, ... in rescue of fellow citizens now subjugated to tyrannical usurpation; in dutiful respect for the early fathers, ... in the name of the Constitution outraged, of the laws trampled down, of justice banished, of humanity degraded, of peace destroyed, of freedom crushed to earth, and in the name of the Heavenly Father, whose service is perfect freedom,—I make this last appeal.

107

Chicago Tribune on the *Dred Scott* v. *Sanford* Decision (1857)

The sectional tensions over slavery spread from the political to the judicial arena in 1857, when the Supreme Court ruled on the case of Dred Scott v. Sanford. *Scott, a slave born in Southampton County, Virginia, moved with owner Peter Blow to St. Louis, Missouri, in 1827. Purchased by army surgeon John Emerson in 1833, Scott went wherever his new master was stationed, spending three years in Illinois and two in the Wisconsin Territory. In 1846, a white friend sued for Scott's freedom, arguing that residence in a free territory emancipated the slave. The case ultimately came before the Supreme Court, presided over by Roger B. Taney, a Maryland native appointed by Andrew Jackson. The court divided along sectional lines, with Chief Justice Taney deciding that (1) African Americans' inherent inferiority precluded them, whether slave or free, from the rights of a citizen—including bringing a case before the Supreme Court; (2) the Missouri Compromise was an abridgment of property rights and was, therefore, unconstitutional; and (3) a territory could not prohibit the introduction of slaves. The following excerpt provides the reaction of the* Chicago Tribune.

Questions to Consider

1. How does the *Chicago Tribune* view the Supreme Court's decision?
2. What does the newspaper suggest that citizens do?
3. In what ways did the Supreme Court's decision help further divide the nation?
4. How might Francis Pickens ("Inaugural Address of South Carolina Governor Francis Pickens," Document 111) have responded to this article?

. . . We must confess we are shocked at the violence and servility of the Judicial Revolution caused by the decision of the Supreme Court of the United States. We scarcely know how to express our detestation of its inhuman dicta, or to fathom the wicked consequences which may flow from it. The blood of the early day—of the times that tried mens souls—was all healthful and strong, and lived, or was shed, for Liberty as freely as water. That is now changed legally. This decision has sapped the constitution of its glorious and distinctive features, and seeks to pervert it into a barbarous and unchristian channel.

Jefferson feared this Supreme Court, and foretold its usurpation of the legislative power of the Federal Government. His prophecy is now reality. The terrible evil he dreaded is upon us.

To say or suppose, that a Free People can respect or will obey a decision so fraught with disastrous consequences to the People and their Liberties, is to dream of impossibilities. No power can take away their rights. They will permit no power to abridge them. No servility of Judges or of Presidents, no servility of Congresses can taint their spirit or subdue it. The contest has come, and in that contest, the Supreme Court, we are sorry to say, will be shorn of its moral power—will lose that prestige, that authority, which instinctively insures respect and commands obedience. By its own bad act it has impaired its organization. Fortunate will it be, if that act does not destroy its utility. . . .

That there has been for long years a conspiracy against Freedom in this Republic, and that certain members of the Supreme Court were engaged in it, we do not doubt. How this has happened, or why, it is needless to discuss now. It is enough to know, that a continued residence at Washington—the breathing in of its central and polluted atmosphere makes, or tends to make, those in authority, at once obedient and servile to the ruling dynasty, and callous to the purer and higher instincts and principles of the people. The Judiciary has proven no exception. We would, therefore, apply the remedy which JEFFERSON urged, and JACKSON recommended—decentralization. Strip the President of every power which the people can exercise. Let every office which they are able to fill, be filled by them. Confide into their hands the election of the Judges of the United States, and thus infuse into these Judges a knowledge of their interests, a spirit and a purposeful kindred with theirs, an independence of the Executive worthy of them.

"The Past and Present," *Chicago Tribune,* March 12, 1857, p. 2.

108

The Freeport Doctrine (1858)

*With the nation teetering closer to conflict, the 1858 U.S. Senate races took on addi-
tional importance. At first glance, the result of the Illinois contest seemed a foregone
conclusion. Incumbent Democrat Stephen A. Douglas was one of his party's national
leaders. The key figure in securing passage of the Compromise of 1850 and the 1854
Kansas-Nebraska Act, Douglas was a champion of popular sovereignty, a democratic
device that called for the citizens of a territory to determine whether to admit slavery.
His opponent was Abraham Lincoln, a relative unknown representing the new Republican party. Although a vote by the Illinois legislature would determine the state's next
senator, the candidates met in seven different towns to debate the issues in the summer
and fall of 1858. During the Freeport debate, Lincoln asked his opponent to reconcile
his stance on popular sovereignty with the recent* Dred Scott *decision. An excerpt of
Douglas's response follows.*

Questions to Consider

1. To what audience is Stephen Douglas directing this speech?
2. Where would Douglas stand in a conflict between the U.S. Supreme
   Court and the wishes of a territorial legislature?
3. What is Douglas's response to Lincoln's view that "A House divided
   against itself cannot stand"?
4. How might Francis Pickens ("Inaugural Address of South Carolina
   Governor Francis Pickens," Document 111) have responded to this
   speech?

. . . The next question propounded to me by Mr. Lincoln is, can the people
of a Territory in any lawful way, against the wishes of any citizen of the
United States, exclude slavery from their limits prior to the formation of a
State Constitution? I answer emphatically, as Mr. Lincoln has heard me
answer a hundred times from every stump in Illinois, that in my opinion the
people of a Territory can, by lawful means, exclude slavery from their limits
prior to the formation of a State Constitution. Mr. Lincoln knew that I had
answered that question over and over again. He heard me argue the Nebraska
bill on that principle all over the State in 1854, in 1855, and in 1856, and he
has no excuse for pretending to be in doubt as to my position on that question. It matters not what way the Supreme Court may hereafter decide as to
the abstract question whether slavery may or may not go into a Territory

"Mr. Douglas's Speech," *Political Debates between Hon. Abraham Lincoln and Hon. Stephen A. Douglas* (New York,
1860), 93–105.

under the Constitution, the people have the lawful means to introduce it or exclude it as they please, for the reason that slavery cannot exist a day or an hour anywhere, unless it is supported by local police regulations. Those police regulations can only be established by the local legislature, and if the people are opposed to slavery they will elect representatives to that body who will by unfriendly legislation effectually prevent the introduction of it into their midst. If, on the contrary, they are for it, their legislation will favor its extension. Hence, no matter what the decision of the Supreme Court may be on that abstract question, still the right of the people to make a slave Territory or a free Territory is perfect and complete under the Nebraska bill. I hope Mr. Lincoln deems my answer satisfactory on that point. . . .

The third question which Mr. Lincoln presented is, if the Supreme Court of the United States shall decide that a state of this Union cannot exclude slavery from its own limits, will I submit to it? I am amazed that Lincoln should ask such a question. ["A school-boy knows better."] Yes, a school-boy does know better. Mr. Lincoln's object is to cast an imputation upon the Supreme Court. He knows that there never was but one man in America, claiming any degree of intelligence or decency, who ever for a moment pretended such a thing. It is true that the Washington *Union,* in an article published on the 17th of last December, did put forth that doctrine, and I denounced the article on the floor of the Senate, in a speech which Mr. Lincoln now pretends was against the President. The *Union* had claimed that slavery had a right to go into the free States, and that any provision in the Constitution or laws of the free States to the contrary were null and void. I denounced it in the Senate, as I said before, and I was the first man who did. Lincoln's friends, Trumbull, and Seward, and Hale, and Wilson, and the whole Black Republican side of the Senate were silent. They left it to me to denounce it. And what was the reply made to me on that occasion? Mr. Toombs, of Georgia, got up and undertook to lecture me on the ground that I ought not to have deemed the article worthy of notice, and ought not to have replied to it; that there was not one man, woman or child south of the Potomac, in any slave State, who did not repudiate any such pretension. Mr. Lincoln knows that that reply was made on the spot, and yet now he asks this question. He might as well ask me, suppose Mr. Lincoln should steal a horse, would I sanction it; and it would be as genteel in me to ask him, in the event he stole a horse, what ought to be done with him. He casts an imputation upon the Supreme Court of the United States, by supposing that they would violate the Constitution of the United States. I tell him that such a thing is not possible. It would be an act of moral treason that no man on the bench could ever descend to. Mr. Lincoln himself would never in his partisan feelings so far forget what was right as to be guilty of such an act. . . .

[A voice—"How will you vote?"]

Mr. Douglas—"I will vote for the admission of just such a State as by the form of their Constitution the people show they want; if they want slavery, they shall have it; if they prohibit slavery it shall be prohibited. They can form their institutions to please themselves, subject only to the Constitution;

and I for one stand ready to receive them into the Union. Why cannot your Black Republican candidates talk out as plain as that when they are questioned?

I do not want to cheat any man out of his vote. No man is deceived in, regard to my principles if I have the power to express myself in terms explicit enough to convey my ideas. Mr. Lincoln made a speech when he was nominated for the United States Senate which covers all these Abolition platforms. He there lays down a proposition so broad in its abolitionism as to cover the whole ground.

In my opinion it [the slavery agitation] will not cease until a crisis shall have been reached and passed. 'A House divided against itself cannot stand.' I believe this Government cannot endure permanently half slave and half free. I do not expect the house to fall—but I do expect it will cease to be divided. It will become all one thing or all the other. Either the opponents of Slavery will arrest the further spread of it, and place it where the public mind shall rest in the belief that it is in the course of ultimate extinction, or its advocates will push it forward till it shall become alike lawful in all the States— old as well as new, North as well as South."

There you find that Mr. Lincoln lays down the doctrine that this Union cannot endure divided as our fathers made it, with free and slave States. He says they must all become one thing, or all the other; that they must all be free or all slave, or else the Union cannot continue to exist. It being his opinion that to admit any more slave States, to continue to divide the Union into free and slave States, will dissolve it. I want to know of Mr. Lincoln whether he will vote for the admission of another slave State.

He tells you the Union cannot exist unless the States are all free or all slave; he tells you that he is opposed to making them all slave and hence he is for making them all free, in order that the Union may exist; and yet he will not say that he will not vote against another slave State, knowing that the Union must be dissolved if he votes for it. I ask you if that is fair dealing? The true intent and inevitable conclusion to be drawn from his first Springfield speech is, that he is opposed to the admission of any more slave States under any circumstance. . . .

109

Cartoonists Depict the Issues of the Day

The 1860 presidential election was one of the most momentous in American history. The divisions that dominated the political landscape of the 1850s could no longer be contained; armed conflict marred the contest over popular sovereignty in Kansas; politicians had resorted to violence in the Sumner-Brooks affair. The issues of the 1850s shattered the Second Party system of Democrats and Whigs and left a divided democracy and several fledgling new parties. The emergence of the Republican party (Abraham Lincoln), with its purely northern appeal, was perceived as a dire threat to many southerners. The ensuing election campaign was further complicated by the division of the Democrats and subsequent selection of a main Democratic candidate (Stephen A. Douglas) and a candidate from the Deep South (John C. Breckinridge). A fourth ticket also ran, promising nothing more than the preservation of the Union (John Bell). The ensuing images depict the major issues of the day as portrayed by cartoonists.

Questions to Consider

1. What does the cartoonist see as the central issue in the first image?
2. Who are the different candidates appealing to in the first image?
3. In the second image, what is the cartoonist predicting will happen as a result of the presidential election?
4. How accurate is this prediction?

"The Political Quadrille, Music by Dred Scott"

"Dividing the National Map" In this 1860 election cartoon, Lincoln and Douglas fight for control of the country while Breckinridge tears away the South. John Bell tries to repair the damage to the torn nation.

110

Republican Party Platform (1860)

No American political party has ever emerged so quickly nor had a more immediate impact than that of the Republican party. It was a product of northern outrage over the Kansas-Nebraska Act, and its founders rapidly put together a league of Free Soilers, antislavery Democrats, Conscience Whigs, workingmen, and nativists to form a new, sectional coalition. Southerners and many northern Democrats branded them as radicals, but the party grew. In 1856, John C. Fremont ran as the Republican candidate for president. Fremont's status as a Western hero did not win him the election, but he carried 11 of the 16 free states. At the 1860 convention, the party passed over better-known men such as William H. Seward (NY) in favor of Illinois' Abraham Lincoln, who was considered an electable moderate. The following selection contains excerpts from the Republican platform of 1860.

Questions to Consider

1. What are the key issues of the Republican party platform?
2. Why does Kansas figure prominently in several planks of the platform?
3. Besides its stance on slavery, what would attract voters to the Republican party in 1860?
4. How might a slave owner respond to this selection? Why?

Resolved, That we, the delegated representatives of the Republican electors of the United States, in Convention assembled, . . . unite in the following declarations:

1. That the history of the nation, during the last four years, has fully established the propriety and necessity of the organization and perpetuation of the Republican party, and that the causes which called it into existence are permanent in their nature, and now, more than ever before, demand its peaceful and constitutional triumph.

2. That the maintenance of the principles promulgated in the Declaration of Independence and embodied in the Federal Constitution, "That all men are created equal; that they are endowed by their Creator with certain inalienable rights; that among these are life, liberty and the pursuit of happiness; that; to secure these rights, governments are instituted among men, deriving their just powers from the consent of the governed," is essential to the preservation of our Republican institutions; and that the Federal Constitution, the Rights of the States, and the Union of the States, must and shall be preserved.

3. That to the Union of the States this nation owes its unprecedented increase in population, its surprising development of material resources, its rapid augmentation of wealth, its happiness at home and its honor abroad; and we hold in abhorrence all schemes of Disunion so often made by Democratic members, . . . and we denounce those threats of Disunion, in case of a popular overthrow of their ascendancy, as denying the vital principles of a free government, and as an avowal of contemplated treason, which it is the imperative duty of an indignant People sternly to rebuke and forever silence.

4. That the maintenance inviolate of the rights of the States, and especially the right of each State to order and control its own domestic institutions according to its own judgement exclusively, is essential to that balance of powers on which the perfection and endurance of our political fabric depends; and we denounce the lawless invasion by armed force of the soil of any State or Territory, no matter under what pretext, as among the gravest of crimes.

Francis Curtis, *The Republican Party* (New York, 1904), 1: 355–358.

5. That the present Democratic Administration has far exceeded our worst apprehensions, in its measureless subserviency to the exaction of a sectional interest, as especially evinced in its desperate exertions to force the infamous Lecompton constitution upon the protesting people of Kansas; in construing the personal relation between master and servant to involve an unqualified property in persons; in its attempted enforcement, everywhere, on land and sea, through the intervention of Congress and the Federal Courts of the extreme pretensions of a purely local interest; and in its general and unvarying abuse of the power intrusted to it by a confiding people. . . .

7. That the new dogma that the Constitution, of its own force carries Slavery into any or all of the Territories of the United States, is a dangerous political heresy, at variance with the explicit provisions of that instrument itself, . . . is revolutionary in its tendency, and subversive of the peace and harmony of the country.

8. That the normal condition of all the territory of the United States is that of freedom; That as our Republican fathers, when they had abolished slavery in all our national territory, ordained that "no person should be deprived of life, liberty, or property, without due process of law," it becomes our duty, by legislation, whenever such legislation is necessary, to maintain this provision of the Constitution against all attempts to violate it; and we deny the authority of Congress, of a territorial legislature, or of any individuals, to give legal existence to Slavery in any Territory of the United States.

9. That we brand the recent re-opening of the African slave-trade, under the cover of our national flag, . . . as a crime against humanity and a burning shame to our country and age; and we call upon Congress to take prompt and efficient measures for the total and final suppression of the execrable traffic.

10. That in the recent vetoes, by their Federal Governors, of the acts of the Legislatures of Kansas and Nebraska, prohibiting Slavery in those Territories, we find a practical illustration of the boasted Democratic principle of Non-Intervention and Popular Sovereignty embodied in the Kansas–Nebraska bill, and a demonstration of the deception and fraud involved therein.

11. That Kansas should, . . . be immediately admitted as a State under the Constitution recently formed and adopted by her people, and accepted by the House of Representatives.

12. That, while providing revenue for the support of the General Government by duties upon imports, sound policy requires such an adjustment as to encourage the development of the industrial interests of the whole country; and we commend that policy of national exchanges which secures to the working men liberal wages, to agricultural remunerating prices; to mechanics and manufacturers an adequate reward for their skill, labor and enterprise, and to the nation commercial prosperity and independence.

13. That we protest against any sale or alienation to others of the Public Lands held by actual settlers, . . . and we demand the passage by Congress of the complete and satisfactory Homestead measure which has already passed the house.

14. That the Republican Party is opposed to any change in our Naturalization Laws or any State legislation by which the rights of our citizenship hitherto accorded to immigrants from foreign lands shall be abridged or impaired; and in favor of giving a full and efficient protection to the rights of all classes of citizens, whether native or naturalized, both at home and abroad.

15. The appropriations by Congress for River and Harbor improvements of a National character, . . . are authorized of Government to protect the lives and property of its citizens.

16. That a Railroad to the Pacific Ocean is imperatively demanded by the interests of the whole country; that the Federal Government ought to render immediate and efficient aid in its construction; and that, as preliminary thereto, a daily Overland Mail should be promptly established. . . .

111

Inaugural Address of South Carolina Governor Francis Pickens (1860)

Abraham Lincoln's election brought a howl of protest from the South. In South Carolina, a convention of delegates began meeting in December to consider whether the state should secede. The following selection contains excerpts of an address delivered by Governor Francis W. Pickens shortly before South Carolina left the Union. A member of a prominent state family, Pickens had been an outspoken supporter of his state during the 1832–33 nullification crisis. Years of service in the Congress made him increasingly wary of compromise with the North, and by 1850, he had emerged as one of his state's leading secessionists. By the mid-1850s, however, he became more cautious on the issue. After serving two years as American minister to Russia, he returned to South Carolina in the fall of 1860. He initially warned against immediate secession and, with the support of the state's conservative secessionists, was elected governor.

Questions to Consider

1. Why is Francis Pickens wary of the Republican control of Congress and the presidency?

2. What does he advocate for South Carolina and the South?

3. What can you deduce from this document about South Carolina in 1860?

4. Compare and contrast Governor Pickens' views with those expressed in "South Carolina Nullifies the Tariff" (Document 64). What similarities do you note? Differences?

Gentlemen of the Senate and House of Representatives:

You have called me to preside as Chief Magistrate of South Carolina at a critical juncture in our public affairs. I deeply feel the responsibilities of the position I am about to assume.

For seventy-three years this State has been connected by a federal compact with co-States, under a bond of union, for great national objects, common to all. In recent years there has been a powerful party organized upon principles of ambition and fanaticism, whose undisguised purpose is to divert the Federal Government from external, and turn its power upon the internal interests and domestic institutions of these States. They have thus combined a party exclusively in the Northern States, whose avowed objects not only endanger the peace, but the very existence of near one-half the States of this Confederacy; and in the recent election for President and Vice President of these States, they have carried the election upon principles that make it no longer safe for us to rely upon the powers of the Federal Government or the guarantees of the Federal Compact. This is the great overt act of the people in the Northern States at the ballot-box, in the exercise of their sovereign power at the polls, from which there is no higher appeal recognized under our system of Government, in its ordinary and habitual operations—They thus propose to inaugurate a Chief Magistrate at the head of the army and navy, with vast powers, not to preside over the common interests and destinies of all the States alike, but upon issues of malignant hostility and uncompromising war to be waged upon the rights, the interests and the peace of half the States of this Union.

In the Southern States these are two entirely distinct and separate races, and one has been held in subjugation to the other by peaceful inheritance from worthy and patriotic ancestors, and all who know the races well know that it is the only form of Government that can preserve both, and administer the blessings of civilization with order and in harmony.

Anything tending to change or weaken this government and the subordination between the races, not only endangers the peace, but the very existence of our security. We have for years warned the Northern people of the dangers they were producing by their wanton and lawless course. We have often appealed to our sister States of the South to act with us in concert upon some firm but moderate system, by which we might be able, if possible,

---

"The News From Columbia," *Charleston Mercury,* December 18, 1860, p. 1.

to save the Federal Constitution, and yet feel safe under the general compact of Union. But we could obtain no fair hearing from the North, nor could we see any concerted plan proposed by our co–States of the South, calculated to make us feel safe and secure.

Under all these circumstances, we now have no alternative left but to interpose our sovereign power as an independent State, to Protect the rights and ancient privileges of the people of South Carolina.

This State was one of the original parties to the Federal Compact of the Union. We agreed to it as a state under peculiar circumstances, when we were surrounded with great external pressure for purposes of national protection and for the general welfare of all the States equally and alike; and when it ceases to do this it is no longer a perpetual Union. It would be an absurdity to suppose it was a perpetual Union for our ruin. The Constitution is a compact between Co-states, and not with the Federal Government. On questions vital, and involving the peace and safety of the parties to the compact from the very nature of the instrument, each State must judge of the mode and measure of protection necessary for her peace and the preservation of local and domestic institutions, South Carolina will therefore decide for herself, and will, as she has a right to do, resume her original powers of government as an independent State, and, as such will negotiate with other powers such treaties, leagues or covenants, as she may deem proper. . . .

There is one thing certain, and I think it due to the country say in advance, that South Carolina is resolved to assert her separate independence, and, as she acceded separately to the compact of the Union, so she will most assuredly secede, separately and alone, be the consequences what they may; and I think it right to say, with no unkind feeling whatever, that on this point there can be no compromise, let it be offered from where it may. The issues are too grave, and too momentous, to admit of any counsel that looks to anything but direct and straight forward independence. In the present emergency, the most decided measures are the safest and wisest. To our sister States who are identified with us in interest and feeling, we will cordially and kindly look for co-operation and for a future Union; but it must be after we have asserted and resumed our original and inalienable rights and powers of sovereignty and independence. We can then form a government with them, having a common interest with people of homogenous feelings, united together by all the ties that can bind States in one common destiny. From the position we may occupy towards the Northern States, as well as from our own internal structure of society, the government may, from necessity, become strongly military in its organization. When we look back upon the inheritance, the common glories and triumphant power of this wonderful Confederacy, no language can express the feelings of the human heart, as we turn from the contemplation, and sternly look to the great future that opens before us. It is our sincere desire to separate from the States of the North in peace, and leave them to develop their own civilization, according to their own sense of duty and of interest. But if, under the guidance of ambition and fanaticism, they decide otherwise, then be it so. We are prepared for any event, and, in humble reliance upon that Providence who presides over the destiny of men and of nations, we will endeavor to do our duty faithfully, bravely and honestly.

I am now ready to take the oath of office, and swear undivided allegiance to South Carolina.

15

The Civil War

By the time Abraham Lincoln assumed the presidency in March 1861, seven states of the Deep South had left the Union. Determined to maintain the integrity of the Union, the new president soon challenged the secessionists, an act that caused four states of the upper South to join the Confederacy. Many thought it would be a short war, but it quickly developed into a bloodbath, which required enormous sacrifices on the homefront to support the struggle in the field. By 1863, northern war aims had evolved from a conflict to save the Union into a crusade to end slavery. The following documents reveal the motives of those involved in the war and help illustrate the transformation of the conflict.

112

Mary Boykin Chesnut, the Attack on Fort Sumter (1861)

The Union first tested secession in South Carolina, where Fort Sumter in Charleston harbor remained in Union hands. South Carolina officials, determined to confiscate federal property, declared their refusal to allow the Union to provision the fort. On April 4, President Lincoln, resolved to hold Union property in the South, ordered that Fort Sumter (as well as Fort Pickens in Florida) be resupplied. South Carolina, with the support of the Confederate government, decided to resist these efforts. Mary Boykin Chesnut was the daughter of Mary Boykin and Stephen Miller (one of South Carolina's leading political figures); she married James B. Chesnut, Jr., whose father was one of the state's largest landowners. Following James's election to the U.S. Senate in 1858, Mary quickly established herself in the social circles of other southern politicians' wives. In 1860, the Chesnuts left the nation's capital to return to South Carolina, where James played a prominent role in the state's secession. Her diary, from which this account is excerpted, provides an excellent description of Charleston society just before and during the attack on Fort Sumter.

Questions to Consider

1. Why does Mary B. Chesnut's diary move from excitement about the attack to a more subdued assessment the following day?
2. What does Chesnut anticipate about the coming war?
3. Why does Chesnut comment on the reaction of the slaves?
4. In what ways do Chesnut's views contrast with those of "The Southern Homefront" (Document 117) How do you account for these differences?

April 12th.—Anderson will not capitulate. Yesterday's was the merriest, maddest dinner we have had yet. Men were audaciously wise and witty. We had an unspoken foreboding that it was to be our last pleasant meeting. Mr. Miles dined with us to-day. Mrs. Henry King rushed in saying, "The news, I come for the latest news. All the men of the King family are on the Island," of which fact she seemed proud. . . .

I do not pretend to go to sleep. How can I? If Anderson does not accept terms at four, the orders are, he shall be fired upon. I count four, St. Michael's bells chime out and I begin to hope. At half-past four the heavy booming of a cannon. I sprang out of bed, and on my knees prostrate I prayed as I never prayed before.

There was a sound of stir all over the house, pattering of feet in the corridors. All seemed hurrying one way. I put on my double-gown and a shawl and went, too. It was to the housetop. The shells were bursting. In the dark I heard a man say, "Waste of ammunition." I knew my husband was rowing about in a boat somewhere in that dark bay, and that the shells were roofing it over, bursting toward the fort. If Anderson was obstinate, Colonel Chesnut was to order the fort on one side to open fire. Certainly fire had begun. The regular roar of the cannon, there it was. And who could tell what each volley accomplished of death and destruction?

The women were wild there on the housetop. Prayers came from the women and imprecations from the men. And then a shell would light up the scene. To-night they say the forces are to attempt to land. We watched up there, and everybody wondered that Fort Sumter did not fire a shot. . . .

April 13th.—Nobody has been hurt after all. How gay we were last night. Reaction after the dread of all the slaughter we thought those dreadful cannon were making. Not even a battery the worse for wear. Fort Sumter has been on fire. Anderson has not yet silenced any of our guns. So the aides, still with swords and red sashes by way of uniform, tell us. But the sound of those guns makes regular meals impossible. None of us go to table. Tea-trays pervade the corridors going everywhere. Some of the anxious hearts lie on their beds and moan in solitary misery. Mrs. Wigfall and I solace ourselves

Mary Boykin Chesnut, *A Diary from Dixie,* eds. Isabella D. Martin and Myrta Lockett Avary (New York, 1905), 30–41.

with tea in my room. These women have all a satisfying faith. "God is on our side," they say. When we are shut in Mrs. Wigfall and I ask "Why?" "Of course, He hates the Yankees, we are told. You'll think that well of Him."

Not by one word or look can we detect any change in the demeanor of these negro servants. Lawrence sits at our door, sleepy and respectful, and profoundly indifferent. So are they all, but they carry it too far. You could not tell that they even heard the awful roar going on in the bay, though it has been dinning in their ears night and day. People talk before them as if they were chairs and tables. They make no sign. Are they stolidly stupid? or wiser than we are; silent and strong, biding their time?

. . . [April 15th—] Mrs. Frank Hampton knows already what civil war means. Her brother was in the New York Seventh Regiment, so roughly received in Baltimore. Frank will be in the opposite camp. . . .

113

"A War to Preserve the Union" (1861)

A child of the frontier, Abraham Lincoln was born in Kentucky and lived in Indiana before finally settling in Illinois. Primarily self-taught, he began a legal career in Springfield in the mid-1830s and quickly gained notoriety as a trial lawyer. A Whig, he served in the Illinois legislature from 1834 until 1842, and was elected to the U.S. Congress in 1846. He joined the new Republican party in 1856 and, two years later, ran against Stephen A. Douglas for the U.S. Senate. Although he lost this race, it propelled him to national prominence. When Abraham Lincoln became president in March 1861, seven states of the Deep South had already left the Union. With Congress in recess, Lincoln had to act unilaterally to meet the secession crisis. His decisions to supply Fort Sumter and his later call for troops led to the secession of four more southern states. In the following excerpted selection, the president informs a special session of Congress of his motives and war aims.

Questions to Consider

1. What was Lincoln's initial response to the seizure of federal property throughout the South?

2. What is Lincoln's purpose in fighting the war?

3. Is Lincoln convinced that most southerners support secession and the attack on federal property?

4. To what extent do Lincoln's views reflect those expressed by Daniel Webster in his "Second Reply to Robert Y. Hayne" (Document 63)?

"Message to Congress in Special Session, July 4, 1861," *Complete Works of Abraham Lincoln,* eds. John G. Nicolay and John Hay (Lincoln, PA, 1894), 6: 297–325.

MESSAGE TO CONGRESS IN SPECIAL SESSION, JULY 4, 1861

Fellow-citizens of the Senate and House of Representatives: Having been convened on an extraordinary occasion, as authorized by the Constitution, your attention is not called to any ordinary subject of legislation.

At the beginning of the present presidential term, four months ago, the functions of the Federal Government were found to be generally suspended within the several States of South Carolina, Georgia, Alabama, Mississippi, Louisiana, and Florida, excepting only those of the Post-office Department.

Within these States all the forts, arsenals, dockyards, custom-houses, and the like, including the movable and stationary property in and about them, had been seized, and were held in open hostility to this government, excepting only Forts Pickens, Taylor, and Jefferson, on and near the Florida coast, and Fort Sumter, in Charleston Harbor, South Carolina. The forts thus seized had been put in improved condition, new ones had been built, and armed forces had been organized and were organizing all avowedly with the same hostile purpose.

The forts remaining in the possession of the Federal Government in and near these States were either besieged or menaced by warlike preparations, and especially Fort Sumter was nearly surrounded by well-protected hostile batteries, with guns equal in quality to the best of its own, and outnumbering the latter as perhaps ten to one. . . .

Finding this condition of things, and believing it to be an imperative duty upon the incoming executive to prevent, if possible, the consummation of such attempt to destroy the Federal Union, a choice of means to that end became indispensable. This choice was made and was declared in the inaugural address. The policy chosen looked to the exhaustion of all peaceful measures before a resort to any stronger ones. It sought only to hold the public places and property not already wrested from the government, and to collect the revenue, relying for the rest on time, discussion, and the ballot-box. . . .

[T]he assault upon and reduction of Fort Sumter was in no sense a matter of self-defense on the part of the assailants. . . . They knew that this government desired to keep the garrison in the fort, not to assail them, but merely to maintain visible possession, and thus to preserve the Union from actual and immediate dissolution. . . . By the affair at Fort Sumter, with its surrounding circumstances, that point was reached. Then and thereby the assailants of the government began the conflict of arms, without a gun in sight or in expectancy to return their fire, save only the few in the fort sent to that harbor years before for their own protection, and still ready to give that protection in whatever was lawful. In this act, discarding all else, they have forced upon the country the distinct issue, "immediate dissolution or blood."

And this issue embraces more than the fate of these United States. It presents to the whole family of man the question whether a constitutional republic or democracy—a government of the people by the same people—can or cannot maintain its territorial integrity against its own domestic foes.

It presents the question whether discontented individuals, too few in numbers to control administration according to organic law in any case, can always,
upon the pretenses made in this case, or on any other pretenses, or arbitrarily
without any pretense, break up their government, and thus practically put an
end to free government upon the earth. It forces us to ask: "Is there, in all
republics, this inherent and fatal weakness?" "Must a government, of necessity,
be too strong for the liberties of its own people, or too weak to maintain its
own existence?". . .

114

Jefferson Davis Responds to the Emancipation Proclamation (1862)

*Many southerners insisted that the election of a Republican president would lead to
the emancipation of slaves. During the first phase of the Civil War, however, the North
fought only to preserve the Union. By late 1862, the need for additional manpower,
the determination to undermine the South economically, and the desire to make the war
a moral crusade led northern leaders to announce their plan for emancipation. On January 1, 1863, the Emancipation Proclamation freed all slaves behind Confederate lines,
in effect making the war a crusade against slavery. In the following selection, Confederate President Jefferson Davis responds to the proclamation in his annual message to
the Confederate Congress. Jefferson Davis had enjoyed an impressive career before
becoming the Confederacy's only president. A West Point graduate, the Kentucky
native briefly served in the military before becoming a Mississippi planter. He served
his adopted state in the Congress and the Senate, and was secretary of war in the
Franklin Pierce administration.*

Questions to Consider

1. In what ways does Jefferson Davis react to the Emancipation
   Proclamation?
2. How does he use the occasion to justify secession and re-establish the
   fear of the Republican party?
3. What can you deduce about southern attitudes toward slavery?

The public journals of the North have been received, containing a proclamation, dated on the 1st day of the present month, signed by the President of
the United States, in which he orders and declares all slaves within ten of the
States of the Confederacy to be free, except such as are found within certain

---

"The President's Message," *Richmond Daily Dispatch*, January 15, 1863, p. 2.

districts now occupied in part by the armed forces of the enemy. We may well leave it to the instincts of that common humanity which a beneficent Creator has implanted in the breasts of our fellowmen of all countries to pass judgment on a measure by which several millions of human beings of an inferior race, peaceful and contented laborers in their sphere, are doomed to extermination, while at the same time they are encouraged to a general assassination of their masters by the insidious recommendation "to abstain from violence unless in necessary self-defense." Our own detestation of those who have attempted the most execrable measure recorded in the history of guilty man is tempered by profound contempt for the impotent rage which it discloses. So far as regards the action of this Government on such criminals as may attempt its execution, I confine myself to informing you that I shall, unless in your wisdom you deem some other course more expedient, deliver to the several State authorities all commissioned officers of the United States that may hereafter be captured by our forces in any of the States embraced in the proclamation, that they may be dealt with in accordance with the laws of those States providing for the punishment of criminals engaged in exciting servile insurrection. The enlisted soldiers I shall continue to treat as unwilling instruments in the commission of these crimes, and shall direct their discharge and return to their homes on the proper and usual parole.

In its political aspect this measure possesses great significance, and to it in this light I invite your attention. It affords to our whole people the complete and crowning proof of the true nature of the designs of the party which elevated to power the present occupant of the Presidential chair at Washington and which sought to conceal its purpose by every variety of artful device and by the perfidious use of the most solemn and repeated pledges on every possible occasion. . . .

The people of this Confederacy, then, cannot fail to receive this proclamation as the fullest vindication of their own sagacity in foreseeing the uses to which the dominant party in the United States intended from the beginning to apply their power, nor can they cease to remember with devout thankfulness that it is to their own vigilance in resisting the first stealthy progress of approaching despotism that they owe their escape from consequences now apparent to the most skeptical. This proclamation will have another salutary effect in calming the fears of those who have constantly evinced the apprehension that this war might end by some reconstruction of the old Union or some renewal of close political relations with the United States. These fears have never been shared by me, nor have I ever been able to perceive on what basis they could rest. But the proclamation affords the fullest guarantee of the impossibility of such a result; it has established a state of things which can lead to but one of three possible consequences—the extermination of the slaves, the exile of the whole white population from the Confederacy, or absolute and total separation of these States from the United States.

This proclamation is also an authentic statement by the Government of the United States of its inability to subjugate the South by force of arms, and as such must be accepted by neutral nations, which can no longer find any justification in with holding our just claims to formal recognition. It is also in effect an intimation to the people of the North that they must prepare to submit to a separation, now become inevitable, for that people are too acute not to understand a restoration of the Union has been rendered forever impossible by the adoption of a measure which from its very nature neither admits of retraction nor can coexist with union. . . .

115

New York City Draft Riots (1863)

The loss of life occasioned by the Civil War demanded that the federal government take extraordinary measures. Perhaps none represented a greater intrusion of federal power into the lives of ordinary people than the decision to draft young men into the army. While such a measure was considered a wartime necessity in many parts of the North, the decision was unpopular among some groups. For recently arrived immigrants, especially the Irish, the Republican party with its vestiges of anti-immigrant "Know Nothingism" was their enemy. Because most immigrants were poor urban dwellers whose status was artificially elevated by the intense racism aimed at free blacks, the transition to a war against slavery potentially meant additional competition for jobs and status. Finally, the working poor realized that a draft was likely to fall much more heavily on them than other groups in society. Nowhere was the situation more acute than in New York City, and among no immigrant group were these feelings more prevalent than the Irish. Fear of the draft, coupled with lingering urban problems, led to the worst riots in American history. The following account from The New York Herald *describes the cause of the disturbances.*

Questions to Consider

1. According to this account, what are the underlying causes of the riots?

2. After reading this document, what can you deduce about Civil War–era attitudes concerning class, race, and ethnicity?

3. Compare and contrast this account with that found in "Urban Riots" (Document 77). What similarities do you note? Differences? What conclusions might be drawn concerning middle-class Americans' view of property rights?

Now that the smoke and the dust and the noise and confusion of the late riots in this city have cleared away we may without much difficulty get at their true character, their causes and the elements involved in them. We are

---

"The Late Riots—A Mountain Reduced to a Molehill," *The New York Herald,* July 24, 1863, p. 4.

all satisfied that while under the general panic which they created throughout Manhattan Island they were greatly magnified—that, in brief, what was
supposed to be a prodigious mountain has dwindled down to a contemptible
molehill.

These riots were commenced by a body of laboring men in an active,
lawless demonstration against the draft, including a number of enraged individuals turned over to the army by the first day's working of the wheel in
the disaffected district. Carrying everything before them in the outset, and
finding neither policemen nor soldiers on hand in sufficient numbers to
check them, the rioters were rapidly joined by all the thieves, burglars, pick-
pockets, incendiaries and jailbirds of all descriptions in the neighborhood,
until a large proportion of the villains and vagabonds of every part of the
island and every hole and corner of the city had joined the original mob, and
completely changed its character into carious hordes of rogues and ruffians,
seizing the occasion for a carnival of terrorism, fire, blood and plunder.

A single regiment of our State militia on Monday morning would have
been sufficient to quell the original disturbance. Certainly the troops and
policemen collected by Monday afternoon, if managed with anything like
skill and system, would have been sufficient in a few hours to put down
every vestige of a lawless assemblage. But between our supreme federal military officer, General Wool, and Governor Seymour and Mayor Opdyke, all of
whom made a great parade of doing wonderful things, while, in fact, they
were doing little or nothing, there was so much of confusion in the management of our soldiers and policemen that it was not until Wednesday that the
war was turned decisively against the rioters.

It is due, however, to Commissioner Acton, of the Metropolitan board, to
say that from the moment he assumed the general direction of the police to
the end of the disturbances, his conduct was that of a skilful, fearless, energetic and able officer. He has nobly earned the gratitude of the whole community. Captain Wilson, too, of the Fort Washington Precinct, operated
among the rioters after the fashion of General Grant, breaking up one gang
here, another there, and so on from point to point with his faithful squad,
giving the enemies of law and order no rest, but smiting them hip and thigh,
right and left, till his work was done. There were several other detachments
of the police which did good service against great odds in various encoun-
ters with the rioters; but still there is a considerable number of these
grenadier Metropolitans who seem to be fit for little else in their vocation
than to escort the ladies safely across Broadway "among those horrid
omnibuses."

Mayor Opdyke would doubtless have done something had not this func-
tionary been deprived of the power to do anything by our tinkering Albany
politicians. They have by their tinkering, in fact, given us such divided counsels and departments in our city government as to render it almost completely helpless in any emergency like that of a carnival of rogues and ruffians. It is to be hoped that this fact will not be forgotten by our city members
at the next meeting of the State Legislature.

But these late riots which have so disgraced our city have been exaggerated by our radical abolition organs into a grand rebel conspiracy in behalf of Jeff. Davis. Nothing could be more absurd, except the absurd speculations of some of the newspapers of rebeldom. The *Richmond Dispatch,* for instance, supposes that these New York disturbances are but the beginnings of a general Northern rebellion against the Lincoln despotism, and that by these outbreaks the Davis confederacy is to be lighted to its national independence. Such are the straws that drowning men will snatch at. It will not be long before these Southern newspaper philosophers discover their folly and stupidity in believing for a moment the partisan claptrap of our abolition organs in regard to these late riots. They are ended; for we are sure that President Lincoln, in returning to the business of the draft, will, in a liberal application of the law, render it acceptable even to the working man, who has nothing but his daily labor to depend upon for the subsistence of his family.

The New York riots are ended. They will not be renewed; and the sooner the newspaper organs of Jeff. Davis at Richmond dismiss the idea that he has a great political conspiracy in the North moving for his support the sooner will the misery and the suspense of Davis and his fellows be ended.

116

African-American Troops in Combat (1863)

Legislation passed in July 1862 and the ensuing Emancipation Proclamation opened the Union army to African Americans. Despite wretched treatment in the army and the threat of execution if captured by Confederate forces, black soldiers quickly demonstrated their willingness to fight. The following account by William Wells Brown describes an engagement between African-American troops and Confederate soldiers at Milliken's Bend, Mississippi. Brown, a former slave born near Lexington, Kentucky, spent his early years in St. Louis, Missouri, where he worked a variety of odd jobs. In 1834, he escaped slavery and, by the mid-1840s, lived near Rochester, New York, where he gave antislavery lectures and was active in the Underground Railroad. After spending five years in Great Britain, where he became a featured abolitionist speaker, he returned to the United States in 1854. In 1863, he helped recruit African-American troops for the Union cause.

Questions to Consider

1. What made the battle so "desperate" for the participants?
2. What was the irony that Brown observed in the capturing of the "rebel prisoner"?

William Wells Brown, *The Negro in the American Rebellion: His Heroism and His Fidelity* (Boston, 1867), 137–138.

3. Why were African Americans eager to fight in the Civil War?

4. What can you deduce from this document about northern attitudes toward African Americans?

. . . My informant states that a force of about five hundred negroes, and two hundred men of the Twenty-third Iowa, belonging to the second brigade, Carr's division (the Twenty-third Iowa had been up the river with prisoners, and was on its way back to this place), was surprised in camp by a rebel force of about two thousand men. The first intimation that the commanding officer received was from one of the black men, who went into the colonel's tent, and said, "Massa, the secesh are in camp." The colonel ordered him to have the men load their guns at once. He instantly replied, "We have done did dat now, massa." Before the colonel was ready, the men were in line, ready for action. As before stated, the rebels drove our force towards the gunboats, taking colored men prisoners and murdering them. This so enraged them that they rallied, and charged the enemy more heroically and desperately than has been recorded during the war. It was a genuine bayonet-charge, a hand-to-hand fight, that has never occurred to any extent during this prolonged conflict. Upon both sides men were killed with the butts of muskets. White and black men were killed with the butts of muskets. White and black men were lying side by side, pierced by bayonets, and in some instances transfixed to the earth. In one instance, two men—one white and the other black—were found dead, side by side, each having the other's bayonet through his body. If facts prove to be what they are now represented, this engagement of Sunday morning will be recorded as the most desperate of this war. Broken limbs, broken heads, the mangling of bodies, all prove that it was a contest between enraged men: on the one side, from hatred to a race; and, on the other, desire for self-preservation, revenge for past grievances, and the inhuman murder of their comrades. One brave man took his former master prisoner, and brought him into camp with great gusto. A rebel prisoner made a particular request, that his own negroes should not be placed over him as a guard. . . .

117

The Southern Homefront (1863)

By 1863, the initial enthusiasm of two years earlier had given way to the harsh reality of struggle and privation for many southerners. The ever-tightening Union naval blockade, the need for huge quantities of food to feed a modern army, the lack of a reliable transportation infrastructure to easily move supplies, and the lack of manpower to work southern farms all contributed to the growing shortages. These would contribute to bread riots in Richmond, Virginia, during the spring of 1863. In the ensuing document, "Southern Lady" Sallie Putnam recounts the difficulties faced during the war and how women on the homefront sought to contribute to the Confederate war effort.

Questions to Consider

1. Does the author of this selection remain enthusiastic about the war effort?
2. What can you deduce about public support for the war from this document?
3. In what ways has life changed in Richmond?
4. What can you deduce about the importance of social class from this document? In what ways have attitudes changed?

At this time our Richmond workshops were turning out large supplies of valuable arms and weapons of warfare, and our Nitre Bureau was made effective in contributions of valuable ammunition. While our financial interests were going to ruin, and our navy doing comparatively nothing for our assistance, our people were striving, by their own energies, and by the development of their personal resources, to neutralize, as far as possible, the maladministration of certain departments of the government, which, properly conducted, might have remedied many of the evils and inconveniences entailed upon us. While the men were in the field branches of female industry were faithfully attended to. We were carried back to the times of our grandmothers.

Our women were actively interested in discovering the coloring properties of roots, barks, and berries, and experimenting with alum, copperas, soda, and other alkalies and mineral mordants in dying cotton and wool for domestic manufacture. On approaching a country house rather late, the ear would be greeted, not with the sound of the piano or the Spanish guitar, but with the hum of the spinning-wheel brought out from the hiding-place to which it had been driven before the triumph of the mechanical skill, and the "bang-bang" of the old-fashioned and long-disused loom. The whereabouts of the mistress of the mansion might be inferred from the place whence the sound proceeded; for she was probably herself engaged in, or superintending, the work of a servant, in the weaving or spinning-room. . . . With commendable pride we beheld the Southern gentlemen clad in the comfortable homespun suit, and our ladies wearing domestic dresses that challenged comparison with the plaids and merinos of commercial manufacture. To the rustic and virtuous simplicity of the times the honored wife of our President nobly conformed.

The winter evenings' exercises of knitting for the soldiers were varied by the braiding of straw for bonnets and hats, many of which would compare favorably with those of English manufacture. For gloves, knitting was resorted to, and they were also made of soft, thin cloth, and those rather rude in appearance, were cheerfully exhibited as ingenious evidences that necessity develops resources.

Kid gloves were rarely seen. On a gentleman they were considered as only little more than disgusting relics of dandyism. Confederate simplicity was

A Richmond Lady [Sallie A. Putnam], *Richmond During the War: Four Years of Personal Observation* (New York, 1867).

rigidly austere. The Paris gloves remaining in possession of our ladies were carefully preserved to be the accompaniment to well-cared-for silks and laces of the abundance of days gone by and a costume so magnificent was only donned for some momentous occasion.

Our style of living was quite as simple as our dress. Hotels and boarding-houses, in consequence of the high prices and scarcity of provisions, had ceased to furnish a *"table d'hote,"* and "keeping apartments" was the fashionable mode of living in Richmond. "We are living in the Paris style," did not mean, however, the luxury of a suit[e] of magnificent apartments where could be served to all the delicacies and luxuries of the season, but generally the renting of a single room, which served at the same time the purposes of kitchen, dormitory, and parlor for the lucky family that could secure even such comfortable accommodations. The simple dinner was cooked in a sauce-pan on the grate, and often consisted only of potatoes and a very small quantity of meat and bread, varied with occasionally a fowl, and tea. At weddings we were served with unfrosted cake, and drank the health of the fair bride in domestic wine, if wine at all could be procured. We knew nothing of dyspepsia, and the thousand ailments of an overcharged stomach were unheard of. We practiced a compulsory system of "Banting," and amused ourselves at the many laughable, yet instructive inconveniences to which we were subjected. When invited to breakfast with an intimate friend, the inducement to accept the kind invitation was frequently, "I'll give you a cup of nice pure coffee," and for dinners we would sometimes ask, "Will you give me something sweet?" (meaning a dessert.) "Yes." "Then I'll come." There was something romantic, something novel in this mode of life, and the remembrance, though associated with much that is painful, is on the whole rather pleasant. We were taught many lessons of forbearance and economy, the value of which to us must be tested by their influence on our future lives. We were, in our poverty, prepared fully to realize the truth—

"Man wants but little here below—"

but our trials only served to make us regret every piece of economy practiced when goods were plentiful, and at such prices that we could with ease obtain them.

The situation of the refugees was often painful in the extreme. It was no unusual thing to have presented at our doors a basket in the hands of a negro servant who sold on commission articles disposed of by the necessitons to obtain food. Handsome dresses, patterns of unmade goods, purchased perhaps before the commencement or in the beginning of the war, a piece of silver, or sets of jewelry, accompanied by a note anonymously sent, attested to the poverty and noble pride of some woman who doubtless wore a cheerful face, and when asked if she desired peace, would reply, "Only with liberty." In the stores of our jewelers were frequently seen diamonds and pearls, watches and valuable plate for sale, placed there by some unfortunate, who disposed of these articles of former wealth, luxury and taste, to procure necessary articles of food and raiment.

118

General William T. Sherman on War (1864)

In the western theater, Union commanders not only achieved important victories, but also developed new military strategies in the process. One of the most effective of these generals was William T. Sherman. An Ohio native, Sherman was a graduate of West Point and later served in the Mexican-American War. During the Civil War, Sherman quickly rose through the ranks and, in March 1864, succeeded Grant as commander of Union armies in the West. Sherman sought to defeat the enemy by destroying its economic infrastructure; his interest in Atlanta resulted from its strategic significance as a transportation hub and supply center. In the following account, Sherman responds to Atlanta's leaders with a description of his view of warfare and his role in it.

Questions to Consider

1. Why was William T. Sherman fighting the war?
2. What is his definition of war, and how does he hope to prosecute it?
3. Why does Sherman have little sympathy with the mayor of Atlanta?
4. How might Sallie Putnam ("The Southern Homefront," Document 117) have responded to General Sherman?

> Headquarters Military Division of the Mississippi,
> In the Field, Atlanta, Georgia, September 12, 1864

James M. Calhoun, Mayor, E. E. Rawson and S. C. Wells,
representing City Council of Atlanta.

GENTLEMEN: I have your letter of the 11th, in the nature of petition to revoke my orders removing all the inhabitants from Atlanta. I have read it carefully, and give full credit to your statements of the distress that will be occasioned, and yet shall not revoke my orders, because they were not designed to meet the humanities of the case, but to prepare for the future struggles in which millions of good people outside of Atlanta have a deep interest. We must have peace, not only at Atlanta, but in all America. To secure this, we must stop the war that now desolates our once happy and favored country. To stop war, we must defeat the rebel armies which are arrayed against the laws and Constitution that all must respect and obey. To defeat those armies, we must prepare the way to reach them in their recesses, provided with the arms and instruments which enable us to accomplish our purpose. Now, I know the vindictive nature of our enemy, that we may have many years of military

---

William T. Sherman, "William T. Sherman to James M. Calhoun (Mayor), E. E. Rawson and S. C. Wells, September 12, 1864," *Memoirs* (New York, 1892), 2: 125–127.

operations from this quarter; and, therefore, deem it wise and prudent to prepare in time. The use of Atlanta for warlike purposes is inconsistent with its character as a home for families. There will be no manufactures, commerce, or agriculture here, for the maintenance of families, and sooner or later want will compel the inhabitants to go. Why not go now, when all the arrangements are completed for the transfer, instead of waiting till the plunging shot of contending armies will renew the scenes of the past month? Of course, I do not apprehend any such thing at this moment, but you do not suppose this army will be here until the war is over. I cannot discuss this subject with you fairly, because I cannot impart to you what we propose to do, but I assert that our military plans make it necessary for the inhabitants to go away, and I can only renew my offer of services to make their exodus in any direction as easy and comfortable as possible.

You cannot qualify war in harsher terms than I will. War is cruelty, and you cannot refine it; and those who brought war into our country deserve all the curses and maledictions a people can pour out. I know I had no hand in making this war, and I know I will make more sacrifices to-day than any of you to secure peace. But you cannot have peace and a division of our country. If the United States submits to a division now, it will not stop, but will go on until we reap the fate of Mexico, which is eternal war. The United States does and must assert its authority, wherever it once had power; for, if it relaxes one bit to pressure, it is gone, and I believe that such is the national feeling. This feeling assumes various shapes, but always comes back to that of Union. Once admit the Union, once more acknowledge the authority of the national Government, and, instead of devoting your houses and streets and roads to the dread uses of war, I and this army become at once your protectors and supporters, shielding you from danger, let it come from what quarter it may. I know that a few individuals cannot resist a torrent of error and passion, such as swept the South into rebellion, but you can point out, so that we may know those who desire a government, and those who insist on war and its desolation.

You might as well appeal against the thunder-storm as against these terrible hardships of war. They are inevitable, and the only way the people of Atlanta can hope once more to live in peace and quiet at home, is to stop the war, which can only be done by admitting that it began in error and is perpetuated in pride.

We don't want your negroes, or your horses, or your houses, or your lands, or any thing you have, but we do want and will have a just obedience to the laws of the United States. That we will have, and, if it involves the destruction of your improvements, we cannot help it.

You have heretofore read public sentiment in your newspapers, that live by falsehood and excitement; and the quicker you seek for truth in other quarters, the better. I repeat then that, by the original compact of Government, the United States had certain rights in Georgia, which have never been relinquished and never will be; that the South began war by seizing forts, arsenals, mints, custom-houses, etc., etc., long before Mr. Lincoln was installed, and before the South had one jot or tittle of provocation. I myself have seen in Missouri, Kentucky, Tennessee, and Mississippi, hundreds and thousands of women and children fleeing from your armies and desperadoes, hungry and with bleeding feet. In Memphis, Vicksburg, and Mississippi, we fed thousands upon thousands of the families of rebel soldiers left on our hands, and whom we could not see starve. Now that war comes home to you, you feel very different. You deprecate its horrors, but did not feel them when you sent car-loads of soldiers and ammunition, and moulded shells and shot, to carry war into Kentucky and Tennessee, to desolate the homes of hundreds and thousands of good people who only asked to live in peace at their old homes, and under the Government of their inheritance. But these comparisons are idle. I want peace, and believe it can only be reached through union and war, and I will ever conduct war with a view to perfect and early success.

But, my dear sirs, when peace does come, you may call on me for any thing. Then will I share with you the last cracker, and watch with you to shield your homes and families against danger from every quarter.

Now you must go, and take with you the old and feeble, feed and nurse them, and build for them, in more quiet places, proper habitations to shield them against the weather until the mad passions of men cool down, and allow the Union and peace once more to settle over your homes at Atlanta.
Yours in haste,
—W. T. Sherman, Major-General commanding.

119

Lincoln's Second Inaugural Address (1865)

By March 1865, Union military successes in Virginia and Georgia had brought the North to the brink of victory. With triumph in sight, postwar issues now became increasingly central to the national agenda. In the midst of the debates over the nation's future, President Abraham Lincoln delivered his second inaugural address, which appears as follows.

Questions to Consider

1. How have President Lincoln's views changed since he proclaimed "A War to Preserve the Union" (Document 113)? What has remained unchanged?

2. How would you describe President Lincoln's views toward the South?

"Second Inaugural Address, March 4, 1865," *Complete Works of Abraham Lincoln,* eds. John G. Nicolay and John Hay (New York, 1894), 11: 44–47.

3. What does the president see as the major issues confronting the nation after the war?

4. What can you deduce about the religious sensibilities of President Lincoln?

FELLOW-COUNTRYMEN: At this second appearing to take the oath of the presidential office, there is less occasion for an extended address than there was at the first. Then a statement, somewhat in detail, of a course to be pursued, seemed fitting and proper. Now, at the expiration of four years, during which public declarations have been constantly called forth on every point and phase of the great contest which still absorbs the attention and engrosses the energies of the nation, little that is new could be presented. The progress of our arms, upon which all else chiefly depends, is as well known to the public as to myself; and it is, I trust, reasonably satisfactory and encouraging to all. With high hope for the future, no prediction in regard to it is ventured.

On the occasion corresponding to this four years ago, all thoughts were anxiously directed to an impending civil war. All dreaded it—all sought to avert it. While the inaugural address was being delivered from this place, devoted altogether to saving the Union without war, insurgent agents were in the city seeking to destroy it without war—seeking to dissolve the Union, and divide effects, by negotiation. Both parties deprecated war; but one of them would make war rather than let the nation survive; and the other would accept war rather than let it perish. And the war came. One-eighth of the whole population were colored slaves, not distributed generally over the Union, but localized in the southern part of it. These slaves constituted a peculiar and powerful interest. All knew that this interest was, somehow, the cause of the war. To strengthen, perpetuate, and extend this interest was the object for which the insurgents would rend the Union, even by war; while the government claimed no right to do more than to restrict the territorial enlargement of it.

Neither party expected for the war the magnitude or the duration which it has already attained. Neither anticipated that the cause of the conflict might cease with, or even before, the conflict itself should cease. Each looked for an easier triumph, and a result less fundamental and astounding. Both read the same Bible, and pray to the same God; and each invokes his aid against the other. It may seem strange that any men should dare to ask a just God's assistance in wringing their bread from the sweat of other men's faces; but let us judge not, that we be not judged. The prayers of both could not be answered—that of neither has been answered fully.

The Almighty has his own purposes. "Woe unto the world because of offenses! For it must needs be that offenses come; but woe to that man by whom the offense cometh." If we shall suppose that American slavery is one of those offenses which, in the providence of God, must needs come, but which, having continued through his appointed time, he now wills to remove, and that he gives to both North and South this terrible war, as the woe due to those by whom the offense came, shall we discern therein any departure from those divine attributes which the believers in a living God always ascribe to him? Fondly do we hope—fervently do we pray—that this mighty scourge of war may speedily pass away. Yet, if God wills that it continue until all the wealth piled by the bondsman's two-hundred and fifty years of unrequited toil shall be sunk, and until every drop of blood drawn with the lash shall be paid by another drawn with the sword, as was said three thousand years ago, so still it must be said, "The judgements of the Lord are true and righteous altogether."

With malice toward none; with charity for all; with firmness in the right, as God gives us to see the right, let us strive on to finish the work we are in; to bind up the nation's wounds; to care for him who shall have borne the battle, and for his widow, and his orphan—to do all which may achieve and cherish a just and lasting peace among ourselves, and with all nations.

16

Reconstruction

After the Civil War, the nation faced the enormous task of reconstructing the republic. In particular, policy makers had to determine the status of the former Confederate states and what to do with the recently freed slaves. Devastated by the war, the South also had to cope with the influx of northern troops, reformers, and profiteers, many of whom had their own ideas concerning the region's future. The diversity of opinions over Reconstruction deeply divided the North and occasionally brought a violent response from some southern whites. The ensuing selections reveal how Americans of different races and regions responded to Reconstruction.

120

A Northern Teacher's View of the Freedmen (1863–65)

Early in the Civil War, Union troops occupied the sea islands along South Carolina's coast near Beaufort. All property—plantations, cotton, and slaves—was confiscated and placed under the jurisdiction of Secretary of the Treasury Salmon P. Chase. Of particular concern was the welfare of the slaves, who at this early stage of the war were considered "contraband" if they were behind Union lines and were not returned to their owners. Sensing the opportunity to use these islands as an experiment for the future reconstruction of the South, Chase permitted benevolent organizations to send teachers, many of whom were women, to help educate the former slaves. In October 1863, the New England Freedmen's Aid Society sponsored Elizabeth Hyde Botume as a teacher in this experiment. Hyde became more than a teacher in the several years she spent among the ex-slaves, as her book, First Days Amongst the Contrabands, *revealed. Excerpted as follows is Hyde's description of the freedmen.*

Questions to Consider

1. In what ways did the slaves react to freedom?
2. What are the initial problems facing the freedmen?
3. What social, political, and economic issues confronting Reconstruction does Elizabeth Hyde Botume observe?

. . . Contrabands were coming into the Union lines, and thence to the town, not only daily, but hourly. They came alone and in families and in gangs,— slaves who had been hiding away, and were only now able to reach safety. Different members of scattered families following after freedom, as surely and safely guided as were the Wise Men by the Star of the East.

On New Year's Day I walked around amongst these people with Major Saxton. We went to their tents and other quarters. One hundred and fifty poor refugees from Georgia had been quartered all day on the wharf. A wretched and most pitiable gang, miserable beyond description. But when we spoke to them, they invariably gave a cheerful answer. Usually to our question, "How do you do?" the response would be, "Thank God, I live!"

Sometimes they would say, "Us ain't no wusser than we been."

These people had been a long time without food, excepting a little hominy and uncooked rice and a few ground-nuts. Many were entirely naked when they started, and all were most scantily clothed and we had already had some extremely cold days, which we, who were fresh from the North, found hard to bear.

It was the same old story. These poor creatures were covered only with blankets, or bits of old carpeting, or pieces of bagging, "crocus," fastened with thorns or sharp sticks. . . .

I went first to the negro quarters at the "Battery Plantation," a mile and a half away. A large number of Georgia refugees who had followed Sherman's army were quartered here. Around the old plantation house was a small army of black children, who swarmed like bees around a hive. There were six rooms in the house, occupied by thirty-one persons, big and little. In one room was a man whom I had seen before. He was very light, with straight red hair and a sandy complexion, and I mistook him for an Irishman. He had been to me at one time grieving deeply for the loss of his wife, but he had now consoled himself with a buxom girl as black as ink. His sister, a splendidly developed creature, was with them. He had also four sons. Two were as light as himself, and two were very black. These seven persons occupied this one room. A rough box bedstead, with a layer of moss and a few old rags in it, a hominy pot, two or three earthen plates, and a broken-backed chair, comprised all the furniture of the room. I had previously given one of the women a needle and some thread, and she now sat on the edge of the rough bedstead trying to sew the dress she ought, in decency, to have had on. . . .

The winter of 1864–1865 was a sad time, for so many poor creatures in our district were wretchedly ill, begging for help, and we had so little to give them. Many of the contrabands had pneumonia. Great exposure, with scanty clothing and lack of proper food, rendered them easy victims to the encroachments of any disease. I sent to Beaufort for help. The first doctor who came was exasperatingly indifferent. He might have been a brother of a "bureau officer," who was sent down especially to take care of the contrabands, and

Elizabeth Hyde Botume, *First Days Amongst the Contrabands* (Boston, 1893), 78–79, 82–83, 117–118, 168–169, 176–177.

who wished all the negroes could be put upon a ship, and floated out to sea and sunk. It would be better for them and for the world. When we expressed our surprise that he could speak so of human beings, he exclaimed, "Human beings! They are only animals, and not half as valuable as cattle."

When the doctor came, I went from room to room and talked with the poor sick people, whose entire dependence was upon us. Finally I could endure his apathy and indifference no longer.

"Leave me medicines, and I will take care of these people as well as I can," I said. . . .

I could not, however, excuse the doctor, a man in government employ, drawing a good salary with no heart in his work. Beaufort was reported to be a depot for officials whom government did not know what to do with. . . .

Early in February we went to Savannah with General and Mrs. Saxton, and members of the general's staff, and other officers. How it had become known that we were to make this trip I cannot tell, but we found a crowd of our own colored people on the boat when we went aboard. To our exclamations of surprise they said with glee,—

"Oh, we're goin' too, fur us has frien's there."

We found the city crowded with contrabands who were in a most pitiable condition. Nearly all the negroes who had lived there before the war had gone away. A large number went on with the army; those left were the stragglers who had come in from the "sand hills" and low lands. The people from the plantations too had rushed into the city as soon as they knew the Union troops were in possession.

A crowd of poor whites had also congregated there. All were idle and destitute. The whites regarded the negroes as still a servile race, who must always be inferior by virtue of their black skins. The negroes felt that emancipation had lifted them out of old conditions into new relations with their fellow beings. They were no longer chattels, but independent creatures with rights and privileges like their neighbors. . . .

Nothing in the history of the world has ever equalled the magnitude and thrilling importance of the events then transpiring. Here were more than four millions of human beings just born into freedom; one day held in the most abject slavery, the next, "de Lord's free men." Free to come and to go according to the best lights given them. Every movement of their white friends was to them full of significance, and often regarded with distrust. Well might they sometimes exclaim, when groping from darkness into light, "Save me from my friend, and I will look out for my enemy."

Whilst the Union people were asking, "Those negroes! what is to be done with them?" they, in their ignorance and helplessness, were crying out in agony, "What will become of us?" They were literally saying, "I believe, O Lord! help thou mine unbelief."

They were constantly coming to us to ask what peace meant for them? Would it be peace indeed? or oppression, hostility, and servile subjugation? This was what they feared, for they knew the temper of the baffled rebels as did no others.

121

Charleston, South Carolina at the Conclusion of the Civil War (1865)

The Civil War brought destruction to the South. With much of the fighting taking place in southern states, armies of both sides laid waste to the countryside and burned or destroyed communities as they struggled to win the war. While often not directly involved in the fighting, the civilian population felt the brunt of the war. The war also brought a dislocation of trade and business activities in the South, often resulting in shortages of food and clothing. Furthermore, the Civil War shattered the plantation economy of primarily cotton production based on the labor of African-American slaves. When the Confederacy surrendered in April 1865, the southern states faced significant social, political, and economic adjustments. At the war's conclusion, several northern journalists traveled throughout the South to report on conditions and people's reactions to the beginnings of Reconstruction. Sidney Andrews was one of these journalists; his observations appeared in the Chicago Tribune *and the* Boston Advertiser. *The reports from his three-month southern tour attracted such attention that they were compiled in book form,* The South Since the War, *which is excerpted as follows. Andrews' direct and well-written accounts were among the best commentaries on the immediate post-war South.*

Questions to Consider

1. What conditions did Andrews find in Charleston?
2. In what ways did residents of Charleston react to northerners? To Reconstruction policies? Would this be expected?
3. What issues and attitudes does Andrews reveal that become critical in Reconstruction?

A city of ruins, of desolation, of vacant houses, of widowed women, of rotting wharves, of deserted warehouses, of weed-wild gardens, of miles of grass-grown streets, of acres of pitiful and voiceful barrenness,—that is Charleston, wherein Rebellion loftily reared its head five years ago, on whose beautiful promenade the fairest of cultured women gathered with passionate hearts to applaud the assault of ten thousand upon the little garrison of Fort Sumter! . . .

We will never again have the Charleston of the decade previous to the war. The beauty and pride of the city are as dead as the glories of Athens. Five millions of dollars could not restore the ruin of these four past years; and that sum is so far beyond the command of the city as to seem the boundless measure of immeasurable wealth. Yet, after all, Charleston was

---

Sidney Andrews, *The South Since the War* (Boston, 1866), 1-9.

Charleston because of the hearts of its people. St. Michael's Church, they held, was the center of the universe; and the aristocracy of the city were the very elect of God's children of earth. One marks now how few young men there are, how generally the young women are dressed in black. The flower of their proud aristocracy is buried on scores of battlefields. If it were possible to restore the broad acres of crumbling ruins to their foretime style and uses, there would even then be but the dead body of Charleston. . . .

Of Massachusetts men, some are already in business here, and others came on to "see the lay of the land," as one of them said. "That's all right," observed an ex-rebel captain in one of our after-dinner chats,—"that's all right; let's have Massachusetts and South Carolina brought together, for they are the only two States that amount to anything."

"I hate all you Yankees most heartily in a general sort of way," remarked another of these Southerners; "but I find you clever enough personally, and I expect it'll be a good thing for us to have you come down here with your money, though it'll go against the grain of us pretty badly."

There are many Northern men here already, though one cannot say that there is much Northern society, for the men are either without families or have left them at home. Walking out yesterday with a former Charlestonian, . . . he pointed out to me the various "Northern houses"; and I shall not exaggerate if I say that this classification appeared to include at least half the stores on each of the principal streets. "The presence of these men," said he, "was at first very distasteful to our people, and they are not liked any too well now; but we know they are doing a good work for the city."

I fell into some talk with him concerning the political situation, and found him of bitter spirit toward what he was pleased to denominate "the infernal radicals." When I asked him what should be done, he answered: "You Northern people are making a great mistake in your treatment of the South. We are thoroughly whipped; we give up slavery forever; and now we want you to quit reproaching us. Let us back into the Union, and then come down here and help us build up the country." . . .

It would seem that it is not clearly understood how thoroughly Sherman's army destroyed everything in its line of march,—destroyed it without questioning who suffered by the action. That this wholesale destruction was often without orders, and often against most positive orders, does not change the fact of destruction. The Rebel leaders were, too, in their way, even more wanton, and just as thorough as our army in destroying property. They did not burn houses and barns and fences as we did; but, during the last three months of the war, they burned immense quantities of cotton and rosin. . . .

The city is under thorough military rule; but the iron hand rests very lightly. Soldiers do police duty, and there is some nine-o'clock regulation; but, so far as I can learn, anybody goes anywhere at all hours of the night without molestation. "There never was such good order here before," said an old colored man to me. The main street is swept twice a week, and all garbage is removed at sunrise. "If the Yankees was to stay here always and keep the city so clean, I don't reckon we'd have 'yellow jack' here any more," was a remark I overheard on the street. "Now is de fust time sense I can 'mem'er when brack men was safe in de street af'er nightfall," states the negro tailor in whose shop I sat an hour yesterday.

On the surface, Charleston is quiet and well-behaved; and I do not doubt that the more intelligent citizens are wholly sincere in their expressions of a desire for peace and reunion. The city has been humbled as no other city has been; and I can't see how any man, after spending a few days here, can desire that it shall be further humiliated enough for health is another thing. Said one of the Charlestonians on the boat, "You won't see the real sentiment of our people, for we are under military rule; we are whipped, and we are going to make the best of things; but we hate Massachusetts as much as we ever did." This idea of making the best of things is one I have heard from scores of persons. I find very few who hesitate to frankly own that the South has been beaten. "We made the best fight we could, but you were too strong for us, and now we are only anxious to get back into the old Union and live as happily as we can," said a large cotton factor. I find very few who make any special profession of Unionism; but they are almost unanimous in declaring that they have no desire but to live as good and quiet citizens under the laws.

122

African Americans Seek Protection (1865)

The emancipation of 4 million slaves in the South brought significant social, political, and economic adjustment for both African Americans and whites. Despite obtaining freedom from their masters and the rigors of plantation life, the former slaves lost their source of shelter, food, clothing, and occupation. In short, they had little but their freedom. Realizing that they remained at the mercy of their previous owners, many African Americans gathered in conventions in cities throughout the South to discuss the best methods of protecting their fragile freedom. Some of these conventions petitioned Congress for assistance, whereas others turned to local officials for help. Excerpted following is a petition from a convention of African Americans meeting in Alexandria, Virginia, in August 1865, which demonstrates the precarious position of the freedmen and how they proposed to protect themselves. This petition was the typical result of the conventions.

Questions to Consider

1. What types of protection does this convention seek?
2. For what reasons was the convention critical of "loyalty oaths" and the Freedmen's Bureau?
3. What does this document reveal about the situation for the freedmen at this time?

4. Compare and contrast the views of the post-war South expressed in this document with those in found in "A White Southern Perspective on Reconstruction" (Document 124).

We, the undersigned members of a convention of colored citizens of the State of Virginia, would respectfully represent that, although we have been held as slaves, and denied all recognition as a constituent of your nationality for almost the entire period of the duration of your government, and that by your permission we have been denied either home or country, and deprived of the dearest rights of human nature; yet when you and our immediate oppressors met in deadly conflict upon the field of battle—the one to destroy and the other to save your government and nationality, we, with scarce an exception, in our inmost souls espoused your cause, and watched, and prayed, and waited, and labored for your success. . . .

When the contest waxed long, and the result hung doubtfully, you appealed to us for help, and how well we answered is written in the rosters of the two hundred thousand colored troops now enrolled in your service; and as to our undying devotion to your cause, let the uniform acclamation of escaped prisoners, "Whenever we saw a black face we felt sure of a friend," answer.

Well, the war is over, the rebellion is "put down," and we are declared free! Four-fifths of our enemies are paroled or amnestied, and the other fifth are being pardoned, and the President has, in his efforts at the reconstruction of the civil government of the States, late in rebellion, left us entirely at the mercy of these subjugated but unconverted rebels, in everything save the privilege of bringing us, our wives and little ones, to the auction block. He has, so far as we can understand the tendency and bearing of his action in the case, remitted us for all our civil rights, to men, a majority of whom regard our devotions to your cause and flag as that which decided the contest against them! This we regard as destructive of all we hold dear, and in the name of God, of justice, of humanity, of good faith, of truth and righteousness, we do most solemnly and earnestly protest. Men and brethren, in the hour of your peril you called upon us, and despite all time-honored interpretation of constitutional obligations, we came at your call and you are saved; and now we beg, we pray, we entreat you not to desert us in this the hour of our peril!

We know these men—know them well—and we assure you that, with the majority of them, loyalty is only "lip deep," and that their professions of loyalty are used as a cover to the cherished design of getting restored to their former relation with the Federal Government, and then, by all sorts of "unfriendly legislation," to render the freedom you have given us more intolerable than the slavery they intended for us.

We warn you in time that our only safety is in keeping them under Governors of the military persuasion until you have so amended the Federal Constitution that it will prohibit the States from making any distinction

"The Late Convention of Colored Men," *New York Times,* August 13, 1865, p. 3.

between citizens on account of race or color. In one word, the only salvation for us besides the power of the Government, is in the possession of the ballot. Give us this, and we will protect ourselves. No class of men relatively as numerous as we were ever oppressed when armed with the ballot. But, 'tis said we are ignorant. Admit it. Yet who denies we know a traitor from a loyal man, a gentleman from a rowdy, a friend from an enemy? . . .

. . . All we ask is an equal chance with the white traitors varnished and japanned* with the oath of amnesty. Can you deny us this and still keep faith with us? "But," say some, "the blacks will be overreached by the superior knowledge and cunning of the whites." Trust us for that. We will never be deceived a second time. "But," they continue, "the planters and landowners will have them in their power, and dictate the way their votes shall be cast." We did not know before that we were to be left to the tender mercies of these landed rebels for employment. Verily, we thought the Freedmen's Bureau was organized and clothed with power to protect us from this very thing, by compelling those for whom we labored to pay us, whether they liked our political opinions or not! . . .

We are "sheep in the midst of wolves," and nothing but the military arm of the Government prevents us and all the truly loyal white men from being driven from the land of our birth. Do not then, we beseech you, give to one of these "wayward sisters" the rights they abandoned and forfeited when they rebelled until you have secured our rights by the aforementioned amendment to the Constitution.

Let your action in our behalf be thus clear and emphatic, and our respected President, who, we feel confident, desires only to know your will, to act in harmony therewith, will give you his most earnest and cordial cooperation; and the Southern States, through your enlightened and just legislation, will speedily award us our rights. Thus not only will the arms of the rebellion be surrendered, but the ideas also.

123

Thaddeus Stevens on Reconstruction and the South (1865)

The debate over Reconstruction began during the Civil War and became increasingly acute as the North moved toward victory. The lines were quickly drawn between the president and Congress, although various factions within the Republican party argued vociferously for certain positions. Some of the more important issues were: How should the secessionist states be reunited with the Union; what political and social status should be conveyed to the 4 million freedmen; how should whites who supported the Confederacy be treated; and who should control Reconstruction? Presidential Reconstruction, begun by Abraham Lincoln in December 1863 and slightly modified when

---

*A varnish that yields a hard brilliant finish.

Andrew Johnson assumed the presidency, was declared too lenient by Republicans. Within Congress, a powerful group called the Radical Republicans challenged presidential Reconstruction and began advocating their own agenda. Among the leaders of the Radical Republicans was Thaddeus Stevens, a representative from Lancaster, Pennsylvania, whose quick wit, honesty, political savvy, and belief that Reconstruction offered an opportunity to establish a better country made him a powerful supporter of Congressional Reconstruction. The following excerpt is Stevens' speech on the status of the South and what Congressional Reconstruction should encompass.

Questions to Consider

1. What political actions does Thaddeus Stevens propose for the South?

2. What does Stevens believe Congress should do for the freedmen?

3. In what ways do Stevens' proposals help shape Reconstruction policies?

. . . No one doubts that the late rebel states have lost their constitutional relations to the Union, and are incapable of representation in Congress, except by permission of the Government. It matters but little, with this admission whether you call them States out of the Union, and now conquered territories, or assert that because the Constitution forbids them to do what they did do, that they are therefore only dead as to all national and political action, and will remain so until the government shall breathe into them the breath of life anew and permit them to occupy their former position. In other words, that they are not out of the Union, but are only dead carcasses lying within the Union. In either case, it is very plain that it requires the action of Congress to enable them to form a State government and send representatives to Congress. Nobody, I believe, pretends that with their old constitutions and frames of government they can be permitted to claim their old rights under the Constitution. They have torn their constitutional States into atoms, and built on their foundations fabrics of a totally different character. Dead men cannot raise themselves. Dead States cannot restore their own existence "as it was." Whose especial duty is it to do it? In whom does the Constitution place the power? Not in the judicial branch of government, for it only adjudicates and does not prescribe laws. Not in the Executive, for he only executes and cannot make laws. Not in the Commander-in-Chief of the armies, for he can only hold them under military rule until the sovereign legislative power of the conqueror shall give them law. . . .

Congress alone can do it. But Congress does not mean the Senate, or the House of Representatives, and President, all acting severally. Their joint action constitutes Congress. . . . Congress must create States and declare when they are entitled to be represented. Then each House must judge whether the members presenting themselves from a recognized State possess the requisite qualifications of age, residence, and citizenship; and whether the election and returns are according to law. The Houses, separately, can judge of nothing

"Reconstruction," *Congressional Globe*, 39th Congress, 1st session, part 1 (December 18, 1865), 72–74.

else. It seems amazing that any man of legal education could give it any larger meaning.

It is obvious from all this that the first duty of Congress is to pass a law declaring the condition of these outside or defunct States, and providing proper civil governments to them. Since the conquest they have been governed by martial law. Military rule is necessarily despotic, and ought not to exist longer than is absolutely necessary. As there are no symptoms that the people of these provinces will be prepared to participate in constitutional government for some years, I know of no arrangement so proper for them as territorial governments. There they can learn the principles of freedom and eat the fruit of foul rebellion. Under such governments, while electing members to the Territorial Legislatures, they will necessarily mingle with those to whom Congress shall extend the right of suffrage. In Territories Congress fixes the qualifications of electors; and I know of no better place nor better occasion for the conquered rebels and the conqueror to practice justice to all men, and accustom themselves to make and obey equal laws. . . .

According to my judgment they ought never to be recognized as capable of acting in the Union, of being counted as valid States, until the Constitution shall have been so amended as to make it what its framers intended; and so as to secure perpetual ascendancy to the party of the Union; and so as to render our republican Government firm and stable forever. The first of those amendments is to change the basis of representation among the States from Federal numbers to actual voters. . . .

But this is not all that we ought to do before these inveterate rebels are invited to participate in our legislation. We have turned, or are about to turn, loose four million slaves without a hut to shelter them or a cent in their pockets. The infernal laws of slavery have prevented them from acquiring an education, understanding the commonest laws of contract, or of managing the ordinary business of life. This Congress is bound to provide for them until they can take care of themselves. If we do not furnish them with homesteads, and hedge them around with protective laws; if we leave them to the legislation of their late masters, we had better have left them in bondage. Their condition would be worse than that of our prisoners at Andersonville. If we fail in this great duty now, when we have the power, we shall deserve and receive the execration of history and of all future ages.

124

A White Southern Perspective on Reconstruction (1868)

Congressional or Radical Reconstruction imposed a new set of requirements on the South. It divided the region into five military districts and outlined how new governments were to be created—especially granting suffrage to African Americans. Complying with these guidelines, every southern state was readmitted into the Union by 1870. A Republican party coalition of African Americans, recently arrived northerners (carpet-baggers), and southern whites (scalawags) controlled nearly all of these state governments. Many former supporters of the Confederacy found these Republican governments to be offensive, corrupt, and expensive (they raised taxes to pay for new services like public education). One of the most outspoken and uncompromising opponents of Radical Reconstruction was Howell Cobb. Born into a wealthy Georgia cotton plantation family, Cobb devoted his life to public service. He served in the House of Representatives, was elected speaker in 1849, was governor of Georgia, served as secretary of the treasury under President James Buchanan, was a prominent secessionist, helped form the Confederate government, and was an officer in the war. After the war, Cobb maintained a self-imposed silence on political matters, which he broke with the following excerpted letter. Many white southerners would have agreed with Cobb's attack on Radical Reconstruction.

Questions to Consider

1. What are Howell Cobb's reasons to oppose Reconstruction policies?
2. Which policies does he particularly dispute? Why?
3. In what ways did white southerners react to Reconstruction?
4. In what ways might Howell Cobb have reacted to Sidney Andrews's commentary on conditions in Charleston, South Carolina ("Charleston, South Carolina at the Conclusion of the Civil War," Document 121)?

Macon [GA], 4 Jany., 1868

We of the ill-fated South realize only the mournful present whose lesson teaches us to prepare for a still gloomier future. To participate in a national festival would be a cruel mockery, for which I frankly say to you I have no heart, however much I may honor the occasion and esteem the association with which I would be thrown.

The people of the south, conquered, ruined, impoverished, and oppressed, bear up with patient fortitude under the heavy weight of their burdens. Disarmed and reduced to poverty, they are powerless to protect themselves against wrong and injustice; and can only await with broken spirits that destiny which the future has in store for them. At the bidding of their more powerful conquerors they laid down their arms, abandoned a hopeless struggle, and returned to their quiet homes under the plighted faith of a soldier's honor that they should be protected so long as they observed the obligations

Howell Cobb to J. D. Hoover, 4 January 1868, *Annual Report of the American Historical Association for the Year 1911*, vol. 2, *The Correspondence of Robert Toombs, Alexander H. Stephens, and Howell Cobb*, ed. U. B. Phillips (Washington DC, 1913), 690–694.

imposed upon them of peaceful law–abiding citizens. Despite the bitter charges and accusations brought against our people, I hesitate not to say that since that hour their bearing and conduct have been marked by a dignified and honorable submission which should command the respect of their bitterest enemy and challenge the admiration of the civilized world. Deprived of our property and ruined in our estates by the results of the war, we have accepted the situation and given the pledge of a faith never yet broken to abide it. Our conquerors seem to think we should accompany our acquiescence with some exhibition of gratitude for the ruin which they have brought upon us. We cannot see it in that light. Since the close of the war they have taken our property of various kinds, sometimes by seizure, and sometime by purchase,—and when we have asked for remuneration have been informed that the claims of rebels are never recognized by the Government. To this decision necessity compels us to submit; but our conquerors express surprise that we do not see in such ruling the evidence of their kindness and forgiving spirit. They have imposed upon us in our hour of distress and ruin a heavy and burthensome tax, peculiar and limited to our impoverished section. Against such legislation we have ventured to utter an earnest appeal, which to many of their leading spirits indicates a spirit of insubordination which calls for additional burthens. They have deprived us of the protection afforded by our state constitutions and laws, and put life, liberty and property at the disposal of absolute military power. Against this violation of plighted faith and constitutional right we have earnestly and solemnly protested, and our protest has been denounced as insolent;—and our restlessness under the wrong and oppression which have followed these acts has been construed into a rebellious spirit, demanding further and more stringent restrictions of civil and constitutional rights. They have arrested the wheels of State government, paralized the arm of industry, engendered a spirit of bitter antagonism on the part of our negro population towards the white people with whom it is the interest of both races they should maintain kind and friendly relations, and are now struggling by all the means in their power both legal and illegal, constitutional and unconstitutional, to make our former slaves *our masters,* bringing these Southern states under the power of *negro supremacy.* To these efforts we have opposed appeals, protests, and every other means of resistance in our power, and shall continue to do so until the bitter end. If the South is to be made a pandemonium and a howling wilderness the responsibility shall not rest upon our heads. Our conquerors regard these efforts on our part to save ourselves and posterity from the terrible results of their policy and conduct as a new rebellion against the constitution of our country, and profess to be amazed that in all this we have failed to see the evidence of their great magnanimity and exceeding generosity. Standing today in the midst of the gloom and suffering which meets the eye in every direction, we can but feel that we are the victims of cruel legislation and the harsh enforcement of unjust laws. . . . We regarded the close of the war as ending the relationship of enemies and the beginning of a new national brotherhood, and in the light of that conviction felt and spoke of constitutional equality. . . . We claimed that the result of the war left us a state in the Union, and therefore under the protection of the constitution, rendering in return cheerful obedience to its requirements and bearing in common with the other states of the Union the burthens of government, submitting even as we were compelled to do to *taxation without representation;* but they tell us that a successful war to keep us in the Union left us out of the Union and that the pretension we put up for constitutional protection evidences bad temper on our part and a want of appreciation of the generous spirit which declares that the constitution is not over us for the purposes of protection. . . . In such reasoning is found a justification of the policy which seeks to put the South under negro supremacy. Better, they say, to hazard the consequences of negro supremacy in the south with its sure and inevitable results upon Northern prosperity than to put faith in the people of the south who though overwhelmed and conquered have ever showed themselves a brave and generous people, true to their plighted faith in peace and in war, in adversity as in prosperity. . . .

With an Executive who manifests a resolute purpose to defend with all his power the constitution of his country from further aggression, and a Judiciary whose unspotted record has never yet been tarnished with a base subserviency to the unholy demands of passion and hatred, let us indulge the hope that the hour of the country's redemption is at hand, and that even in the wronged and ruined South there is a fair prospect for better days and happier hours when our people can unite again in celebrating the national festivals as in the olden time.

125

The Ku Klux Klan during Reconstruction (1872)

The original Ku Klux Klan was formed in 1866 in Pulaski, Tennessee, as a social organization, but several former Confederates made the Klan a terrorist group. The Klan espoused white supremacy, the defeat of the Republican party in the South, and keeping African Americans "in their place." Incensed with the Republican party's control of state governments, especially African Americans voting and holding public office, and intrigued with the secrecy, unusual names, and disguises of the Klan, thousands joined the organization in the late 1860s. The Klan embarked on a terrorist campaign with intimidation, whippings, beatings, property destruction, shootings, or simply riding disguised in the countryside as its hallmarks. Blacks who affirmed their rights were the most common Klan targets, but white Republicans were also singled out. Much of the South was spared Klan activity, but locations where both races or political parties were almost equally balanced often witnessed Klan terrorism, especially near election time. In 1871, a congressional committee traveled in the South to investigate Klan activities and take statements from many of its victims. Excerpted as follows is Edward "Ned" Crosby's testimony on Klan intimidation in Mississippi.

Questions to Consider

1. What were the reasons for the Klan's intimidation of African Americans?
2. How were African Americans coerced into voting for the Democratic party?
3. What does this document reveal about race relations in the South during Reconstruction?
4. In what ways might Edward Crosby have reacted to Howell Cobb's commentary on conditions in the South ("A White Southern Perspective on Reconstruction," Document 124)?

Columbus, Mississippi, November 17, 1871

EDWARD CROSBY (colored) sworn and examined.
By the Chairman:
QUESTION. Where do you live?

ANSWER. Right near Aberdeen—ten miles east of Aberdeen.

QUESTION. State whether you were ever visited by the Ku-Klux; and, if so, under what circumstances.

ANSWER. I have been visited by them. They came to my house, and came into my house. . . . It looked like there were thirty-odd of them, and I didn't know but what they might interfere with me, and I just stepped aside, out in the yard to the smokehouse. They came up there and three of them got down and came in the house and called for me, and she told them I had gone over to Mr. Crosby's. . . . She didn't know but they might want something to do to me and interfere with me and they knocked around a while and off they went.

QUESTION. Was this in the night-time?

ANSWER. Yes, sir.

QUESTION. Were they disguised?

ANSWER. Yes, sir.

QUESTION. Had you been attempting to get up a free-school in your neighborhood?

ANSWER. Yes, sir.

QUESTION. Colored school?

ANSWER. Yes, sir.

U.S. Congress, *Testimony Taken by the Joint Select Committee to Inquire into the Condition of Affairs in the Late Insurrectionary States* (Washington, DC, 1872), 12: 1133–1134.

QUESTION. Do you know whether their visit to you had reference to this effort?

ANSWER. No, sir; I don't know only this: I had spoken for a school, and I had heard a little chat of that, and I didn't know but what they heard it, and that was the thing they were after.

QUESTION. Were their horses disguised?

ANSWER. Yes. Sir. . . .

QUESTION. Did you know any of the men?

ANSWER. No, sir; I didn't get close enough to know them. I could have known them, I expect, if I was close up, but I was afraid to venture.

QUESTION. Did they ever come back?

ANSWER. No, sir.

QUESTION. What do you know as to the whipping of Green T. Roberts?

ANSWER. Only from hearsay. He told me himself. They didn't whip him. They took him out and punched him and knocked him about right smart, but didn't whip him.

QUESTION. Was he a colored man?

ANSWER. He was a white man—a neighbor of mine.

QUESTION. Who took him out?

ANSWER. The Ku-Klux. . . .

QUESTION. What if anything do you know of any colored men being afraid to vote the republican ticket and voting the democratic ticket at the election this month, in order to save their property, and to save themselves from being outraged?

ANSWER. Well sir, the day of the election there was, I reckon, thirty or forty; I didn't count them, but between that amount; they spoke of voting the radical ticket. It was my intention to go for the purpose. I had went around and saw several colored friends on that business. . . . I knew some of the party would come in and maybe they would prevent us from voting as we wanted to. I called for the republican tickets and they said there was none on the ground. I knocked around amongst them, and I called a fellow named Mr. Dowdell and asked if there would be any there; he said he didn't know; he asked me how I was going to vote; I told him my opinion, but I was cramped for fear. They said if we didn't act as they wanted they would drop us at once. There is only a few of us, living amongst them like lost sheep where we can do the best; and they were voting and they stood back and got the colored population and pushed them in front and let them vote first, and told them there was no republican tickets on the ground. I didn't see but three after I voted. Shortly after I voted, Mr. James Wilson came with some, and a portion of the colored people had done voting. I met Mr. Henderson; I was going on to the other box at the Baptist church. He asked if there were any colored voters there; I told him there was thirty or forty, and there was no republican tickets there. Mr.

Wilson had some in his pocket, but I didn't see them. I saw that I was beat at my own game, and I had got on my horse and dropped out.

QUESTION. Who told you that unless the colored people voted the democratic ticket it would be worse for them?

ANSWER. Several in the neighborhood. Mr. Crosby said as long as I voted as he voted I could stay where I was, but he says, "Whenever Ned votes my rights away from me, I cast him down."

QUESTION. Was he a democrat?

ANSWER. A dead-out democrat.

QUESTION. Did you hear any other white men make the same declaration?

ANSWER. Not particular; I only heard them talking through each other about the colored population. I heard Mr. Jerome Lamb—he lived nigh Athens—tell a fellow named Aleck that lived on his place, he spoke to him and asked him if he was going to vote as he did; Aleck told him he was—he did this in fear, mind you—and Aleck went and voted, and after he voted he said, "Aleck, come to me;" says he, "Now, Aleck, you have voted?" Aleck says, "Yes sir;" he said, "Well, now, Aleck, you built some very nice houses. Now, I want you to wind your business up right carefully. I am done with you; off of my land."

QUESTION. Had Aleck voted the republican ticket?

ANSWER. Yes, sir.

QUESTION. Did all the colored men except these three vote the democratic ticket that day?

ANSWER. Up at Grub Springs all voted the democratic ticket. There was no republican ticket given to the colored people at all.

QUESTION. Did they vote the democratic ticket from fear that they would be thrown out of employment or injured?

ANSWER. That was their intention. You see pretty nigh every one of them was the same way I was, but there was none there; and them they were all living on white people's land, and were pretty fearful. The Ku-Klux had been ranging around through them, and they were all a little fearful.

QUESTION. Do you think they were all radical in sentiment, and would have been glad to have voted the radical ticket if uninfluenced?

ANSWER. They would. They had a little distinction up amongst themselves—the white and colored people. One of them said, "Ned, put in a republican ticket." Well, there was none on the ground, and I remarked, "If there is any radical tickets on the ground I will take one of them, and I will not take a democratic ticket, and I will fold them up and drop that in the box, and they will never tell the difference," and it got out that I had voted the radical ticket, and some were very harsh about it.

QUESTION. Would the colored people of your county vote the radical ticket if left alone?

ANSWER. Well, sir, I suppose they would have done it.

126

"The Problem at the South" (1871)

The end of the Civil War demanded federal efforts to remake the South, but efforts to bring the southern states back into the Union while helping the former slaves make the transition to freedom proved particularly problematic. By 1871, supporters of Reconstruction grew increasingly frustrated at their inability to achieve these two goals in the face of southern white opposition, weak Reconstruction governments, and Democratic challenges to their policies. As northerners debated Reconstruction policy, E. L. Godkin was a prominent commentator on the issue. A native of Great Britain, Godkin helped found The Nation *in July 1865 as a reform-minded political journal. The following excerpt from an 1871 selection offers his critique of Reconstruction as well as a suggestion concerning future policy toward the South.*

Questions to Consider

1. What does E. L. Godkin see as the major problems facing Reconstruction?
2. Are Godkin's suggested solutions prudent given the situation?
3. What does Godkin's commentary reveal about northern commitment to Reconstruction?

There is no doubt about the multiplicity and atrocity of the outrages committed by what are called the Ku-klux on the negroes and Unionists at the South. It appears to be equally certain that the persons who commit these outrages are not brought to Justice. The sheriffs do not arrest them, or, if they do, juries do not convict them—in other words, through a great part of the South there is no security for either life or property. That some such state of things would come to pass was foreseen after the war. It was said that if legislation and the election of officers were left solely to the Southern whites, the Southern blacks would be left without adequate protection. Consequently, the suffrage was given to the blacks. But this was not felt to be sufficient. A great proportion of the more experienced and intelligent people at the South were excluded by the State constitutions, and by an amendment to the United States Constitution, from all share in the government. In this way not only were the negroes and Unionists guaranteed a voice in the Government, but they were secured in the exclusive control of it. That is, to speak plainly, for the purpose of securing the poor and ignorant against oppression, not only were they admitted to an equality of rights with the rich and educated, but they were put in possession of the whole administrative machinery. Considering that a large body of the voters—in some States a majority—had recently emerged from slavery in its most brutal form, it must be admitted

E. L. Godkin, "The Problem at the South," *The Nation* (March 23, 1871): 192–193.

the experiment was a bold one; in fact, it was the boldest ever known. No similar rearrangement of the social organization has ever been attempted anywhere else. We do not blame those who attempted it. They were hot from a civil war which had ended in a social revolution, and they found themselves charged with the duty of securing a large and helpless population of freemen in possession of common civil rights, in the presence of their late masters, without having recourse to pure military coercion.

The experiment has, however, totally failed. The most influential portion of the Southern population, with whose support no government can in the long run dispense, as has been a thousand times proved, have not only given the new governments at the South no assistance, but have, naturally enough, been bitterly hostile to them. The new political system, indeed, was of a kind to rouse all their prejudices against it. The men who took part in and aided the rebellion, and who are therefore disfranchised, have within the last five years been reinforced by a powerful body of youths who were boys during the rebellion, and who have entered on manhood during a period of great disorder and uncertainty and poverty, in which few careers are open to them, and in which all the circumstances of their lives tend to exasperate and embitter them, and prepare them for turbulence and violence. They may therefore be said, without exaggeration, to have taken the field against the new regime. They have formed organizations somewhat similar to the Irish Whiteboys and Molly Maguires, the express object of which is to drive negroes and union men out of the South, and make all government through their instrumentality impossible. For this purpose they murder, rob, and maltreat, and they are too powerful, too skillful, and too firmly bound together, and enjoy too much of the sympathy of the local population, to make it possible for the State officers to bring them to justice. More than this, and, if possible, worse than this, they have at the North a powerful political party, which, if it cannot be said to be at their back, is certainly not disposed to blame them or call them to account, and whose chances of accession to power seem to improve as the passions excited by the war die out.

On the other hand, the new governments have done nothing to atone for the theoretical defects of their origin. We owe it to human nature to say that worse governments have seldom been seen in a civilized country. They have been largely composed of trashy whites and ignorant blacks. Of course, there have been in them men of integrity and ability of both races; but the great majority of the officers and legislators have been either wanting in knowledge or in principle, or both. That of South Carolina is one of the worst specimens, and, as such, we have often commented on it.

What is to be done? Congress having set those governments up, and having emancipated the negroes, and the negroes being, it is safe to say, the only men at the South who are really devoted to the Union, it seems as if it was the duty of Congress to see to their protection. Moreover, the experiment which is now on trial at the South being of Republican devising, it seems to be necessary to the credit of the party that it should be made to succeed, and at the same time, it seems as if the Ku-klux stories might be made to help the party by showing the necessity of such a prolongation of its power as would enable it to complete the work of Southern pacification. Accordingly, nearly every session of Congress there is a call either from philanthropists under the influence of feelings of humanity, or from mere politicians in search of "capital," for additional legislation "to protect life and property at the South." Of the sort of legislation demanded, the bill recently brought in by Butler is a fair specimen, and it consists simply in attempts to substitute for the state machinery, which is the only means of protecting life and property known to the Constitution of the United States, the machinery in use under the arbitrary and centralized governments of Europe—that is, the withdrawal of criminal cases from the jury, and their committal to single judges appointed by the central authority and armed with extraordinary powers, and the concession to mere official suspicion, and to legal presumptions, of a part in determining the question of guilt or innocence of a prominence hitherto unknown in Anglo-Saxon jurisprudence.

These are momentous changes to introduce into the administrative system of any free country; they are more momentous in this country than they would be in any other, because they not only increase the power of the central government, but they arm it with jurisdiction over a class of cases of which it has never hitherto had, and never pretended to have, any jurisdiction whatever. It would not simply furnish the Government at Washington with additional means of performing one of its well-known duties, such as the suspension of the *habeas corpus* in Ireland furnishes the British Government with, but it would impose upon it altogether new duties. But the separate States are, under the Constitution, as clearly charged with the duty of protecting life and property within their own borders, as the United States with the duty of making treaties with foreign powers. To impose the duty of protecting life and property on the Federal Government is, therefore, just as distinct and well-marked a novelty as, and a far more serious novelty than, the transfer of the power of negotiating treaties to the separate States would be. . . .

Is there, then, no remedy for local disorder at the South? If the state government does not protect a man, can he look nowhere else for redress? We answer, that if there be any value whatever in the theory on which American polity is based, the remedy of Southern disorders must come from the Southern people, through their experience of the folly and suffering of disorder. If this be not true, the whole American system is a mistake, and is destined ere long to perish. Our business is now to leave every Southern State to its own people, first, because this is the only practicable course, and secondly, because it is the only wise one. If they are so demoralized that they go on robbing, and murdering, and "Kukluxing" each other, we cannot interfere effectively, and had better not interfere at all. The American punishments for a State which permits these things are two—impoverishment and emigration. If a man cannot have freedom, security, and light taxation in New York, let him go to New Jersey; if he cannot have them in South Carolina, let him go to Virginia; if he cannot have them in either, let him go to Missouri. Those who stay behind, on seeing capital and population steadily leaving their State, and their property declining in value, will gradually mend their ways. This may be a slow remedy, but it is a sure one. It goes to the root of the disorder, while under coercion from the outside no state of things can grow up, or ever has grown up, in which coercion ceases to be necessary. Of course there is nothing in this theory to prevent the United States enforcing the Federal Constitution and laws. This ought to be done, *at whatever cost—* that is, by officers, and not by bill and resolution. If it be true that black men are kept from the polls by intimidation, we ought to see that going to the polls is made as safe as going to church; but to pass bills providing for this, without voting the men or the money to execute them, is a wretched mockery, of which the country and the blacks have had enough . . .

127

African-American Suffrage in the South (1867, 1876)

One of the critical and hotly debated issues of Reconstruction was the extension of civil rights to the freedmen. Mainly to protect the former slaves from possible retaliation at the hands of their former masters, the initial Reconstruction plans called for the protection of African-Americans' rights. Led by some Radical Republicans, Congress implemented its plan of Reconstruction, which required the new state governments in the South to guarantee the right to vote for male African Americans. In 1867, African Americans voted for the first time, often casting their ballots for Republican candidates and helping to establish the Republican party's control of state government. For white southerners, who mainly belonged to the Democratic party, this represented a revolutionary change and caused bitter resentment toward black voters and the Republican party. Some southern whites joined the Ku Klux Klan to intimidate Republicans, and other whites used their economic influence as landowners to intimidate African Americans. The two images that follow from Harper's Weekly, *a well-respected newspaper of the era, reflect the optimism of African Americans participating in the political process for the first time, as well as the reality of voter manipulation. The first image was the cover of the November 16, 1867 issue; the second image was a double-page illustration in the October 21, 1876 issue.*

Questions to Consider

1. How do the images differ in their depiction of African Americans' right to vote?

2. What appears to be the status of African Americans voting in the first image? How is the African American portrayed in the second image different? What might you deduce from these differences?

3. How does the second image portray southern whites? How do you account for this portrayal?

4. How do you think Howell Cobb, author of "A White Southern Perspective on Reconstruction" (Document 124), would respond to these images?

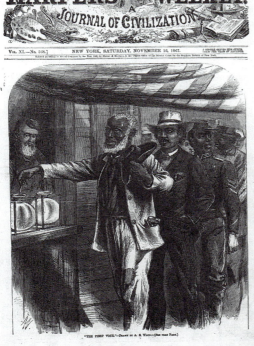

"The First Vote"

"Of Course He Wants to Vote the Democratic Ticket!"
Democratic "Reformer." "You're as free as air, ain't you? Say you are, or I'll blow yer black head off!"